# Innovation, Entrepreneurship und Digitalisierung

**Reihe herausgegeben von**

Mario Schaarschmidt, Northumbria University, Amsterdam Campus, The Netherlands

Harald von Korflesch, Institut für Management, Universität Koblenz-Landau, Koblenz, Deutschland

Kern dieser Schriftenreihe ist die empirische und praxisnahe Betrachtung des Zusammenspiels von Innovation, Entrepreneurship und Digitalisierung in verschiedenster Ausprägung. Dies beinhaltet Themen wie Geschäftsmodellinnovation, Soziale Medien, Technologiemanagement sowie neuere Themenblöcke wie beispielsweise Sharing Economy. Ein besonderer Fokus liegt bei der Bearbeitung der Themen auf den Veränderungen, die durch Digitalisierung hervorgerufen wurden. Ziel dieser Reihe ist es, insbesondere innovative Forschungsergebnisse, welche zu neuen wissenschaftlichen Erkenntnissen führen, gebündelt dem geneigten Leser zu präsentieren. Publiziert werden nationale und internationale wissenschaftliche Arbeiten.
Die Reihe Innovation, Entrepreneurship und Digitalisierung wird herausgegeben von Mario Schaarschmidt und Harald von Korflesch.

Sonja Christ-Brendemühl

# Digital Technology in Service Encounters

## Effects on Frontline Employees and Customer Responses

Sonja Christ-Brendemühl
Universität Koblenz-Landau
Koblenz, Germany

Universität Koblenz-Landau, Dissertation, 2021
Vollständiger Abdruck der vom Fachbereich 4: Informatik der Universität Koblenz-Landau genehmigten Dissertation mit dem Titel "The Effects of Digital Technology on Frontline Employees and Customer Responses in Service Encounters. Evidence from Four Empirical Studies".

ISSN 2524-5783 ISSN 2524-5791 (electronic)
Innovation, Entrepreneurship und Digitalisierung
ISBN 978-3-658-37884-4 ISBN 978-3-658-37885-1 (eBook)
https://doi.org/10.1007/978-3-658-37885-1



Responsible Editor: Marija Kojic
This Springer Gabler imprint is published by the registered company Springer Fachmedien Wiesbaden GmbH, part of Springer Nature.
The registered company address is: Abraham-Lincoln-Str. 46, 65189 Wiesbaden, Germany

*Thank you to my entire family for their patience and support, to my friends and colleagues for their encouragement, and to my supervisor for giving me the opportunity to study such an exciting topic and discuss it with service researchers from around the world.*

# Abstract

Digital technology is disrupting the prerequisites for most firms in the service industry and frequently forces them to adapt their strategy to the technological developments. Even service providers that traditionally put great emphasis on making personal customer contact are reassessing the ratio of human interaction and technology use for service encounters. To retain competitiveness, it seems mandatory to increase service encounter efficiency by embedding technology into the existing processes.

However, there is little empirical evidence on how such technological implementations affect the sentiments, attitudes, and behaviors of frontline employees (FLEs). Likewise, research on interrelated customer responses is scarce. To address this matter, this thesis presents four distinct yet related studies to investigate the impact of digital technology on frontline employees, customers, and ultimately service firms.

Study A focuses on the factors that foster or hinder frontline employees' technology-induced role ambiguity and process deviance when an online reservation system for restaurants is in use. The answers of 123 frontline employees participating in the online survey featured in this study are analyzed.

Study B implements a qualitative approach to achieve a 360-degree view of technology deployment in full-service restaurants. For this purpose, 36 semi-structured interviews were conducted with technology providers, restaurant managers, frontline employees, and customers.

Study C uses dyadic data gathered from a field survey with 147 frontline employees and 373 customers of full-service restaurants. This study aims to investigate how technology induces frontline employee technostress and customer orientation and whether this affects customer satisfaction and delight with the frontline employee.

Study D compares customer fairness perceptions and behavioral intentions after making a purchase that either involves purchase advisory service in a branch store or a virtual try-on service in an online shop. This 2x2 between-subject experimental study includes 215 participants.

To summarize, this thesis contributes to the research on digital technology in service encounters by revealing employee outcomes of using frontline service technology and interrelated customer responses. The derivation of implications provides meaningful insights for theory and practice.

# Contents

# Abbreviations

| | |
|---|---|
| AGFI | Adjusted Goodness of Fit Index |
| AMOS | Analysis of Moment Structures |
| ANOVA | Analysis of Variance |
| AR | Augmented Reality |
| AVE | Average Variance Extracted |
| ß | Beta (Greek alphabet); standardized regression weight |
| b | Regression weight |
| CFI | Comparative Fit Index |
| COR | Conservation of Resources |
| COVID-19 | Coronavirus Disease 2019 |
| C.R. | Critical Ratio |
| CR | Composite Reliability |
| df | Degrees of freedom |
| e.g. | Exempli gratia (Latin); 'for example' (English) |
| et al. | Et alii (Latin); 'and others' (English) |
| eWOM | Electronic Word-of-Mouth |
| FL | Factor Loading |
| FLE | Frontline Employee |
| GDP | Gross Domestic Product |
| GPS | Global Positioning System |
| H | Hypothesis |
| i.a. | Inter alia (Latin); 'among other things' (English) |
| IBM | International Business Machines Corporation |
| ICT | Information and Communication Technology |
| i.e. | Id est (Latin); 'that is' (English) |
| IFI | Incremental Fit Index |

| | |
|---|---|
| IRA | Interrater Agreement |
| IS | Information Systems |
| IT | Information Technology |
| ITC | Item-Total Correlation |
| JD-R | Job Demands-Resources |
| JOSM | Journal of Service Management |
| JSM | Journal of Services Marketing |
| JSR | Journal of Service Research |
| LLCI | Lower Level for Confidence Interval |
| M | Mean |
| MANOVA | Multivariate Analysis of Variance |
| MTurk | Mechanical Turk (Amazon's crowdsourcing web service) |
| N | Number of participants (sample size) |
| n/a | Not applicable |
| NFI | Normed Fit Index |
| n.s. | Not significant |
| OECD | Organization for Economic Cooperation and Development |
| OFR | Organizational Frontline Research |
| p | Probability |
| P-E fit | Person-environment fit |
| QDA | Qualitative Data Analysis |
| QR | Quick Response |
| QUIS | Quality in Services |
| R&D | Research and Development |
| RMSEA | Root Mean Square Error of Approximation |
| RQ | Research Question |
| RTC | Resistance to Change |
| SD | Standard Deviation |
| S.E. | Standard Error |
| SEM | Structural Equation Modeling |
| SERVSIG | Services Special Interest Group |
| SPSS | Superior Performing Software Systems |
| TLI | Tucker-Lewis Index |
| TRI | Technology Readiness Index |
| ULCI | Upper Level for Confidence Interval |
| U.S. | The United States |
| VIF | Variance Inflation Factor |
| VR | Virtual Reality |
| WOM | Word-of-Mouth |

# List of Figures

# List of Tables

# Introduction

# 1

## 1.1 Motivation

Digital technology is disrupting the established structures in the marketplace at a fast pace (Subramaniam, Iyer, and Venkatraman, 2019). Consequently, the prerequisites of most industries and firms are fundamentally changing (Kunz, Heinonen, and Lemmink, 2019). For firms in the service industry, it has become essential to incorporate digital technology into their **business strategy** and also to determine which backend processes, service offerings, and customer interactions should be enhanced by technology (Huang and Rust, 2017). This is because many established service firms have been surpassed by more digitized competitors in the past years (Verhoef *et al.*, 2021). Particularly, those firms that traditionally put great emphasis on personal customer contact have long lagged behind in introducing new technology (Tan and Netessine, 2020). Thus, to improve productivity gains, it seems mandatory for service firms to reassess their ratio of human interaction and technology use in service encounters.

The term **service encounter** depicts the occasions when customers directly interact with a service firm (Ostrom, Fotheringham, and Bitner, 2019). For decades, these interactions were considered as a "game of persons" (Bowen, 2016, p. 5) between customers and **frontline employees (FLEs)**. FLEs are those employees who directly interact with customers at the forefront of service firms (Stock, de Jong, and Zacharias, 2017). By forming pleasant and mutually rewarding relationships with customers, FLEs play a key role in driving successful service encounters (Giebelhausen *et al.*, 2014). Their attitudes and customer-interactive behaviors determine customer satisfaction and service quality perceptions (Bowen, 2016; Yoon, Seo, and Yoon, 2004). Accordingly, FLEs


S. Christ-Brendemühl, *Digital Technology in Service Encounters*, Innovation, Entrepreneurship und Digitalisierung, https://doi.org/10.1007/978-3-658-37885-1_1

are often considered as the most important asset of service firms and a source of competitive advantage (Wirtz and Lovelock, 2016).

However, even service encounters that were historically characterized by intense social interactions between FLEs and customers are becoming increasingly infused by **technology interfaces** (Giebelhausen *et al.*, 2014). Technology infusion refers to the incorporation of "technological elements into the customer's frontline experience" (van Doorn *et al.*, 2017, p. 43). Technology operated by FLEs can accelerate customer information transmission and order processing and, thereby, augment service interactions (Kunz *et al.*, 2019). The interfaces operated by customers can be used to reduce waiting time and complement personal customer service (Tan and Netessine, 2020). At the same time, such interfaces reduce the labor costs of service firms and potentially attract customers who strive for convenience and fast service delivery (Hilken *et al.*, 2017). Accordingly, most service encounters today are not limited to mere dyadic interactions between FLEs and customers anymore; rather, they encompass human actors as well as interrelated technologies and service processes (Larivière *et al.*, 2017).

As a matter of course, a technology-induced transformation of service encounters involves a fundamental **redesign of organizational processes**. In service firms, FLEs are the ones who are ultimately responsible for embedding redesigned or new processes into their daily work (Cadwallader *et al.*, 2010). Yet, FLEs face several challenges when organizational processes involve the use of digital technology (Rafaeli *et al.*, 2017). These challenges include learning how to operate specific user interfaces, convincing customers of their usefulness, coping with sometimes non-functioning technological equipment, and trusting new processes wherein technology partly replaces human interaction. Moreover, service firms need to align FLEs' tasks with digital processes in order to ensure efficient workflows and, in turn, increased productivity (Larivière *et al.*, 2017). Consequently, the roles of FLEs undergo severe changes (Subramony *et al.*, 2017).

On the one hand, technology has the potential to enhance the **role performance** of FLEs by enabling them to focus on core tasks such as personal interactions with customers (de Keyser *et al.*, 2019; Larivière *et al.*, 2017). On the other hand, technology may evoke skepticism and anxiety among FLEs (Meuter *et al.*, 2003). This anxiety can result from job security concerns (Frey and Osborne, 2017) or from an employee's disposition to react emotionally to imposed change. After all, technology-induced changes frequently force employees to adopt new routines (Thatcher, Stepina, and Boyle, 2002). In addition, digital technologies often come alongside increasingly sophisticated customer demands and a more and more complex work environment (Selzer *et al.*, 2021). Accordingly, digital technologies are confronting FLEs with additional demands.

Selzer *et al.* (2021), for instance, propose that digital technology used to mediate customer interactions elicits FLE **role ambiguity**. Technology-induced role ambiguity arouses when FLEs lack clarity about whether and to which extent they have to deal with technology-related issues rather than with their core tasks (Maier *et al.*, 2015). Role ambiguity is considered as a job demand that hinders FLEs from performing their role and impairs their commitment to organizational guidelines (Podsakoff, LePine, and LePine, 2007). In turn, this ambiguity might cause FLEs to deviate from the prescribed processes in service encounters and, thereby, harm the organization.

Moreover, technology-induced role ambiguity can instigate **technostress** (Ayyagari, Grover, and Purvis, 2011). Technostress is defined as the stress that an individual experiences when using technologies (Ragu-Nathan *et al.*, 2008). It can impair employee well-being and poses a risk to employee health (Ayyagari *et al.*, 2011). In daily work, technostress reduces FLEs' ability to concentrate and frequently diverts their attention from satisfying customer needs (Arnetz and Wiholm, 1997; La Torre *et al.*, 2019).

Customers are likely to detect signs of FLE technostress, particularly when it mitigates FLEs' ability to provide quality interactions (Netemeyer, Maxham, and Pullig, 2005). Consequently, technostress might negatively affect **customer responses** in terms of their satisfaction levels and delight with the FLE service. Similarly, customer-operated technology interfaces can function as a barrier to service encounters and, thereby, impair customer responses. In particular, the use of technology may cause dissatisfaction in those customers who still seek human touch since the latter can differentiate one service encounter from another (Keating, McColl-Kennedy, and Solnet, 2018). For instance, Giebelhausen *et al.* (2014) contend that technology operated by customers distracts from FLEs' attempts to build a personal connection. Establishing connections is vital because those customers who feel connected to a firm spend more money on its services than those who are merely satisfied with a firm's service (Dvorak and Robison, 2020; Gallup, 2014).

Against this background, service firms are trying to find ways to deliver service in a more digitized way while still connecting, or rather engaging, with customers. One attempt to **engage customers**—particularly their senses—is the adoption of augmented reality (AR). By interactively embedding virtual objects into the customer's current environment, AR is meant to compensate for the impossibility of touching, feeling, or trying on items that are not physically present (Heller *et al.*, 2019b; Hilken *et al.*, 2017). For services, AR is mainly integrated into mobile applications or online services in which technology-based offerings completely substitute personal encounters (de Keyser *et al.*, 2019). Such

AR-enabled services are characterized by high-degree customer participation since customers invest effort, cognitive resources, and sensitive data. However, those customers are not automatically engaged. Thus, academic research as well as practitioners are still searching for the ideal approach to engage customers through AR in a way that personal encounters would (Heller *et al.*, 2021).

In summary, technological advancements are transforming the nature of service encounters and the experiences of both FLEs and customers (de Keyser *et al.*, 2019; Rust and Huang, 2012; van Doorn *et al.*, 2017). Yet, little research has been conducted on technology-mediated interactions between FLEs and customers (Marinova *et al.*, 2017). Accordingly, Ostrom *et al.* (2015) asserted that the **integration of humans and technology** is a major priority of service research. In their online survey conducted with 330 service researchers from 37 countries, "integrating the roles of customers, employees, and technology for value creation" was rated as the second important aspect out of a list of 80 topics (Ostrom *et al.*, 2015, p. 132). This dissertation thesis intends to further investigate these interdependent roles.

## 1.2 Research Question and Research Design

In academic literature, several recent conceptual papers make **technology in service encounters** a topic of discussion. For instance, Huang and Rust (2017) develop a typology of four service strategies that aim to respond to rapid technological changes. Marinova *et al.* (2017) conceptualize mechanisms that foster service effectiveness and efficiency in technology-mediated interactions between FLEs and customers. Larivière *et al.* (2017) elaborate on the changing interdependent roles of employees, technologies, and customers. Based on the degree to which technology either substitutes or augments personal interactions in service encounters, de Keyser *et al.* (2019) propose a set of eight different technology infusion archetypes.

Although these conceptual papers partly address the **role of FLEs** in the context of technology-infused service encounters, FLEs seldom are the main focus of research endeavors (Subramony *et al.*, 2017). Through a semantic analysis of 5,118 technology-related service management articles, Kunz *et al.* (2019) find that the keyword "employee" is highly underrepresented in service literature. More specifically, neither service journals nor conference papers and business magazines such as *The Economist* contain the keyword "employee" in their concept networks, demonstrating that employee-related research is scarce. Instead, business journals such as *Harvard Business Review* or *Sloan Management Review* appear to be the only medium where articles on service technology include the employee perspective (Kunz *et al.*, 2019). Thus, only few conceptual and empirical research in service management has been conducted on how FLEs are affected by the integration of digital technology.

According to Subramony *et al.* (2017), one potential reason for the underexplored **employee-related research** in service management may be the lack of awareness that FLEs are the key to recognizing and resolving customer issues. Furthermore, most current conceptualizations on technology in service encounters differentiate between technologies that either augment or substitute personal interactions or serve as network facilitators (de Keyser *et al.*, 2019; Larivière *et al.*, 2017). These particular differentiations assume that technology—as long as it does not replace FLEs—is expected to positively affect FLEs by providing them with assistance and freeing time for performing core tasks (Marinova *et al.*, 2017; van Doorn *et al.*, 2017). However, not everyone will equally embrace and value technology in service encounters. This is particularly true when technology confronts FLEs with additional demands or diminishes the value of human touch in service encounters.

Therefore, it seems essential to study how FLEs perceive the support of and the demands arising from digital technology and how these affect the sentiments and behavioral patterns of FLEs in service encounters. Since FLEs directly interact with customers, it is equally important to understand how customers respond to the technology-induced sentiments and behaviors of FLEs. Moreover, customers are frequently in control of deciding whether they want to personally interact with FLEs or use digital technology for service transactions (Sands *et al.*, 2020). Accordingly, service firms need to understand how customers evaluate the aspects of service when it either involves personal interactions with FLEs or is completely delivered via technology. Hence, this dissertation thesis pursues the following overall **objective**:

> **This thesis aims to further examine the impact of digital technology on frontline employees and customer responses in service encounters that are traditionally characterized by personal interactions.**

To achieve this objective, this thesis encompasses the perspectives of four interrelated stakeholder groups on digital technology in service encounters. FLEs constitute the first stakeholder group. This group has a particular kind of importance because the existing conceptualizations mainly neglect the fact that digital technology might also hinder FLEs in properly performing their tasks rather than supporting them. The employee perspective instantly relates to the second stakeholder group, which is formed by customers. It is worth noting that customers' evaluations of service encounters that are either mediated by or completely carried out through technology are essential for service firms.

The ways FLEs handle and customers evaluate technology, together, substantially impact the effectiveness and success of service firms. Hence, service firms constitute the third stakeholder group. The fourth stakeholder group is made up of technology providers. They must know the needs of FLEs, customers, and, concomitantly, service firms in order to effectively design, customize, and market their technological solutions. The integration of these four perspectives is reflected in the given **central research question**:

> How do frontline employees and customers respond to digital technology in service encounters, and what do these responses mean for service firms and technology providers?

This central research question will be further itemized throughout a set of four studies within this thesis. Correspondingly, Table 1.1 provides an overview of the study design, research method, and sample size of the four studies. Furthermore, this table presents the respective service industry, the kind of technology, and stakeholder groups. Finally, Table 1.1 also depicts the theoretical framework used for each study as well as the outcomes considered. Each study could be viewed as standing for itself. Yet, as the studies were conducted consecutively, their findings inspired the development of subsequent studies. The four studies and their connections to one another will be described in the following sections.

**Study A** investigates to what degree intrapersonal determinants such as self-efficacy and resistance to change (RTC) determine technology-induced role ambiguity and process deviance of FLEs. An earlier version of Study A entitled "Frontline backlash: Service employees' deviance from digital processes" has been published in the Journal of Services Marketing (Christ-Brendemühl and Schaarschmidt, 2019). With the example of online reservation systems for restaurants, technology that substitutes the remote interactions between FLEs and customers is considered in this study. However, since the reservation process only initiates restaurant visits, FLEs are not completely substituted. Rather, they continue interacting with customers when the latter express their wish to make changes to their reservation and also during the core service encounter. During

**Table 1.1** Overview of the four empirical studies

| | **Study A** | **Study B** | **Study C** | **Study D** |
|---|---|---|---|---|
| **Study design** | Quantitative | Qualitative | Quantitative | Quantitative |
| **Research method** | Online survey | Semi-structured interviews | Dyadic field survey | Scenario-based online experiment |
| **Sample size** | N = 123 | N = 36 | N = 147 data sets | N = 215 |
| **Service industry** | Hospitality | Hospitality | Hospitality | Retail |
| **Technology considered** | Online reservation system | Frontline service technology | Frontline service technology | Augmented reality (video try-on) |
| **Intended role of technology** | Substituting remote interactions | Mediating personal interactions | Mediating personal interactions | Substituting personal interactions |
| **Stakeholder groups** | | | | |
| Frontline employees | ● | ● | ● Dyads | |
| Technology providers | | ● | ↕ | |
| Managers | | ● | | |
| Customers | | ● | ● | ● |

(continued)

**Table 1.1** (continued)

| | Study A | Study B | Study C | Study D |
|---|---|---|---|---|
| **Theoretical framework** | Transactional theory of stress and coping | Job demands-resources (JD-R); expectancy-disconfirmation | Conservation of resources; JD-R; expectancy-disconfirmation, equity theory | Equity theory, fairness theory |
| **Outcomes considered** | Employee role ambiguity; constructive and destructive process deviance | Adoption barriers and benefits; customer responses to technology | Employee technostress; customer satisfaction and delight | Customer fairness perceptions; behavioral intentions |

these interactions, FLEs are expected to comply with the processes that aim to increase the efficiency of managing reservations.

Using Lazarus and Folkman's (1984) transactional theory of stress and coping as a theoretical framework, Study A aims to develop and test a research model to investigate the antecedents and consequences of technology-induced role ambiguity. The data was collected via an online survey from 123 FLEs working in restaurants that use online reservation systems. The results of structuring equation modeling (SEM) confirm that employee resistance to change fosters role ambiguity, while self-efficacy reduces this ambiguity. Technology-induced role ambiguity leads to both constructive and destructive process deviance. The existence of strict service scripts strengthens the influence of FLE technology-induced role ambiguity on destructive process deviance. Furthermore, there is a direct effect of resistance to change on destructive process deviance.

Despite the significant relationships among the constructs investigated in Study A, it is apparent that most FLEs indicate moderate absolute levels of technology-induced role ambiguity in the online survey. Based on this finding, **Study B** follows a holistic approach to explore not only the potential negative effects of technology in service encounters but also the positive ones. Again, the restaurant industry serves as a use case. Through a qualitative approach, interviews were conducted with three technology providers, seven restaurant managers, eleven FLEs, and fifteen customers in full-service restaurants. These interviews were designed to assess these interviewees' attitudes toward technology and individual experiences. The integration of all the above-mentioned four stakeholder groups aims to attain a 360-degree view of digital technology that is meant to augment personal interactions in service encounters.

Therefore, Study B investigates the benefits and barriers regarding the deployment of digital technology and its impact on FLEs, firms' internal processes and financials, and customer responses. In line with the basic principles of Bakker and Demerouti's (2007) job demands-resources (JD-R) model, FLEs were asked under which circumstances they perceived digital technology as either demanding or enhancing. The interviews with customers provided insights into their perceived relevance of personal interactions with frontline employees. Moreover, several questions on customer satisfaction and delight with technology-mediated service encounters were inspired by Oliver's (1980) expectancy-disconfirmation paradigm. Complementarily, restaurant managers and technology providers were asked to share their appraisals on how FLEs and dining customers handle and value technology.

These interviews were transcribed and then coded using the Straussian coding technique. The qualitative data analysis software MAXQDA was utilized to systematically explore the content of the 36 interviews. The findings of Study B indicate that FLEs predominantly agree with restaurant managers and technology providers' certainty that technology increases their work productivity. This is especially the case when FLEs display a general optimism toward technology, receive clear instructions on their roles, and indicate that their management is highly committed to digital technology. It was indicated that solely system unreliability and the resulting role overload cause strain and stress for FLEs. Customers particularly value digital technology that is easy to use and provides fast service. Yet, customer satisfaction with a service is likely to decrease when technology interfaces are less effective than what the customers had expected.

The findings of the qualitative research in Study B served as a basis and inspiration for the development of a research model for **Study C**. With the help of Hobfoll's (1989) conservation of resources (COR) as its theoretical framework, Study C yet again applies Bakker and Demerouti's (2007) JD-R model to investigate the employee perspective on technology-induced service encounters. According to the JD-R model, each job characteristic can be classified as either resource or demand. In line with the potential stressors identified in Study B, technology-induced role overload and role ambiguity represent job demands that potentially promote FLE technostress. Optimism toward technology is conceptualized to mitigate the relationship between job demands and technostress. On the other hand, managerial commitment and FLE self-efficacy are conceptualized as resources that foster customer orientation.

Through a dyadic approach, FLE technostress and customer orientation behaviors are brought together with customer satisfaction and delight with the FLE. Again, Oliver's (1980) expectancy-disconfirmation paradigm was used as a theoretical framework for considering the customer perspective. Moreover, the equity theory served as a basis for investigating how customer satisfaction and delight impact the respective tip level and customer intention to engage in positive (electronic) word-of-mouth (WOM). For this purpose, dyadic data was gathered using a field survey in full-service restaurants that use frontline service technology. The data sets include 147 FLEs and 373 customers of 73 full-service restaurants in 14 cities and were analyzed using structural equation modeling with IBM SPSS AMOS.

The results of the analysis confirm that technology-induced job demands lead to FLE technostress, whereas job and personal resources foster customer orientation. Technostress reduces customer satisfaction and delight with the FLE, while customer orientation has a positive effect on them. On the other hand, customer delight relates positively to customer tip level and customer intention to engage in positive electronic WOM, but there is no such effect in the case of customer satisfaction. Excerpts of Study C have been published in the Journal of Business Research (Christ-Brendemühl and Schaarschmidt, 2020). This article is entitled "The impact of service employees' technostress on customer satisfaction and delight: A dyadic analysis."

As depicted in Table 1.1, studies A, B, and C address technology that is either meant to mediate personal interactions or to substitute remote interactions that precede the core service encounter. To supplement these applications of digital technology in service encounters, **Study D** compares customer responses to a purchase that either involves purchase advisory service in a branch store or video try-on in an online shop. Based on augmented reality (AR) technology, video try-on features offer customers the opportunity to place virtual objects on a moving picture captured through their (smartphone) cameras. While this digital technology is meant to enable customers to better imagine what items look like in reality, it requires a high level of customer participation. After all, customers are the ones who provide the necessary electronic device, operate the video try-on interface, share sensitive data, and make purchase decisions without receiving any advisory from FLEs.

Thus, it is essential to understand whether AR-enabled online services could achieve equal levels of perceived fairness and engagement intention as personal service encounters with FLEs. Ultimately, it would be worthless for service firms to invest in digital technology without attaining a comprehensive understanding of how customers value such technologies (Lee, Verma, and Roth, 2015). Additionally, it is also important to know how cross-channel price comparisons affect customer responses. Thus, Study D contains a 2×2 between-subject online experiment to compare customer responses after purchasing a pair of sunglasses in a branch store as opposed to making an AR-enabled online purchase.

In Study D, based on the fairness theory and equity theory, hypotheses on customer fairness perceptions and behavioral intentions are derived. Moreover, the answers of 215 participants were analyzed. The study results demonstrate that the participants in video try-on scenarios reported significantly lower levels of distributive, procedural, and price fairness as well as lower engagement intentions. At the same time, they reported higher intentions to spread negative WOM, particularly when a cross-channel price comparison revealed that the same pair of sunglasses cost 20 percent less in one of the retailer's branch stores.

In summary, the four studies encompass quantitative as well as qualitative research works. They were conducted in two service industries that are traditionally characterized by personal interactions between FLEs and customers—hospitality and retail. To gather data from different sources, the research methods included online data collection, telephone interviews, face-to-face interviews, and also a field survey. Digital technologies that differ in maturity level, market penetration, and intended role were considered. Four stakeholder groups were integrated in order to capture different perspectives. Overall, the four studies contribute to answering the research question pertaining to how FLEs and customers respond to digital technology in service encounters.

## 1.3 Structure of the Thesis

As made evident in the introduction section of **Chapter 1**, digital technology in service encounters is a research field that deserves further attention. Accordingly, Section 1.1 ends with the claim that research focusing on the integration of the roles of FLEs, customers, and technology needs to be prioritized. Resulting from this need, Section 1.2 outlines the overall research objective of this dissertation thesis. Following the derivation of the central research question, the research designs of all the four studies that constitute the empirical part of this thesis are introduced. Section 1.3 presents an overview of the thesis structure. Figure 1.1 illustrates this structure.

Following this section, **Chapter 2** begins with an overview of the characteristics of service in Section 2.1, including the evolution of service management as a research discipline. Furthermore, the roles of both FLEs and customers in service encounters are highlighted. Thereupon, Section 2.2 depicts the phenomenon of the technology-induced transformation of service encounters. In this section itself, the changing nature of service encounters from mere dyadic interactions to complex systems is depicted. As an integral element of service encounters today, the role of technology as an enabler of service innovation is discussed. Lastly, Section 2.2 illustrates the meaning of augmented reality (AR) to technology-based services and how this digital technology possibly enhances service encounters.

**Chapter 3** is presented in three sections to illustrate the theoretical foundations of this thesis. First, Section 3.1 provides an overview of two recognized theories on stress and strain in the occupational context. Both Lazarus and Folkman's (1984) transactional theory of stress and coping and Hobfoll's (1989) conservation of resources (COR) theory are introduced in this section. Based on the COR theory, Bakker and Demerouti's (2007) JD-R model is presented. Section 3.2 contrasts two different concepts depicting an individual's predisposition toward technology, that is, Oreg's (2003) concept of resistance to change (RTC) and Parasuraman's (2000) concept of technology readiness. Finally, the underlying mechanisms of technostress are discussed. While the concepts in Section 3.2 are

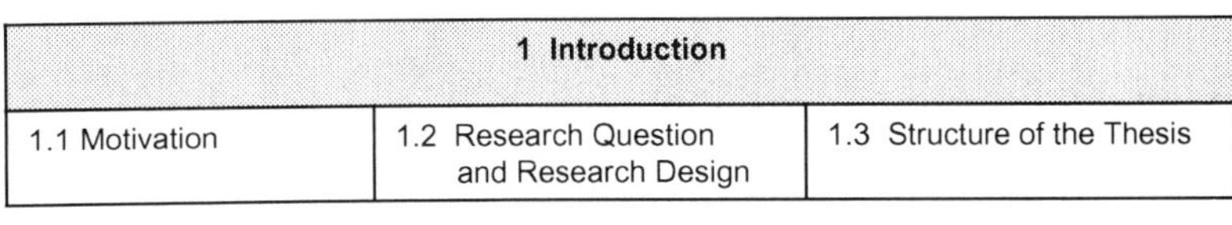

2 Technology in Service Management
2.1 The Characteristics of Service
2.2 The Technology-induced Transformation of Service Encounters

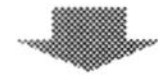

3 Theoretical Foundations
3.1 Theories on Stress and Strain in the Occupational Context
3.2 Individual Predisposition and Appraisal of Technology
3.3 Formation of Customer Evaluations of Service Encounters

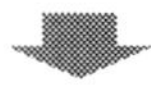

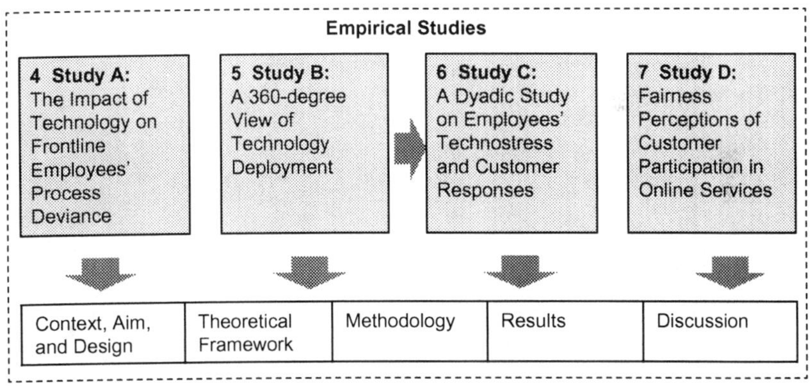


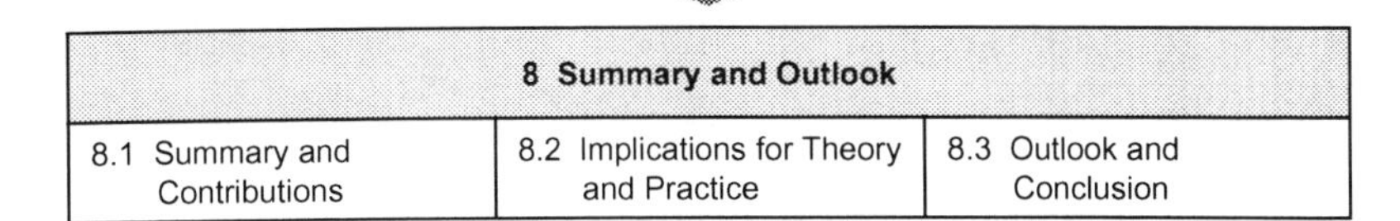


**Figure 1.1** Structure of the thesis. (Source: Own illustration)

mainly applicable to the perspective of FLEs throughout this thesis, Section 3.3 is dedicated to the theoretical foundations of customer evaluations and responses. To this end, Oliver's (1980) expectancy-disconfirmation paradigm, the equity theory, and the concept of service fairness are presented.

The four empirical studies in this thesis are each discussed in Chapters 4, 5, 6, and 7. Study A in **Chapter 4** is entitled "The Impact of Technology on Front-line Employees' Process Deviance" and, accordingly, focuses on the employee perspective in technology-induced service encounters. In contrast, Study B in **Chapter 5** aims at providing "A 360-degree View of Technology Deployment" through qualitative research. Thereby, it provides the framework for a quantitative field survey in Study C, which is depicted in **Chapter 6**. Accordingly, Study C is entitled "A Dyadic Study on Employees' Technostress and Customer Responses". It investigates customer responses to FLEs' technology-induced sentiments and behaviors. Finally, Study D in **Chapter 7** explores "Fairness perceptions of customer participation in online services" in the context of AR features that aim to enhance the customer experience in online retail.

Each of the four studies begins with an outline of their respective context, aim, and research design. Following this, a theoretical framework is presented in order to derive particular research models and hypotheses for the three quantitative studies as well as the focus of the interviews for the qualitative study. Thereupon, the methodology of each study is depicted, followed by a section that summarizes the results or findings. Each of these four chapters is complemented by a discussion section, which encompasses the implications for theory and practice as well as the limitations and avenues for further research.

As illustrated in Figure 1.1, **Chapter 8** concludes this thesis with a summary and outlook. Given the quadripartite empirical research design, this thesis offers important contributions theoretically, empirically, as well as practically. Section 8.1 summarizes the key findings and central contributions of the four presented studies. Then, Section 8.2 combines the implications for theory and practice of all the four studies in order to provide collective implications concerning the integration of the roles of FLEs, customers, and technology. Lastly, Section 8.3 transfers the findings of the thesis to make them relevant for the current and future challenges regarding digital technology in service management.

# Technology in Service Management 2

## 2.1 The Characteristics of Service

Services are central to the global economy and are increasingly becoming essential for fostering sustainable growth (Deloitte Insights, 2018; Wirtz and Lovelock, 2016). In 2017, services accounted for approximately 63 percent of the global gross domestic product (GDP) and 74 percent of the GDP in high-income countries (OECD, 2017). Primarily driven by the demand for services related to information and communication technology (ICT), even the number of exports of commercial services is constantly accelerating and has already outpaced the export of merchandise trade in terms of annual growth rate (World Trade Organization, 2019). Globally, in 2019, services accounted for half of the total employment (The World Bank, 2020). This share is expected to rise as most new jobs are being created in the service sector (International Labour Office, 2019).

The **service sector** includes governmental services as well as commercial services, such as retail, hospitality, real estate, consultation, transport, finance and insurance, healthcare, and entertainment (Fitzsimmons and Fitzsimmons, 2011). However, service provision is not limited to the aforementioned sectors and became an integral part of manufactures' offerings more than three decades ago (Grönroos, 1990b). After all, additional services such as maintenance or counseling can increase the core product's value and serve as a means of differentiation (Raddats *et al.*, 2019). Due to the manifoldness of services, several **definitions** of the term exist.



S. Christ-Brendemühl, *Digital Technology in Service Encounters*, Innovation, Entrepreneurship und Digitalisierung,
https://doi.org/10.1007/978-3-658-37885-1_2

As depicted in Table 2.1, many definitions conceptualize the term service as an interactional process that aims to satisfy customer needs. In line with this process-focused conceptualization of service, an early classification made by Lovelock (1983) determines whether services are directed at people or their possessions and whether the service activity is tangible or intangible. Accordingly, four **categories of services** have been established: people-processing (e.g., healthcare), possession-processing (e.g., maintenance), mental stimulus-processing (e.g., education), and information-processing services (e.g., banking) (Wirtz and Lovelock, 2016).

Despite the rapid evolution of service, this classification still seems to be applicable to today's service landscape. At the same time, it challenges the assumption that services are intangible by nature. Traditionally, service research uses four **characteristics** to separate services from products—intangibility, heterogeneity, inseparability, and perishability (Zeithaml, Parasuraman, and Berry, 1985). Yet, researchers today mainly regard the narrowness of these four characteristics as misleading for the effective management of services (Edvardsson, Gustafsson, and Roos, 2005; Lovelock and Gummesson, 2004; Vargo and Lusch, 2004b).

**Table 2.1** Different definitions of the term service

| Source | Definition |
|---|---|
| Grönroos (1990a, p. 27) | "A service is an activity or series of activities of more or less intangible nature that normally, but not necessarily, take place in interactions between the customer and service employees and/or physical resources or goods and/or systems of the service provider, which are provided as solutions to customer problems." |
| Vargo and Lusch (2004b, p. 326) | "We define services as the application of specialized competences (skills and knowledge), through deeds, processes, and performances for the benefit of another entity or the entity itself (self-service)." |
| Fitzsimmons and Fitzsimmons (2011, p. 4) | "A service is a time-perishable, intangible experience performed for a customer acting in the role of co-producer." |
| Qiu (2013, p. 1) | "[S]ervice is a process of transformation of the customer's needs utilizing the operations' resources, in which dimensions of customer experience manifest themselves in the themes of a service encounter or service encounter chain." |
| Wirtz and Lovelock (2016, p. 21) | "Services are economic activities performed by one party to another. Often time-based, these performances bring about desired results to recipients, objects, or other assets. [...] However, [customers] do not normally take ownership of the physical elements involved." |

(continued)

**Table 2.1** (continued)

| Source | Definition |
|---|---|
| Zeithaml, Bitner, and Gremler (2017, p. 4) | "Services are deeds, processes, and performances provided, coproduced, or co-created by one entity or person for and/or with another entity or person." |

Coincidently, the effective management of services is vital to a firm's productivity and can create a competitive edge in increasingly contested markets (Fitzsimmons and Fitzsimmons, 2011). To better understand the nature of services, Section 2.1.1. first presents an overview of the **evolution of service management** as a research discipline. This overview includes brief introductions to prevalent terminologies in service management. Subsequently, this chapter covers the characteristics of those services that are particularly directed at people and typically require interactions between customers and FLEs. Therefore, Section 2.1.2 examines the **role of FLEs** in service management. Likewise, Section 2.1.3 depicts the **role of customers** and their contributions to service.

### 2.1.1 The Evolution of Service Management as a Research Discipline

During the 1970s, western countries began to deregulate major parts of the transportation, telecommunication, banking, and electronic power industries (Winston, 1993). Along with this **deregulation of service segments**, formerly protected monopolies transitioned into competitive markets (Brock, 1998). Thus, the strive for growth in productivity through effective management methods became increasingly prevailing in the service sector (Pilat, 1996). However, management theories that targeted the requirements of the manufacturing industry turned out to generate only limited applicability and value for service firms. Accordingly, the development of new concepts and the advancement of theoretical frameworks based on service-specific issues started in the 1970s (Grönroos, 1994).

Marketing researchers were among the first to examine the specific requirements of service firms and thereby created the foundations of a new academic field (Berry and Parasuraman, 1993). Wilson's (1972) book entitled 'The marketing of professional services' and Rathmell's (1974) book 'Marketing in the service sector' marked the early cornerstones of **service marketing** research.

With the introduction of the customer contact model, Chase (1978) initially differentiated the organizational frontline from the back office and played a pivotal role in acknowledging the customer's role in service delivery. Thereafter, researchers in North America as well as in Europe evolved models to further examine the nature of service delivery, customer relationships, and service quality (Grönroos, 1984; Lovelock, 1983; e.g., Parasuraman, Zeithaml, and Berry, 1985).

Normann (1984) specifically dedicated his research to **service management** and published the eponymous book in Swedish in 1982 and in English two years later. Inspired by the Swedish approach, U.S.-based management consultant Karl Albrecht recorded a definition of service management that became formative for linking theory and practice in this field. He stated that "[s]ervice management is a total organizational approach that makes quality of service, as perceived by the customer, the number one driving force for the operation of the business" (Albrecht, 1988, p. 20).

Quite simultaneously, the Decision Science Institute[1], a U.S.-based international association of academics and practitioners, recognized service (operations) management as a **stand-alone academic field** in 1987 (Fitzsimmons and Fitzsimmons, 2011). In the same year, the Journal of Services Marketing (JSM)[2]was inaugurated. Its publishing house, Emerald, then additionally launched the International Journal of Service Industry Management[3] in 1990 to emphasize service management topics. The latter journal was renamed into the Journal of Services Management (JOSM)[4] in 2009. Although the publishing house SAGE first published the Journal of Service Research (JSR)[5] as late as in the year of 1998, the JSR soon became the **leading journal** in the academic field (Fitzsimmons and Fitzsimmons, 2011). Figure 2.1 depicts the cornerstones of the evolution of service management as a research discipline in the 1980s and 1990s.

[1] https://decisionsciences.org/ [05.06.2020]

[2] https://www.emerald.com/insight/publication/issn/0887-6045 [05.06.2020]

[3] https://www.emerald.com/insight/publication/issn/0956-4233 [05.06.2020]

[4] https://www.emerald.com/insight/publication/acronym/JOSM [05.06.2020]

[5] https://journals.sagepub.com/home/jsr [05.06.2020]

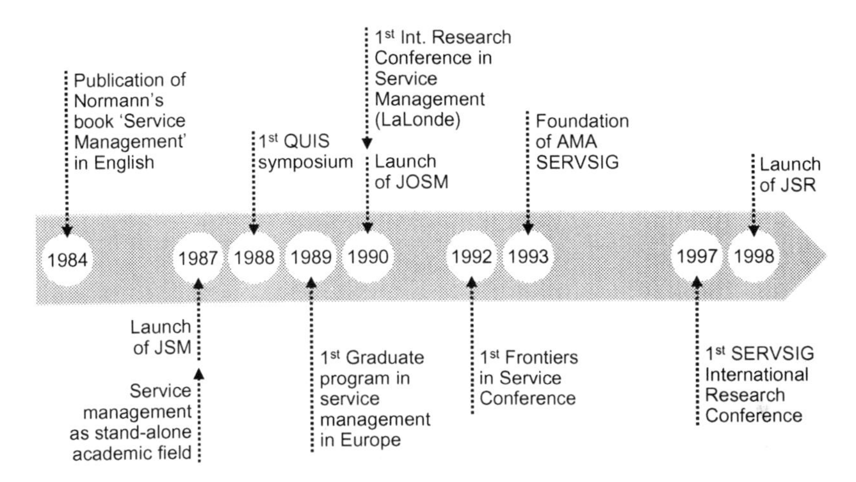


**Figure 2.1** The evolution of service management in the 1980s and 1990s. (Source: Own illustration)

As demonstrated in Figure 2.1, service management started to become a part of management studies at universities in the late 1980s. Concurrently, Bo Edvardsson, Evert Gummesson, and Stephen W. Brown established the 'Quality in Services' (QUIS) symposium. The first edition in 1988 brought together service researchers in Karlstad, Sweden[6] by invitation only. In 1989, the 'Institut d'Administration des Entreprises d'Aix-en-Provence' in Aix-Marseille had been the first university in Europe to offer a **graduate program** in service management[7]. The same institution hosted the first 'International Research Conference in Service Management' in 1990. This initiative, known today as the 'La Londe Conference' in the South of France, has aimed at uniting multidisciplinary research from its beginnings[8].

Besides the QUIS symposium and 'La Londe Conference', multiple renowned **academic conferences** today focus on services. Founded in 1992, the 'Frontiers in Service Conference' is considered one of the leading annual conferences on service research[8]. The global conference is sponsored by the Institute for Operations Research and the Management Sciences (INFORMS), the Center for

[6] https://www.kau.se/en/ctf/about-ctf/ctf/seminars-events/quis-symposium-1988-2019 [29.06.2020]

[7] https://www.servsig.org/wordpress/2019/09/la-londe-conference-2020/ [05.06.2020]

[8] https://www.frontiersinservice.com/about [05.06.2020]

Excellence in Service at the University of Maryland, and the American Marketing Association (AMA). In addition, the AMA's Services Special Interest Group (SERVSIG), founded by Ray Fisk in 1993, hosts the biennial 'SERVSIG International Research Conference' since 1997[9].

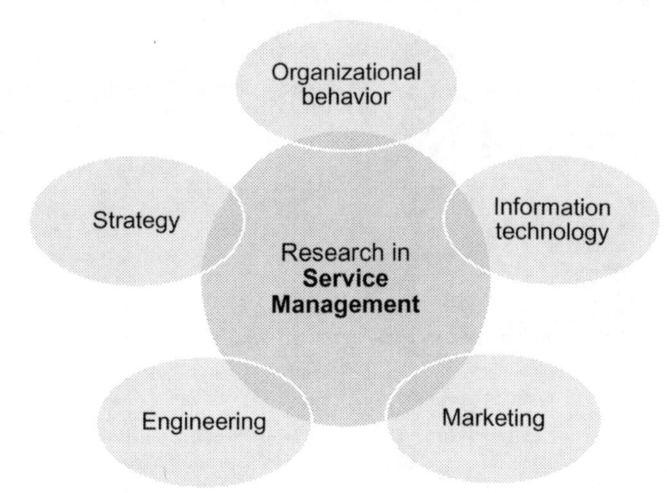


**Figure 2.2** The multidisciplinary of service research. (Source: Adapted from Brady, 2019)

Figure 2.2 compiles multiple disciplines that influence research in service management today. The illustration is adapted from a presentation at the 'Let's Talk about Service Conference' 2019 by Michael K. Brady, editor of the Journal of Service Research at that time. In his presentation, he postulated that service research is **multidisciplinary by definition** (Brady, 2019). Similarly, Spohrer, Kwan, and Fisk (2014) state that more than 20 academic disciplines are investigating services from their perspective. Fitzsimmons and Fitzsimmons (2011) propose that the integration of various perspectives is essential to effective service management. The multidisciplinary of service management becomes prevalent in a concept that will be further elaborated in Section 2.1.2, namely Heskett *et al.*'s (1994) service-profit chain. The latter links human resources management, operations, and service marketing to the financial performance of service firms (Loveman, 1998).

[9] https://www.servsig.org/wordpress/2018/07/servsig-history-and-a-future-perspective/ [05.06.2020]

Vargo and Lusch (2004a) emphasize that the performance of a service firm results from the value created for customers. The creation of value is central to a theoretical framework that Vargo and Lusch (2004a) have entitled **service-dominant logic**. According to this framework, services are the fundamental form of exchange in any transaction between firms and customers. Today, service-dominant logic encompasses eleven foundational premises (Vargo and Lusch, 2016). One of these foundational premises proposes that the value of service is not solely determined by the service provider, but is always co-created by the active participation of the customer (Vargo and Lusch, 2004a). The concept of co-creation will be further elaborated in Section 2.1.3. Still, the concept is of importance regarding the evolution of service management depicted in this section since service-dominant logic is seen as the basis of service science (Kim, 2019).

**Service science** examines how service systems advance to co-create value (Maglio and Spohrer, 2008). Maglio and Spohrer (2008) are considered as the originators of the term service science. By integrating multiple academic disciplines into a new domain, they aimed at building the foundation for service innovation through the systematic study of service systems (Kim, 2019). **Service systems**, in turn, are composed of customers and service firms that interact to reciprocally achieve beneficial outcomes (Feldmann *et al.*, 2019). As these interactions are increasingly induced by digital solutions, technology is considered to be an integral part of service systems (Patrício *et al.*, 2011). Despite the importance of technology, however, the research field of service science has recently emphasized a more human-centered approach of studying service systems that require intense personal interactions between customers and frontline employees (Sangiorgi *et al.*, 2019). Such human-centered service systems share an immanent complexity that is driven by human needs, emotions, cognition, and behavior (Breidbach, Antons, and Salge, 2016).

Similarly, Subramony and Pugh (2015) emphasize the relevance of individual antecedents for both individual-level and organization-level service outcomes. More specifically, they propose that employee characteristics like knowledge, skills, and abilities as well as their emotions and cognitions form customer responses through inter-and intrapersonal processes (Subramony and Pugh, 2015). These 'inter- and intrapersonal processes' represent one of four **research domains** that Subramony and Pugh (2015) classify by distinguishing between the individual and the organizational level as well as between antecedents and outcomes of different service constructs. Table 2.2 depicts these domains. According to this classification, 'micro-foundations' encompass organizational-level effects like financial performance that result from individual-level constructs (Felin *et al.*, 2012).

**Table 2.2** Domains of service management research. (Source: Adapted from Subramony and Pugh, 2015, p. 351)

| | | **Outcomes** | |
|---|---|---|---|
| | | **Individual-level** (e.g., process deviance, customer responses) | **Organization-level** (e.g., financial performance) |
| **Antecedents** | **Individual-level** (e.g., predispositions, emotions, skills) | Interpersonal and intrapersonal processes | Micro-foundations |
| | **Organization-level** (e.g., service climate, leadership practices) | Multilevel effects | Macro linkages |

At the same time, individual-level and organizational-level outcomes can result from organizational-level antecedents. Organizational-level antecedents encompass human resource management and established leadership practices as well as the aggregation of employees' characteristics and individual beliefs (Ployhart *et al.*, 2014). Depending on whether individual-level or organizational-level outcomes are considered, these domains are either termed 'multilevel effects' or 'macro linkages'. Although Subramony and Pugh (2015) state that an integrative theory of service management has not yet been established, they claim that their proposed classification is overarching. This is because almost all research in service management investigates the connection between organizations, employees, and customers either within or across the depicted four domains (Subramony and Pugh, 2015).

One research stream in service management that equally focuses on these connections is **organizational frontline research** (OFR). The term frontline is originated in the military, where 'front' denominated the boundary between conflicting armies and 'line' referred to the particular points of contact (Singh *et al.*, 2017). In the 1960s, the term frontline was first introduced to the management literature by Black and Ford (1963). Thereafter, Smith (1965) described frontline organizations as those whose locus of initiative is in frontline units. In general, these frontline units perform tasks independently from each. Their activities are thus considered to be difficult to supervise (Smith, 1965).

About fifty years later, Singh *et al.* (2017, p. 3) view organizational frontlines as "the **intersection of interfaces and interactions** that connect organizations and their customers." In turn, organizational frontline research encompasses scholarship that systematically investigates how such interfaces and interactions stimulate or enhance value creation and exchange (Singh *et al.*, 2017). Hence, the transdisciplinary research field of organizational frontline research examines the roles of humans and technology to address customer needs and thereby achieve organizational goals (Rafaeli *et al.*, 2017).

As illustrated in this section, service management has considerably evolved over the decades. The research discipline has put forth theoretical frameworks that aim at enabling a comprehensive understanding and effective management of services. While it had been questioned in the early 2000s whether existing service concepts were applicable to technology-based services at all (Edvardsson *et al.*, 2005), technology today represents an integral part of service research (Huang and Rust, 2017). As technology has essentially changed the context of service delivery, the roles of employees working in the frontline need to be fundamentally redesigned to integrate technology into their behaviors (Rafaeli *et al.*, 2017). Thus, the following section provides an overview of the role that frontline employees play in service management.

### 2.1.2 The Role of Frontline Employees in Service Management

As depicted in the previous section, the origins of service research lie in the marketing literature. Accordingly, a customer-driven perspective still dominates scholarship in service (Groth *et al.*, 2019). Although the potential of **employee-related research** in service management may thus be considered as unfulfilled (Subramony *et al.*, 2017), there is a broad consensus that frontline employees can have a vast impact on customers in service settings (Barnes, Ponder, and Hopkins, 2015; Grönroos, 2020). Research investigating the role of frontline employees has started to evolve about four decades ago. Particularly, Leonard L. Berry is considered as the first scholar to introduce the term 'frontline employee' to service research (Singh *et al.*, 2017). In his seminal paper, Berry (1981) called for acknowledging the important role of employees who work at the frontline of organizations since they are responsible for customer contact and service (Singh *et al.*, 2017).

In line with this, Grönroos (1990b) formulated six **principles of service management** of which four particularly emphasize the relevance of effectively managing employees to leverage customer-related outcomes. These principles are part of an article published in the very first issue of the International Journal of

Service Industry Management in 1990 (Subramony *et al.*, 2017). The journal is today known as the Journal of Service Management (JOSM). In this particular article, Grönroos (1990b) postulated that the main goal of a service firm should be the support of frontline operations. This requires managers to encourage frontline employees. Moreover, the authority of making decisions should be moved as close as possible to the frontline. Finally, reward systems should recognize frontline employees' responsibility and effort to deliver quality service to customers (Grönroos, 1990b). Thirty years later, it still applies that employees are responsible for serving, satisfying, and retaining customers (Grönroos, 2020).

Today, the term frontline employee is widely used (Giebelhausen *et al.*, 2014; Schepers and van der Borgh, 2020; Subramony *et al.*, 2017; Wilder, Collier, and Barnes, 2014). However, there is no fully consistent terminology. Rather, researchers use the concepts 'service employee' (e.g., Groth *et al.*, 2019), 'customer-contact service employee' (e.g., Chebat and Kollias, 2000), 'service worker' (e.g., Sirianni *et al.*, 2009), and 'frontline service employee' (Beatty *et al.*, 2016; Elmadağ, Ellinger, and Franke, 2008; Sok *et al.*, 2018) interchangeably. To emphasize the immediate touchpoints between a customer and an employee at a service firm's frontline, the term **frontline employee (FLE)** will be used hereafter. Throughout this thesis, frontline employees (FLEs) are defined as those employees who personally interact with customers in service encounters (Ellinger, Elmadağ, and Ellinger, 2007; Schaarschmidt, 2016; Stock *et al.*, 2017).

These **personal interactions** shape a customer's impression of a service firm and are an essential facet of service experience (Groth *et al.*, 2019; Hartline, Maxham, and McKee, 2000). After all, an FLE's performance is regarded as a major element of a service (Hennig-Thurau, 2004). In line with this, Zeithaml *et al.* (2017, p. 320) state that employees "*are* the service" in many personal services like haircutting or professional ones like tax consultancy. In such service settings, FLEs autonomously provide the entire service and thereby determine the value delivered to the customer (Zhang *et al.*, 2011). Accordingly, FLEs are still viewed as an organization's most important asset in many service industries (Wirtz *et al.*, 2018).

Even in service industries in which components like the food served in a full-service restaurant or the value of goods sold in a retail store mainly contribute to the perceived quality of service, customers view FLEs as **representatives of the service firm** (Berry, 2009). Accordingly, aligning FLE behavior with a service firm's positioning is expected to positively influence customer responses to those service firms (Sirianni *et al.*, 2013). The awareness of this effect is crucial as everything FLEs say or do can influence a customer's perception of an organization (Zeithaml *et al.*, 2017). Hence, FLEs that demonstrate counterproductive behaviors in service encounters can constitute a liability to customer interactions (Wirtz and Lovelock, 2016).

The pivotal role frontline employees play in service firms becomes prevalent in the service-profit chain. The latter is illustrated in Figure 2.3. The **service-profit chain** proposes that a service firm's revenue growth and profitability primarily depend on customer loyalty, which is conceptualized as resulting from customer satisfaction (Heskett *et al.*, 1994). Heskett *et al.* (1994) expect customer satisfaction to derive from the provided value of service. In turn, value is leveraged when service employees are satisfied, loyal, and thus work productively (Heskett *et al.*, 1994). Finally, Heskett *et al.* (1994) suggest that service employee satisfaction predominantly results from internal service quality. The latter is reflected in work conditions and service scripts that enable employees to deliver high-quality services to customers. Taken together, employees who are satisfied, loyal, and productive represent a key opportunity for service differentiation (Heskett, Sasser, and Schlesinger, 2015).

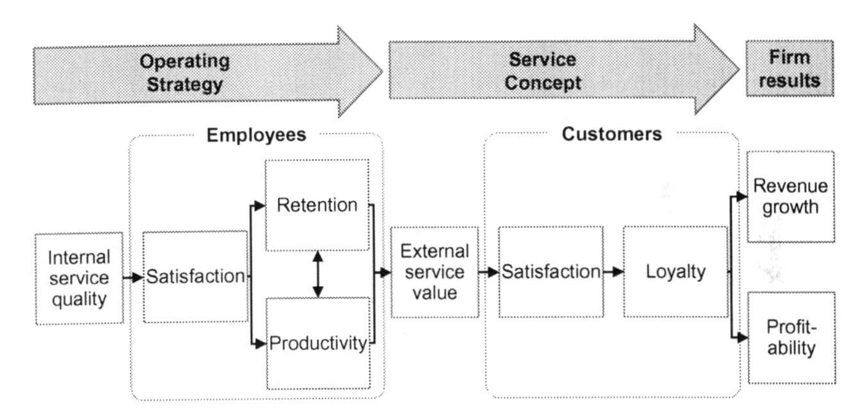


**Figure 2.3** Links in the service-profit chain. (Source: Adapted from Heskett *et al.*, 1994, p. 166)

Meta-analyses confirm that the links postulated by the service-profit chain appear substantial and statistically significant, particularly the relationships among employee job satisfaction, perceived service quality, and customer satisfaction (Brown and Lam, 2008; Hogreve *et al.*, 2017). More recent research has extended the service-profit chain and proposes that customer loyalty is stimulated even stronger by customer-company identification (Homburg, Wieseke, and

Bornemann, 2009) or customer delight (Stock *et al.*, 2017). These extensions share the common ground that the identified antecedents to **customer loyalty** highly depend on FLEs. More specifically, FLE customer orientation (Homburg *et al.*, 2009) and innovative service behavior (Stock *et al.*, 2017) build the basis for customer satisfaction, delight, and identification with the firm. Accordingly, as one result of their meta-analysis, Hogreve *et al.* (2017) emphasize the relevance of personal encounters and customer relationships for customer responses.

In the long-term, a primary success factor for strong customer-firm relationships is **customer rapport** (Gremler and Gwinner, 2008). Gremler and Gwinner (2000, p. 83) consider rapport to be "the customer's perception of having an enjoyable interaction with a service provider employee" that is characterized by a personal connection between the FLE and the customer. As most service encounters involve social interactions, these should feel pleasant and amicable for both parties to establish and maintain a relationship (Bradley *et al.*, 2010). FLEs can display various behaviors to build rapport with customers. For instance, they can seek and address similarities with the customer to build common ground. Furthermore, FLEs can develop a connection to the customer through smiling, using humor, or being particularly friendly and warm (Gremler and Gwinner, 2008). Moreover, rapport-building behaviors can be reflected in courtesy, attentiveness, and responsiveness to customer requests as well as in sharing information about the service offerings (Giebelhausen *et al.*, 2014).

Due to their constant contact with customers, FLEs are in a good position to build rapport and to identify and address **customer needs** (Rafaeli, Ziklik, and Doucet, 2008). Today, customers expect FLEs to meet their individual needs and fulfill their special requests (Beatty *et al.*, 2016). However, it requires empathy and anticipation to recognize customer needs. Secondly, FLEs must possess adequate skills and creativity to offer satisfactory choices to the customer (Wilder *et al.*, 2014). Moreover, service firms that expect FLEs to deliver customized service offerings have to allocate appropriate resources, empower, and support FLEs in manifesting adaptive behaviors (Gwinner *et al.*, 2005). Through such behaviors, FLEs can contribute to establishing strong relationships between their service firm and customers and thus enhance customer loyalty (Bove and Johnson, 2001; Wirtz and Jerger, 2016). Furthermore, FLEs offering additional service components or products that best match customer needs can generate additional revenue through cross- and upselling (Jasmand, Blazevic, and de Ruyter, 2012; Yu, Patterson, and de Ruyter, 2013).

On the other hand, FLE adaptive behavior may as well have negative consequences for service firms. In most service settings, FLEs carry the responsibility to tailor a service experience to customers' needs (Wilder *et al.*, 2014). The heterogeneity of service delivery frequently entices FLEs to deviate from preplanned and scripted behavior (Groth *et al.*, 2019). FLE behavior that breaks norms or rules with the intent to solve a problem or to satisfy customers' needs is referred to as **constructive deviance** (Galperin, 2012). For instance, Brady, Voorhees, and Brusco (2012) claim that FLEs giving unauthorized discounts or free supplements to customers cause substantial revenue losses to service firms. Moreover, customers perceive preferential treatment as relatively unjust although receiving something extra as compared to other customers can enhance customer satisfaction (Söderlund *et al.*, 2014). Thus, FLE constructive deviance is a two-sided phenomenon as it harms the operational profitability of a service firm in the short-term. In the long-term, it may evoke positive effects through increased customer satisfaction, loyalty, and positive word-of-mouth (Brady *et al.*, 2012).

Figure 2.4 sums up the findings illustrated in this section. Taken together, the way FLEs feel and act in service encounters strongly impacts the quality of and customer responses to service delivered by a firm (Gemmel, van Looy, and van Dierdonck, 2013). FLEs that contribute to the provision of excellent service can constitute a competitive advantage and thus enhance a service firm's success (Groth *et al.*, 2019). The important role FLEs play in service encounters will be further elaborated in the empirical studies constituting this thesis.

### 2.1.3 The Contribution of Customers to Service

In the service sector, customers have initially represented "an untapped productive resource" (Fitzsimmons, 1985, p. 60). Along with the recognition that **customer contribution** distinguishes service delivery from the production of goods, service research has started to investigate the shift of activities from service providers onto the customer (Bitner *et al.*, 1997; Bowen and Jones, 1986). Although the service-profit chain is still widely applied to investigate the links between internal service quality and service performance (Hogreve *et al.*, 2017), the paradigm of unilateral service delivery by the firm or its service employees has been challenged. Rather, it has been acknowledged that customers contributing their time, effort, and other resources bear the potential to increase a service provider's productivity and performance (Haumann *et al.*, 2015). As this creates a competitive advantage, it has become crucial for service providers to foster customer contribution to service innovation and development (Blut, Wang, and Schoefer, 2016) as well as to service delivery (Fliess, Dyck, and Schmelter, 2014).

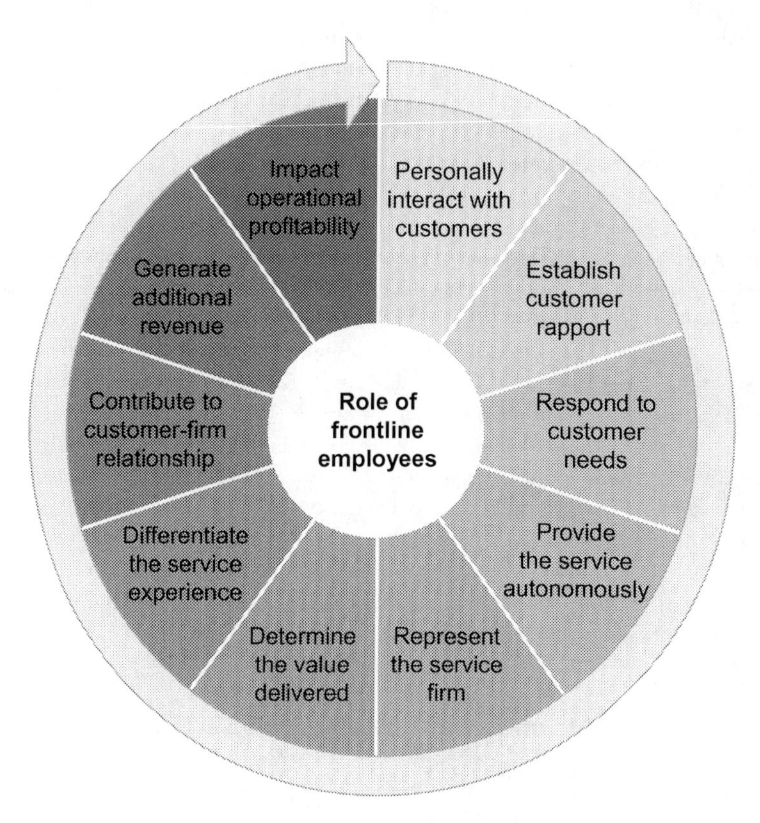


**Figure 2.4** The role of frontline employees in service encounters. (Source: Own illustration)

Prior research has applied inconsistent conceptualizations and terms to describe customer contribution to services (Fliess *et al.*, 2014). Hence, the following section aims at defining and distinguishing the terminologies most commonly used in extant service literature. Figure 2.5 serves as guidance through the different concepts and visualizes their interrelationships (Moeller, 2008). As illustrated, the concepts are hereafter classified according to the respective degree of customer contribution and the service stage they are relevant for. In line with Fliess *et al.* (2014), customer contribution serves as an umbrella term for the different concepts discussed in this section.

The first concept considered is a customer's involvement. The latter is positioned at the bottom of Figure 2.5. It spans all three service stages as it can be of importance for service innovation, service delivery, and recovery as well as for the promotion of services after service delivery. In the service *innovation* literature, **customer involvement** stands for the incorporation of customers into the development of new services. This aims at understanding customer needs before designing new services (Melton and Hartline, 2010). More precisely, Edvardsson *et al.* (2011, p. 301) define customer involvement as "being proactive and 'coming close to customers' to learn from and with them throughout the service innovation process." Hence, the customer is viewed as a subject that a service provider may wish to include in the innovation processes.

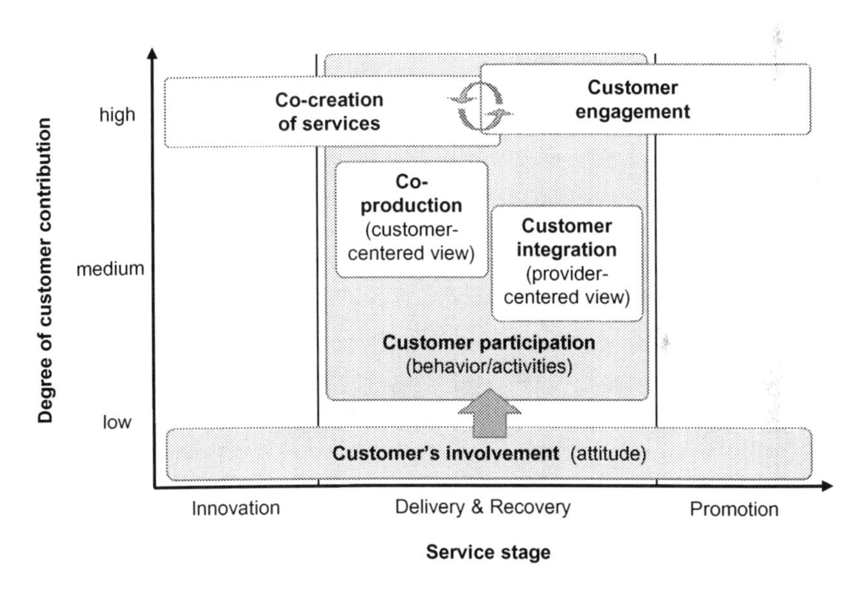


**Figure 2.5** Framework of customer contribution to services. (Source: Own illustration inspired by Bitner *et al.*, 1997 and Fliess *et al.*, 2014)

Instead, in *customer behavior* research, involvement is defined as "a person's perceived relevance of the object based on inherent needs, values, and interests" (Zaichkowsky, 1985, p. 342). Hence, the customer is viewed as a subject that forms an *attitude* toward a service offering and toward contributing actively to it (Fliess *et al.*, 2014). Following this conceptualization, a **customer's involvement** is positioned at the bottom of Figure 2.5, representing a low degree of (tangible) customer contribution. At the same time, a customer's involvement constitutes the basis of all other forms of customer contribution. This is in line with the presumption that motivation—as a behavioral intention resulting from positive attitudes—is one prerequisite of customer contribution (Bettencourt *et al.*, 2002).

First and foremost, a customer's involvement potentially results in **customer participation**, which focuses on actual behaviors and thus customer activities during service delivery or recovery (Moeller, 2008). Dong and Sivakumar (2017, p. 944) define customer participation as "the extent to which customers are involved in service production and delivery by contributing effort, knowledge, information, and other resources." Bitner *et al.* (1997) were among the first to describe three different levels of customer participation.

At a low level of customer participation, services solely require the physical presence of a customer, for instance, when going to the movies. Besides the mere presence, money may be the only resource customers need to contribute to this kind of service provision (Bitner *et al.*, 1997). At a moderate level of participation, the provision and/or customization of a service offering requires customer inputs such as information, effort, or tangible possessions (Bitner *et al.*, 1997). For instance, a customer with a broken car has to transport the vehicle to the repair shop—which involves effort. Furthermore, he or she needs to share information on what should be fixed and has to leave his or her possession there until it is repaired. Still, as with low participation levels, the core service is traditionally conducted by the service provider and its employees (van Birgelen, Dellaert, and de Ruyter, 2012).

Nonetheless, customer participation can as well supplement or even substitute employee labor (Lovelock and Young, 1979), suggesting that customers act as 'partial employees' of service providers (Mills and Morris, 1986). Fliess and Kleinaltenkamp (2004) disagree with the proposition that customers can be seen as members of service firms. Instead, customers participating in service provision contribute additional and necessary resources (Fliess and Kleinaltenkamp, 2004). At a high level of participation, customers are actively included in co-creating the service and thereby affect the outcome (Bitner *et al.*, 1997). Moreover, the service cannot effectively be delivered unless the customer complies with the requirements of his contribution role, for instance, in education and training (Bitner *et al.*, 1997).

As depicted in Figure 2.5, customer participation captures different degrees of customer effort (Silpakit and Fisk, 1985). Although the concept is widely recognized in marketing research (Dong and Sivakumar, 2017), Moeller (2008) suggests that the term **customer integration** is better able to depict customer contribution to service provision. More specifically, she states that supplementary to the activity focus of customer participation, customers contribute to services by initiating and enabling service provision through their personal data or resources (Moeller, 2008).

However, the conceptualization of customer participation has evolved over the decades (Mustak, Jaakkola, and Halinen, 2013). More recent literature does not limit customer participation to activities. Moreover, a considerable number of researchers recognize the importance of further customer resources like needs- and solution-based knowledge (Chang and Taylor, 2016), labor and tasks (Dong *et al.*, 2015), or information (Dong and Sivakumar, 2017). Accordingly, in this thesis, customer integration is considered to be one form of customer participation when participation ranges at a moderate level. Hibbert, Winklhofer, and Temerak (2012, p. 248) define customer resource integration as "the processes by which customers deploy their resources as they undertake bundles of activities that create value." Thus, from a provider-centered view, customers are seen as a resource contributor to the service provider's value-creating process (Fliess *et al.*, 2014).

A concept similar to customer integration is **customer co-production**. The latter "involves the participation in the creation of the core offering itself" (Lusch, Vargo, and O'Brien, 2007, p. 11). This definition demonstrates that co-production is considered as a further form of customer participation as well (Etgar, 2008). As it derives from a customer-centered view of services (Fliess *et al.*, 2014), co-production is positioned as the counterpart of customer integration in Figure 2.5. However, since customer co-production is rather attributed to service provisions that are "independent of direct service employee involvement" (Haumann *et al.*, 2015, p. 19), it tends to involve higher degrees of customer contribution than customer integration. Consequently, it is positioned at some higher degree of customer contribution in Figure 2.5. The maximum form of customer co-production is self-service (Hilton *et al.*, 2013). In this case, the 'co-' refers to the interaction between the customer and either a system or infrastructure provided by the service firm (Oertzen *et al.*, 2018).

Similarly, **co-creation** describes the "joint creation of value by the company and the customer" (Prahalad and Ramaswamy, 2004, p. 8). The term co-creation is embedded into a customer-centered view, regarding customers "as an integral and at least equal actor in service provision" (Fliess *et al.*, 2014, p. 437). Customers are expected to be willing to share personal data and invest substantial effort in exchange for a customized service experience (Etgar, 2008). Yet, their contribution to co-created services partly depends on personality traits and demographic factors (Oertzen, Odekerken-Schröder, and Mager, 2020). As with co-production, in highly co-created services, customers partly take over tasks that are typically performed by service employees (Heidenreich and Handrich, 2015).

At first sight, the co-creation of services is closely affiliated to the sixth foundational premise of service-dominant logic, stating that the value of a service offering is always co-created and thus determined by the customer (Lusch and Vargo, 2006). However, literature inspired by the service-dominant logic approach assumes that the customer takes control over the value creation process and that the provider solely joins this process (Grönroos and Voima, 2012). Opposing, the **co-creation of services** perspective promoted by Oertzen *et al.* (2018, p. 642) "does not specify whether the provider joins the customer's sphere or vice versa; instead, it concentrates on the mutual creation of services during service processes and service innovation activities."

The above-mentioned definition implies that co-creation is not limited to service delivery and consumption. Instead, the concept is as well used to explain the role of customers in service innovation (Gustafsson, Kristensson, and Witell, 2012) and the development of new products or services (Hoyer *et al.*, 2010). Co-creation of services thus stretches over two stages of service in Figure 2.5. The bent arrow pointing from customer engagement to co-creation of services reflects the consideration that besides involvement and participation, engagement is one necessary prerequisite for the co-creation of services (Oertzen *et al.*, 2018).

In academic literature, various definitions of **customer engagement** exist. Bowden (2009) conceptualizes customer engagement as a psychological process eliciting customer loyalty toward a service brand. Hollebeek (2011) specifies that customer engagement is a tripartite construct encompassing cognitive, emotional, and behavioral brand-related activities. Vivek, Beatty, and Morgan (2012) add a social element to these three levels and depict that the intensity of a customer's participation and connection with the service offering determine customer engagement. Similarly, Brodie *et al.* (2011) describe customer engagement as a psychological state resulting from interactive, co-created customer experiences. The iterative process between customer engagement and co-creation of services is symbolized by the circle of bent arrows in Figure 2.5. A customer's involvement and customer participation are necessary antecedents of this process (Brodie *et al.*, 2011).

A further literature stream emphasizes the "behavioral manifestations" (van Doorn *et al.*, 2010, p. 253) of customer engagement that result from motivational drivers and go beyond the purchase. Whereas the purchase represents a direct contribution to the service firm, indirect customer contributions can include (incentivized) referral behavior, influencing activities through social media channels, feedback, or provided suggestions to improve service (Kumar *et al.*, 2010; Kumar and Pansari, 2016). Thus, customer engagement is a multi-dimensional concept going beyond service delivery (Pansari and Kumar, 2017). Since customer engagement requires cognitive and behavioral resources as well as emotional and social ones (Vivek *et al.*, 2012), the concept is positioned at a higher degree of customer contribution than the co-creation of service in Figure 2.5. Overall, this section aimed at providing an overview of the different specifications of customer contribution, its differences, and interrelationships.

## 2.2 The Technology-induced Transformation of Service Encounters

Over the past few decades, the nature of service encounters has profoundly changed in many respects (Ostrom *et al.*, 2015). Today, service innovations and advancements in technology enable service firms to provide a highly personalized service experience to their customers while simultaneously integrating them into service delivery (Groth *et al.*, 2019). Through customers' integration into technology-based services, they partly take over the role of performing the tasks that were traditionally done by FLEs (Heidenreich and Handrich, 2015). Moreover, technology facilitates customers to search for information, make comparisons among different service providers, and share experiences with others. Accordingly, the implementation of ICT in organizations is transforming how customers interact with a service firm before, during, and after service delivery (Ostrom *et al.*, 2015). This evolution has distorted the traditional roles of FLEs and customers in service encounters (Groth *et al.*, 2019).

The following chapter further elaborates on the technology-induced transformation of service encounters. To this end, Section 2.2.1 begins by presenting a conceptualization of the terminology 'service encounter' and discuss the traditional centricity of dyadic interactions between FLEs and customers. Then, the ways through which technology has changed the nature of service encounters are outlined. Next, Section 2.2.2 examines the role of technology in service innovation and outlines that it can be viewed as a trigger or an enabler of innovation or even as an innovator in its own right. Finally, Section 2.2.3 presents augmented reality (AR) as one technology that is meant to enhance the experience in service encounters.

### 2.2.1 The Changing Nature of Service Encounters

In academic literature, conceptual and empirical research on service encounters has only started to accelerate during the 1980s (Czepiel, Solomon, and Surprenant, 1985; Solomon *et al.*, 1985). These early works are largely based on prior research on the **dyadic interaction** between firm representatives and customers that conceptualizes the sales process as a social situation (e.g., Evans, 1963). In line with this conceptualization, early definitions refer to the term service encounter as "the dyadic interaction between a customer and a service provider" (Surprenant and Solomon, 1987, p. 87). The originators of the latter definition, Michael R. Solomon and Carol F. Suprenant, belong to a group of researchers who led the efforts to develop research on service encounters and thus bundled their expertise in a book entitled 'The Service Encounter' (Czepiel *et al.*, 1985). Together with this book, a paper published in the *Journal of Marketing* by Solomon *et al.* (1985) that investigates service encounters from a role theory perspective is considered a seminal work on this topic (Bitner and Wang, 2014).

Although Solomon *et al.* (1985) acknowledge that service encounters may involve more than two actors, these typically consist of dyadic person-to-person interactions that differentiate one service encounter from another. Since service encounters frequently determine customer perceptions of the service as such (Bitner, Booms, and Tetreault, 1990), they are often referred to as **'moment of truth'** that determines a customer's evaluation of service quality and thus the service firm's overall success (Grönroos, 1990a; Groth *et al.*, 2019). The declaration as '*moment* of truth' indicates a further characteristic of the service encounter. The latter is considered as "a discrete event" (Bitner and Hubbert, 1994, p. 74) that is "often brief" (Fitzsimmons and Fitzsimmons, 2011, p. 213). This characteristic distinguishes service encounters from the concept of service experience (Bitner and Wang, 2014). While service encounters are discrete, service experience emerges over time and is continuous by nature (Voorhees *et al.*, 2017).

Similarly, sequential service encounters build and nurture service relationships that are established through the exchange and fulfillment of promises (Bitner, 1995). As illustrated in the **service encounter triad** in Figure 2.6, service firms make promises to customers and form their expectations, for instance, through external marketing activities (Zeithaml *et al.*, 2017). At the same time, service firms need to enable their employees to deliver the promise when personally interacting with customers during a service encounter (Bitner, 1995; Zeithaml *et al.*, 2017).

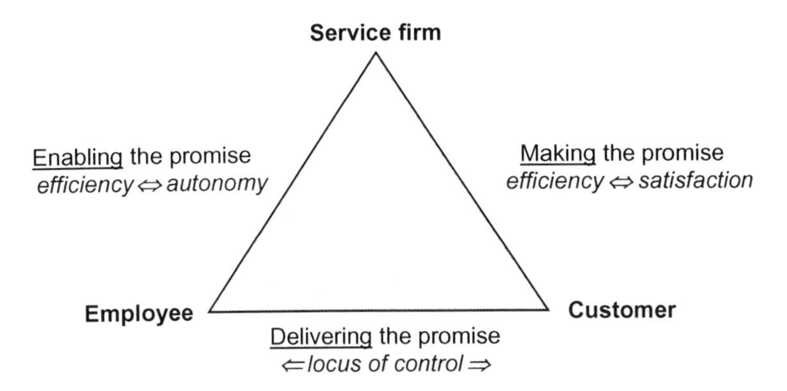


**Figure 2.6** The service encounter triad. (Source: Adapted from Zeithaml *et al.*, 2017, p. 321 and Fitzsimmons and Fitzsimmons, 2011, p. 214)

The service encounter triad captures the relationships and potential areas of tension between employees, customers, and the service firm. The arrows in Figure 2.6 symbolize these areas of tension. For instance, service firms strive to grant employees autonomy and to satisfy customers while simultaneously operating their business efficiently (Cook *et al.*, 2002). Cook *et al.* (2002) claim that it is mutually beneficial for each party to collaborate and thereby create a positive service encounter. The closest **collaboration** within the service encounter triad is required for personal interactions between the employee and the customer. During such interactions, the employee might try to control customer behavior to make the encounter more manageable and less stressful while the customer wants to gain control to maximize the derived benefit (Fitzsimmons and Fitzsimmons, 2011).

Besides the need for control, Bradley *et al.* (2010) identify seven further psychological needs that should be met for service encounters to become successful. These are the needs for cognition, competence, power, justice, trust, respect, and pleasant relations (Bradley *et al.*, 2010). The focus on psychological needs as an essential complement to functional needs (e.g., service outcome and price) is based on the proposition that service encounters "are first and foremost social encounters" (McCallum and Harrison, 1985, p. 35) and that customers tend to respond emotionally to service encounters (Price, Arnould, and Deibler, 1995).

While the service encounter triad is still used to demonstrate the interplay between employees, customers, and service firms to develop, promote, and deliver services (e.g., Zeithaml *et al.*, 2017), the original version does not explicitly encompass technology. To emphasize the technology-induced changes of the nature of service encounters, Parasuraman (2000) extended the service encounter triad by incorporating technology as a new dimension that is included in Figure 2.7.

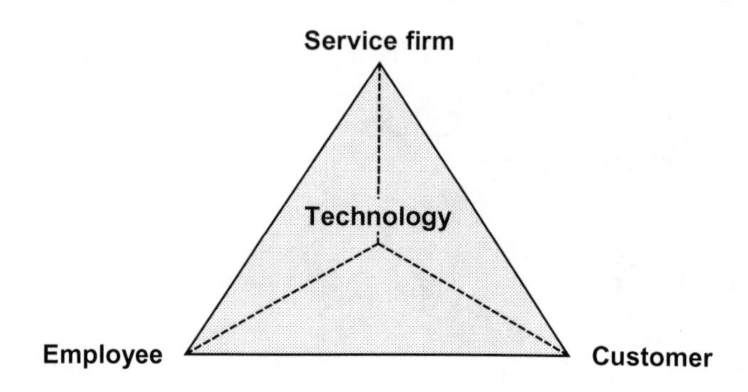


**Figure 2.7** The service encounter pyramid. (Source: Parasuraman, 2000, p. 308)

The **service encounter pyramid** illustrated in Figure 2.7 underlines the importance of effectively managing the links between technology and the service firm, its employees, and customers (Parasuraman, 2000; Ramaseshan, Kingshott, and Stein, 2015). Particularly, Parasuraman (2000) notes that despite the benefits of technology-based services, customers as well as employees may get frustrated when dealing with them. It is proposed that, in such cases, the effective handling of technology depends on an individual's technology readiness (Parasuraman, 2000; Parasuraman and Colby, 2015). This concept capturing the individual predisposition toward technology will be further elaborated in Section 3.2.2.

In line with Parasuraman (2000), Bitner, Brown, and Meuter (2000) acknowledge that technology in service encounters may not be embraced by everyone and may even bear negative outcomes. However, according to their **'technology infusion matrix'**, a technology that is thoughtfully and effectively managed can drive service encounter satisfaction through customization, improved service recovery, and delighting customers (Bitner *et al.*, 2000). Along with Parasuraman (2000), Bitner *et al.* (2000) were among the first researchers to conceptualize a framework for technology in service encounters. Initiated by these conceptualizations, the term service encounter has evolved to comprise remote, technology-mediated, and face-to-face encounters (Zeithaml *et al.*, 2017). While remote encounters typically occur without any physical contact between customers and employees, technology-mediated encounters encompass personal interactions that are supported by technology. For instance, mobile devices operated either by employees or customers increasingly become part of the service provision (Giebelhausen *et al.*, 2014).

Taking into account the increasing **prevalence of technology**, Larivière *et al.* (2017, p. 239) define service encounters nowadays as "any customer-company interaction that results from a service system that is comprised of interrelated technologies (either company- or customer-owned), human actors (employees and customers), physical/digital environments and company/customer processes." In their conceptual framework, they propose that technology can either augment or substitute employees or serve as network facilitator (Larivière *et al.*, 2017). Similarly, Kunz *et al.* (2019, p. 480) define service technologies as "networked technology interfaces or devices that enable and augment customer–business interactions and relationships".

Figure 2.8 depicts the three different **roles of technology** following Larivière *et al.* (2017, p. 239). Technology is referred to as augmenting when it assists or complements FLEs and enables them to focus on their core activities and the interaction with customers (Marinova *et al.*, 2017; van Doorn *et al.*, 2017). Still, employees may fear being substituted when service encounters become highly standardized and could completely be generated by technology (Frey and Osborne, 2017). Finally, technology may enable more personalized relationships and connect service firms, customers, and employees (Larivière *et al.*, 2017). In contrast, Giebelhausen *et al.* (2014) propose that technology functions as a barrier for interpersonal exchanges when customers are occupied with a digital interface while employees try to engage in building rapport.

Thus, different types of technology can have very different effects on frontline employees as well as on customers. These effects can be distinguished by the intensity of human interaction between FLEs and customers (low versus high touch) and the degree of complexity (low versus high tech) of the respective technology (Keating *et al.*, 2018). Figure 2.9 combines the latter classification with two different frontline service technology archetypes evolved by de Keyser *et al.* (2019). The first archetype is characterized by intense interactions between customers and FLEs.

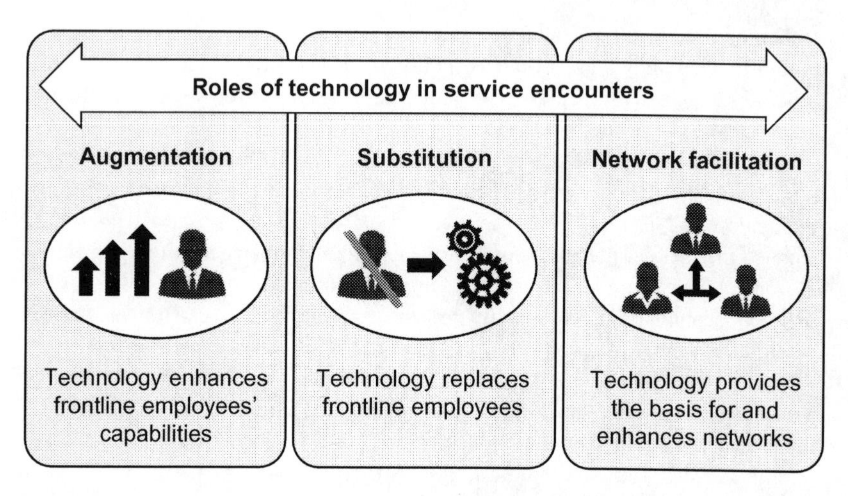


**Figure 2.8** The roles of technology in service encounters. (Source: Adapted from Larivière *et al.*, 2017)

The upper two quadrants of Figure 2.9 encompass service encounters with such intense interactions. Within this upper part, and in line with Larivière *et al.* (2017)'s conceptualization depicted above, frontline service technology is referred to as 'augmenting' when it supports FLEs (de Keyser *et al.*, 2019). Restaurant ordering devices represent one example of **augmented services** in the upper left quadrant since these devices enable FLEs to process customer orders faster. Such technologies are characterized by low to moderate levels of technical complexity. In addition, the upper right quadrant represents **blended services**. Here, technology provides the platform for exchange between FLEs and customers. One example with a high potential for the tourism and hospitality industry is wireless speech recognition devices that facilitate personal interactions with foreign speakers through simultaneous translation (Schwartz, 2019).

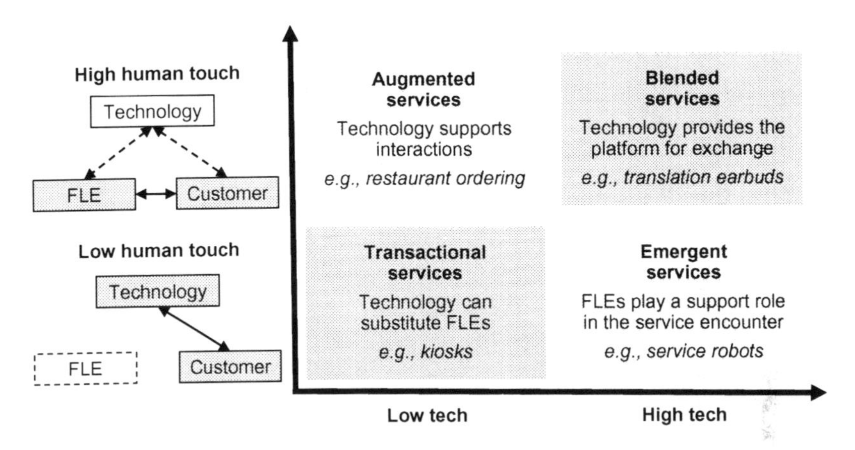


**Figure 2.9** Classification of technology-induced services. (Source: Adapted from de Keyser *et al.*, 2019, p. 159 and Keating *et al.*, 2018, p. 768)

The bottom part of Figure 2.9 represents service encounters in which FLEs are either partly or completely substituted because customers directly interact with technology (de Keyser *et al.*, 2019). For many **transactional services** in the lower left quadrant, self-service technology has already substituted FLEs that had formerly completed highly standardized tasks (Huang and Rust, 2017). Moreover, artificial intelligence (AI) increasingly substitutes FLEs in service encounters as AI agents like chatbots are programmed to speak or write like a human in customer conversations (Robinson *et al.*, 2020). Contrarily, humanoid service robots are only commencing to take over tasks like room service delivery or navigating customers that enter a firm site (Qiu *et al.*, 2019; van Doorn *et al.*, 2017). Often, these technologies still need to be supported or complemented by FLEs today (Meyer, Jonas, and Roth, 2020). This kind of service—characterized by low human touch and high tech in the lower right quadrant—is thus classified as **emergent services** (Keating *et al.*, 2018).

Overall, the interdependent roles of technology, frontline employees, and customers are changing (Larivière *et al.*, 2017). This section demonstrates that service encounters have evolved from mere dyadic to more **complex interactions** comprising both human and technological aspects. While there is a consensus among service researchers that not every type of service will be or should be carried through technology in the future (Keating *et al.*, 2018), technology is already fundamentally transforming service encounters (Robinson *et al.*, 2020). Thus, it has become increasingly important for service firms to effectively manage the interactions between technology, customers, and FLEs to pave the way for satisfying service encounters (Bitner and Wang, 2014).

### 2.2.2 Technology as an Enabler of Innovation in Service Encounters

Service firms must constantly reconsider their service offerings to attract and satisfy customers (Dotzel, Shankar, and Berry, 2013; Ryu and Lee, 2018). Thus, innovation increasingly impacts service firms' capabilities to build a **competitive advantage** (Witell *et al.*, 2016). As a result, both technological, as well as non-technological service innovations, are expected to enhance firm performance in terms of revenue growth and profitability (Ordanini and Parasuraman, 2011). Despite the recognized importance of service innovation, however, theory building in this field is comparatively novel and there is no common conceptualization of service innovation in academic literature (Flikkema, Jansen, and van der Sluis, 2007).

Among others, this dissent is reflected in the interchangeable use of service innovation and new service development as well as in the insufficient distinction between service innovation and new services (Witell *et al.*, 2016). Therefore, Gustafsson, Snyder, and Witell (2020, p. 114) claim that the process of developing a service should undoubtedly be separated from the concept of service innovation. They define **service innovation** "as a new process or offering that is put into practice and is adopted by and creates value for one or more stakeholders" (Gustafsson *et al.*, 2020, p. 114).

Twenty years ago, Coombs and Miles (2000) classified existing research on service innovation into three approaches; assimilation, demarcation, and synthesis. These three are contrasted in Table 2.3. At its core, the **assimilation** approach regards service innovation as similar to product innovation and assumes that existing theories and instruments can be applied to services with only minor modifications (Coombs and Miles, 2000). The proposed equal treatment of services and products becomes prevalent in the definition that is cited in Table 2.3, stating that service innovation is "a type of product innovation" (Giannopoulou, Gryszkiewicz, and Barlatier, 2014, p. 25). As a result of their literature review of service innovation research, Witell *et al.* (2016) find that the assimilation approach has been widest used between 1979 and 2014. The assimilation approach focuses on service innovation that is new to the market and is mainly driven by new technologies (Witell *et al.*, 2016).

**Table 2.3** Three approaches to service innovation. (Source: Adapted from Witell *et al.*, 2016, p. 2870)

| | **Assimilation** | **Demarcation** | **Synthesis** |
|---|---|---|---|
| **Proposition** | Theories on and instruments for product innovation can be adapted to processes and services. | Service innovation fundamentally differs from product innovation and requires specific theories. | Service as an integrated perspective can be used to understand innovation in all types of offerings. |
| **Exemplary definition** of service innovation | "[...] a type of product innovation involving the introduction of a service that is new or significantly improved with respect to its characteristics or to its intended uses" (Giannopoulou *et al.*, 2014, p. 25) | "[...] new ways of delivering a benefit, new service concepts, or new service business models through continuous operational improvement, technology, investment in employee performance, or management of the customer experience" (Enz, 2012, p. 187) | "[...] a new service or such a renewal of an existing service which is put into practice and which provides benefit to the organization that has developed it; the benefit usually derives from the added value that the renewal provides the customers"[10] (Toivonen and Tuominen, 2009, p. 893) |
| **Role of technology** | Technology as the main driver of innovation | Technology as a trigger, enabler, or innovator | Not limited to technological innovations |
| **Scope of innovation** | Technical innovation new to the market | Process adaption new to the firm and/or the customer | Service new to the firm and/or the customer |

The second approach, **demarcation,** acknowledges the idiosyncrasies of service. In contrast to the assimilation approach, the former supposes that service innovation is highly distinctive and thus requires specific theories and instruments (Coombs and Miles, 2000). The substantial differences between service and product innovation concern both the character of research and development (R&D) activities as well as the actual implementation of innovations in service firms

[10] The style of English was changed from British to American

(Hipp and Grupp, 2005). Firstly, R&D activities are seldom formally embedded into the organizational structure of service firms through a dedicated R&D department (Miles, 2007). Rather, the customers' unmet needs are seen as the primary source of service innovation (Heidenreich *et al.*, 2015; Ostrom *et al.*, 2010). Moreover, for services in which provision and consumption are inseparable, the customer is actively integrated into service offerings that have changed (Hipp and Grupp, 2005). In contrast to the assimilation approach, the demarcation approach encompasses not only radical but also rather small process adaptions and their impact on customers (Witell *et al.*, 2016).

Along with an increasing interest in customer centricity, research in service innovation has shifted from assimilation through demarcation to a **synthesis** approach (Carlborg, Kindström, and Kowalkowski, 2014). The latter is seen as a critique of both the assimilation and the demarcation approach (Witell *et al.*, 2016). It calls for an integration of insights from product innovation research with formerly neglected aspects that have been brought fore by service innovation (Coombs and Miles, 2000). Thereby, the synthesis approach aims at creating a unified conceptual framework that is applicable to any tangible or intangible offering (Gallouj and Savona, 2009). The exemplary definition by Toivonen and Tuominen (2009) demonstrates that this approach separates the development process of service innovation from its outcome. Moreover, the approach emphasizes the benefit for the firm that results from the value a new service has from the customer perspective.

The propensity to implement service innovations and thereby create value has become an essential capability of service firms (Dotzel *et al.*, 2013). The **role of technology** with regard to service innovations is controversially discussed in academic literature (Ryu and Lee, 2018). While some researchers postulate that technology is the major source of service innovation (Huang and Rust, 2017), others acknowledge that people are equally important to enable innovation, particularly in service industries that are characterized by intense personal interactions between employees and customers (Dotzel *et al.*, 2013). However, advances in technology can support service firms to serve their customers more effectively since new technology enables the collection, storage, and analysis of big data (Rust and Huang, 2014). Service innovations thus bear the potential to personalize communication and offerings according to customer needs and thereby strengthen the relationship with customers (Huang and Rust, 2017).

As Table 2.3 demonstrates, the assimilation approach of service innovation focuses on the impact of new technology on service innovation. Within this approach, service firms have often been considered passive adopters rather than active creators of innovative technology and have thus been rated as non-innovative (Tether, 2005). In contrast, both the demarcation and the synthesis approach acknowledge that service innovation is not limited to the implementation of new technology, but can also be reflected in operational improvements, increased employee performance, or enhancement of the customer experience (Enz, 2012). In a **model of service innovation** based on the demarcation approach, den Hertog, van der Aa, and de Jong (2010) declare six dimensions in which service firms can take action to establish new solutions and service experiences. These six dimensions comprise the service concept, customer interactions and interfaces, business partners, a firm's revenue model, and service delivery systems either regarding organizational and cultural aspects, or technology (den Hertog *et al.*, 2010).

Based on an earlier model of service innovation by den Hertog (2000), Ryu and Lee (2018) empirically investigate the role of technology as an innovator, trigger, or enabler of service innovation. They center their model around a firm's **service innovation orientation**. The latter refers to a strategic direction of creating, conducting, and effectively managing service innovations to achieve a sustainable superior performance (Ryu and Lee, 2018). Service innovation orientation is conceptualized as resulting from the interplay of a service firm's technology orientation on the one hand and people and organization on the other hand. As illustrated in Figure 2.10, the component 'people and organization' encompasses three dimensions. These are new ways of delivering service, the creation of new service concepts, and innovative ways to interact with customers.

Prior research has considered **technology as an innovator** in its own right, particularly when embedded into physical products or service delivery (Huang and Rust, 2017). Opposing, Ryu and Lee (2018) find no evidence for a direct effect of technology orientation on firm performance. However, technology might as well be considered as a trigger of innovation that initiates idea generation and the innovation process (Nambisan, 2013). Indeed, Ryu and Lee (2018) point out that technology orientation indirectly effects firm performance through triggering service concept orientation and service delivery orientation. Moreover, technology orientation supports the relationship between a firm's customer interaction orientation and firm performance (Ryu and Lee, 2018). This is in line with the view of technology as a complementary factor that enables and facilitates innovation implementation (Storey *et al.*, 2016). Technology thus plays multiple roles in service innovation. Ryu and Lee (2018) conclude that technology alone can barely leverage firm performance, but is an essential antecedent for encouraging service innovation.

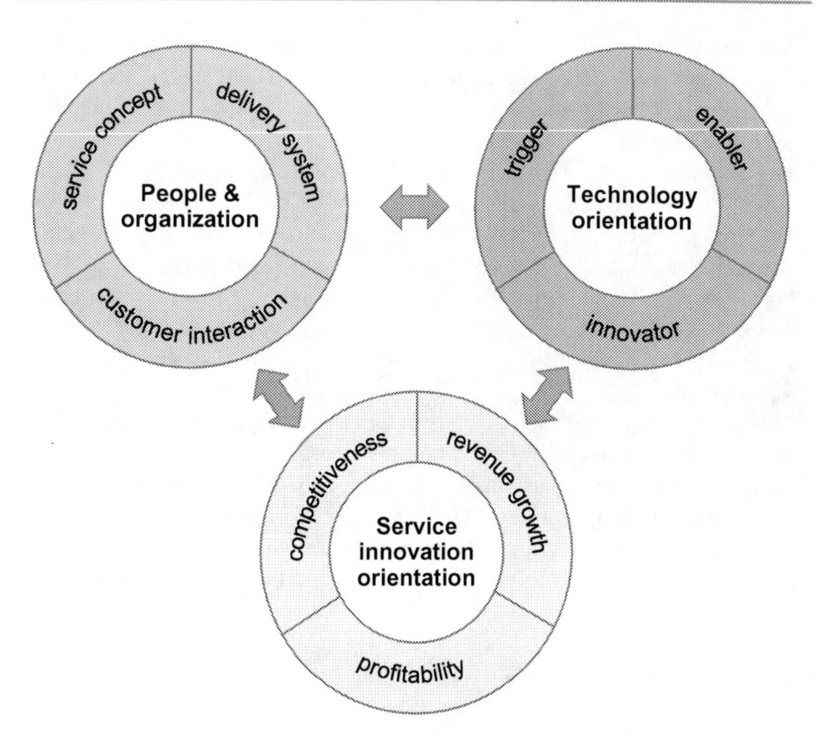


**Figure 2.10** Service innovation orientation as an interplay of people and technology. (Source: Own illustration inspired by Ryu and Lee, 2018 and Dotzel *et al.*, 2013)

Throughout this thesis, different technology-based service innovations and their effect on frontline employees and customer responses will be regarded. Study A concentrates on online reservation systems in the restaurant industry that change customer interactions and the roles of frontline employees. Study B uses a qualitative approach to explore the effects of technology deployment in full-service restaurants from the perspectives of technology providers, restaurant managers, frontline employees, and customers. It considers well-established technology like contactless payment as well as innovations that are currently being tested to prepare their market launch. Among these are, for instance, tableside ordering devices with speech recognition that a German start-up is developing. Study C investigates the effects of restaurant technology through a quantitative field survey. Finally, Study D broaches the issue of service innovations that are based on augmented reality (AR). More specifically, it aims at revealing differences in customer responses between personal service encounters in retail stores and online shopping that includes AR-based video try-on. Thus, this thesis covers a spectrum from widespread to newly developed technology-based service innovations.

### 2.2.3 Augmented Reality as a Means to Enhance Service Encounters

Along with virtual reality (VR), **augmented reality (AR)** is regarded as a technology with a high potential to change and enhance the relationships among customers, firms, and their brands (Nayyar *et al.*, 2018; Scholz and Duffy, 2018). Augmented reality interactively embeds virtual objects into the customer's current environment in real-time (Hilken *et al.*, 2017). Information about the physical environment is captured through cameras and eventually supplemented by GPS technology. This information is then overlaid with virtual objects that aim at augmenting the user's sensory experience (Buhalis *et al.*, 2019). As a result, these computer-generated objects "appear to coexist in the same space as the real world" (Azuma *et al.*, 2001, p. 34). Augmented reality is thus classified as 'mixed reality' in Milgram and Kishino's (1994) reality-virtuality continuum depicted in Figure 2.11.

In contrast, **virtual reality (VR)** marks the most extreme form of virtuality within the continuum. VR consists exclusively of "computer-generated, interactive, and highly vivid environments that enable the user to achieve a state of immersion through the ultimate experience of telepresence" (Boyd and Koles, 2019, p. 442). This definition acknowledges the central role of technology in creating virtual environments. At the same time, the definition by Boyd and Koles (2019) pays tribute to an early claim from Steuer (1992) to shift the emphasis of virtual reality applications to the importance of user experience. In the service sector, both virtual and augmented reality are evolving to capture and leverage customers' attention and thereby influence purchase decisions (Pantano, 2014).

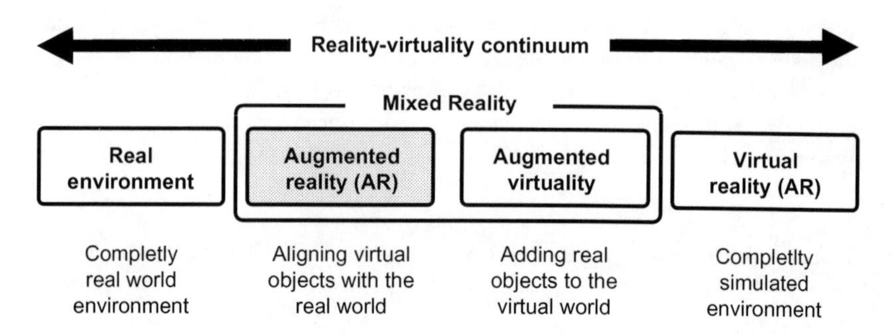


**Figure 2.11** Reality-virtuality continuum. (Source: Adapted from Milgram and Kishino, 1994)

For service firms, AR can increase the dynamics of the service encounter and enable customers to actively create their personal service experience (Rafaeli *et al.*, 2017). Thus, many service providers are adopting AR to enhance service delivery both online and offline (Heller *et al.*, 2021). For instance, AR allows visitors in cultural heritage or historical sites to see what these looked like in former times (tom Dieck and Jung, 2017). Similarly, AR is deployed in museums or during events to provide immersive experiences (Buhalis *et al.*, 2019). For commercial purposes, several car dealerships offer their customers the opportunity to customize accessories directly onto certain car models with AR[11]. Another example of AR in services is the application Kabaq[12]. The latter creates three-dimensional models of selected dishes to facilitate customer choices and to support non-native customers when they order in restaurants or online (Heller *et al.*, 2021; Nayyar *et al.*, 2018).

In online environments, AR features aim at stimulating aspects of the service experience that are typically reserved for personal service encounters (Brynjolfsson, Hu, and Rahman, 2013). For instance, the mobile application 'IKEA Place'[13] allows customers to virtually place furniture in their homes. Similarly, U.S. customers can preview home items in their preferred surroundings with the mobile application of *Magnolia Market*[14]—a lifestyle brand that runs one

[11] https://www.re-flekt.com/portfolio-item/bmw-product-genius [20.08.2020]

[12] https://www.kabaq.io/ [20.08.2020]

[13] https://ikea-unternehmensblog.de/article/2019/ikea-place-app [11.03.2020]

[14] https://shop.magnolia.com/collections/arkit [11.03.2020]

single brick and mortar store. For such **marker-based** mobile applications, customers must first capture a QR code, barcode, or another hard-coded object with their smartphone camera (Rese *et al.*, 2017). With the help of a visual marker, mobile applications can determine the center, orientation, and range of a three-dimensional coordinate system and hence display a virtual object (Katiyar, Kalra, and Garg, 2015). The left part of Figure 2.12 visualizes this approach.

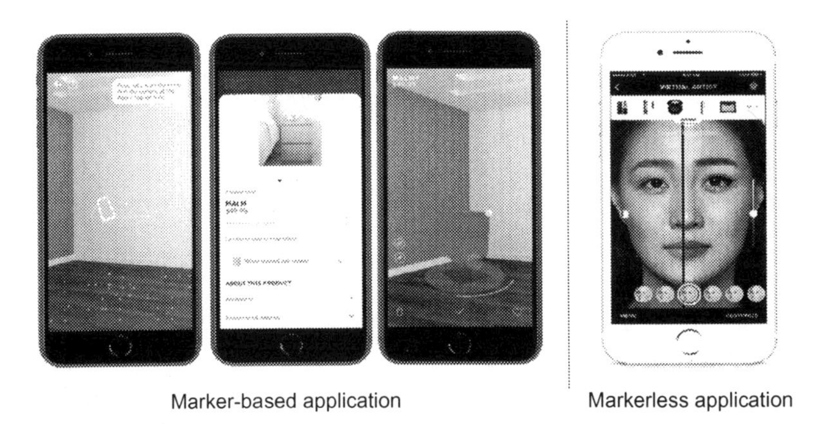


**Figure 2.12** Examples of augmented reality-enhanced mobile applications. (Sources: Case Study IKEA Place[15] (left); Sephora Virtual Artist[16] (right))

In contrast, **markerless** applications are based on more complex augmented reality features to recognize real environments (Rese *et al.*, 2017). These environments include images that have not been provided to the application beforehand. Thus, the algorithm has to automatically identify patterns, colors, or other characteristics of objects in front of the camera (Brito and Stoyanova, 2018). Markerless AR technology places virtual objects like fashion items on the tracked environments in real-time (Rese *et al.*, 2017). Customers turn their heads, move their feet, or use gestures to interact with the application and thereby perceive it as a natural interface (Brito and Stoyanova, 2018). Overall, such AR interfaces are meant to reshape service experiences by making online services more effective and enjoyable (Heller *et al.*, 2019a; Scholz and Duffy, 2018).

---

[15] https://medium.com/@HausJiang/ux-case-study-ikea-place-a66319510023 [11.03.2020]

[16] https://sephoravirtualartist.com/ [11.03.2020]

Examples of markerless applications can be found in diverse service industries, such as retail. As shown in Figure 2.12, customers can try out makeup using a web or smartphone camera with *Sephora*'s 'Virtual Artist'. Other retailers offer both mobile applications and web versions of **virtual mirrors**. Especially for eyewear, multiple online retailers have already adopted AR solutions. For instance, *Mister Spex*[17] originated in Germany and U.S.-based *Warby Parker*[18] both have launched video try-on options for large parts of their glasses and sunglasses assortments (Hilken *et al.*, 2017). The French start-up *Jeeliz*[19] is one technology provider of virtual try-on solutions for eyewear. Moreover, the Indian mobile application developer Quy Technologies[20] today offers virtual try-on solutions for eyewear, jewelry, watches, or hats for the retail industry. A detailed overview of AR solutions in retailing by Heller *et al.* (2019a) demonstrates the wide range of applications that are already available.

Despite the growing supply, the penetration of AR applications with regard to the actual use by customers lags behind. For instance, most online retail AR applications achieve low total numbers of installs on customer smartphones compared to gaming AR applications with a more playful purpose (Dacko, 2017). However, the above-mentioned examples demonstrate that there is an increasing variety of available AR applications both for online and offline service encounters. To increase customer engagement with such AR applications, Heller *et al.* (2021) claim that service managers should build a conceptual understanding of AR as a service enabler rather than focusing on mere technical aspects. After all, AR holds the unique potential to engage customer senses, create a compelling experience, and thereby generate value both for customers and service firms (Heller *et al.*, 2019a).

---

[17] https://www.misterspex.de/brillen/brillen-mit-webcam-anprobe [11.03.2020]

[18] https://www.warbyparker.com/app [11.03.2020]

[19] https://jeeliz.com/blog/virtual-try-on/ [11.03.2020]

[20] https://www.quytech.com/augmented-reality-solutions/virtual-try-on-solutions.php [11.03.2020]

# Theoretical Foundations

# 3

## 3.1 Theories on Stress and Strain in the Occupational Context

As discussed in Chapter 2, technology can enhance FLEs' role performance by helping them focus on carrying out their core activities (de Keyser *et al.*, 2019; Larivière *et al.*, 2017). Conversely, when technology confronts FLEs with additional demands or arises job security concerns, it may also arouse work stress (Frey and Osborne, 2017; Hamborg and Greif, 2015). Yet, the term 'work stress' does not have a consistent definition in academic literature. It is either used to capture an environmental event (i.e., a stimulus), an individual's reaction to that event (i.e., a response), or the relationship between stimulus and response (Bliese, Edwards, and Sonnentag, 2017; Jex, Beehr, and Roberts, 1992).

Accordingly, research on stress in the occupational context distinguishes the key terms as follows: A job stressor denotes a demanding aspect of the job that requires an employee's attention and adaptive response (Bliese *et al.*, 2017; Spector and Jex, 1998). An individual appraisal of job stressors is referred to as perceived stress (Bliese *et al.*, 2017). Job strains encompass an individual's psychological, physiological, and behavioral reactions to job stressors, for instance, exhaustion (Bliese *et al.*, 2017; Spector, Chen, and O'Connell, 2000). Finally, the characteristics of an individual or a workplace that alter the relationship among job stressors, perceived stress, and job strains are subsumed as moderators (Bliese *et al.*, 2017).

In this thesis, the term **stress** is used to capture the overall process that an employee goes through upon being exposed to a job stressor. The following three sections discuss the different theories that can be applied to investigate



S. Christ-Brendemühl, *Digital Technology in Service Encounters*, Innovation, Entrepreneurship und Digitalisierung,
https://doi.org/10.1007/978-3-658-37885-1_3

and understand this process. Section 3.1.1 depicts Lazarus' (1966) appraisal-based transactional theory of stress and coping that conceptualizes stress as an individual's perception. In contrast, Hobfoll's (1989) COR theory introduced in Section 3.1.2 considers the objective characteristics of an event as the causes of stress. Both theories were developed as frameworks in order to explain stress in general. However, as outlined throughout the sections, they are certainly applicable to the occupational context. Based on the COR theory, Bakker and Demerouti's (2007) JD-R model discussed in Section 3.1.3 specifically focuses on stress at work and its organizational outcomes.

### 3.1.1 Transactional Theory of Stress and Coping

Until the 1950 s, research on stress has primarily focused on external stimuli and how an organism responds *physiologically* to threats, for instance, through varying stress hormone levels (Cooper and Dewe, 2005). In the 1960 s, the focus of stress research shifted to major social and life events and their physical as well as *psychological* consequences (Holmes and Rahe, 1967). As part of this shift, Lazarus (1966) developed the **transactional theory of stress and coping** that was later expanded by Lazarus and Folkman (1984). Transactional theory ranks among the most influential theoretical frameworks of psychological stress as it recognizes the relevance of subjective factors in the stress process (Bliese *et al.*, 2017). The theory assumes that each individual appraises specific situations differently and that stress results from the interplay between an individual and the environment (Dewe, Cox, and Ferguson, 1993). Figure 3.1 visualizes the processes within the transactional theory that will be outlined hereafter.

When a **potential stressor** occurs, Lazarus and Folkman (1984) distinguish between two forms of cognitive appraisal. By cognitive appraisal, they mean the process of evaluating the significance of an event for individual well-being. Well-being is viewed as encompassing an individual's general health as well as the satisfaction at work and outside work (Danna, 1999; Nielsen *et al.*, 2017). Among others, satisfaction and well-being at work are shaped by job characteristics, role clarity, pay and equity, job security, work hours, perceived autonomy or control, and support by supervisors or co-workers (Cartwright, 2018; Sparks, Faragher, and Cooper, 2001). In the context of this thesis, frontline employees may evaluate the impact of frontline service technologies on their well-being differently.

The evaluation of potential stressors is referred to as **primary appraisal** (Bliese *et al.*, 2017). Within this process, an individual classifies an external event as **irrelevant** when there are no expected implications for individual well-being (Lazarus and Folkman, 1987). For instance, the introduction of digital technology operated by customers may be perceived as irrelevant by frontline employees. However, when an event potentially preserves or even enhances individual well-being, it is classified as **benign-positive** (Lazarus and Folkman, 1984). As outlined in Section 2.2.1, frontline service technology may facilitate work tasks and thereby exert a positive effect on frontline employees (Larivière *et al.*, 2017). On the contrary, **stressful** appraisals will occur when an individual fears an event to threaten, challenge, or harm the individual well-being (Dewe *et al.*, 1993). Such feelings may arise when frontline employees are apprehensive of the impact of technology on their workload, role clarity, perceived autonomy, or job security.

In contrast to the primary appraisal, the **secondary appraisal** refers to an individual's considerations of whether available resources are sufficient to manage stressful situations (Bliese *et al.*, 2017). Lazarus and Folkman (1984) emphasize that the secondary appraisal is a complex evaluative process encompassing the available coping options as well as an individual's expectancy regarding the accomplishments. Following Bandura (1977), **outcome expectancy** refers to the probability that a particular behavior will lead to the desired outcome while **efficacy expectations** reflect an individual's belief that he or she can effectively perform the behavior required to achieve the accomplishment.

Secondary and primary appraisals interact with each other and thereby determine the level of perceived stress as well as the response (Lazarus and Folkman, 1984). Regarding this **reciprocal relationship**, Lazarus and Folkman admit themselves that the "choice of terminology, 'primary' and 'secondary', was unfortunate" (Lazarus and Folkman, 1984, p. 31). After all, neither form of appraisal is more relevant than the other and—more importantly—it is essential to recognize that the primary appraisal does not necessarily precede the second appraisal in time (Folkman, Lazarus, and Dunkel-Schetter *et al.*, 1986). Rather, both cognitive processes occur simultaneously because an individual dynamically evaluates and re-evaluates potential stressors and available coping resources as both the stressor and the coping responses evolve (Turner-Cobb and Hawken, 2019). This reciprocal relationship is symbolized by the bidirectional arrow between primary and secondary appraisals in Figure 3.1.

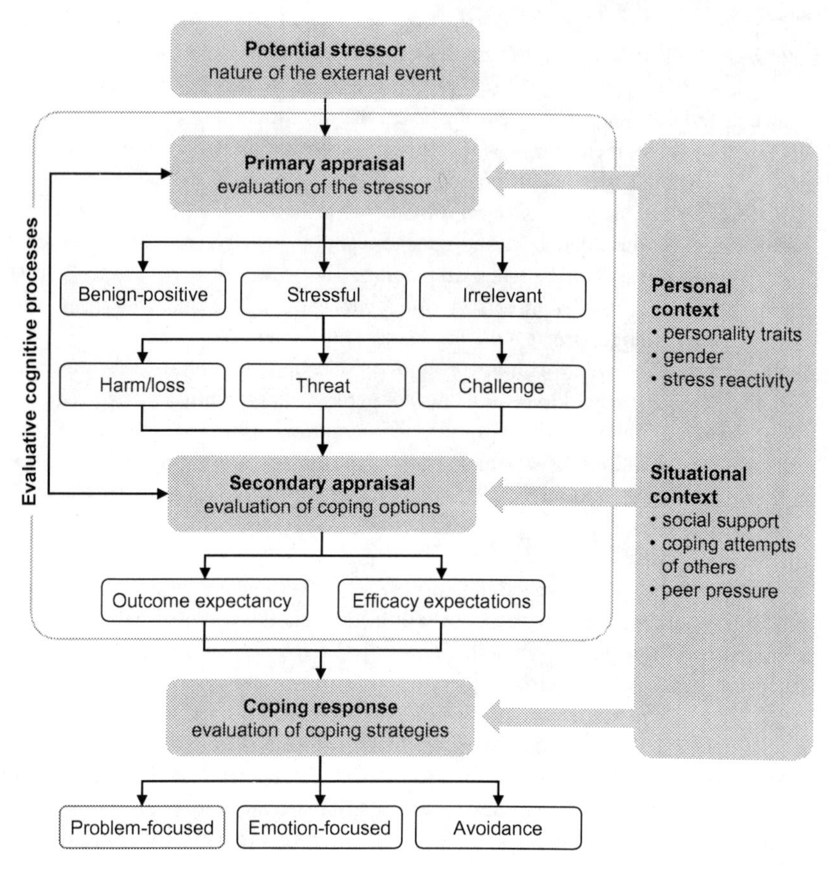


**Figure 3.1** Appraisal and coping processes within the transactional theory. (Source: Own illustration based on Turner-Cobb and Hawken, 2019, p. 230, DeLongis and Holtzman, 2005, p. 1635, and descriptions by Lazarus and Folkman, 1984)

Hence, both appraisal processes equally predict the coping strategy an individual will pursue. Coping is defined as "adaptively changing cognitive and behavioral efforts to manage psychological stress" (DeLongis and Holtzman, 2005, p. 1634) and can be distinguished into three coping strategies. Taking direct actions to manage or relieve the stress is referred to as **problem-focused coping** (Lee-Baggley, Preece, and DeLongis, 2005). Individuals are expected to pursue this coping strategy when environmental conditions are perceived as changeable

(Lazarus and Folkman, 1984). For instance, frontline employees that can rely on their supervisors and co-workers can actively ask for help when they struggle with operating a technological device.

In contrast, when an individual has the feeling that nothing can be done to change the current conditions, **emotion-focused coping** is applied to regulate or reduce an individual's emotional response to stressful situations (Lee-Baggley *et al.*, 2005). The predominant form of emotion-focused coping is the reappraisal of a stressor by which the meaning and importance of a situation are changed (Lazarus and Folkman, 1984). The avoidance of a situation can be seen as a particular form of emotion-focused coping. However, Cox and Ferguson (1991) conceptualize **avoidance** as a third and separate form of coping to acknowledge its distinctiveness. Avoidance is one of the least effective forms of coping since wishful thinking or direct escape routes often worsen the situation (Feldman, 2019).

The appraisal of potential stressors, the likelihood of engaging in a certain coping strategy as well as the effectiveness of the latter depend on the **nature of the external event**, the **personal context** of the individual, and the situational context in which the event occurs (DeLongis and Holtzman, 2005). The nature of stressful events at work is primarily determined by the intensity, frequency, and meaning attributed to the event (Dewe, 1989). These characteristics are assumed to particularly affect an individual's coping response (DeLongis and Holtzman, 2005). Moreover, Matud (2004) investigates gender differences in coping responses and postulates that women tend to engage in emotion-focused and avoidant coping more often than men. Besides gender, personality traits play an important role in the appraisal and coping process since they determine an individual's stress reactivity and belief in coping effectiveness (Lee-Baggley *et al.*, 2005).

Finally, the role of personality in the appraisal and coping process depends on the **situational context** in which stress arises (DeLongis and Holtzman, 2005). More specifically, observable coping attempts of others, peer pressure, and the satisfaction or disappointment with social support shape an individual's response to potential stressors (DeLongis and Holtzman, 2005). At work, co-workers and supervisors are the most important source of support when new digital technology is implemented or when issues occur with an existing one. At the same time, frontline employees can either learn from or build resistances against the coping attempts of others. Overall, the transactional theory of stress and coping seems appropriate to investigate frontline employees' responses to technology because the theory reflects intra-individual and inter-individual differences that emerge from the context and nature of a potential stressor as well as from the personal and situational context (Turner-Cobb and Hawken, 2019).

### 3.1.2 Conservation of Resources Theory

The **conservation of resources (COR) theory** by Hobfoll (1989) was framed as an alternative to appraisal-based theories such as Lazarus' (1966) transactional theory of stress and coping. The central assumption of COR theory is that individuals strive to obtain, retain, foster, and protect resources (Hobfoll, 1989; Hobfoll *et al.*, 2018). Although cognitive appraisal plays a central role in the evaluation of resources and in the perception of whether resources are at risk, COR theory primarily emphasizes the objective elements of an event as determinants of stress (Bliese *et al.*, 2017). Thus, whereas transactional theory conceptualizes stress as individual perception, COR theory assumes external events to have a common level of impact on individuals within or even across cultures (Hobfoll *et al.*, 2018).

According to COR theory, psychological stress occurs when valued **resources** are lost or threatened with loss, or when individuals fail to gain new resources despite investing significant resources (Hobfoll, 1989; Hobfoll *et al.*, 2018). Orginally, Hobfoll (1989) refers to resources as material objects, personal characteristics, conditions, or energies that individuals value or that enable them to attain the former mentioned. This conceptualization has been criticized because the term 'value' implies that only things leading to a positive outcome can be categorized as a resource (Halbesleben *et al.*, 2014). Opposing, Halbesleben *et al.* (2014, p. 1338) propose to "define resources as anything perceived by the individual to help attain his or her goals." The latter definition fits well with other motivation theories.

Indeed, COR theory is not solely applicable to explain stress. Moreover, it also counts as a **theory of motivation** since it implies when and why individuals are motivated to invest resources at all (Halbesleben *et al.*, 2014). The motivational aspect of COR theory is best reflected in its 'resource investment principle'. Figure 3.2 includes the resource investment principle in the upper left corner. This principle states that individuals are motivated to invest resources to recover from losses, to avoid the loss of further resources, and to gain new ones (Hobfoll *et al.*, 2018). A resource loss would lead to negative psychological states. Thus, individuals enrich their resource pool to protect themselves, gain self-esteem, and ensure their status (Stock *et al.*, 2017).

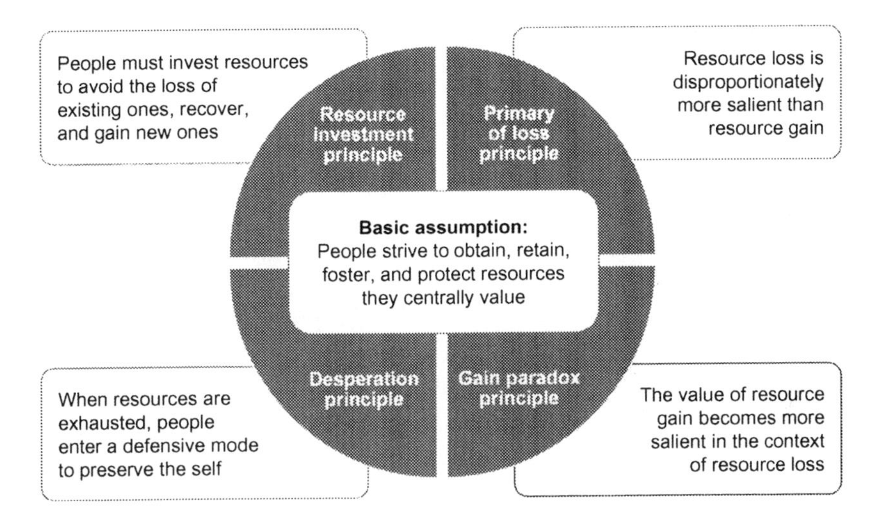


**Figure 3.2** Principles of the conservation of resources theory. (Source: Own illustration based on Hobfoll *et al.*, 2018, p. 106)

In total, COR theory encompasses **four principles** that are depicted in Figure 3.2. The 'primary of loss principle' in the upper right corner refers to the evolutionary-based cognitive bias that individuals overweigh resource loss while underweighting resource gain (Hobfoll *et al.*, 2018). In the context of work, the latter principle proposes that feared losses (e.g., losses of pay, time, or autonomy) will be perceived as more harmful by employees than comparable gains would be perceived as helpful (Halbesleben *et al.*, 2014).

However, the value of resource gain becomes more salient when resources have currently been lost, as proposed by the gain paradox principle in the lower right corner (Hobfoll *et al.*, 2018). For instance, employees whose resources have recently been outstretched appreciate the support from supervisors or co-workers to a greater extent than those employees not needing help. Finally, the 'desperation principle' in the lower left corner proposes that individuals pass over to a defensive mode when their resources are outstretched or exhausted. This attempt to preserve remaining resources is often characterized by aggressive or irrational behaviors (Hobfoll *et al.*, 2018).

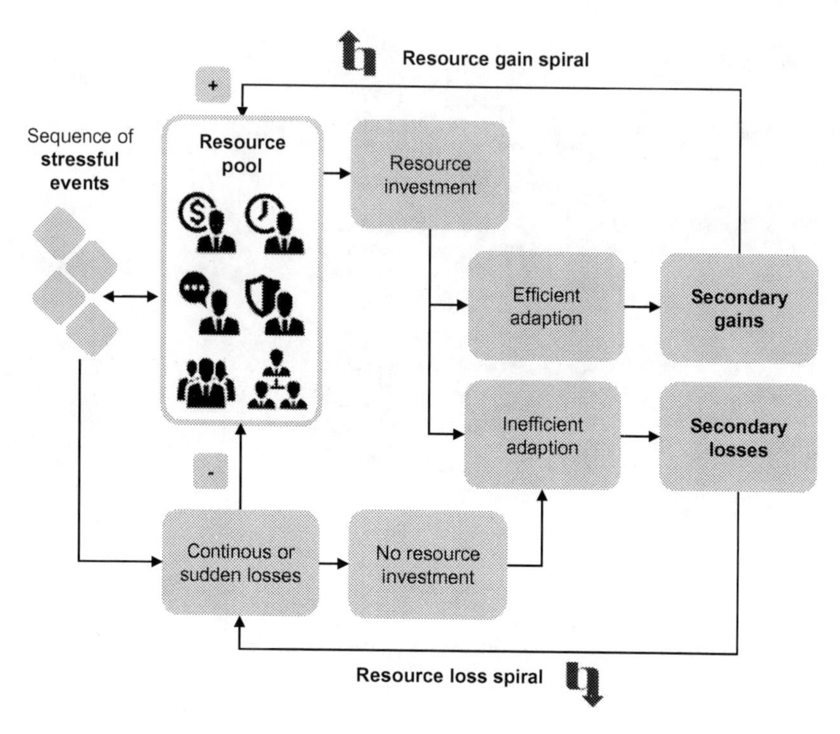


**Figure 3.3** Mechanisms of the conservation of resources theory. (Source: Own illustration based on Hobfoll, 1989)

The depicted principles of COR theory imply three main mechanisms. First, individuals with a greater pool of resources are less vulnerable to the loss of resources and more capable to gain new ones (Hobfoll *et al.*, 2018). When a stressful event or a sequence of stressful events occurs, the existence of sufficient resources is a prerequisite to investing resources at all. The **resource pool** in Figure 3.3 contains six symbols of resources that help individuals achieve their goals, particularly in the context of work. From top to bottom and left to right, these are

- pay and financial rewards (Halbesleben, Harvey, and Bolino, 2009; Shin, Taylor, and Seo, 2012),
- time to perform tasks at work as well as recovery breaks (Trougakos *et al.*, 2014),

- autonomy and participation in decision making (Ito and Brotheridge, 2003),
- job security (de Cuyper *et al.*, 2012),
- social support from supervisors and co-workers (Park *et al.*, 2014),
- and finally decision authority and status (Park *et al.*, 2014).

When individuals invest resources but adapt them inefficiently or when they are affected by continuous or sudden losses and cannot invest resources at all, secondary losses are precipitated (Hobfoll *et al.*, 2018). Since each resource loss triggers stress, individuals are decreasingly worse positioned to counterbalance further threats to their resources, which leads to a **resource loss spiral** (Stock *et al.*, 2017). This second mechanism of COR theory is illustrated in the lower section of Figure 3.3. The third mechanism represents the equivalent of the second. When individuals invest resources and adapt them efficiently, secondary gains are generated. This leads to a **resource gain spiral** in which individuals are increasingly capable to invest and gain further resources (Halbesleben *et al.*, 2014). Yet, resource gain takes more time than resource loss and is of less magnitude to the individual. Thus, resource gain spirals develop slowly and tend to be fragile (Hobfoll *et al.*, 2018).

Hobfoll *et al.* (2018) claim that COR theory has become one of the most widely cited theories in organizational behavior. Indeed, a considerable number of studies have investigated how resource loss in the occupational context affects employees' job performance, the intensity with which they approach their tasks, and job satisfaction (see Halbesleben *et al.*, 2014 for an overview). Surprisingly, neither Hobfoll *et al.*'s (2018) review of the application of COR theory in organizational behavior research nor Halbesleben *et al.*'s (2014) retrospective on the role of resources in COR theory specifically addresses the subject of technology. However, the implementation of digital technology at work can be regarded as having a common impact on employees that can be examined from a resource perspective.

### 3.1.3 Job Demands-Resources Model

Demerouti *et al.* (2001) used Hobfoll's (1989) conservation of resources (COR) theory as a basis to develop the **job demands-resources (JD-R) model**. Originally aimed at explaining employee burnout, the JD-R model is now recognized as an appropriate framework for explaining effective organizational functioning and various facets of stress and employee well-being (Bakker and Demerouti, 2017). Since 2011, the model has matured into the JD-R theory which considers more work-specific aspects of organizational stress than COR theory (Hobfoll *et al.*, 2018). From the beginnings, the central assumption of the JD-R model has been that working conditions can be classified into two general categories; job demands and job resources (Demerouti *et al.*, 2001).

**Job demands** are defined as those organizational, physical, psychological, and social characteristics of the job that require considerable cognitive and emotional effort or specific skills (Bakker and Demerouti, 2007). Examples include organizational aspects like the implementation of new processes, unfavorable physical conditions like heat, psychological demands like role ambiguity, or emotionally demanding conflicts with customers. Despite these undesirable examples, job demands are not necessarily negative per se. For instance, conflicts with customers can be perceived as a chance to develop skills or to gain respect from co-workers in case of a successful conflict resolution.

Accordingly, **challenge job demands** are referred to as demands that arouse effort but potentially stimulate personal achievement and growth (Podsakoff *et al.*, 2007). Yet, job demands might turn into stressors when coping requires a substantial investment of resources that the employee does not have at disposal or is not willing to devote (Halbesleben *et al.*, 2014). In line with this, stressful demands that unnecessarily hinder employees from achieving their goals through excessive or undesirable constraints are classified as **hindrance job demands** (Cavanaugh *et al.*, 2000). Such hindrance job demands often refer to an employee's role within the organization and include role ambiguity and role conflict (Podsakoff *et al.*, 2007).

Similar to job demands, **job resources** encompass organizational, physical, psychological, and social aspects. More specifically, job resources are defined as those characteristics of the job that enable employees to reduce job demands and to achieve their goals at work or stimulate personal development and growth (Bakker and Demerouti, 2007). When bridging the gap to the examples of job demands mentioned earlier, job resources include an employer's offerings to fundamentally train employees when new processes are implemented. Likewise, supervisors can shape job resources by clearly communicating role expectations to reduce employees' role ambiguity or by granting employees more autonomy to resolve conflicts on their responsibility. Thus, job resources function as a means to cope with job demands on the one hand. On the other hand—and equally important—job resources have a motivational potential (Bakker and Demerouti, 2007).

In their retrospective on the JD-R model and JD-R theory, Bakker and Demerouti (2017) propose that employees' **personal resources** such as optimism and self-efficacy can instigate similar processes as job resources. That is because employees who actively utilize their personal resources on the job are in a better position to cope with job demands (van Woerkom, Bakker, and Nishii, 2016). Moreover, personal resources encompass the belief in their abilities to handle existing and unforeseen demands (Xanthopoulou *et al.*, 2007). In a further study, Xanthopoulou *et al.* (2009a) find that personal resources and work engagement (as one facet of employee motivation) predicted job resources and that the reversed causal effects existed from job resources to work engagement and personal resources.

Similar to Hobfoll's (2001) concept of the resource gain spiral depicted in Section 3.1.2, JD-R theory proposes that employees can generate a gain spiral of resources and work engagement through job crafting (Bakker and Costa, 2014; Bakker and Demerouti, 2017). This concept refers to proactively increasing job resources (e.g., asking for clarification) and challenge job demands (e.g., occupying oneself with a new project) or to decreasing hindrance job demands (e.g., rejecting additional workload) (Tims, Bakker, and Derks, 2012). Bakker and Demerouti (2017) postulate that such job crafting behaviors result from motivation and in turn lead to higher levels of job and personal resources. The reciprocal relationships among job resources, personal resources, and motivation are reflected by dotted-line arrows in Figure 3.4.

As illustrated in Figure 3.4, job demands and resources unleash two very distinct main processes. First, job demands instigate a health-impairment process and are assumed to be the unique predictors of **job strain**—from the lack of energy over exhaustion to burnout (Bakker and Demerouti, 2007; Demerouti *et al.*, 2001). Longitudinal research has revealed that employees suffering from organizational strain perceive more job demands over time or even create additional job demands like work overload (ten Brummelhuis *et al.*, 2011). That is because strained employees tend to make more mistakes and to communicate poorly, which in turn evokes more conflicts. Thereby, they self-undermine their performance and further intensify the already high job demands (Bakker and Costa, 2014). Again, the reciprocal relationship between job demands and strain is reflected by a dotted-line arrow in Figure 3.4.

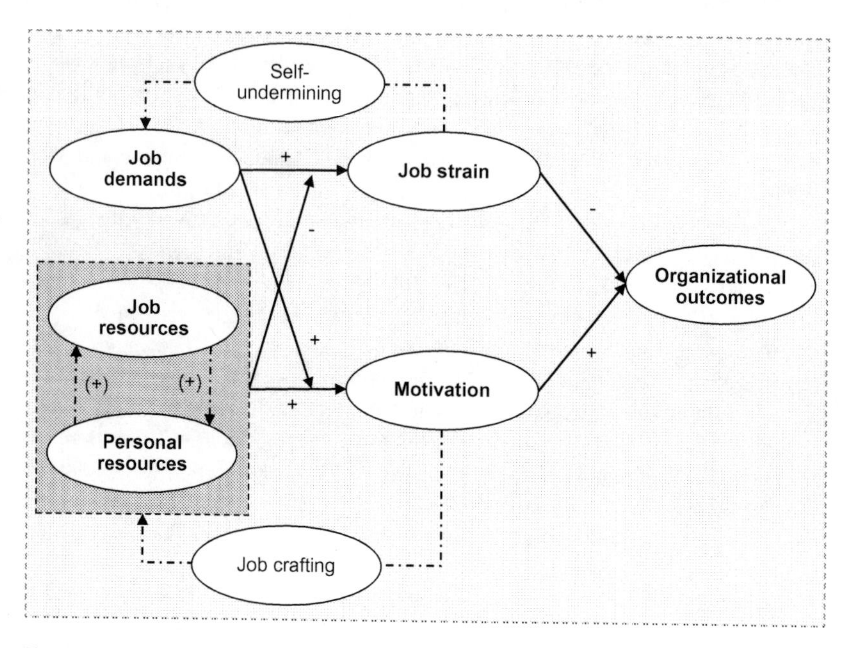


**Figure 3.4** The job demands-resources model. (Source: Adapted from Bakker and Demerouti, 2017, p. 275)

The second main process within the JD-R theory is a motivational process instigated by job resources. Resources are assumed to be the unique predictors of **motivation**, employee engagement, and commitment (Demerouti *et al.*, 2001). Besides the two main effects instigated by job demands and resources, the JD-R theory encompasses two moderating effects. On the one hand, resources have the potential to buffer the influence of job demands on strain (van Woerkom *et al.*, 2016). Accordingly, employees with sufficient resources at their disposal are better able to cope with job demands. On the other hand, high job demands enhance the effect of resources on motivation. This proposition is in line with the principle of COR theory that resources become more salient and particularly unfold their motivational potential when resources are threatened or have currently been lost (Hobfoll *et al.*, 2018). Thus, JD-R theory proposes that job resources especially influence employee motivation in the presence of high job demands (Bakker and Demerouti, 2017).

The final proposition of JD-R theory states that motivation is a source of energy that supports employees in focusing on their tasks and thereby influences **organizational outcomes** positively (Bakker and Demerouti, 2017). Contrarily, strained employees have less energetic resources to achieve their work goals and thus, job strain harms organizational outcomes (Bakker and Demerouti, 2017; Bakker, van Emmerik, and van Riet, 2008). The organizational outcomes that have been investigated by research on the JD-R model are manifold and include in-role performance (Hopstaken *et al.*, 2016), extra-role behavior (Bakker, Demerouti, and Verbeke, 2004), deep and surface acting of frontline employees (Yoo and Arnold, 2016), service climate (Salanova, Agut, and Peiró, 2005), innovativeness (Schaufeli and Taris, 2014), financial results (Xanthopoulou *et al.*, 2009b), absenteeism (van Woerkom *et al.*, 2016), and employee turnover intentions (Babakus, Yavas, and Karatepe, 2017).

The broadness of potential organizational outcomes reflects the broad scope the JD-R model generally claims to encompass. Bakker and Demerouti (2017) state that the JD-R model is applicable to employees with different occupations—independent from whether they work with objects, information, or humans. Moreover, Schaufeli and Taris (2014) remark that the JD-R model is not restricted to specific job demands and resources. Rather, the model assumes that any demand and any resource may affect employee motivation and strain (see the Appendix of Schaufeli and Taris, 2014 for an overview). Although the broadness of the JD-R model and JD-theory has been criticized, it allows its application to various organizational settings and can be assumed to be an appropriate framework to investigate antecedents and outcomes of job strain and employee motivation.

## 3.2 Individual Predisposition and Appraisal of Technology

Although organizational change might have manifold reasons, technology is regarded as its key driver (Akingbola, Rogers, and Baluch, 2019). Certainly, the 'technological imperative' which assumes technology to determine and constrain human behavior and organizational structures (Markus and Robey, 1988), is obsolete today. Rather, organizations now have a sheer unlimited number of choices in terms of technological solutions. They can select the solutions that best fit the respective tasks, infrastructural requirements, and organizational goals. Despite these opportunities, the implementation of new ICT in organizations is often associated with high failure rates (Kivijärvi, 2020; Lee, Keil, and Shalev, 2019).

This is because workplace technology only enhances employee performance and, consequently, organizational performance when it exhibits a good task-technology fit and when it is actually utilized (Goodhue and Thompson, 1995; Howard and Rose, 2019).

Non-utilization or inappropriate utilization of technology can stem from employee resistance (i.e., lack of willingness) or from their inability to cope with technological demands (i.e., lack of resources). Moreover, academic literature proposes that employee resistance to using workplace technology is the predominant reason for failure during or even after the implementation of technology (Heidenreich and Talke, 2020). Accordingly, Section 3.2.1 discusses Oreg's (2003) concept of RTC as an approach to explain an individual's unwillingness to cope with technological demands. Section 3.2.2 considers Parasuraman's (2000) concept of technology readiness as the propensity to adopt and effectively use new technologies. Hence, technology readiness encompasses an individual's beliefs on technology prior to its adoption as well as during its actual use. Finally, and in line with the conceptualization of Ayyagari (2007) and Ayyagari *et al.* (2011), Section 3.2.3 regards employee appraisal of technology-in-use as a potential stressor affecting technostress. Technostress is likely to arouse when individuals lack the necessary resources to cope with technological demands. Figure 3.5 provides an overview of these three concepts and their classification.

### 3.2.1 Dispositional Resistance to Change

Research on the adoption of workplace technology has long focused on individual technology acceptance decisions (Laumer and Eckhardt, 2012). Following the introduction of the **technology acceptance** model (TAM) by Davis (1986, 1989), the links between perceived ease of use and usefulness of technology, behavioral intentions, and an individual's initial decision to use a particular technology have extensively been investigated (Pantano, Rese, and Baier, 2017; Williams *et al.*, 2009). Co-authored by the initiator of the technology acceptance model, Venkatesh *et al.* (2003) extended the existing model toward a Unified Theory of Acceptance and Use of Technology (UTAUT). This theory proposes that performance expectancy, effort expectancy, and social influence determine employee behavioral intentions to use workplace technology (Venkatesh *et al.*, 2003).

In contrast to technology acceptance, Laumer and Eckhardt (2012) remark that an individual's resistance to the use of technology remains an under-investigated research area. However, this research area is of importance because resistance

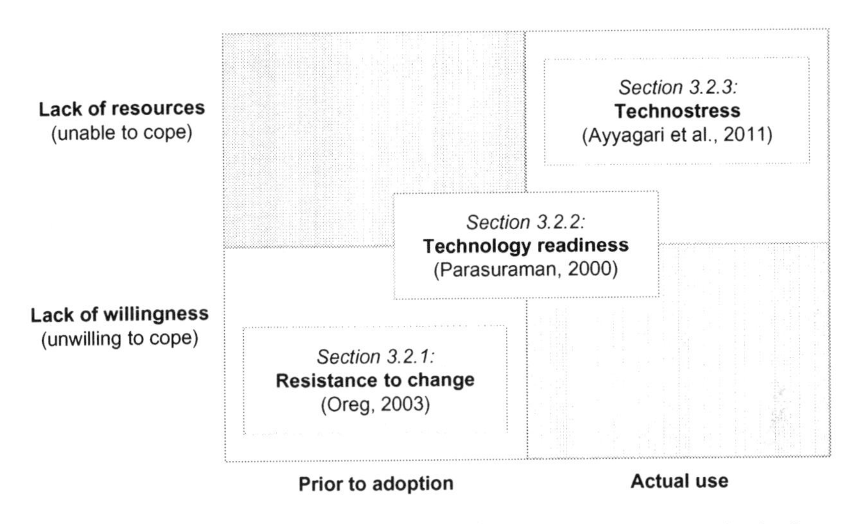


**Figure 3.5** Concepts depicting an individual's predisposition and appraisal of technology. (Source: Own illustration)

is conceptually different from adoption as well as from **non-adoption**. *Non-adoption* decisions seem to be based on barriers like lack of knowledge or an ongoing evaluation process due to the pace of change (Venkatesh and Brown, 2001). This takes into account that undesired employee responses to technology-induced change might even occur despite the employee's best of intentions (Piderit, 2000). In contrast, *resistance* implies that individuals have already considered technology and deliberately reject it (Bhattacherjee and Hikmet, 2007).

One appropriate theoretical framework to explore an individual's resistance and the resulting rejection or inappropriate use of technology is the concept of **resistance to organizational change** by Oreg (2003). This concept is frequently used to explain why efforts to introduce organizational changes do not meet with expectations, for instance, when new technology fails to unfold the desired benefits for users or the organization (Oreg, 2006). For the service industry, technology becomes increasingly important in service encounters, fundamentally changing processes and the roles of frontline employees (Singh *et al.*, 2017). Resistance to change (RTC) can be seen as a predisposition determining how individuals respond to the introduction of digital technology that potentially changes their role and well-practiced routines (Nov and Ye, 2009).

In line with Piderit (2000), Oreg (2003) anticipates that resistance to change encompasses cognitive, affective, and behavioral components. The cognitive component regards the thoughts and opinions of employees affected by organizational change. The affective component involves feelings about change. Finally, the behavioral component comprises behavioral intentions or particular actions to respond to the change (Oreg, 2006). The behavioral responses can be distinguished into open or expressive ('overt') and concealed or hidden ('covert') as well as into active and passive behaviors (Kim and Kankanhalli, 2009). Although these components are in line with the work of Piderit (2000), Oreg (2003) conceptualizes the multifaceted construct as a disposition rather than an attitude toward change.

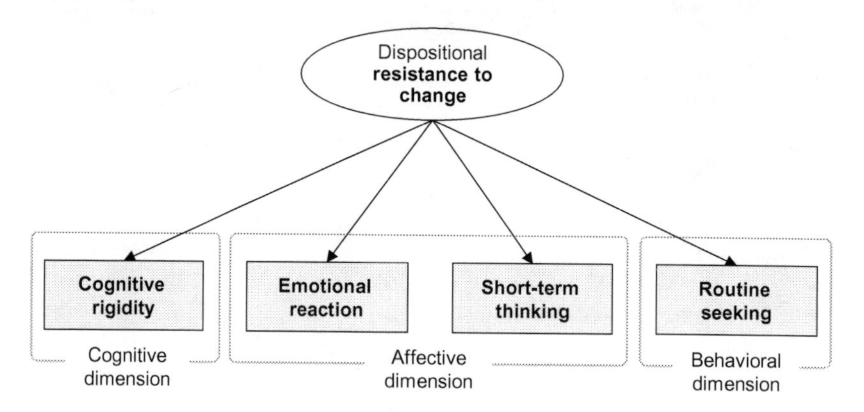


**Figure 3.6** Dispositional resistance to change and its underlying factors. (Source: Own illustration based on Oreg, 2003)

With a particular focus on sources of resistance, Oreg (2003) identifies four factors that appear to be rooted in an individual's personality. Figure 3.6 illustrates these four factors. The first one, **cognitive rigidity**, denotes the cognitive dimension of RTC. It refers to the habitualness of how frequently and easy individuals change their minds (Oreg, 2003). The affective dimension of RTC comprises two factors. On the one hand, the factor **emotional reaction to imposed change** represents an individuals' psychological resilience and the fear to lose control (Oreg, 2003). Conner (1993, p. 127) emphasizes the importance of this feeling by stating that people do not resist the intrusion of something new into their lives as much as they resist the resulting loss of control. Likewise, the factor **short-term thinking** reflects an individual's immediate inconvenience or anxiety about the detrimental effects of changes even when they potentially bear long-term benefits (Oreg, 2003).

Finally, the fourth factor, **routine seeking**, represents the behavioral dimension of RTC. The latter encompasses an individual's unwillingness to give up old habits and is thereto comparable with the inclination to favor low levels of novelty (Oreg, 2003). Since these four factors are assumed to reflect an unobserved, underlying concept, dispositional RTC is illustrated as a reflective construct in Figure 3.6 (Hulland, 1999). The interchangeability of the four factors and the moderate to high intercorrelations among them are indicators of this reflective relationship (Oreg, 2003).

Laumer *et al.* (2016) propose that the four factors depicted in the previous two paragraphs have an even stronger effect on employees' **resistance to technology-induced change** than individual characteristics such as age, gender, or working experiences. In line with this, dispositional resistance to change is seen as an influential peculiarity that explains a large proportion of the variance in beliefs about technology and potential user resistance (Laumer *et al.*, 2016). Likewise, Heidenreich and Spieth (2013) suggest that resistance to change is one determining factor of passive innovation resistance. As such, RTC can be applied to explore why individuals are less likely to adopt an innovation regardless of how beneficial it objectively would be. Due to negative emotional and cognitive responses to changes accompanying innovations, individuals with a high disposition to resist changes evaluate new things less favorable (Heidenreich and Spieth, 2013). Accordingly, Oreg's (2003) concept of dispositional resistance to change can be equally applied to the private as well as to the occupational context.

### 3.2.2 Technology Readiness

**Technology readiness** reflects an individual's propensity to willingly accept and effectively use new technology (Parasuraman, 2000). The construct is based on Mick and Fournier's (1998) conceptual framework on the paradoxes of technological devices and their impact on customer emotions and coping strategies. In line with this framework, Parasuraman (2000) adopted the assumption that individuals may simultaneously hold favorable and unfavorable feelings about technological products or technology-based services. Since the relative dominance of either feeling is expected to vary across individuals, the propensity to willingly accept and effectively use technology should vary as well (Parasuraman and Colby, 2015). Thus, technology readiness reflects a configuration of psychological **motivators** and **inhibitors** that collectively determine an individual's predisposition to use new technologies (Parasuraman, 2000).

More precisely, Parasuraman (2000) identified four dimensions that compose an individual's technology readiness. These are illustrated in Figure 3.7. Among the motivators of technology readiness, **optimism** describes a positive attitude toward technology, as well as the belief that it offers individuals more control, efficiency, and flexibility in life. The second motivator, **innovativeness**, reflects an individual's inclination to act as a thought leader and be among the first to use new technology. On the contrary, individuals will suffer **discomfort** when they feel overwhelmed by technology and think that they lack control over the course of events. Thus, discomfort accounts as an inhibitor of technology readiness together with **insecurity**. The latter encompasses skepticism about a technology's capability to function properly as well as worries about potential harmful consequences that result in mistrust of technology (Parasuraman, 2000).

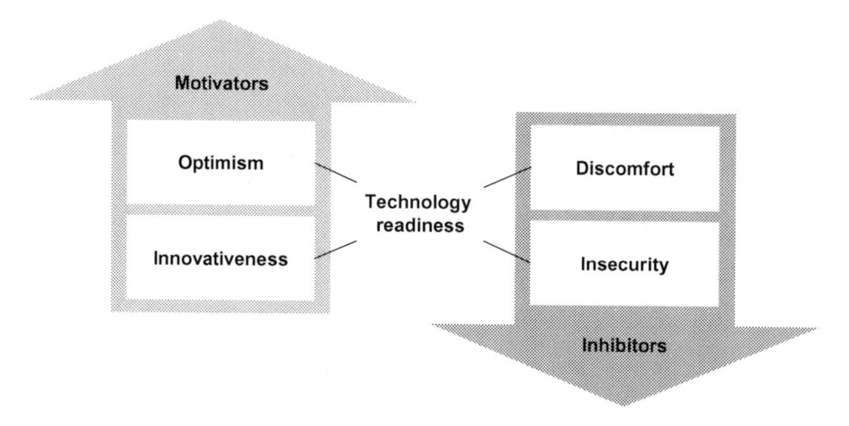


**Figure 3.7** Technology readiness and its underlying factors. (Source: Own illustration based on Parasuraman, 2000)

While optimism and innovativeness contribute to technology readiness, discomfort and uncertainty detract individuals from the latter. The four dimensions are regarded as being comparatively distinct from one another because an individual can exhibit different and partly paradoxical configurations of motivators and inhibitors as they possibly occur simultaneously (Mick and Fournier, 1998).

At the same time, Parasuraman and Colby (2015) expect these **individual characteristics** to be relatively stable over time and thus predicting the adoption of new technology, the intensity of use, as well as the perceived ease of use. Thus, in contrast to Oreg's (2003) concept of resistance to change, technology readiness is not limited to the decision *whether* to embrace technology or not, but also considers *how* individuals operate technology and integrate it into their daily routines.

To assess such technology-related attitudes and behaviors, Parasuraman (2000) developed 36 items that constituted the first version of the **technology readiness index (TRI)**. Since then, both the concept of technology readiness as well as the index have broadly been applied to understand and predict customers' predisposition toward technology. For instance, the concept has been connected to the technology acceptance model (Lin, Shih, and Sher, 2007). Furthermore, the index has been refined and adopted to particular technologies like self-service technology (Liljander *et al.*, 2006; Lin and Hsieh, 2012). Moreover, the index can be used to classify customers into different segments depending on their technology readiness (Colby and Parasuraman, 2001). The aim of such a classification is to apply distinctive marketing strategies or offer specific support regarding technology-based products and services (Tsikriktsis, 2004).

Although the concept of technology readiness is based on Mick and Fournier's (1998) paradoxes of technology and further research in the consumer behavior field (Cowles and Crosby, 1990; in particular, Dabholkar, 1996), the four dimensions of technology readiness are applicable to both private and **occupational settings**. Parasuraman (2000) acknowledges this scope by stating that the use of technology supports individuals in achieving goals in their private lives as well as at work. Furthermore, Parasuraman and Colby (2015) emphasize that employees should be regarded as internal customers when organizations design, implement, and manage their technological infrastructure. After all, frontline employees who rate high on technology readiness will be more willing to operate technology and help customers to resolve potential problems with technology interfaces (Parasuraman and Colby, 2015).

Despite its eligibility, however, the technology readiness index has seldom been applied to employees (see Walczuch, Lemmink, and Streukens, 2007 for an exception). Potentially, the updated and streamlined version of the index that Parasuraman and Colby (2015) claim **technology readiness index 2.0** (TRI 2.0) can serve as a stimulus to empirically investigate employees' predisposition toward technology more systematically. The technology readiness index 2.0 comprises four items for each of the four dimensions optimism, innovativeness, discomfort, and insecurity. The TRI 2.0 takes into account the increasing technology penetration in private lives as well as in occupational settings (Parasuraman and Colby, 2015).

### 3.2.3 Technostress

Particularly in the information system (IS) literature, the phenomenon of **technostress** represents an emerging research field (La Torre *et al.*, 2019). Research on technostress considers why and how the use of technology poses demands on the individual (Tarafdar, Cooper, and Stich, 2019). It was first made a subject of discussion by Brod (1984) who viewed technostress as a 'modern disease' reflecting employees' inability to cope with new technologies in a healthy manner. From his perspective as a clinical psychologist, Brod (1984) assumes that employees struggling with computer technology feel pressured to accept and use it. In turn, they would suffer from physical symptoms like headaches or form a psychological resistance to learning how to operate technology (Brod, 1984). Weil and Rosen (1997) broaden this perspective and refer to technostress as any negative effect on attitudes, behaviors, or physical states caused by technology either directly or indirectly. Today, a widely accepted, yet broad definition is that technostress captures the experience of stress when using technologies (Ragu-Nathan *et al.*, 2008).

The experience of stress is initiated by an individual's perception of technology-related demands or events that can be subsumed as **technology stressors** (La Torre *et al.*, 2019). According to Tarafdar *et al.* (2007), five technostress creators can be distinguished. Among these, techno-overload refers to the pressure technology may put on employees to work more and faster while techno-invasion describes employees' felt obligation to stay constantly connected (Tarafdar *et al.*, 2007). Techno-complexity denotes employees' feelings that their skills are insufficient to master technology and techno-insecurity depicts the perceived threat of being replaced by technology (Tarafdar *et al.*, 2007). Finally, techno-uncertainty is associated with constant changes and upgrades of installed systems that force employees to continuously learn and adapt (Tarafdar *et al.*, 2007). Taken together, these technology stressors are found to decrease employee productivity, job satisfaction, and organizational commitment (Ragu-Nathan *et al.*, 2008; Tarafdar *et al.*, 2007).

However, the research by Tarafdar, Ragu-Nathan, and colleagues offers little specifications on which **technology *characteristics*** ultimately determine technology stressors. To address this issue, Ayyagari *et al.* (2011) investigate various technology characteristics depicted in Figure 3.8. Usability characteristics comprise the degree to which technology enhances an employee's job performance (usefulness), the effort needed to use technology (complexity), as well as system stability (reliability). Dynamism reflects the perceived speed with which employees are confronted with new technology features (pace of change). Intrusive characteristics include the reachability of employees (presenteeism) and the degree of usage traceability (anonymity) for each employee (Ayyagari *et al.*, 2011).

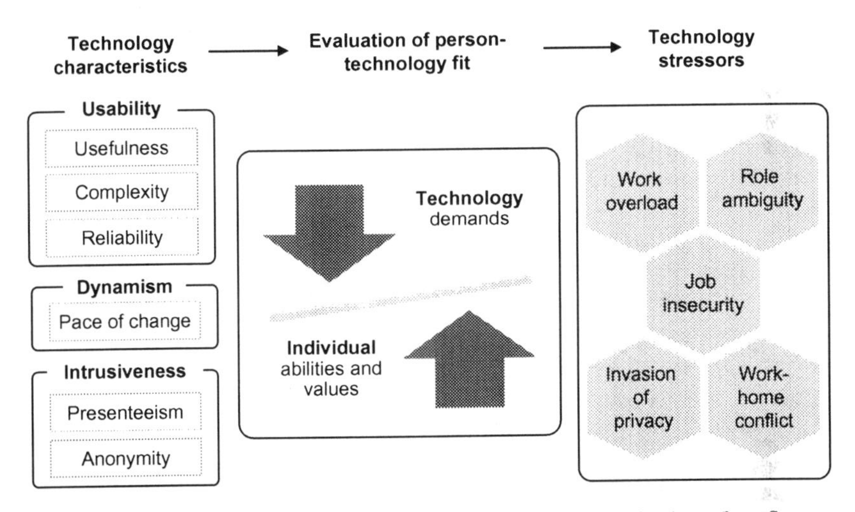


**Figure 3.8** Impact of technology characteristics on the person-technology fit. (Source: Own illustration inspired by Ayyagari *et al.*, 2011)

Ayyagari *et al.* (2011) propose that the degree to which technology characteristics form technology stressors depends on the fit between a person and the environment or, more specifically, the fit between a person and technology. The **person-environment (P-E) fit** refers to the congruence between a person and the environment and represents a central concept in organizational behavior research (Edwards, 2008). Among others, the P-E fit can be used to explain job stress. French and Kahn (1962) postulate that the P-E fit depends on the degree to which available environmental supplies meet the requirements of the person. These requirements encompass personal needs, goals, and values (Edwards, 2008). Focusing on the fit between demands and abilities, McGrath (1970) defines stress as an individual's perception of a substantial misfit between demands from the environment and response capabilities. Stress can occur when abilities deviate from demands in either direction and when the individual believes that the consequences of this misfit are of importance (Edwards, 2008).

By integrating the fit between supplies and needs as well as demands and abilities, Ayyagari *et al.* (2011) suggest that each technology characteristic can influence the evaluation of a potential misfit between technology demands and individual values and abilities. This evaluation process is illustrated in the center of Figure 3.8. For instance, the pace of change with which technology changes in the occupational context could exceed an employee's cognitive abilities. Likewise, intrusive characteristics might be perceived as being incompatible with personal values regarding privacy issues.

Finally, the individual evaluation of the person-technology misfit is the originator of five technology stressors that Ayyagari *et al.* (2011) identify: Work overload, role ambiguity, job insecurity, invasion of privacy, and work-home conflict. Thus, although the approach and focus differ from Tarafdar *et al.* (2007), there is a considerable overlap concerning technology stressors. As a result of their empirical study, Ayyagari *et al.* (2011) find that work overload and role ambiguity are the most prevailing stressors leading to **technostrain**. The latter is conceptualized as "the individual's psychological response" (Ayyagari *et al.*, 2011, p. 834) to demands that are perceived as stressful, whereas technostress refers to the transactional process while using technology (Maier *et al.*, 2019). Throughout this thesis, the term technostress rather than technostrain is used to capture the overall process.

Similarly to the concept of challenge job demands and hindrance job demands depicted in Section 3.2.3 (Podsakoff *et al.*, 2007), technology characteristics can be appraised as a challenge and thus evoke **techno-eustress** (Tarafdar *et al.*, 2019). This positive facet of stress can motivate employees to tackle demands and may even result in increased job satisfaction (Califf *et al.*, 2015). However, academic research has focused on **techno-distress** in the past, explaining employees' appraisals of technology as hindrance or threat (Tarafdar *et al.*, 2019). From a neurobiological perspective, technostress increases technology user's stress hormones (Riedl *et al.*, 2012). Furthermore, it is reflected in cognitive symptoms, such as poor concentration or bad temper (Arnetz and Wiholm, 1997).

Various outcomes of the undesirable physical and psychological state of technostress are compiled in Table 3.1. As the table demonstrates, most research on technostress in the workplace so far is rooted in the information systems (IS) literature. Prior empirical studies focus on employee outcomes of technostress such as job satisfaction, turnover intentions, or burnout. Yet, they lack the consideration of potential customer outcomes. More specifically, technostress, which

**Table 3.1** Empirical research on the outcomes of technostress in occupational settings

| Study | Empirical Analysis *(Study Context)* | Theoretical explanation | Outcomes considered | Key findings |
|---|---|---|---|---|
| Tu, Wang, and Shu (2005) | Survey among N = 437 employees using ICTs at work *(miscellaneous)* | Technostress literature | · Individual productivity | Overall technostress has no significant effect on employee productivity; techno-overload increases productivity, techno-invasion and techno-insecurity decrease productivity |
| Ragu-Nathan *et al.* (2008) | Survey among N = 608 end users of ICTs *(government, financial services, manufacturing)* | Transactional theory | · Job satisfaction<br>· commitment<br>· intention to stay | Technostress creators decrease job satisfaction, leading to decreased organizational and continuance commitment |
| Fuglseth and Sørebø (2014) | Online survey among N = 216 employees *(government)* | Transactional theory | · Satisfaction with use of ICT<br>· intention to extent use of ICT | Technostress creators decrease satisfaction with, and thereby the intention to extend the use of, ICTs |
| Califf *et al.* (2015) | Survey among N = 402 nurses in hospitals *(healthcare)* | Organizational stress cycle | · Job satisfaction<br>· turnover intention | Techno-eustress increases job satisfaction, techno-distress decreases job satisfaction and increases turnover intention |

(continued)

**Table 3.1** (continued)

| **Study** | **Empirical Analysis *(Study Context)*** | **Theoretical explanation** | **Outcomes considered** | **Key findings** |
|---|---|---|---|---|
| Maier, Laumer, and Eckhardt (2015) | Online survey among N = 306 full-time employees using ICTs at work *(miscellaneous)* | Stressor-strain-outcome model | · Job satisfaction<br>· organizational commitment<br>· turnover intention | Techno-exhaustion only indirectly impacts job satisfaction, organizational commitment, and turnover intention negatively through work-exhaustion |
| Srivastava, Chandra, and Shirish (2015) | Online survey, N = 152 senior organizational managers *(miscellaneous)* | Transactional theory | · Job burnout<br>· job engagement | Agreeableness and extraversion buffer the effect of technostress on job burnout; neuroticism intensifies the effect of technostress on job engagement while openness buffers the latter |
| Tarafdar, Pullins, and Ragu-Nathan (2015) | Survey among N = 237 sales professionals *(B2B sales)* | Social cognitive theory | · Techno-enabled innovation<br>· sales performance | Technostress creators decrease technology-enabled innovation and sales performance |
| Khedhaouria and Cucchi (2019) | Online survey among N = 161 senior managers *(industrial sector, commerce, services)* | Transactional theory; complexity theory | · Job burnout | Different combinations of personality traits elicit different reactions to technostress creators, leading to different levels of job burnout |

*Notes: ICT = Information and communication technology*

may arise due to the increasing adoption of technologies in service encounters, has neither been considered as a result of technology-induced job demands nor as an antecedent to customer responses. This thesis aims at filling this gap by investigating technostress with a qualitative approach in Study B and a dyadic field survey in Study C.

## 3.3 Formation of Customer Evaluations of Service Encounters

The three concepts related to an individual's predisposition toward technology depicted in Section 3.2 are applicable to the acceptance and use of technology in occupational settings (i.e., from an employee perspective) as well as in private settings (i.e., from a customer perspective). Despite the applicability of the aforementioned concepts to both employees and customers, technology use in the private context is supposed to be different from the occupational context. Today, the market share of 'smart' products constantly rises (Hubert *et al.*, 2019; Mani and Chouk, 2017), and service strategies are increasingly becoming technology-driven (Huang and Rust, 2017). Nevertheless, customers—in contrast to employees—still have more choices in making use of technology and evaluating technology-induced service encounters. Even when service providers force customers to use a technology interface instead of personally interacting with an FLE, customers can switch providers fairly easily (Reinders, Dabholkar, and Frambach, 2008). Moreover, customers can easily voice their evaluations of a service encounter and, thereby, influence others and ultimately act as a determiner of a service firm's success (Beatty *et al.*, 2012).

Therefore, service providers need to anticipate customers' evaluation of technology-induced service encounters to effectively implement digital technology and to design digital customer-facing processes. Accordingly, this chapter explores three concepts that can be applied to **customer evaluations** of service encounters. These evaluations encompass customer satisfaction and delight, equity, and fairness. Customer intentions regarding purchase behavior, loyalty, or word-of-mouth often result from the aforementioned concepts and can also be subsumed as customer evaluations (Maxham, Netemeyer, and Lichtenstein, 2008). First, Section 3.3.1 discusses Oliver and DeSarbo's (1988) **expectancy-disconfirmation paradigm** to explain the mechanisms leading to customer satisfaction and delight. Thereafter, Section 3.3.2 describes how individuals compare the perceived ratio of their own inputs and outcomes to that of a reference person, group, or institution using Adams' (1965) **equity theory**. Finally,

Section 3.3.3 discusses the multiple dimensions of Seiders and Berry's (1998) concept of **service fairness** as perceived by the customer and outlines the relationship between fairness evaluations and customer satisfaction.

### 3.3.1 Expectancy-Disconfirmation Paradigm

Within academic research on customer evaluations of a product or service, Oliver's (1980) **expectancy-disconfirmation paradigm** is the dominant framework to understand the mechanisms underlying customer satisfaction and delight (Barnes, Ponder, and Dugar, 2011). The paradigm expresses customer satisfaction as a result of confirmed expectations (Oliver, 1980). Through the advancement of earlier propositions on disconfirmed expectations, the paradigm aims at providing further evidence for "the seemingly obvious conclusion that satisfaction increases as the performance/expectation ratio increases" (Oliver, 1980, p. 460). It is mainly based on the results of a seminal experimental study on customer expectation and satisfaction by Cardozo (1965).

Furthermore, Oliver and DeSarbo (1988) designate assimilation and contrast theory as precursors of the expectancy-disconfirmation paradigm. They state that some customers are more expectations-influenced in their satisfaction response, some are rather disconfirmation-influenced and others emphasize both expectations and disconfirmation. Similar to Festinger's (1957) theory of cognitive dissonance, **assimilation theory** assumes that customers strive for a cognitive state of balance and are reluctant to acknowledge any disconfirmation (Hovland, Harvey, and Sherif, 1957). When a comparison between expectations and perceptions results in disconfirmation, expectations-influenced customers are predicted to assimilate their evaluation toward their initial expectations (Olson and Dover, 1979).

On the other hand, **contrast theory** assumes that any disconfirmation triggers customers to magnify their evaluations in either direction of the particular disconfirmation (Dawes, Singer, and Lemons, 1972). Thus, disconfirmation-influenced customers are predicted to evaluate performance below expectations poorer than reasonable whereas performance exceeding expectations is likely to be rated extremely high (Oliver and DeSarbo, 1988). Finally, the **assimilation-contrast approach** proposes that a customer's reaction depends on the magnitude of disconfirmation. While minor disconfirmation will be assimilated by the customer, major disconfirmation that exceeds a customer's latitude of acceptance is expected to elicit the contrast effect (Anderson, 1973). The expectancy-disconfirmation paradigm considers these various customer responses (Oliver and DeSarbo, 1988).

Although primarily developed to explain customer evaluations of *product* performance, the paradigm is also considered as the basis of **service quality** theory (Brady and Cronin, 2001). More specifically, Grönroos (1984) states that perceived service quality results from the comparison of customer expectations with the perceived technical and functional quality of the received service. Technical quality refers to the instrumental performance of the service and captures *what* the customer receives as the service outcome (Grönroos, 1984). In comparison, functional quality reflects *how* the outcome is delivered and thus captures aspects of the interaction between the customer and a frontline employee or the service firm's technology interfaces (Brady and Cronin, 2001; Grönroos, 1984).

The expectancy-disconfirmation paradigm also forms the foundations of Parasuraman *et al.*'s (1985) service quality model (SERVQUAL). The latter conceptualizes perceived service quality as the correspondence of customer expectations with actual perceptions. These perceptions encompass the reliability, responsiveness, assurances, empathy, and tangibility of the service experience (Parasuraman, Zeithaml, and Berry, 1988). For technology-based services delivered through websites, the dominant quality dimensions are efficiency, fulfillment, system availability, and privacy (Parasuraman, Zeithaml, and Malhotra, 2005).

Figure 3.9 illustrates the application of the expectancy-disconfirmation paradigm to the evaluation of service performance. The paradigm considers customer evaluations to result from two processes: the formation of expectations prior to purchasing a good or a service and the comparison of those expectations with the perceived performance (Oliver and DeSarbo, 1988). A customer's initial **expectations** derive from individual needs, prior experiences, a firm's traditional marketing activities including pricing as well as from external influences from one's network, media, or online review platforms (Grönroos, 1984; Voorhees *et al.*, 2017; Zeithaml, Berry, and Parasuraman, 1993). Moreover, the initial contact with a service firm via the phone, electronic channels, or in person is regarded as part of a customer's information search and is thus expected to shape expectations regarding the core service encounter (Bitner, 1995; Voorhees *et al.*, 2017; Whiting and Donthu, 2006).

With regard to services, the **cognitive comparison** process takes place during or after the core service encounter. At this state, customers compare their perceptions of service quality with their expectations either consciously or unconsciously (Krüger, 2016). If this comparison results in confirmation, the expectancy-disconfirmation paradigm proposes that **customer satisfaction** will arouse (Oliver, 1980). However, when the customer is either not motivated or not able to conduct a conscious comparison, the accordance of expectations and perceptions is likely to result in latent satisfaction. In this case, the customer is not necessarily aware of being satisfied (Bloemer and de Ruyter, 1998). In contrast, a conscious comparison will result in manifest satisfaction that the customer deliberately appreciates (Bloemer and de Ruyter, 1998). As depicted in Figure 3.9, a negative disconfirmation will result in dissatisfaction whilst a positive disconfirmation will arouse customer delight (Kotler and Keller, 2016).

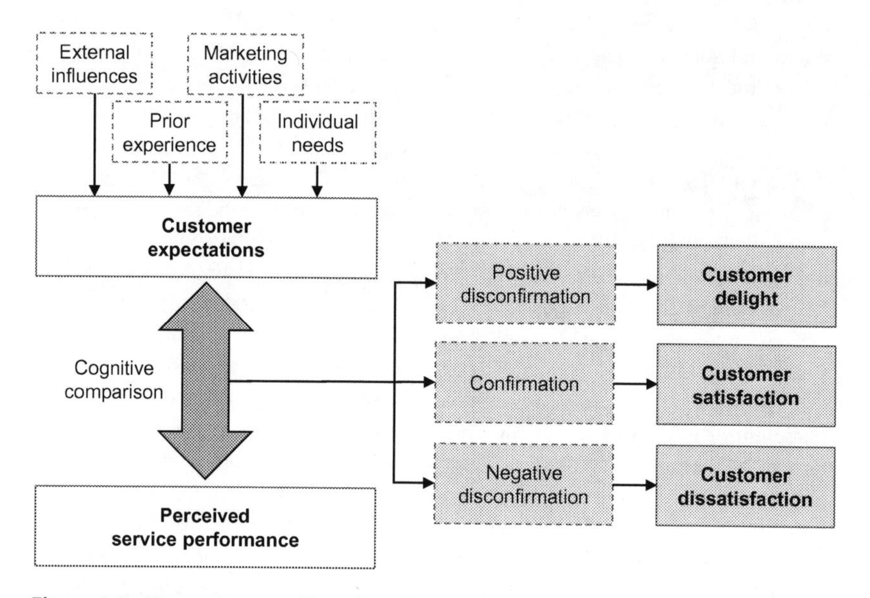


**Figure 3.9** The expectancy-disconfirmation paradigm applied to service performance. (Source: Own illustration based Oliver, 1980)

There are two distinct perspectives on **customer delight** in academic literature. The first one postulates that customer delight represents an extraordinarily high level of customer satisfaction (Anderson and Mittal, 2000). This conceptualization as the "zone of delight" is based on a proposition by Rust, Zahorik, and Keiningham (1995) that at upper levels of customer satisfaction, there is a zone in which customer loyalty increases disproportionately. The expectancy-disconfirmation paradigm suggests that delight is only possible when service exceeds customer expectations to a surprising degree (Barnes *et al.*, 2016).

The second perspective in academic literature conceptualizes customer delight as a separate construct with different antecedents and underlying mechanisms as compared to customer satisfaction. Based on insights from emotion psychology, delight is conceived as an **affective customer response** involving surprise as well as positive emotions such as joy or excitement (Collier *et al.*, 2018; Finn, 2012; Oliver, Rust, and Varki, 1997). Barnes *et al.* (2011) postulate that customers pursue a 'cognitive route' to delight as proposed by the expectancy-disconfirmation paradigm when they can easily form expectations. In contrast, when customers cannot easily form expectations, positive affect and emotions are expected to arouse delight (Barnes *et al.*, 2011).

Transferred to customer evaluations of technology-induced services, the expectancy-disconfirmation paradigm is appropriate to explain why customers value personal service and technology differently (Scherer, Wünderlich, and von Wangenheim, 2015). Customers have distinct expectations regarding the **interactions with frontline employees** (FLEs) that determine satisfaction and delight (Hennig-Thurau, 2004). Rust, Zahorik, and Keiningham (1996) state that personal interactions between FLEs and customers often are the primary determinants of customer satisfaction. Similarly, Barnes *et al.* (2011) find that employee affect (e.g., being caring and friendly) and effort (e.g., being attentive and helpful) have the strongest impact on arousing customer delight.

However, **digital technology** operated by the FLE may distract from providing quality customer interactions (Netemeyer *et al.*, 2005). Likewise, technology devices operated by customers can draw their attention away from FLE rapport-building efforts like smiling during the service encounter (Giebelhausen *et al.*, 2014). On the other hand, technology has the potential to enhance FLEs' role performance by helping them focus on core activities and speeding up service delivery (Kumar *et al.*, 2016; Larivière *et al.*, 2017). Thus, service performance as perceived by the customer may deviate from their initial expectations in both directions when service encounters are supplemented by technology.

### 3.3.2 Equity Theory

Equity theory builds on the foundations of the **theory of cognitive dissonance** by Festinger (1957). At its core, the theory of cognitive dissonance postulates that each individual strives for consistency, thus an inner equilibrium, among cognitions. Cognitions include "any knowledge, opinion, or belief about the environment, about oneself, or about one's behavior" (Festinger, 1957, p. 3). If these cognitions are inconsistent, the psychologically uncomfortable state of cognitive dissonance arises, driving the individual to try to reduce the dissonance (Festinger, 1957).

Based on the former assumptions, Adams (1963) develops the **theory of inequity** as a special case of Festinger's theory of cognitive dissonance. First applied to employee-employer relationships, inequity is supposed to exist when an employee's *perceived* inputs as compared to the outcomes stand in reverse relation to the *perceived* inputs and outcomes of a comparable reference person, group, or institution (Adams, 1963). Routed in social psychology, equity theory applies to various exchange relationships (Adams, 1965; Walster, Berscheid, and Walster, 1973). Figure 3.10 symbolizes that in these exchange relationships, individuals weigh their individual **ratio of inputs and outcomes** against other's ratio. Inputs include all individual contributions to an exchange relationship, whereas outcomes can be either positive or negative consequences of this relationship (Walster *et al.*, 1973).

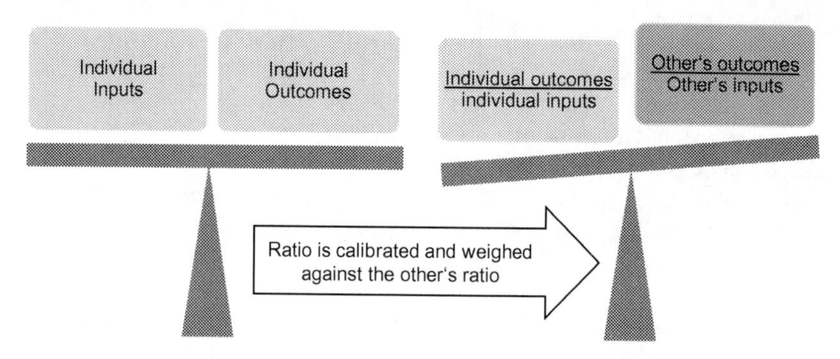


**Figure 3.10** The principle of equity theory. (Source: Own illustration based on Adams, 1965)

Like in the case of cognitive dissonance, individuals perceiving inequity in **social exchange** will feel a sense of dissatisfaction or a negative emotional state like anger if the inequity is unfavorable to them (Lapidus and Pinkerton, 1995). Söderlund *et al.* (2014) call this form of inequity 'under-reward'. At the same time, receiving more than others likewise creates inequity. This form of inequity can be referred to as 'over-reward' (Söderlund *et al.*, 2014). Although the bias of equity theory proposes that an individual perceives less inequity when it is in the individual's favor, such inequity may still evoke feelings of guilt toward the exchange partner (Lapidus and Pinkerton, 1995). Overall, the tension created by perceived inequity motivates individuals to strive for a fair distribution of inputs and outcomes (Adams, 1963). The desire to reduce this tension depends on the degree of inequity between an individual and the respective exchange partner (Adams, 1965).

As the exchange between a customer and a firm is one form of social exchange (Lapidus and Pinkerton, 1995), the patterns of equity theory have been transferred to **marketing research** in the late 1970 s. Huppertz, Arenson, and Evans (1978) investigate customer ratings of different prices and service quality levels and name several strategies to reduce inequity in retail exchange. Namely, exchange partners can increase, decrease or psychologically re-evaluate inputs and outcomes, change the reference point, or leave the exchange situation (Huppertz *et al.*, 1978). Although their study does not explicitly focus on customer satisfaction, it has initiated further research on equity and satisfaction in social exchanges (Oliver and Swan, 1989).

Overall, equity theory assumes that **satisfaction** arises when the customer perceives "that his/her outcome-to-input ratio is proportionate to that of the partner" (Oliver and DeSarbo, 1988, p. 496). Since equity theory explicitly considers inputs and outcomes of all parties involved in the exchange, it is unique as compared to other theoretical frameworks like the expectancy-confirmation paradigm described in Section 3.3.1 or the earlier-mentioned theory of cognitive dissonance (Oliver and Swan, 1989). Accordingly, equity theory is not limited to the perspective of one actor in the marketplace (e.g., the customer) but focuses on the equitable distribution of benefits in dyadic relationships (Huppertz *et al.*, 1978).

In the dyadic relationship between a customer and a service provider, the customer's input is composed of monetary and non-monetary **resources** (Haumann *et al.*, 2015). Monetary resources include the price paid for a service as well as costs associated with the transaction (e.g., fuel or public transport for offline environments and technical equipment for online environments). Time, effort, competencies, and personal data represent the most prevalent non-monetary resources and are especially high if customers actively participate in the provision of services (Fliess and Kleinaltenkamp, 2004).

This is particularly true for **technology-based services** in which customers interact with a firm-provided system either online or in-store (Oertzen *et al.*, 2018). For instance, customers use online reservation systems (see Study A) or self-ordering devices as part of their restaurant experience (see Study B and C) or buy eyewear after virtually trying it on instead of claiming personal purchase advisory (see Study D). In these cases, customers perceive their input and productivity to be high because they partly take over tasks that would otherwise be performed by service employees (Anitsal and Schumann, 2007; Heidenreich and Handrich, 2015).

In turn for their inputs, customers derive value from the received service as the outcome of the exchange (Etgar, 2008). Besides quality and price, a service provider's effort to increase customer convenience and thus reduce non-monetary resources leverages **value equity** (Lemon, Rust, and Zeithaml, 2001). Thus, presuming high customer inputs to technology-based services are expected to be compensated through reduced waiting times (Kokkinoua and Cranage, 2013) and increased convenience (Hilken *et al.*, 2017) to achieve value equity. In turn, value equity increases customer satisfaction and loyalty (Vogel, Evanschitzky, and Ramaseshan, 2008).

### 3.3.3 Service Fairness

Research on fairness has examined various aspects of customer behavior in customer-firm relationships (Nguyen and Klaus, 2013). Yet, fairness is of particular interest to service firms because the "intangibility of services heightens customers' sensitivity to fairness issues" (Berry, Parasuraman, and Zeithaml, 1994, p. 40). Berry (1995) proposes that service offerings implicitly comprise the promise to treat customers fairly. Based on this proposition, Schneider and Bowen (1999) assume that customers form psychological contracts in which they expect a service provider to engage in fair behaviors. Accordingly, **service fairness** reflects the perceived degree of justice in that behavior (Seiders and Berry, 1998).

Prior studies provide empirical evidence that fairness is imperative to service firms because it affects customer satisfaction (Han *et al.*, 2019), loyalty intentions (Chiu *et al.*, 2009), and different forms of customer engagement behaviors such as word-of-mouth or customers helping customers as well as the company (Roy *et al.*, 2018). Within this research stream, there is a consensus that fairness comprises three interdependent, yet distinct, dimensions. That is distributive, procedural, and interactional fairness (Devlin, Roy, and Sekhon, 2014). These three dimensions are visualized as three pillars in Figure 3.11.

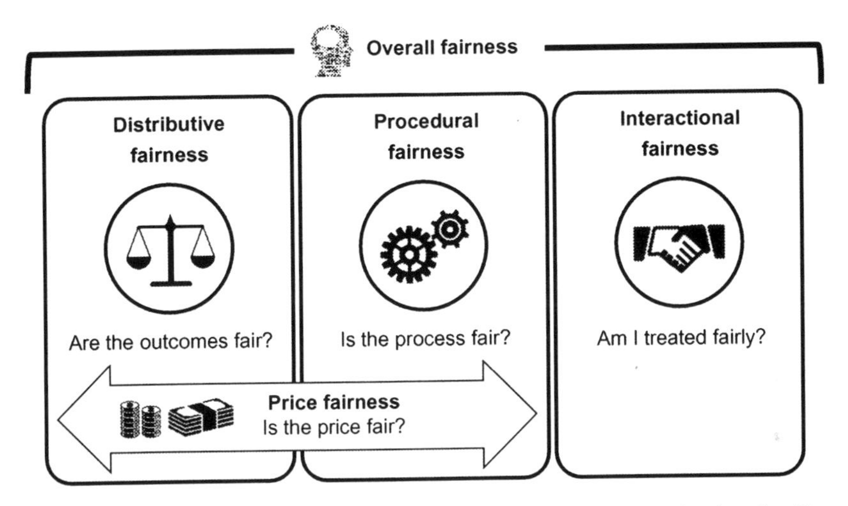


**Figure 3.11** The multi-dimensionality of fairness. (Source: Own illustration based on Ferguson, Ellen, and Bearden, 2014 and Cropanzano *et al.*, 2001)

The first dimension is **distributive fairness**. It refers to the perceived correctness of the allocation of outcomes to different exchange partners in relation to the inputs (Franke, Keinz, and Klausberger, 2013). Hence, equity theory can be understood as a specification of the principle of distributive fairness (Adams, 1963). Though, equity theory has been criticized to be unidimensional because it solely focuses on the fair distribution of outcomes but disregards the procedures leading to that distribution (Leventhal, 1980). In this regard, the concept of fairness expands equity theory by considering **procedural fairness** as the second dimension. The latter relates to whether the processes used to allocate the outcomes are consistent with general norms and represent the interests of all involved exchange partners (Ferguson *et al.*, 2014). The third dimension, **interactional fairness**, encompasses the degree to which service employees behave politely, integer, and concerned toward customers (Han *et al.*, 2019).

The importance of these three dimensions for the formation of overall fairness is discussed conversely in literature. According to **fairness theory**, all three elements are used to assess a situation as opposed to alternative scenarios (Folger and Cropanzano, 1998; Folger and Cropanzano, 2001). However, fairness theory postulates that interactional fairness might be a stronger predictor of outcome evaluations than distributive or procedural fairness (Collie, Bradley, and Sparks,

2002). By focusing on potential alternative situations, fairness theory assumes that individuals ask themselves 'what might have been' by weighing which alternative courses of action the exchange partners would, could, and should have taken (Cropanzano *et al.*, 2001). These cognitive mechanisms are referred to as 'counterfactual reasoning' (McColl-Kennedy and Sparks, 2003).

On the contrary, **fairness heuristics theory** assumes that due to the lack of transparency regarding exchange partners' inputs and outcomes (i.e., distributive fairness), individuals rely more strongly on information regarding the process (i.e., procedural fairness) to evaluate an exchange (van den Bos *et al.*, 1997). In such situations, individuals apply procedural fairness in a heuristic manner and thereby use "a psychological shortcut" (Lind *et al.*, 1993, p. 225) to determine overall fairness. In social and organizational psychology, this is referred to as **'fair process effect'** (Collie *et al.*, 2002). When individuals believe that the applied procedures are fair, "they are likely to be satisfied with the outcomes—even if the outcomes are considered unfair" (Chiu *et al.*, 2009, p. 350). Yet, when information on outcomes is available and transparent, the **'fair outcome effect'** proposes that distributive fairness will overweigh procedural fairness in determining overall fairness (van den Bos *et al.*, 1997).

Concerning **price fairness**, it is considered that the latter results from customer evaluations of both distributive and procedural fairness (Ferguson *et al.*, 2014). Thus, price fairness is represented as an arrow spanning these two dimensions of fairness in Figure 3.11. More precisely, customers compare a price and procedures applied to set a price with a certain reference point that either stems from the past (e.g., prior purchases), the market (e.g., competitor prices), or from a firm's costs as estimated by the customer (Bolton, Warlop, and Alba, 2003). Based on this comparison, customers evaluate whether the price offered to them is acceptable, reasonable, and just (Xia, Monroe, and Cox, 2004).

For technology-induced service encounters, the importance of each of the three fairness dimensions depends on the **degree of human touch**. In augmented and blended services (see Figure 2.9 for an overview), customers directly interact with frontline employees (Keating *et al.*, 2018). These interactions allow customers to evaluate interactional fairness based on whether the frontline employee provides reasonable explanations or behaves truthful, respectful, and appropriately (Ting, 2013). For transactional or emergent services, interactional fairness evaluations are limited to cases in which customers contact an employee either in person, via phone, or using an online platform (Chiu *et al.*, 2009).

Thus, fairness evaluations of technology-based services are mainly based on distributive and procedural fairness when the human touch is low. Since customers interact with technology in such service settings, distributive fairness evaluations take into account the time and effort invested to operate technology (Roy *et al.*, 2018). As outlined for value equity in Section 3.3.2, higher customer inputs might be counterbalanced by higher convenience of technology-based service (Hilken *et al.*, 2017). However, the fairness concept considers further aspects that go beyond equity theory. For services, fairness evaluations also comprise procedural aspects like waiting procedures, service efficiency, timely delivery, or the degree of personalization (Han *et al.*, 2019). These components of procedural fairness apply to different types of technology-induced services (Chiu *et al.*, 2009). At the same time, a high degree of perceived procedural fairness increases the probability of long-term customer satisfaction with a service provider (Maxham and Netemeyer, 2002).

# Study A: The Impact of Technology on Frontline Employees' Process Deviance

4

## 4.1 Context, Aim, and Design of Study A

Service sectors with a high degree of personal customer contact, including the restaurant industry, have long been comparatively reluctant to invest in technologies for digital customer integration (Gandhi, Khanna, and Ramaswamy, 2016; Tan and Netessine, 2020). For most wide-spread technologies today, market-leading restaurant chains were the first to discover their benefits and to leverage the necessary financial resources. Owing to large chains forging ahead, restaurants of every size are now adopting technological solutions to increase sales and gain productivity advantages (National Restaurant Association, 2018).

Among others, restaurant operators are widely using online reservation systems (Schaarschmidt and Hoeber, 2017). Through multi-restaurant reservation sites such as Yelp, Quandoo, OpenTable, or Bookatable, customers can compare multiple restaurants and pursue reservations for free (Harvard Business School, 2018). In a restaurant technology survey among United States citizens, 83 percent of diners say online reservations are "very important" or "somewhat important" to their dining experience (Toast Inc., 2017), implying a large demand for reserving a table independently from restaurant opening hours (Kimes, 2009).

---

A version of Study A with a narrower focus has been published in the Journal of Services Marketing: Christ-Brendemühl, S. and Schaarschmidt, M. (2019), "Frontline backlash: Service employees' deviance from digital processes", Journal of Services Marketing, Vol. 31(7), pp. 936–945.

---

**Supplementary Information** The online version contains supplementary material available at https://doi.org/10.1007/978-3-658-37885-1_4.


S. Christ-Brendemühl, *Digital Technology in Service Encounters*, Innovation, Entrepreneurship und Digitalisierung, https://doi.org/10.1007/978-3-658-37885-1_4

Traditionally, restaurant reservations used to be handled by frontline employees (FLEs), giving the reservation process a personal touch and allowing FLEs to talk directly to customers about their seating preferences or special requests (Kimes, 2008). For FLEs, managing the mix between online reservations, phone reservations and customers walking in without reservations can be challenging and time-consuming (Kimes and Kies, 2012). On the one hand, FLEs need to operate the reservation system's interface to overlook the number of online reservations and to integrate phone reservations into the digital table plan. On the other hand, FLEs frequently need to adjust the automatized allocation of customers to the tables, for instance, to respond to special requests or comply with the habits of regular customers (Kimes, 2008). Figure 4.1 depicts the demands that potentially arise in the different stages of the reservation process.

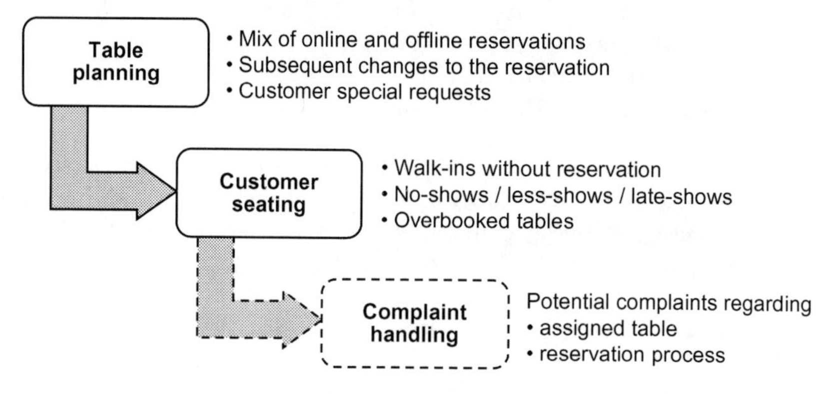


**Figure 4.1** Potential demands along the table reservation process. (Source: Own illustration)

The process stage of seating customers involves situations in which customers show up late, stay away, or enter the restaurant with fewer people than indicated in the reservation (Kimes and Wirtz, 2007). When restaurants are booked out in peak times, reserved tables that remain empty due to customers showing up late or not at all will evoke the desire of walk-in customers to be seated at those tables. FLEs then have to allay walk-in customers' impatience either until the customers who had reserved the table show up or until a certain time has passed so that FLEs can unblock the table. Additionally, restaurant managers frequently overbook their tables during peak times to compensate for no-shows (Kimes and Chase, 1998). In case every customer shows up, this confronts FLEs with the challenge to speed up their service and to kindly ask customers to free tables as soon as they have finished their food.

Finally, as shown in the third stage of the reservation process in Figure 4.1, customers may complain about reservation policies. A restaurant's seating policy often results in customer disappointment or anger that FLEs are expected to resolve, for instance, when customers need to wait for 'their' table or are dissatisfied with the assigned table (Kimes and Wirtz, 2007). Likewise, customers may also complain about the (online) reservation process itself. FLEs are the first ones to receive such complaints and may perceive this as demanding. These examples show that issues related to restaurant reservations can have a considerable impact on FLEs' daily work.

With regard to their market penetration, online reservation systems represent one pervasive technology in the restaurant industry. Financial investments in such platform-based technologies are comparatively minor for small and medium businesses (Luca, Mohan, and Rooney, 2016). Still, restaurant managers strive to pay-off arising reservation fees by reducing their employees' effort with handling reservations (Kimes, 2009). However, FLEs will hardly be relieved when customers who have reserved a table online call the restaurant to change their reservation or to make sure they will be seated at their preferred table.

Consequently, restaurant managers frequently try to implement the rule that customers who have reserved a table online should not be allowed to change or cancel their reservation via the phone. This aims at preventing FLEs from spending their time on tasks that are meant to be automated. In situations when customers still call to make changes to their online reservations, FLEs are torn between fulfilling customers' needs and complying with processes set up to ensure efficiency. This may result in FLE role ambiguity (Kohli and Jaworski, 1994). The degree to which FLEs perceive role ambiguity due to the demands from technology is expected to depend on intrapersonal determinants like self-efficacy (Fida *et al.*, 2015) or an individual's resistance to change (Mulki *et al.*, 2012).

Due to the demands arising from working with online reservation systems, FLEs may depart from formal procedures in order to satisfy customers' needs—a strategy referred to as constructive process deviance (Galperin, 2012). This type of deviance increases the overall costs of the reservation process, for instance, when FLEs offer help via phone although customers should use the online reservation system for changing reservations. Apart from constructive process deviance, other deviating behaviors could harm the organization even stronger. For instance, FLEs not reporting customer complaints regarding the online reservation system hinder the organization to evaluate the effectiveness of digital technology and to improve their service. Such behavior would classify as destructive process deviance (Hammes and Walsh, 2017).

Prior research in the field of digitization has predominantly investigated the restaurant return on investment in technology (Creamer, 2018; Lee *et al.*, 2015), adoption barriers for independent restaurateurs (Ashcroft *et al.*, 2019), and consumer acceptance of, or trust in, online reservation systems (Kimes and Kies, 2012; Schaarschmidt and Hoeber, 2017). Frontline employees—who play a critical role in service encounters (Hüttel *et al.*, 2019; Karatepe and Karadas, 2016)—have seldom been the focus of research endeavors (Montargot and Ben Lahouel, 2018). Yet, FLEs are responsible for the implementation of new processes that come along with digital technology (Cadwallader *et al.*, 2010). Therefore, FLEs need to be integrated more stringently into research on technology in service encounters. Against this backdrop, Study A addresses the following **research questions**:

| | |
|---|---|
| $RQ_A$-1 | To which degree do intrapersonal determinants like self-efficacy and resistance to change determine frontline employee's technology-induced role ambiguity? |
| $RQ_A$-2 | How does frontline employee's technology-induced role ambiguity relate to their constructive and destructive process deviance? |

To provide initial empirical evidence on these questions, Study A uses a quantitative approach. FLE self-efficacy and resistance to change (RTC) are conceptualized as antecedents of FLE technology-induced role ambiguity when working with an online reservation system. Concomitantly, two types of process deviance are investigated as customer-facing outcomes of role ambiguity. Furthermore, it is considered how the existence of service scripts as one form of organizational control (Brach *et al.*, 2015) influences the relationship between role ambiguity and process deviance. For this purpose, data from 123 FLEs with experience in using online reservation systems is collected via a quantitative online survey. The results reveal that technology-induced role ambiguity influences both constructive and destructive process deviance. Likewise, the results show that FLE self-efficacy reduces role ambiguity, while RTC fosters it. Additionally, an analysis of direct and indirect effects reveals a direct effect of RTC on destructive process deviance.

Given this approach, this research offers at least four important **contributions**. First, digitization in more traditional service sectors is examined from the employee perspective. Second, the construct of workplace deviance is adapted to work processes, which are increasingly influenced by digital technologies. Third, the influence of technology-induced role ambiguity on deviant behaviors regarding newly implemented processes is empirically tested. This is of importance because digital interfaces have become an integral part of service management as they are key to provide consistent customer experiences. However, an increase in productivity can only be achieved when FLEs comply with redesigned processes that reflect the requirements of digital interfaces. Fourth, it is examined whether service scripts affect the influence of role ambiguity on process deviance. The results of Study A depict a promising start to the investigation of employee role ambiguity and process deviance as consequences of the introduction of digital technology in people-intensive service industries.

## 4.2 Theoretical Framework

### 4.2.1 Conceptual Model

For Study A, the transactional theory of stress and coping (Folkman, Lazarus, Gruen, and DeLongis, 1986; Lazarus and Folkman, 1984, 1987) serves as a framework for developing a research model and hypotheses. Rapid changes in the business environment lead to continuous adjustments of organizational processes, thereby creating working conditions that employees increasingly perceive as stressful (Bordia *et al.*, 2004; Fida *et al.*, 2015). Technology frequently forces employees to work more and adapt their routines (Thatcher *et al.*, 2002). As organizations' expectations toward employees rise, this can cause tension and role ambiguity.

Traditionally, role ambiguity is defined as "lack of the necessary information available to a given organizational position" (Rizzo, House, and Lirtzman, 1970, p. 151). This comprises others' expectations toward a role as well as the uncertainty about one's role performance (Netemeyer, Johnston, and Burton, 1990). Transferred to the context of digitization, employees have to spend working time on learning how to operate new digital solutions and to resolve issues occurring from (unreliable) technology. This often results in an excess of information and tasks described as overflow (Król, 2017). The lack of clarity about how much time should be spent on technology-related issues in contrast to core activities of the specific job intensifies role ambiguity (Yang *et al.*, 2017). Hereafter, **technology-induced role ambiguity** is specified as the perceived lack of clarity about whether and to what extent an employee has to deal with technology-related issues rather than with work activities (Ayyagari *et al.*, 2011).

Since role ambiguity is one of the main components of role stress (Harris and Fleming, 2017; Jackson and Schuler, 1985; Kahn *et al.*, 1964), the transactional theory of stress and coping is expected to appropriately explain the main effects of Study A. In recent studies, transactional theory has been used to explore stress and coping strategies in the work environment (Bowling and Eschleman, 2010; Johnstone and Feeney, 2015; Podsakoff *et al.*, 2007) and, more specifically, among FLEs in the hospitality industry (Babakus *et al.*, 2017; Wireko-Gyebi, Adu-Frimpong, and Ametepeh, 2017). As outlined in Section 3.1.1, transactional theory recognizes the relevance of individual appraisals of specific situations in the stress process (Bliese *et al.*, 2017). Stress will occur when demands are appraised as harmful, challenging, or threatening to the individual's well-being, and when effort is needed to resolve the demand (Dewe *et al.*, 1993).

### 4.2.2 Main Effect Hypotheses

Figure 4.2 illustrates the research model, including the relationships to be examined in Study A. At its core, this model handles role ambiguity (here induced by online reservation systems) as a central driver of both constructive and destructive process deviance. In turn, role ambiguity is determined by self-efficacy and resistance to change. Service scripts are expected to moderate the relationship among technology-induced role ambiguity and both types of process deviance. To complement the research model, Table 4.1 illustrates the definitions of the three key concepts used in Study A to provide an overview of what they mean. Thereafter, the main effect hypotheses are derived.

***Self-efficacy and technology-induced role ambiguity***

The first hypothesis suggests that self-efficacy relates negatively to technology-induced role-ambiguity. Self-efficacy is defined as an individual's expectation of "how well one can execute courses of action required to deal with prospective situations," (Bandura, 1982, p. 122). On the one hand, this expectation is influenced by experiences from the past. On the other hand, an individual's perception of whether success derives from external aids, fortune, or skills impacts self-efficacy (Bandura, 1977, p. 201). Consequently, individuals differ in their level of self-efficacy and resultant attitudes and behaviors (Sherer and Adams, 1983).

Relying on the transactional theory, self-efficacy can be seen as a protective factor when individuals face potential stressors at work. FLEs who believe

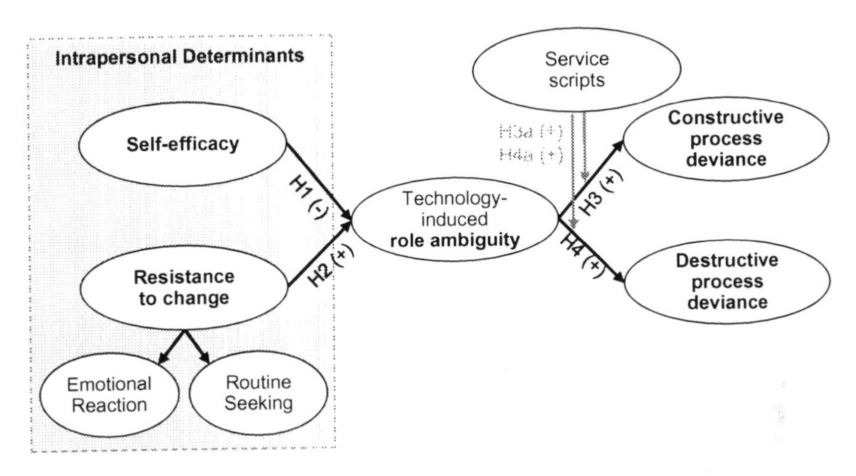


**Figure 4.2** Research model of Study A

**Table 4.1** Key concepts of Study A and their definitions

| Concept | Definition |
|---|---|
| **Technology-induced role ambiguity** | Perceived lack of clarity about whether and to which extent an employee has to deal with technology-related issues rather than with work activities (Ayyagari *et al.*, 2011; Maier *et al.*, 2015). |
| **Constructive process deviance** | Voluntary behavior that breaks norms or rules with the intent to solve a problem or to satisfy customers' needs (Galperin, 2012). |
| **Destructive process deviance** | Unwillingness to perform duties of the job or comply with prescribed processes, e.g., reporting complaints to management (Hammes and Walsh, 2017). |

in their skills and report a high level of self-efficacy should be more confident when dealing with newly implemented technologies at work, thereby reducing technology-induced role ambiguity. Several studies have examined the relationship between self-efficacy and role ambiguity, or rather role clarity, as an antonym of the latter (Teas, Wacker, and Hughes, 1979). Shoemaker (1999) states that employees with high self-efficacy might be better able to seek relevant information and clarify role expectations thanks to their greater task focus. In contrast, employees who disbelieve in their ability to accurately interpret information invest more cognitive resources into searching for and interpreting information, leading to ineffectiveness (Brown, Ganesan, and Challagalla, 2001). This may also lead to uncertainty concerning one's role—which is the core of role ambiguity.

Additionally, research by Fida *et al.* (2015) indicates that employees with higher levels of work self-efficacy report lower levels of role ambiguity. Finally, Kim and Byon (2018) predict that employees with high self-efficacy are better able to address challenges and are, thus, less affected by role ambiguity. Accordingly, it is hypothesized:

> *$H_1$: Frontline employees' self-efficacy relates negatively to their technology-induced role ambiguity.*

***Resistance to change and technology-induced role ambiguity***

Other than self-efficacy, resistance to change can be seen as an intrapersonal determinant of technology-induced role ambiguity. Current research conceptualizes resistance to proposed organizational change as a multidimensional construct reflecting negative attitudes toward change (Oreg, 2006). Based on a literature review, Oreg (2003) aggregates six different sources of resistance to change to the following four factors: routine seeking, emotional reaction, short-term focus, and cognitive rigidity. Oreg's disposition of four related, yet distinct dimensions of resistance to change (RTC) has been applied and confirmed by other researchers (e.g., Heidenreich and Spieth, 2013; Mulki *et al.*, 2012).

As in prior research by Vos and Rupert (2018), Study A includes two of the four dimensions of RTC. These are routine seeking as the behavioral component and emotional reaction as an affective component of RTC (Piderit, 2000). Emotional reaction to imposed change reflects an individual's unwillingness to lose control over an important aspect of the situation. As a further component of RTC, the incorporation of routines reflects an individual's reluctance to give up old habits (Oreg, 2003). Routine-seeking individuals perform best under familiar and well-defined conditions (Kirton, 1980). Faced with technology-induced changes, individuals who seek routines and react emotionally toward changes should encounter a greater technology-induced role ambiguity.

Very little research has been conducted on this specific relationship. Roy *et al.* (2017) investigate how employees' perception of the pace of change in Enterprise Resource Planning (ERP) systems impact technology-induced stressors. In their study, the pace of change has a significant influence on technology-induced role ambiguity. In a different study, Mulki *et al.* (2012) find that a salesperson's resistance to change has a positive impact on stress felt. This result is relevant to the present study because, as illustrated above, role ambiguity is a central component of role stress (Jackson and Schuler, 1985). Accordingly, it is hypothesized:

> *$H_2$: Frontline employees' resistance to change relates positively to their technology-induced role ambiguity.*

***Technology-induced role ambiguity and constructive process deviance***

Technology-induced role ambiguity occurs when demands deriving from technology are cognitively appraised as challenging and when a considerable effort is required to resolve this demand (Dewe et al., 1993). According to the transactional theory of stress and coping, role ambiguity can be classified as a hindrance stressor (Babakus *et al.*, 2017; Podsakoff *et al.*, 2007) that affects work behavior. Although a wide range of research exists on how FLEs experience stress, there is only few evidence on how they cope with stress (Subramony *et al.*, 2017). One coping strategy resulting from role ambiguity is to solve the problem quickly to avoid or reduce stress (Abramis, 1994; Rizzo *et al.*, 1970). Such a strategy may involve bending, stretching, or breaking organizational rules for customers (Evans, 2013; McLean Parks, Ma, and Gallagher, 2010).

Based on the work of Ashforth (2001), McLean Parks *et al.* (2010) argue that role ambiguity can result in employees pretending to understand expectations by "acting out" their roles. By doing so, employees potentially produce an expected outcome without applying the appropriate processes for achieving it. This focus on achieving a desired outcome at the expense of organizational rules or norms (McLean Parks *et al.*, 2010) can be transferred to the relationship between role ambiguity and constructive process deviance.

Constructive process deviance builds on the definition of constructive deviance as voluntary behavior that breaks norms or rules with the intent to solve a problem or to satisfy customers' needs (Galperin, 2012). In the present study, deviance is specifically applied to processes that are linked to online reservation systems in restaurants. Since technology changes the scope and expectations of FLE roles, it can result in role-ambiguity and cause stress. In turn, constructive process deviance can be seen as a potential strategy for coping with the perceived stressor. Accordingly, it is hypothesized:

*$H_3$: Frontline employees' technology-induced role ambiguity relates positively to constructive process deviance.*

***Technology-induced role ambiguity and destructive process deviance***
Stressors, such as role ambiguity, tend to evoke negative attitudes and behaviors (Podsakoff *et al.*, 2007). Negative aspects of deviant behaviors in the workplace have been widely researched and been referred to as counterproductive work behavior (Berry, Carpenter, and Barratt, 2012; Bowling and Eschleman, 2010; Fox, Spector, and Miles, 2001), workplace deviance (Bennett and Robinson, 2003; Neves and Champion, 2015; Peterson, 2002), dysfunctional behavior (Griffin, O'Leary-Kelly, and Collins, 1998; Jaworski and MacInnis, 1989) or service sabotage (Harris and Ogbonna, 2002; Lee and Ok, 2014).

Role ambiguity has been identified as a cause of dysfunctional behaviors in organizations already 50 years ago (Rizzo *et al.*, 1970). In more recent studies, deviant behaviors are also seen as a consequence of work stressors (e.g., Bowling and Eschleman, 2010; Yang and Diefendorff, 2009). Lee and Ok (2014) investigate service sabotage among hotel employees and propose that employees who experience stress and strain are more likely to engage in deviant behaviors in service encounters. Cullen and Sackett (2003) see counterproductive work behaviors as an ineffective, yet common response to work stressors to avoid the latter. The studies listed above are consistent with the proposition that stressors tend to evoke negative attitudes and behaviors (Podsakoff *et al.*, 2007). Employees try to cope with role ambiguity because they consider it to be a threat to their personal growth and goal achievement (Cavanaugh *et al.*, 2000; LePine, Podsakoff, and LePine, 2005).

Among the coping behaviors that have negative impacts on organizations, the present study focuses on destructive process deviance. This specific type of deviant behavior is reflected in FLE unwillingness to perform the duties of the job or comply with prescribed processes. Thereby, FLEs neglect normative actions that have the potential to improve an organization's service (Luria, Gal, and Yagil, 2009), such as reporting customer complaints to management as intended by organizational processes (Hammes and Walsh, 2017). This kind of process deviance is likely to harm organizational goals. Harris and Ogbonna (2006) observe that the intentional violation of processes increases FLEs' self-esteem. Consequently, destructive process deviance is supposed to be one consequence of technology-induced role ambiguity, aiming at regaining self-esteem that has been diminished by the lack of role clarity. Accordingly, it is hypothesized:

> $H_4$: *Frontline employees' technology-induced role ambiguity relates positively to destructive process deviance.*

### 4.2.3 Moderating Effect Hypotheses

Service scripts are a form of management-initiated control designed to increase the probability that employees will behave in ways that support the organization's objectives (Jaworski and MacInnis, 1989). Such scripts specify how FLEs must behave when interacting with customers, and typically include general rules for each step of the service process, comprising verbal (i.e., phrases to use) and visual (i.e., clothing) specifications (Brach *et al.*, 2015). To raise accountability, service scripts are mostly written down and have a formal character. They can be distinguished along a continuum ranging from rigid to weak service scripts. The more rigid a service script, the less flexibility FLEs are meant to have in responding to customer requests and needs (Chebat and Kollias, 2000).

FLEs with a high level of technology-induced role ambiguity feel uncertain about how to react when problems or complaints occur during customer interactions (Fuller, Marler, and Hester, 2006). Service scripts are meant to reduce this uncertainty. However, service scripts confront FLEs with additional role requirements (Nguyen *et al.*, 2014), potentially increasing the existent stress level and even intensifying the effects of role ambiguity (Walsh and Hammes, 2017). The transactional theory implies that individuals who perceive a situation as stressful pursue coping strategies. One way of coping with demands is to solve a problem by bending service scripts or breaking rules for the customer (Evans, 2013; McLean Parks *et al.*, 2010).

Employees particularly execute such forms of constructive process deviance when they tend to dislike the excessive use of scripts during customer interactions (Vella, Gountas, and Walker, 2009). In the context of the present study, rigid service scripts focusing on customer delight, satisfaction, and loyalty should lead FLEs with a high level of role ambiguity to solely focus on the customer. This results in solving customer-related problems arising from technology independently from prescribed processes. Accordingly, it is hypothesized:

*$H_{3a}$: Service scripts strengthen the relationship between frontline employees' technology-induced role ambiguity and constructive process deviance, such that more rigid service scripts result in a higher degree of process deviance.*

Instead of bending service scripts for the satisfaction of customer needs, employees might as well break rules for their own well-being and self-esteem (Harris and Ogbonna, 2006). Consequently, FLE problem-focused coping behavior affects the organization negatively when the FLE is afraid or unwilling to report incidents to management. This is referred to as destructive process deviance and causes damage by hindering an organization's attempts to improve its service (Hammes and Walsh, 2017; Luria *et al.*, 2009). FLEs facing customer complaints or serious problems during service encounters are under higher pressure when rigid service scripts are in place, because they recognize the large discrepancy between the organization's service scripts and the current situation. To keep customers' dissatisfaction secret and to avoid being blamed for it, one coping method is the reluctance to report complaints to management. Accordingly, it is hypothesized:

*$H_{4a}$: Service scripts strengthen the relationship between frontline employees' technology-induced role ambiguity and destructive process deviance, such that more elaborate service scripts result in a higher degree of destructive process deviance.*

## 4.3 Methodology

### 4.3.1 Data Collection and Sample

An anonymous online survey was chosen to test the hypothesized model. Compared to face-to-face surveys, online surveys are considered to be better able to assess undesired behaviors such as process deviance by avoiding a social desirability bias (Heerwegh, 2009). The latter refers to the tendency of research participants "to give socially desirable responses instead of choosing responses that are reflective of their true feelings" (Grimm, 2011, p. 537). The bias is based on the assumption that online surveys are associated with a greater social distance than face-to-face interviews and thus evoke less socially desirable responses (Holbrook, Green, and Krosnick, 2003; Krumpal, 2013).

To reach out primarily to FLEs who work with an online reservation system, Amazon's crowdsourcing web service, Mechanical Turk (MTurk), has been chosen to collect data. The primary reason to choose MTurk for the data collection of Study A is the possibility to address specific subpopulations. In the present study, three criteria were set: (1) U.S. resident, (2) "employment industry—food & beverage" and (3) 95 percent acceptance rate of prior tasks. For an extra fee of 40 percent of participants' pay, MTurk only invites respondents that adhere to such predefined criteria.

The United States were chosen because the local restaurant industry employs 14.7 million people. Half of all adults in the United States have worked in a restaurant at some point during their lives (National Restaurant Association, 2017). According to an industry survey, 25 percent of full-service restaurants offered online reservations in 2016 (National Restaurant Association, 2018). Thus, it can be assumed that the probability of finding a sufficient number of FLEs to report their experiences with online reservation systems is relatively high in the United States.

After five days, 184 participants completed the whole questionnaire and passed the implemented attention check that is recommended when working with MTurk (Goodman, Cryder, and Cheema, 2013). The average time to fill out the questionnaire was 8:26 minutes, corresponding to a reward of 0.98 U.S.-Dollar per task. A total of 61 respondents had to be excluded because they indicated they were too inexperienced with online reservation systems. This led to an effective sample size of 123 FLEs.

All participants within the effective sample indicated working with an online reservation system and having direct customer contact. Most of them worked as front desk employees or waiters/waitresses. Participants included 65 percent men and 35 percent women, with ages ranging from 21 to 75 years (mean of 31.6 years). Organizational tenure stretched from 1 to 219 months with an average of 34.3 months, thus two years and ten months. The majority of participants held a Bachelor degree (50.4%), 15.2 percent held a Master degree. Further 17.1 percent had completed either a technical or vocational training and 17.1 percent had completed high school. Table 4.2 provides an overview of the sample structure.

**Table 4.2** Sample characteristics of Study A

| | FLEs (% of N = 123) |
|---|---|
| *Gender* | |
| Male | 65.0 |
| Female | 35.0 |
| *Age* | |
| <25 years | 10.6 |
| 25–29 years | 43.1 |
| 30–34 years | 23.6 |
| 35–44 years | 14.6 |
| ≥45 years | 8.2 |
| *Organizational Tenure* | |
| < 12 months | 19.5 |
| 12–23 months | 17.9 |
| 24–35 months | 20.3 |
| 36–47 months | 19.5 |
| 48–59 months | 3.3 |
| ≥60 months | 19.5 |
| *Education* | |
| High school or college without degree | 17.1 |
| Technical/vocational training | 17.1 |
| Bachelor degree | 50.4 |
| Master degree | 15.2 |

### 4.3.2 Measures

Unless stated otherwise, each construct was measured with a seven-point Likert scale, anchored at "fully disagree" and "fully agree" (see Appendix A.I in the Electronic Supplementary Material). Work-related self-efficacy was assessed using four items from the generalized self-efficacy scale developed by Schwarzer and Jerusalem (1995). To specifically assess work-related self-efficacy, each of the four items was adjusted to the occupational context, asking participants how they handle difficulties or unexpected events at work. One sample item read "I am confident that I could deal efficiently with unexpected events at work."

Resistance to change (RTC) was operationalized as a second-order construct using the inventory of Oreg (2003). Rather than using four dimensions (e.g., Heidenreich and Spieth, 2013; Mulki *et al.*, 2012), the present study focuses on the two components of routine seeking and emotional reaction, each being assessed with three items. For instance, the item "I like to do the same old things, rather than try new and different ones" was used to assess routine seeking, while the item "when I am informed of a change of plans, I tense up a bit" refers to participants' emotional reaction.

The three-item scale for technology-induced role ambiguity was inspired by measurements of role clarity by Kohli and Jaworski (1994). To reflect technology as a trigger of role ambiguity, participants were asked to answer these questions in relation to the online reservation system their employer had implemented. A sample item read: "After they had implemented the online reservation system, I felt as if I do not know exactly how I am expected to do my job."

The measurement of constructive process deviance depended on five items developed by Galperin (2012). Whilst originally used as a measure for intentions and attitudes toward deviant behaviors, the scale for the present study was adapted to capture actual behaviors working around the online reservation system. In particular, constructive process deviance was assessed by a Likert-type scale with "never" and "many times daily" as anchors. Again, to specifically assess process deviance induced by technology, the questionnaire included the specification that all five items referred to coping with demands that arise from the online reservation system (e.g., "Given the online reservation system you have in use: How often have you departed from organizational procedures to solve a customer's problem?").

The same specification was applied to the measurement of destructive process deviance. Due to the various research streams on employee behaviors having negative impacts on organizations, prior literature does not offer a unique scale to measure destructive process deviance. Following a conceptualization by Luria *et al.* (2009), Study A adapted the four-item scale of Hammes and Walsh (2017) to measure the extent to which employees deviate from the requirement to report customer complaints that are related to the online reservation systems. One sample item read: "I do not report to management about incidents in which customers complain about serious problems with the online reservation system."

The elaborateness of service scripts was measured with five items by Brach *et al.* (2015), reflecting the scope of action FLEs have when interacting with customers (e.g., "My supervisor usually instructs me on what to say and do when serving customers."). In addition to the main constructs of the research model, several control variables have been measured to help ensure the validity of the results of the regression analysis. Gender, age, education, and organizational tenure were assessed. Furthermore, the proportion of reservations made via the online reservation systems compared to desk or phone reservations was used to capture the degree of technology inducement.

### 4.3.3 Quantitative Data Analysis

As proposed by Anderson and Gerbing (1988), the measurement model was assessed for validity and reliability prior to analyzing the proposed structural effects. To evaluate the psychometric properties of the model, a confirmatory factor analysis for all multi-item constructs was conducted with IBM SPSS 25. As a result, the reverse-coded item of the service script scale by Brach *et al.* (2015) was dropped due to a standardized loading below .50. All other loadings were significant with standardized values of at least .69, proving convergent validity. The mean, standard deviation, item-total correlation, and standardized factor loading for each item are listed in Appendix A.I in the Electronic Supplementary Material.

Fornell and Larcker's (1981) criterion was applied to ensure discriminant validity, showing that the correlations between any of the constructs were lower than the square root of the average variance extracted (AVE) for each construct. In Table 4.3, the diagonal elements in bold indicate the square root of the AVE for those constructs measured with multiple items. Table 4.3 also displays the mean and standard deviation for each construct and selected control variables. It further contains correlations and composite reliabilities. For each latent variable, composite reliability ranged between .86 and .94 and thus above the threshold of .60.

**Table 4.3** Correlations and psychometric properties of Study A

| | (1) | (2) | (3) | (4) | (5) | (6) | (7) | (8) | (9) | (10) | (11) |
|---|---|---|---|---|---|---|---|---|---|---|---|
| (1) Self-efficacy | **.79** | | | | | | | | | | |
| (2) RTC | – .30$^{**}$ | **.93** | | | | | | | | | |
| (3) Role ambiguity | – .37$^{**}$ | .69$^{**}$ | **.90** | | | | | | | | |
| (4) Constructive process deviance | – .27$^{**}$ | .59$^{**}$ | .84$^{**}$ | **.87** | | | | | | | |
| (5) Destructive process deviance | – .36$^{**}$ | .71$^{**}$ | .80$^{**}$ | .80$^{**}$ | **.90** | | | | | | |
| (6) Service scripts | .43$^{**}$ | .30$^{**}$ | .11 | .06 | .15 | **.78** | | | | | |
| (7) Gender | .32$^{**}$ | – .27$^{**}$ | – .38$^{**}$ | – .31$^{**}$ | – .32$^{**}$ | .02 | n/a | | | | |
| (8) Age | .20$^{*}$ | – .20$^{*}$ | – .23$^{**}$ | – .23$^{*}$ | – .21$^{*}$ | – .07 | .36$^{**}$ | n/a | | | |
| (9) Tenure | .22$^{*}$ | – .12 | – .09 | – .08 | – .10 | .14 | .02 | .39$^{**}$ | n/a | | |
| (10) Hierarchy | .05 | .06 | .05 | .08 | .06 | .19$^{*}$ | – .07 | – .38$^{**}$ | – .14 | n/a | |
| (11) % online reservations | .08 | – .03 | – .14 | – .10 | .00 | .10 | .06 | – .05 | – .04 | .03 | n/a |
| Mean | 4.20 | 3.51 | 2.93 | 3.36 | 2.98 | 4.28 | 1.36 | 31.59 | 34.30 | 4.69 | 43.49 |
| Standard deviation | .82 | 1.36 | 1.76 | 1.76 | 1.73 | 1.02 | .50 | 8.90 | 33.64 | 3.02 | 26.19 |
| Composite Reliability | .87 | .93 | .93 | .94 | .94 | .86 | n/a | n/a | n/a | n/a | n/a |

Notes: N = 123; $^{*}p < .05$; $^{**}p < .01$; n/a = not applicable; diagonal elements in bold indicate the square roots of the average variance extracted for constructs measured with multiple items.

As a next step, the hypothesized model was assessed with structural equation modeling using AMOS 25. Model fit was evaluated with incremental fit index (IFI), Tucker-Lewis Index (TLI), comparative fit index (CFI), and root mean square error of approximation (RMSEA). Second-order weights and significances of second-order factor resistance to change (RTC) demonstrate that the contribution of both routine seeking and emotional reaction to RTC is significant.

A common latent factor test was used to assess the possibility of common method variance (Podsakoff *et al.*, 2003). The risk of common method bias increases when survey participants respond to items reflecting independent variables as well as to items reflecting dependent variables (Bagozzi and Yi, 1991). The common latent factor technique introduces a new latent variable, which is related to all manifest variables. When comparing factor loadings with or without this common latent factor, substantial differences would indicate a common method bias. After the introduction of the common latent factor for the present sample, all changes in factor loadings were lower than .25. Only four factor loadings changed slightly more than .20, which is most commonly used as a difference value. These results show that common method bias is not a concern for Study A.

## 4.4 Results

### 4.4.1 Main Effects

According to the results, including the control variables, the hypothesized model fits the data well ($\chi^2/df = 1.575$; IFI = .933; TLI = .922; CFI = .932; RMSEA = .069). Second-order weights and significances of second-order factor resistance to change (RTC) show that the contribution of both routine seeking and emotional reaction to RTC is significant. Furthermore, all hypothesized main effects are significant. Figure 4.3 depicts the standardized regression weights of the main effects.

In line with hypothesis $H_1$, FLE self-efficacy relates negatively to technology-induced role ambiguity ($\beta = -.15$; $p < .05$). FLE resistance to change relates strongly and positively to technology-induced role ambiguity ($\beta = .70$; $p < .001$), supporting $H_2$. The two predictors explain 50.6 percent of the variance of technology-induced role ambiguity. Furthermore, the results confirm that FLE technology-induced role ambiguity favors both constructive process deviance ($\beta = .79$; $p < .001$) and destructive process deviance ($\beta = .79$; $p < .001$). Hence, hypothesis $H_3$ and hypothesis $H_4$ are both supported. 63.1 percent of the variance of constructive process deviance and 62.3 percent of the variance of destructive process deviance are explained by technology-induced role ambiguity. The control variables increased the variance explained only slightly by .018. Table 4.4 summarizes the results of the regression analysis.

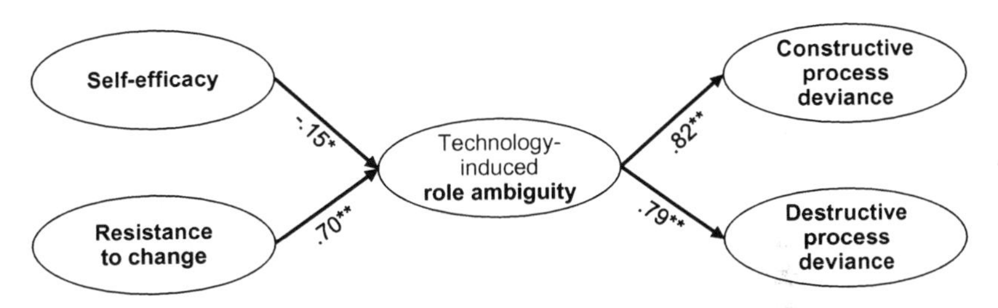


**Figure 4.3** Structural model of Study A including the main effects. (Notes: Standardized regression weights; $^{*}p < .05$; $^{**}p < .01$)

**Table 4.4** Results of structural equation modeling of Study A

| | | ß | S.E. | C.R. | Hypothesis supported |
|---|---|---|---|---|---|
| $H_1$ | Self-efficacy → role ambiguity | $-.151^{*\circ}$ | .151 | − 1.991 | Yes |
| $H_2$ | Resistance to change → role ambiguity | $.695^{**}$ | .106 | 6.846 | Yes |
| $H_3$ | Role ambiguity → constructive process deviance | $.793^{**}$ | .078 | 10.460 | Yes |
| $H_4$ | Role ambiguity → destructive process deviance | $.790^{**}$ | .078 | 9.987 | Yes |

Notes: ß = standardized regression weight; S.E. = Standard Error; C.R. = Critical Ratio; $^{*}p < .05$; $^{**}p < .01$; n.s. = not significant.

### 4.4.2 Moderating Effects

To evaluate the moderating effect of service script using IBM SPSS AMOS, data were mean-centered. An interaction term was added to the direct effect model, showing that rigid service scripts strengthen the relationship between FLE technology-induced role ambiguity and destructive process deviance (b = .16; $p < .05$), as proposed by hypothesis $H_{3a}$. As shown in Figure 4.4, this result suggests that more elaborate service scripts result in a higher degree of constructive process deviance. The variance explained of constructive process deviance increased by .10 after including the moderating effect ($R^2 = .731$). However, the analysis revealed no empirical support for hypothesis H4a. The relationship between FLE technology-induced role ambiguity and destructive process deviance was unattached by the level of existing service scripts. Hypothesis H4a must, therefore, be rejected.

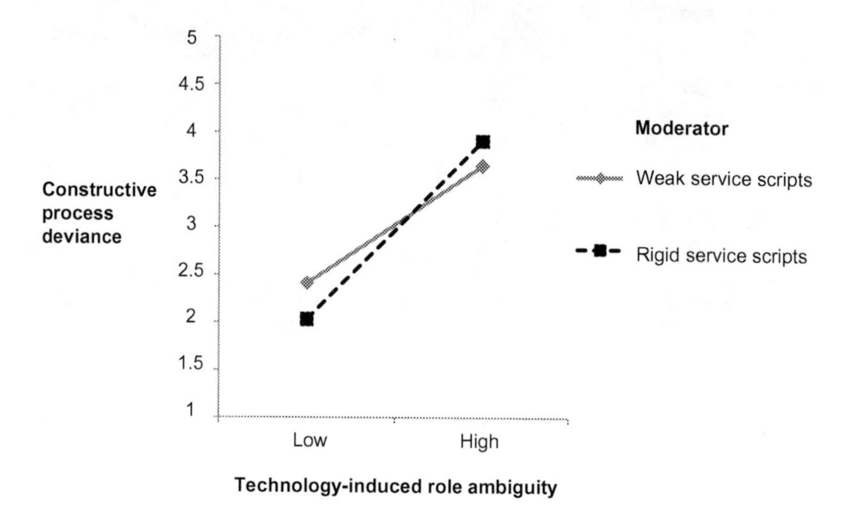


**Figure 4.4** Moderating effect of service scripts on constructive process deviance

## 4.4.3 Alternative Models

A model like the one proposed in Study A suggests that alternative paths may also explain significant proportions of variance in the dependent variables. Figure 4.5 represents the results of the mediation analysis calculated in IBM SPSS AMOS, tested with bootstrapping and 2,000 bootstrap samples. The alternative model revealed a very good model fit ($\chi^2$/df = 1.610; IFI = .953; TLI = .944; CFI = .952; RMSEA = .071).

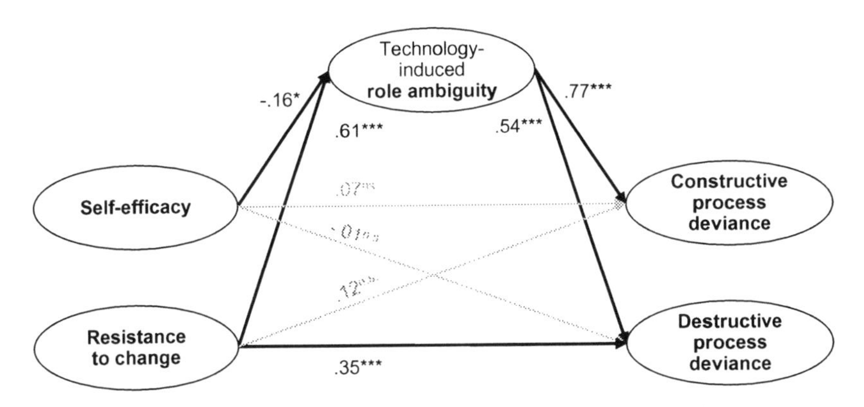


**Figure 4.5** Mediation model of Study A. (Notes: $^{*}p < .05$; $^{***}p < .001$; n.s. = not significant)

As shown in Table 4.5, all indirect effects are significant. The results indicate that for the relationship between self-efficacy and constructive process deviance, both the total effect (ß = − .251, p < .01) and the indirect effect (ß = − .323, p < .001) are significant while the direct effect is insignificant (ß = .073, n.s.). According to this result, a full mediation effect exists (Zhao et al., 2010). The same conclusion applies to the relationship between self-efficacy and destructive process deviance (total effect ß = − .334, p < .01; indirect effect: ß = − .321, p < .001; direct effect: ß = − .013, n.s.) and RTC and constructive process deviance (total effect ß = .581, p < .001; indirect effect: ß = .466, p < .01; direct effect: ß = .115, n.s.). For the relationship between RTC and destructive process deviance, all three effects are significant (total effect ß = .677, p < .001; indirect effect: ß = .329, p < .001; direct effect: ß = .349, p < .001). This result indicates that the relationship between RTC and destructive process is partially mediated by technology-induced role ambiguity (Zhao et al., 2010).

**Table 4.5** Results of mediation analysis of Study A (AMOS/SEM analysis)

| | ß | [LLCI;ULCI] |
|---|---|---|
| Self-efficacy → Constructive process deviance | | |
| Direct effect | $.073^{n.s.}$ | [−.004; .199] |
| Indirect effect | $-.323^{***}$ | [−.436; − .207] |
| Total | $-.251^{**}$ | [−.388; − .121] |
| Self-efficacy → Destructive process deviance | | |
| Direct effect | $-.013^{n.s.}$ | [−.124; .131] |
| Indirect effect | $-.321^{***}$ | [−.435; − .212] |
| Total | $-.334^{**}$ | [−.457; − .199] |
| Resistance to change → Constructive process deviance | | |
| Direct effect | $.115^{n.s.}$ | [−.053; .300] |
| Indirect effect | $.466^{***}$ | [.326; .648] |
| Total | $.581^{***}$ | [.418; .732] |
| Resistance to change → Destructive process deviance | | |
| Direct effect | $.349^{***}$ | [.172; .536] |
| Indirect effect | $.329^{***}$ | [.211; .504] |
| Total | $.677^{***}$ | [.547; .793] |

Notes: ß = Standardized regression weight; LLCI = Lower Level for Confidence Interval; ULCI = Upper Level for Confidence Interval; $^{**}$ $p < .01$; $^{***}$ $p < .001$; n.s. = not significant.

## 4.5 Discussion

In line with prior research (Mulki *et al.*, 2012; Roy *et al.*, 2017), the results of Study A show that resistance to change (RTC) represents an intrapersonal factor leading to FLE role ambiguity when digital technology such as an online reservation system is being implemented. In addition, the results point out that self-efficacy mitigates technology-induced role ambiguity. Employees who are confident about their ability to cope with unexpected situations seem to be better able to cope with role expectations (Shoemaker, 1999).

However, FLE technology-induced behaviors and their consequences on organizational performance have been insufficiently investigated by academic research. Against this background, Study A evaluates FLE customer-facing deviant behaviors regarding technology-related processes. A workplace deviance scale by Galperin (2012) has successfully been adapted to measure constructive process deviance. A scale to evaluate unwillingness to report customer complaints to management has been transferred to the context of destructive process deviance. The results confirm that technology-induced role ambiguity leads to both constructive and destructive process deviance.

Service scripts strengthen the relationship between technology-induced role ambiguity and constructive process deviance. By focusing on the customer, FLEs keep the importance of customer satisfaction and delight in mind. Still, by working around prescribed processes to fulfill customer needs, FLEs frequently deviate from service scripts. In contrast with hypothesis $H_{4a}$, though, the results do not indicate a moderating effect of service scripts on the relationship between technology-induced role ambiguity and destructive process deviance.

### 4.5.1 Implications for Theory

Based on the transactional theory of stress and coping by Lazarus and Folkman (1984), Study A highlights that digital technology can be perceived as a stressor by employees, causing role ambiguity. The perceived level of role ambiguity is forced by an individual's predisposition to resist changes and is mitigated by self-efficacy. Both aspects are therefore suited to be studied in conjunction with role ambiguity. Role ambiguity is one form of role stress that can occur when FLEs perceive additional demands deriving from technology as stressful.

To reduce stress, FLEs who feel ambiguous are more likely to deviate from prescribed processes to solve a problem (Evans, 2013; McLean Parks *et al.*, 2010). The patterns of this coping strategy also explain the relationship between technology-induced role ambiguity and destructive process deviance. An FLE confronted with customer complaints is likely to attribute dissatisfaction to the way the role was performed. To avoid justifying a customer complaint toward the manager, ambiguous FLEs might conceal serious problems related to the online reservation system. Such deviant behaviors hinder organizations' attempts to improve their service (Luria *et al.*, 2009) and to evaluate the effectiveness of newly implemented technologies. This result corresponds with prior research proposing that work stressors, such as role ambiguity, tend to evoke dysfunctional behaviors in organizations (Bowling and Eschleman, 2010; Podsakoff *et al.*, 2003; Rizzo *et al.*, 1970).

Finally, the examination of service scripts confirmed that scripts have ambivalent effects. This form of management-initiated control specifies how FLEs must interact with customers at each step of the service process (Brach *et al.*, 2015). However, it is important to differentiate between prescribed behaviors and desired outcomes. Jaworski and MacInnis (1989) assert that service scripts are considered to increase the probability that employees will behave in ways that support the organization's objectives. Typically, service scripts in industries characterized by intense personal interactions focus rigidly on customer satisfaction and delight. They do contain norms and rules on *how* to interact with customers, but their most tangible aspect is mainly the principle 'the customer is king'—focusing on the desired result rather than on how to achieve it.

For this reason, rigid service scripts strengthen the effect of technology-induced role ambiguity on constructive process deviance. FLEs with high levels of role ambiguity are more likely to deviate from processes to satisfy a customer need when service scripts rigidly put the customer first. On the other hand, service scripts do not affect the relationship between technology-induced role ambiguity and destructive process deviance. Most recently, service scripts imply that customer complaints have to be reported to management. Nevertheless, employees with a high level of role ambiguity do not feel obligated to carry out this duty in the event of complaints. From their perspective, concealing a complaint toward management is the fastest way to solve the problem and, thereby, reduce stress.

### 4.5.2 Implications for Practice

Based on the findings of Study A, managers need to assess whether and why their employees perceive role ambiguity—as one form of role stress— when using digital technologies at work. Given the example of online reservation systems in restaurants, managers should define whose responsibility it is to handle customer (special) requests that depart from their initial online reservation. Such requests should either be passed on to a supervisor or a trained colleague so that FLEs no longer struggle with demanding situations.

The findings of Study A imply that FLEs who are resistant to change are more vulnerable to experience role ambiguity. Methods for reducing resistance to change (RTC) can be divided into methods for building total acceptance among FLEs or a consensus of support (Appelbaum *et al.*, 2015; Darling and Taylor, 1989). However, the starting point of preventing or reducing RTC is to involve FLEs in changes and to explain how digital technology supports the organization's overall strategy. Along with communicating *why* any new technology is implemented, managers must clarify role expectations that come along with changed processes to reduce role ambiguity.

In turn, a lower level of technology-induced role ambiguity reduces the probability of destructive process deviance. Among others, Study A investigates FLEs' unwillingness to report customer complaints to management. An ambiguous FLE confronted with a complaint is likely to attribute customer dissatisfaction to the way the role was performed. Contrarily, FLEs who are clear about their role and feel trusted will develop the ability to cope with customer complaints. This increases their willingness to confidently report complaints to management and thereby helps organizations to improve their service. These implications are in line with a long-established principle of service management articulated by Grönroos (1990b, p. 9), proposing that decision-making should be "decentralized as close as possible to the organization-customer interface."

As one component of decentralized decision-making, it is advisable to reduce service scripts to the desired outcomes. In line with Bowen (2016), managers should then empower employees to make decisions that contribute to organizational goals, rather than insisting on standardized service scripts. Applied to the findings of Study A, promoting FLE decision-making competence in satisfying customer needs will make FLEs feel more valued and more confident. This will be reflected in higher levels of self-efficacy and, thus, reduced technology-induced role ambiguity. In conclusion, identifying potential hassles regarding digital technology, clarifying role expectations, and focusing service scripts on the desired outcome will help employees to effectively cope with technology and reduce deviant behaviors.

### 4.5.3 Limitations and Avenues for Further Research

One limitation of this research might pertain to the nature of the data at hand. Amazon's online platform Mechanical Turk (MTurk) that was used for data collection has been criticized by researchers, assuming that some MTurk workers might click through surveys quickly to receive a predefined monetary compensation (Stritch, Pedersen, and Taggart, 2017). Contrarily, an analysis by Buhrmester, Kwang, and Gosling (2011) suggests that MTurk participants are internally motivated to complete their preferred tasks rather than having the relatively small pay in mind. Moreover, MTurk workers represent a relatively diverse population, and data quality does not seem to be affected by the rate of compensation (Buhrmester *et al.*, 2011; Goodman *et al.*, 2013). Despite its limitations, MTurk is considered to be a reliable source for data collection because participants "exhibit the classic heuristics and biases and pay attention to directions at least as much as subjects from traditional sources" (Paolacci, Chandler, and Ipeirotis, 2010, p. 417).

The fact that the data collection did not involve observing behaviors in real service encounters might be seen as a limitation of the study. On the other hand, prior research on deviant behaviors emphasizes the validity of self-reports, confirming a high correlation between recorded and self-reported behaviors (Bennett and Robinson, 2000; e.g., Lee and Ok, 2014). Concerning the constructs investigated, Study A could serve as a promising starting point to further conceptualize constructive and destructive process deviance. Future research should refine both definitions and further develop appropriate scales to differentiate process deviance more strongly from established constructs, such as counterproductive work behaviors. Along with empirical evidence on process deviance, its antecedents and consequences should be examined in depth.

To fully exploit the potential enhancing effects of digital technology in service encounters, future research should focus more on FLE attitudes toward job-relevant technologies and the resulting customer-facing behaviors. A supplementary avenue for further research thus lies in integrating the perspectives of supervisors and/or customers. For instance, it is of interest how customers perceive deviant behaviors. Additionally, the study could be replicated in cross-cultural settings with different digital maturity levels to assess potential differences in FLE attitudes toward technology.

# 5 Study B: A 360-Degree View of Technology Deployment

## 5.1 Context, Aim, and Design of Study B

As outlined in Section 4.1, the restaurant industry has long been comparatively reluctant to invest in technologies for digital customer integration (Gandhi *et al.*, 2016; Tan and Netessine, 2020). This phenomenon especially applies to full-service restaurants (Oronsky and Chathoth, 2007). The latter are defined as providing waited table service to customers (Gregoire, 2017). Full-service restaurants range from casual to fine dining and accounted for 59 percent of the global consumer spending on eating out in 2016 (Yates, Jodlowski, and Court, 2017). At the same time, all other outlet categories in the food and beverage (F&B) market show stronger actual and expected growth rates (Yates *et al.*, 2017). Figure 5.1 visualizes these proportions. In this highly contested market setting, technology can contribute to building a sustainable competitive advantage for restaurants (Koutroumanis, 2011).

While full-service restaurant chains have meanwhile discovered the benefits of digital technologies and leveraged the necessary financial resources (Puzder, 2016), privately owned restaurants report a considerable backlog in digitizing their businesses (Ashcroft *et al.*, 2019). Among independent restaurateurs, the

---

A version of Study B with a focus on FLEs has been published in the International Journal of Hospitality Management: Christ-Brendemühl, S. (2022). "Bridging the gap: An interview study on frontline employee responses to restaurant technology", International Journal of Hospitality Management, Vol. 102, No. 3, 103,183.

**Supplementary Information** The online version contains supplementary material available at https://doi.org/10.1007/978-3-658-37885-1_5.


S. Christ-Brendemühl, *Digital Technology in Service Encounters*, Innovation, Entrepreneurship und Digitalisierung, https://doi.org/10.1007/978-3-658-37885-1_5

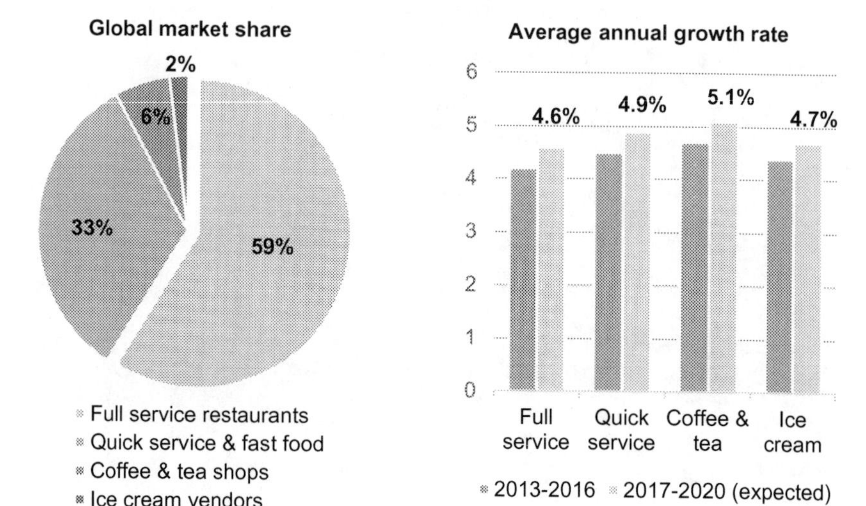


**Figure 5.1** Global market share and growth rate of food & beverage outlet categories. (Source: Yates *et al.*, 2017)

widest-established digital solutions can be assigned to three key business processes. These include payment (e.g., point of sale, card reader, mobile payment), communication with customers (e.g., website, social media, e-mail marketing), and finance including accounting and payroll (Demen-Meier et al. 2018). Still, a survey in Japan, France, Spain, Italy, and Germany reveals that 39 percent of independent restaurants do not use technology at all to support their daily routines. Moreover, 85 percent of respondents do not intend to invest in technology in the near future (Demen-Meier *et al.*, 2018).

One reason for this reluctance might be that restaurants frequently have little financial flexibility to invest in technology. This is due to high operating expenses and low-profit margins around two percent (Mun and Jang, 2018). On the other hand, restaurant managers are cautious about scaling down the value created through human interactions between frontline employees and customers (Solnet *et al.*, 2019). Opposing, technology might as well attract customers who seek for convenience and speed because waiting time is reduced (Kokkinoua and Cranage, 2013). In the United States, 26 percent of consumers state that tableside ordering technology and payment options would make them choose one restaurant over another (National Restaurant Association, 2019).

From the perspective of service firms, the adoption of technology is meant to facilitate workflows and to increase productivity (Larivière *et al.*, 2017). To overcome the obstacles of technology in full-service restaurants, it seems important to deepen the understanding of why and how technology is deployed—or not. Against this backdrop, Study B includes the perspectives of four different stakeholder groups: restaurant technology providers, restaurant managers, frontline employees (FLEs), and customers. The aim is to derive implications for technology deployment by investigating the subsequent **research questions** of Study B:

| | |
|---|---|
| $RQ_B-1$ | Which benefits and barriers exist regarding the deployment of digital technology and its impact on frontline employees, firms' internal processes and financials, and customer relationships? |
| $RQ_B-2$ | Under which circumstances do frontline employees perceive digital technology either as stressful or enhancing? |
| $RQ_B-3$ | To which degree does digital technology influence customer satisfaction and how relevant are personal interactions with frontline employees to customers? |

To answer these questions, a total of thirty-six interviews focusing on frontline service technologies is conducted and analyzed. The interviews with three technology suppliers and seven restaurant managers revealed insights into specific challenges and opportunities of technology deployment in full-service restaurants. Eleven FLEs were interviewed about technology-related job demands, job resources, drivers of motivation and their customer-facing behaviors based on Bakker and Demerouti's job demands-resources (JD-R) model. Additionally, the customers' perspective was integrated by linking the use of technology interfaces to customer satisfaction, delight and recommend intentions through fifteen semi-structured interviews. Oliver and DeSarbo's expectancy-disconfirmation paradigm is applied to investigate customers' expectations of and experiences with technology-induced service encounters.

The interviews were transcribed and thereupon analyzed following Straussian coding principles and using qualitative data analysis (QDA) software MAXQDA.[1] Throughout the analysis, key categories and concepts were identified by open coding, followed by a process of axial and selective coding for all interviewee

[1] https://www.maxqda.com/ [02.10.2019]

groups. The findings indicate that the majority of FLEs agree with operators' and suppliers' certainty that technology makes them more productive in their daily work. Optimism toward technology and managerial commitment are key resources that pave the way to increased employee motivation when digital solutions are deployed. Solely system downtime caused by internet breakdown or empty batteries was indicated to cause strain among full-time employees. Additionally, temporary staff members sometimes struggle with operating the user interface or menu navigation of technological devices when they work infrequently.

From the customer perspective, the most prevalent finding is that satisfaction and delight with a service supported by technology are likely to turn into the opposite if customer expectations regarding the effectiveness of technology interfaces remain unfulfilled. Anger about slow performance of technology-mediated service leads to a higher risk of negative word-of-mouth compared to slow service when fewer technology interfaces are in place. In sum, Study B contributes to research in hospitality by providing a 360-degree view of technology deployment in the restaurant industry.

## 5.2 Theoretical Framework

### 5.2.1 Technology-Induced Job Demands and Resources

Despite the increasing number of conceptual work on technology in service encounters, little empirical research has been conducted on technology-mediated interactions between FLEs and customers (Marinova *et al.*, 2017). Seen from the employee perspective, Bakker and Demerouti's (2007) job demands-resources (JD-R) model proposes that all types of job characteristics—including technology—can be classified either as a job demand or as a job resource. Section 3.1.3 provides a detailed overview of the JD-R model.

Most importantly, whereas job demands have the potential to evoke strain and thereby affect job performance negatively, job resources instigate motivational processes that have positive effects on job performance (Bakker and Demerouti, 2017). On the one hand, technology has the potential to enhance FLEs' role performance by helping them focus on core activities such as personal customer contact (Kumar *et al.*, 2016; Larivière *et al.*, 2017). In that case, FLEs are expected to perceive helpful technology features as a job resource (Bakker and Demerouti, 2017).

On the other hand, technology may evoke strain and anxiety among FLEs (Ayyagari *et al.*, 2011; Meuter *et al.*, 2003). Anxiety "specifically focuses on the user's state of mind regarding their ability and willingness to use technology-related tools" (Meuter *et al.*, 2003, p. 900). This state of mind can result from job security concerns (Frey and Osborne, 2017) or from an individual's predisposition to react emotionally to imposed change. Such emotional reactions occur because people do not resist the intrusion of something new as much as they resist the resulting loss of control over a familiar situation (Conner, 1993). As outlined in Section 3.2.1, emotional reaction is considered as one component of an individual's dispositional resistance to change (RTC).

Based on an extant literature review, Maier *et al.* (2015) identify five technology-induced stressors that employees are facing when operating technology provided by their employers. Among these stressors, technology-induced work overload is defined as the perceived pressure to work faster and longer due to the usage of technologies (Tarafdar, Tu, and Ragu-Nathan, 2010). This is "because IT might cause additional unexpected problems or requests that go beyond the daily stable work routine so that the techno-induced workload increases employees' overall workload" (Maier *et al.*, 2015, p. 356). Thus, digital technologies often force employees to work more and adapt their routines (Thatcher *et al.*, 2002). In turn, the results of the empirical study by Maier *et al.* (2015) reveal that technology-induced work overload significantly influences technology-induced exhaustion. Taken together, such technology-induced job demands have the potential to affect job performance negatively (Bakker and Demerouti, 2017).

### 5.2.2 Customer Expectations in Technology-Induced Service Encounters

The extent to which technology affects the customer experience depends on the role it plays in the respective service encounter. Traditionally, experiences in full-service restaurants are shaped by intense social interactions between FLEs and customers (Im and Qu, 2017). Bitner (1992) categorizes restaurants as elaborated interpersonal services involving both customers' and employees' actions. Hansen, Jensen, and Gustafsson (2005) identify the interaction between customers and staff as a key factor influencing customers' meal experience in à la Carte restaurants. Noone (2008, p. 23) states that "frontline employees often play a central role in customer evaluations of restaurant experiences." Recent research emphasizes the relevance of interpersonal relationships between customers and employees in restaurants (e.g., Jalilvand *et al.,* 2017) and expands empirical findings on "more intangible aspects of the interpersonal service experience between the employees and the customers" (Hanks, Line, and Kim, 2017, p. 37) to various restaurant types.

For customers interacting with a service firm for the first time, "the first encounter—whether in person, over the phone, or by mail—takes on added importance" (Bitner, 1995, p. 248). A customer's first impression and feelings during a pre-service interaction are critical because they affect the subsequent service experience (Albrecht *et al.,* 2016; Bitner, 1995). However, for restaurant technology like online reservation systems and self-ordering devices, the first customer touchpoint will be shifted away from humans to a system, transforming customer-employee relationships (Collier and Kimes, 2013). Similarly, technology can draw customer attention away from FLE rapport-building efforts like smiling (Giebelhausen *et al.,* 2014). In general, technology reduces personal interactions between customers and FLEs and thus diminishes human touch in service encounters (Bitner, 2001).

As each customer values personal service and technology differently (Scherer *et al.,* 2015), Study B applies Oliver and DeSarbo's (1988) expectancy-disconfirmation paradigm to investigate customers' perceptions of the technology-supported service performance. The paradigm depicted in Section 3.3.1 proposes that customers compare their perceptions of service quality with priory formed expectations either consciously or unconsciously (Krüger, 2016). If this comparison results in confirmation, the expectancy-disconfirmation paradigm proposes that customers will be satisfied with a service. A negative disconfirmation will result in dissatisfaction whilst a positive disconfirmation will arouse customer delight (Kotler and Keller, 2016).

## 5.3 Methodology

### 5.3.1 Data Collection and Sample

The interviews for Study B were conducted in Germany, where the restaurant industry represents an important economic sector. Restaurants recorded an annual turnover of 40.3 billion Euro in 2018 (DEHOGA, 2020b) and employed 1.28 million people in 2019 (DEHOGA, 2020a). Coincidently, the ratio of these numbers implies that the restaurant industry is very labor-intense. The share of employee remuneration of the turnover of restaurants amounts to 33.7 percent and is significantly higher than the average of the overall German economy of 28.6 percent

(Lichtblau *et al.*, 2017). At the same time, the restaurant industry is one of the least digitized industries in Germany.

This becomes prevalent through an index published by the IW German institute for economics. The institute's 'digital index'[2] measures the degree of digitization across German firms. It evaluates the technology used, timeliness, available languages, mobile access, speed of access, programming language, and Google page rank. Moreover, the number of companies without any online presence is calculated through a comparison of the data with the national business register. The digital index ranks at only 3.9 for full-service restaurants in Germany while self-service restaurants achieve an index of 16.6 (Lichtblau *et al.*, 2017).

Given that a further technology penetration could contribute to an increase in the competitive capacity of full-service restaurants in Germany, Study B uses a qualitative approach to discover the beliefs and opinions of technology providers specialized in restaurant technology, restaurant managers, FLEs, and customers on technology deployment in full-service restaurants. Technology providers and restaurant managers are integrated into the sample since they are able to depict their own experiences as well as diverse observations and feedback received from customers or employees. In total, thirty-six interviews are conducted to achieve a 360-degree view of the benefits of technology and potential adoption barriers. Figure 5.2 summarizes the structure of the sample.

The approach of the interviews differed between technology providers and the other three stakeholder groups. In the first step, the founder of a German-wide operating foodservice industry network assisted in identifying potential interviewees and established the first contact. Hereafter, the author of this thesis recruited two Chief Executive Officers and one Sales Director of three different companies specialized in restaurant technology. The open-ended interviews were conducted using a broad catalog of questions to meet the idiosyncrasies of the different business models. This approach aimed at gaining a comprehensive understanding of the impact each of the offered solutions has on processes, FLEs, and customers in restaurants. In line with Yeo *et al.*'s (2013) qualitative explorative approach, the findings were used to finish grinding the other three stakeholder groups' semi-structured interview guidelines.

---

[2] https://www.iwconsult.de/aktuelles/projekte/digital-index [10.07.2019]

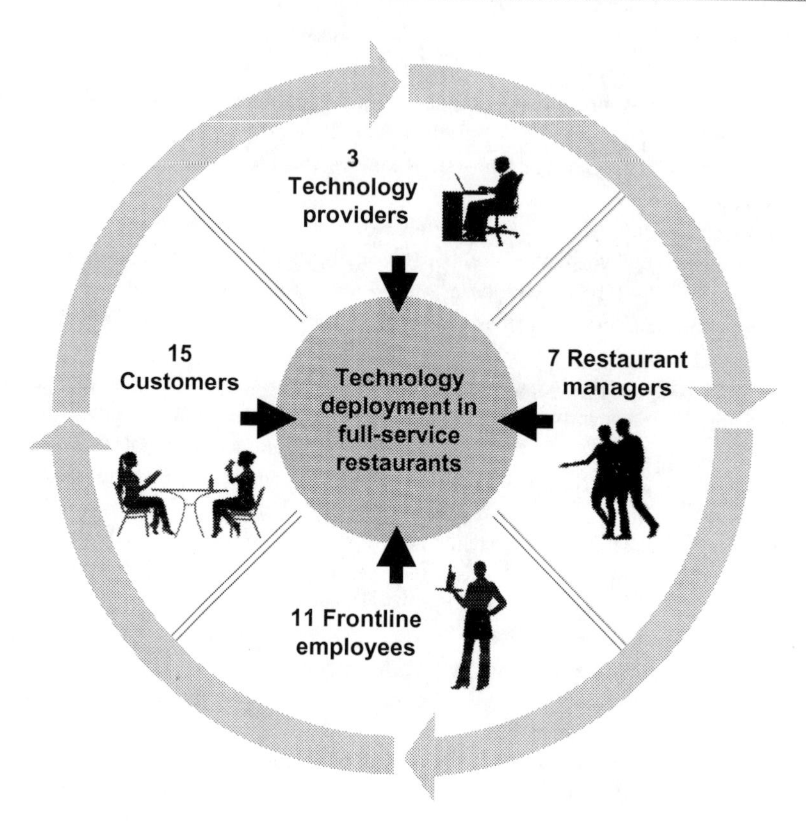


**Figure 5.2** Sample structure and sample size of Study B

In a second step, restaurants with considerably intense use of different digital technologies in the frontline were identified. These digital solutions range from online reservation platforms over handheld ordering systems to interactive tableside devices that enable customers to either call the waiter or place their order directly on a tablet. During six weeks, seven restaurant managers, eleven FLEs, and fifteen customers were interviewed by the author of this thesis and two Bachelor students who were trained in conducting semi-structured interviews.

Restaurant managers were contacted by phone to schedule an interview onsite in case they were willing to participate. One of them preferred to be interviewed on the phone instead. FLEs and customers were approached randomly in different restaurants and then introduced to the study topic. Toward FLEs, the interviewers emphasized that the study was anonymous and that comments and answers would not be shared with FLEs' supervisors. Upon agreement, the interviews were recorded and then transcribed. As for all the other interviewees, no substantive incentive was offered. However, technology providers and restaurant managers had the possibility to leave their email address in case they were interested in a summary of the anonymized results.

The total sample consisted of twenty men and sixteen women, with ages ranging from 15 to 67 years (mean 29.8 years). The interviews span three technology firms and twelve full-service restaurants of which three belonged to a chain and nine were privately owned. Table 5.1 contains a full list including gender and age of the respective interviewees. The sample size can be considered as sufficient since Study B aimed at gaining broad insights into technology deployment rather than testing theory (Creswell and Poth, 2017; Marshall *et al.*, 2013). Data collection ended when data saturation was reached and no new findings were expected of supplementary interviews (Guest, Bunce, and Johnson, 2006).

### 5.3.2 Interview Guideline

The catalog of questions for technology providers offered a high degree of flexibility to take into account their diverse business models. Appendix B.I in the Electronic Supplementary Material contains sample questions. The interviews focused on the providers' experiences with the acceptance of their solutions and enhancing effects reported by restaurant managers. For instance, one sample question specified as follow: "*What are the predominant reasons why restaurant managers choose your solution or decide not to implement it after a testing phase?*". Since technology providers accompany their business-to-business customers through different stages of technology implementation, the interviews also aimed at gaining insights concerning employees, for instance, by asking "*To which extent do your solutions change workflows and employee roles?*" or "*how do your customers prepare their employees to adopt new technologies?*".

For each of the remaining three stakeholder groups, twelve specific questions were developed to serve as a guideline during the interviews. The respective interview guidelines are specified in Appendix B.II (restaurant managers), Appendix B.III (frontline employees), and Appendix B.IV (customers) in the Electronic Supplementary Material. Solely the opening question was homogeneous for all three groups to assess their self-rated technology readiness (Parasuraman and Colby, 2015): "*What do you think about digital technology in general (e.g., smartphone applications, self-service technology, check-in kiosks,* etc.*)?*".

The interviewer guideline for FLEs reflected elements of Bakker and Demerouti's job demands-resources (JD-R) model. Questions on technology-related tasks and underlying processes, drivers of motivation, and customer-facing behaviors aimed at exploring how FLEs perceive technology in their daily work. For instance, FLEs were asked *"To what extent does technology facilitate or impede your work routines and interactions with customers?"* Along with assessing job demands and resources, FLEs were requested to describe to which degree technology enjoys high priority on the part of the management and if and how their employer prepares them for and supports them with the use of technology interfaces. Furthermore, critical incident technique was utilized to unravel potential obstacles of technology, for instance, by asking: *"Please describe a situation in which you have been really annoyed or tired of operating digital technology at work."*

The critical incident technique was introduced to social science by Flanagan (1954). The method relies on a set of procedures to collect, analyze, and classify appraisals of either extremely positive or negative situations (Gremler, 2004). It does not necessitate the specification of potential incidents or behaviors a priori (Bott and Tourish, 2016). Instead of forcing interviewees into a predefined framework, critical incident questions elicit details on situations that are important to the respective respondent (Pina e Cunha, Campos e Cunha, and Rego, 2009).

The questionnaire for restaurant managers widely matched the content of the FLEs' one. One aim was to supplement FLEs' self-ratings with supervisors' appraisal on the importance of managerial commitment and employee involvement concerning new digital technologies. Another aim was to identify potential hindrance factors regarding the adoption of new technologies from the perspectives of firms, employees, and customers by asking, for instance, *"What kind of resistance have you encountered on the part of employees when introducing new digital technologies in the past?"*.

The questions on hindrance factors on a firm level were inspired by the predominant barriers to adopting technology solutions identified by Demen-Meier *et al.* (2018). The three main factors hindering restaurant managers from adopting (more) technologies in their restaurants include that managers set and follow different priorities, that technology is not part of the overall firm strategy, and that expected costs exceed what managers are willing or able to spend (Demen-Meier *et al.,* 2018). Moreover, the questionnaire for restaurant managers sought to identify decision patterns on the firm side when it comes to investing in further digital solutions.

The customers' perspective was integrated by investigating their experiences, satisfaction, and delight with restaurant technology. Again, this involved critical incident questions. Furthermore, online recommend intentions were assessed and brought together with different degrees of technology-infused restaurant experiences. One main interest was to explore how relevant personal interactions with FLEs are to customers. For instance, customers were asked the question *"How important are personal interactions with a waiter or waitress for you compared to the quality of the food and the ambiance of a restaurant?"*.

### 5.3.3 Qualitative Data Analysis

Although existing theoretical models like Bakker and Demerouti's (2007) JD-R model and the expectation-disconfirmation paradigm constituted a framework to develop the semi-structured interview guidelines, a further theoretical foundation is necessary to exploit the effects of technology in service encounters. Thus, data analysis aimed at examining concepts grounded in the data and at understanding underlying patterns and relationships (Corbin and Strauss, 2015). In the first step, the transcribed interviews were broken apart by open coding to delineate concepts that stand for ideas contained in the data (Saldaña, 2016). In a second step, the concepts were related to each other by axial coding. Concepts with shared properties representing relevant phenomena were grouped together to higher-level categories (Saldaña, 2016). Patterns were examined within as well as between the four different stakeholder groups.

The software MAXQDA 2018 was used for coding and categorizing the transcribed interviews. In line with common norms in social science research, pseudonyms for participants' names were chosen to ensure confidentiality (Lahman *et al.*, 2015). As shown in Table 5.1, each of the four stakeholder groups is marked by a different initial letter (pseudonyms starting with C = customer; E = employee, Mg = (restaurant) manager, P = provider). At the same time, Table 5.1 provides an overview of the sample structure. Six arbitrarily chosen interviews—representing 16.7 percent of the total sample—were coded by a second researcher to ensure the objectivity of the analysis (Campbell *et al.*, 2013).

**Table 5.1** Sample description of Study B and pseudonyms used

*Part I: Open-ended interviews with technology providers (P)*

| | No. | Pseudonym | Gender | Age | Technology provided |
|---|---|---|---|---|---|
| | P1 | Peter | m | 49 | I.a., tablets for order processing and administrative tasks |
| | P2 | Paul | m | 30 | Tableside ordering device with speech recognition |
| | P3 | Pascal | m | 50 | I.a., waiter call devices and payment solutions |

*Part II: Semi-structured interviews*

| | No. | Pseudonym | Gender[2] | Age | Chain | Restaurant type | Price level[3] |
|---|---|---|---|---|---|---|---|
| Managers (Mg) | Mg1 | Michael[1] | m | 44 | no | Concert and event location | €€–€€€ |
| | | | | | no | Regional cuisine | €€€ |
| | Mg2 | Matthew[1] | m | 32 | no | Regional cuisine | €€€€ |
| | | | | | no | Steak restaurant | €€–€€€ |
| | Mg3 | Max[1] | m | 51 | no | Regional cuisine | €€€ |
| | | | | | no | Casual dining | €€–€€€ |
| | Mg4 | Martha | f | 31 | yes | Restaurant & bar | €€–€€€ |
| | Mg5 | Mario | m | 43 | no | Italian restaurant | €€–€€€ |
| | Mg6 | Marc | m | 46 | no | Italian restaurant | €€–€€€ |
| | Mg7 | Mohammed | m | 28 | no | Burger restaurant | €€–€€€ |
| Employees (E) | E1 | Elsa | f | 21 | no | Burger restaurant | €€–€€€ |
| | E2 | Elmer | m | 50 | no | Vietnamese restaurant | €€–€€€ |

(continued)

**Table 5.1** (continued)

| | | | | | | | |
|---|---|---|---|---|---|---|---|
| | E3 | Elisa | f | 18 | no | Sushi restaurant | €€–€€€ |
| | E4 | Edward | m | 22 | yes | Café and restaurant | €€–€€€ |
| | E5 | Elinor | f | 23 | no | Café and restaurant | €€–€€€ |
| | E6 | Elliott | m | 25 | no | Regional cuisine | €€–€€€ |
| | E7 | Emily | f | 31 | no | Italian restaurant | €€–€€€ |
| | E8 | Ethan | m | 29 | no | Italian restaurant | €€–€€€ |
| | E9 | Evan | m | 33 | no | Italian restaurant | €€–€€€ |
| | E10 | Eve | f | 25 | no | Italian restaurant | €€–€€€ |
| | E11 | Eric | m | 33 | yes | Restaurant and bar | €€–€€€ |
| Customers (C) | C1 | Cedrick | m | 21 | no | Sushi restaurant | €€–€€€ |
| | C2 | Chris | m | 18 | no | Sushi restaurant | €€–€€€ |
| | C3 | Carla | f | 28 | no | Sushi restaurant | €€–€€€ |
| | C4 | Christina | f | 17 | no | Sushi restaurant | €€–€€€ |
| | C5 | Carina | f | 19 | no | Sushi restaurant | €€–€€€ |
| | C6 | Chrystal | f | 19 | no | Sushi restaurant | €€–€€€ |
| | C7 | Charles | m | 65 | no | Regional cuisine | €€–€€€ |
| | C8 | Charlotte | f | 16 | no | Sushi restaurant | €€–€€€ |
| | C9 | Carlos | m | 37 | yes | Casual dining | €€–€€€ |

(continued)

**Table 5.1** (continued)

| | | | | | | | |
|---|---|---|---|---|---|---|---|
| | C10 | Cassandra | f | 16 | no | Sushi restaurant | €€–€€€ |
| | C11 | Cathy | f | 20 | no | Sushi restaurant | €€–€€€ |
| | C12 | Celina | f | 20 | no | Sushi restaurant | €€–€€€ |
| | C13 | Cindy | f | 19 | no | Sushi restaurant | €€–€€€ |
| | C14 | Claudia | f | 21 | no | Sushi restaurant | €€–€€€ |
| | C15 | Collin | m | 22 | no | Sushi restaurant | €€–€€€ |

Notes: [1]These managers are responsible for (or own) two different restaurants; [2]m = male; f = female; [3]average price of one main course in Euro: €€ = 8–15€; €€€ = 16–25€; €€€€ = > 26€.

## 5.4 Findings

The interviews revealed several aspects of technology deployment in the restaurant industry which are hereafter categorized and then assigned to the three research questions in this section. The first research question addresses (a) benefits of and (b) barriers to technology regarding FLEs, firms' internal processes and financials, and customer relationships from the viewpoint of technology providers and restaurant managers. The second research question seeks to investigate (c) technostress triggers and, opposing, (d) prerequisites for technology to be perceived as an enhancement by FLEs. The third research question addresses (e) customer satisfaction with restaurant technology and, as a consequence of the latter, how technology affects recommend intention. The findings section is complemented by a summary of different viewpoints on (f) the relevance of personal touch in restaurant encounters. Table 5.2 summarizes the key findings that will be outlined in detail in the following sections.

**Table 5.2** Key findings of each category grouped by research question

| | |
|---|---|
| $RQ_B-1$ Which benefits and barriers exist regarding the deployment of digital technology and its impact on frontline employees, firms' internal processes and financials, and customer relationships? | |
| (a) *Benefits*<br>– productivity gains<br>– customer attraction<br>– employee attraction | (b) *Barriers*<br>– expected costs/financial risk<br>– time to select and implement<br>– lack of customizability |
| $RQ_B-2$ Under which circumstances do frontline employees perceive digital technology either as stressful or enhancing? | |
| (c) *Technostress triggers*<br>– system downtime<br>– role overload due to system unreliability<br>– unintuitive user interfaces | (d) *Prerequisites for enhancement*<br>– optimism toward technology<br>– role clarity<br>– managerial commitment |
| $RQ_B-3$ To which degree does digital technology influence customer satisfaction and how relevant are personal interactions with frontline employees to customers? | |
| (e) *Drivers of customer satisfaction*<br>– simplicity<br>– speed<br>– (time) autonomy | (f) *Relevance of personal interactions*<br>– technology paired with value-creating personal interactions<br>– having the choice between digital interface and personal service |

### 5.4.1 Benefits of Restaurant Technology

The main benefits of restaurant technology that both technology providers and restaurant managers mention can be grouped into three concepts. That is productivity gains, customer attraction, and employee attraction. Yet, comparatively simple technologies like online reservation systems facilitate routine tasks, as Matthew states: "*We have made consistently good experiences with online reservations. It is a true relief that not anybody calls, and especially the automated table planning saves us time.*" Time savings and effectiveness also apply to waiter call systems, as Mohammed points out: "*The idea behind it is really good. You know which table actually wants a waiter to come or is finished with choosing from the menu. This is much faster and you don't run to tables in vain, only to hear that they still need a moment to make their choice.*" Max, who owns one casual dining restaurant and one fine dining restaurant, says: "*The use of digital techniques is becoming increasingly important because technology serves to improve or secure processes and also makes the work of employees easier.*" Mario simply summarizes: "*It's all easier and faster and more effective.*"

Peter classifies technology as a prerequisite for business growth: *"Companies can only grow if they establish efficient and mostly digital structures."* One factor for growth is the exploitation of new customer groups. Online marketing tools can help to mobilize both regular and new customers, as Matthew reports experiences from a restaurant that he had co-founded in 2016: *"Social media is very important, especially Facebook, Instagram, and our homepage. In times we didn't take care of our Facebook page because we didn't post new content or didn't comment on posts, sales dropped by ten to twenty percent."* Beyond this, onsite technology bears the potential to increase a restaurants' attractiveness, as Paul states: *"It [tableside devices with fully integrated speech recognition] increases turnover and brings fun to diners, thus increasing the attractiveness of the location. Above all, it shortens the waiting time and thus raises customer satisfaction."*

Although technology partly takes over tasks that used to be handled by employees, all three technology providers emphasize that technology is not meant to substitute employees in service encounters, but frees some of their time to focus on more complex customer needs. Contrarily, restaurant manager Max admits that he aims to reduce human labor through technology: *"In times of a shortage of skilled and unskilled workers, technology is supposed to make work easier in one way or another, and thus also brings along a bit of rationalization in the medium-term."*

However, especially young service workers might explicitly expect the restaurant they apply for to be equipped with modern technology that facilitates workflows. In support of this, Pascal predicts: *"With the constant shortage of skilled workers, it will hardly be possible to run a restaurant without digital systems in two to five years from now because employees can choose in which company they work."* Paul supplements: *"Technology can help train employees. Using a tablet to watch a short video tutorial on how to clean a cream whipping machine properly is far more convenient for new employees than reading operating instructions. Additionally, it is less error-prone and there is no need to disturb colleagues in their work."*

### 5.4.2 Barriers to Technology Deployment

Interestingly, although all interviewed restaurant managers agree that technology increases productivity, none of them is able to quantify the time saved or the approximate return on investment. This is in line with Peter's statement: *"Restaurateurs often tend to make naïve assumptions on costs, because they only see fees and implementation effort for new systems, but they do not contrast this effort with the reduced risk of incorrect bookings, fraud or cash handling. Especially small companies often do not calculate their operations. Pricing is usually based on competition rather than on actual costs. Although there are digital tools that calculate costs and display and control them* via *dashboards."* Accordingly, Paul rates *"the financial risk"* as *"one of the biggest hurdles"* of technology deployment. Peter states as well: *"Cost pressure impedes digitization."*

Indeed, when asking restaurant managers about digital solutions they would like to implement in the future, Michael tells: *"Right now it's contactless payment, but it's just too expensive in relation to the low demand and how many people actually use it."* From Peter's point of view, such hesitation is a wide-spread phenomenon in the restaurant industry: *"For restaurant technology, it's often a chicken-or-egg question. Do I proactively invest in digital infrastructure and thereby create a demand or do I wait until my customers claim technology features to be part of their restaurant experience?".*

From the perspective of technology providers, time is their business-to-business customers' biggest hurdle besides costs. Peter describes: *"Restaurateurs are stuck in their hamster wheel, they are working 60–80 h a week, [...] and simply do not take some time to ask themselves how they could organize themselves better and more efficiently with the help from technology."* Paşcal states: *"Digital solutions are often time-consuming in the beginning because data has to be entered into the software. This is a huge challenge, especially in small businesses where the owner is a hands-on employee himself. During the complimentary test phase, we observe that our prospect customers log in several times late at night and then log out again—they postpone the first obstacle of customizing their account again and again and then give up."*

In spite of this, restaurant managers criticize that certain digital solutions lack customizability to particular firm structures. Max, whose casual dining restaurant is linked to bowling lanes, is still seeking a reservation system fitting his requirements: *"OpenTable turned out to be the best provider, but the system is very restrictive in terms of customization. We haven't heard from them ever since we requested to adapt the table reservation system to our bowling lanes."* Speaking of tableside devices, Paul emphasizes the specific challenges of a restaurant setting for the voice recognition feature he offers. Compared to industries exhibiting a high technology penetration, Paul states that *"it is quite a challenge to recognize voice commands despite the high noise level in restaurants. [...] Moreover, the devices have to be theft-proof, waterproof, and shockproof, in other words, extremely robust."*

### 5.4.3 Technostress Triggers

When it comes to technology-induced job demands as perceived by FLEs, Mohammed differentiates between full-time employees and temporary staff: *"The user interface of the newly implemented iPads is similar but not identical to that of the digital cash register, so some employees had a hard time with the change and it took a while before they could operate it without any loss of time. For temporary staff, the frustration is highest because it naturally takes them longer to gain routine with the devices."* Thus, unintuitive user interfaces may temporarily evoke role overload and increase demands as perceived by FLEs.

When asked about technology-induced stress themselves, FLEs were surprised because they mainly perceive technology as being seamlessly embedded in their workflows and as beneficial to their efficiency. However, the majority of the interviewed FLEs reported about system unreliability. For instance, Elinor states: *"When something doesn't work or breaks down or the cash register goes crazy, it's just annoying."* Elisa reinforces: *"I am strained when the wireless network doesn't work and I can't enter any orders."* Eric depicts: *"When I stand by a table to ask customers for their order and my handheld device doesn't work properly, of course I am angry about that."* Similarly, Edward says: *"If the battery runs out when I'm taking a big group's order, then it's a bit stupid because I have to re-enter it all over again after changing the battery, this is sometimes a bit annoying."* Such system unreliability can cause role overload as FLEs are interrupted in their workflow, may need to fix the occurring issue themselves, and have to replicate tasks.

Restaurant managers also regard system downtime as the major technology-induced stressor for their employees. Michael describes: *"Recently, our server malfunctioned for two days. This means we actually had to work with paper and pencil for two days when processing customer orders. It wasn't pleasant. You just realize that the younger service staff has never learned to work that way."* Marc points out: *"Unfortunately the wireless network connection is interrupted from time to time. This is the disadvantage of using mobile ordering devices."* Max depicts the unexpected need for high additional investments in digital infrastructure to overcome such hurdles: *"The system requires a very stable wireless network, thus we had to rebuild and strengthen the whole network. In the initial phase, this resulted in more errors—orders were not processed—and frustration among employees and unfortunately also customers."*

### 5.4.4 Prerequisites for Technological Enhancement

Apart from the obstacles of unreliability, the vast majority of the interviewed FLEs share restaurant managers' and technology providers' opinion that technology makes them more productive in their work. To overcome potential resistance against technology, Peter emphasizes: "*We do not want to change existing processes as long as they work and are established, but only the data medium—from analog to digital. This must be easy for employees and save them time.*" Indeed, nine out of eleven interviewed FLEs rate technology as "convenient" or "easy". Edward underlines: "*It's easier, it's definitely easier. You don't always have to run to the table and then back to the cash desk and type something, you can do everything right there on the spot.*" Ethan agrees that "*mobile devices save a lot of time that I used to spend walking back and forth.*" Elliot sums up: "*I used to write down orders, now I type. It's faster and more effective.*" This matches Peter's observation among his business-to-business customers: "*In two and a half years there has been one single employee working for one out of our 280 customers who said he would rather want to return to working with paper and pencil.*"

However, the findings demonstrate that FLEs with a positive attitude toward digital technology tend to talk more positively about the respective technology at work. Typically, their descriptions are characterized by an overall optimism toward technology. In contrast, those who complain about unreliable technology at work are often skeptical about technology in general. Edward is one of them: "*Well, technology makes life a lot easier in many ways but there are also some aspects that are not so good about digitization.*" Elisa weighs: "*What I think about digital technology? It depends. Sometimes I find it makes things better, but sometimes I don't. But generally, I think people depend too much on technology. I think too many people are addicted to their smartphones.*"

While restaurant managers can hardly influence FLEs' personal predisposition toward technology, they can shape the relevant workplace-related prerequisites for FLEs to perceive technology as an enhancement. Besides ensuring system reliability, it seems important to clarify role expectations and responsibilities with regard to technology. FLEs report that training helps them to operate a system, as Elliott states: "*For new colleagues or new technology features, everything is shown and explained in detail. It's important that all of us are familiar with the interface and the features.*"

Additionally, (periodic) team meetings are an effective way of resolving potential issues concerning technology. Evan depicts: "*In one month with several system breakdowns, our supervisor drummed up the whole team and made clear that we must not be distracted from caring about our customers. He said the only person caring about technology issues will be him. This way I kept cool during the next interruption."* Eric has made similar experiences: *"There are designated team members who train us and take care of any occurring problems with the devices."* Hence, the clear communication of responsibilities with regard to technology prevents FLEs from experiencing role ambiguity.

Moreover, managers' enthusiasm about technology can inspire employees, as Elsa describes: *"Mohammed always talks about his ideas how this and that system or device could add value for our customers. Of course, the decision has to be made by him as a manager, those things are not cheap. But it's nice that he always wants to know what we think about it and how well we get along with things that he purchases."* Accordingly, managerial commitment to technology seems to be a further prerequisite for achieving enhancing effects.

### 5.4.5 Customer Satisfaction with Restaurant Technology

Especially young interviewees rate technology interfaces as part of their restaurant experience positively. Solely two interviewed customers are rather reserved toward restaurant technology in general. Charles states: *"As long as I don't have to do anything with it, I don't really care. I just think it's nonsense if a waitress is constantly looking at the handheld instead of just listening to what I want, even if I simply order another glass of wine."* Christina also prefers the personal touch: *"I don't use any restaurant technology. Neither for delivery services nor when sitting in a restaurant. I prefer to talk to someone personally and to make sure that I get what I want and that I don't type anything wrong."*

Among the other interviewed customers, interactive tablets are the most popular form of restaurant technology, for three predominant reasons: Simplicity, speed, and autonomy. Carla, Carina, Celina, and Charlotte think that ordering via a tableside tablet *"usually goes faster"* (Carla). Claudia, Cassandra, Chrystal, and Chris appreciate that *"you don't always have to wait for the service staff to come"* (Claudia). This makes *"a lot of things easier"* (Cassandra) *"because it's totally exhausting having to call someone in the restaurant"* (Chrystal). Chris explains: *"I actually find it more relaxed when you can sit there and don't have to constantly shout for a waiter to come."* Carina enjoys being more autonomous: *"You can choose in peace and ask your friends what they are taking. If, for instance, a waiter stands in front of you, you don't always know what you want and wish you could discuss it with your friends without rushing."*

Collin estimates that ordering via tablets decreases the risk of mixed-up orders: *"If you know more or less what you want, you can enter it digitally, then the order is available digitally, easily readable for everyone, and there are fewer careless mistakes, which relieves the service staff."* However, as Collin puts it, the menu navigation of tablets is primarily easy for those who know what they want. Contrarily, Carla says: "It took me quite a while until I found what I wanted, and the handling is a little difficult with this software." Apparently, it is not always common in restaurants to properly introduce tablets, as Carlos points out: "I was really annoyed when the waiter handed out a tablet to us and didn't explain how it works. He just said 'You can order anything with this'." Based on prior experiences with restaurants using self-ordering tablets, Chris suggests: "They need more trained staff that can handle it better."

Along with appreciating the benefits of restaurant ordering technology, the interviewed customers express a clear expectation that technology speeds up the ordering process and ensures shortened waiting times until they can enjoy their food. Although all interviews were conducted in full-service restaurants, four customers mentioned McDonald's' self-service kiosks as a negative example when asked: *"Please describe a situation in which you have been annoyed by a restaurant's digital offer."* Celina answered: *"Yes, for instance, at McDonald's, because there you notice that it takes longer and longer until the orders are ready."* Cindy perceives it similarly: *"At McDonald's, for instance, I didn't like it that much the last times. It just seems to me that the orders still take longer than before."* Christina also pictures her frustration: *"Once at McDonald's these digital kiosks were just full and when I got there the screen malfunctioned. You waited a long time to get to it and suddenly it crashes or it gets stuck all the time or things like that just make it even more difficult to enjoy your meal."* Similarly, Cassandra criticizes having *"to wait forever in line to get to those kiosks."*

For sure, this criticism is inapplicable to full-service restaurants. However, the above quotes emphasize customers' expectation that technology is not only implemented as a means of modernism and gamification but speeds up processes. Customer delight about digital interfaces as part of the restaurant experience can turn into disappointment if expectations remain unfulfilled. The interviews depict that frustration about slow service is greater when customers attribute the responsibility to technology than to humans. In turn, anger and dissatisfaction evoke a higher risk of negative word-of-mouth, as Christina points out: *"Well, in general, I do not write so many online evaluations, but if I did, it would be because something went really wrong."*

Then again, technology can enable restaurant managers to collect more (positive) online evaluations. When, for instance, customers can leave their opinion on a tablet right after paying the bill, the effort is comparatively small. Chris suggests: *"It must be really good until I take the trouble to recommend a restaurant online or a recommend button should pop up directly in the system so that you can rate directly so that a proper, honest rating is submitted."* For Charlotte, this rating option is well-established in her favorite sushi restaurant: *"Actually I almost always give a rating. Today it was like that. Directly after the payment, the option "give us feedback" appeared on the screen. That went relatively fast, that's why we did it."* Such onsite ratings can be linked to incentives, for instance, discount vouchers, to increase the willingness to participate among customers like Carlos: *"I would only give a rating if I have an advantage."*

### 5.4.6 Importance of Personal Touch

For the interviewed restaurant managers, a personal touch is still at the core of their business. Yet, it seems challenging to find the right balance with regard to digital interfaces, as Martha admits: *"The more you use technology, the less eye contact you have with the customer, I'd say. On the other hand, of course, it's much faster and also important for the processes. But indeed, the customer moves to the background a bit."* Max estimates that customer expectations will further change: *"Some customers say it [handheld ordering device] looks too technical and is more impersonal, but it's probably a matter of time. My personal opinion is that there will be fewer and fewer customers who want to be served without technical support."* Matthew has equipped service staff with the iPad mini, *"but it should not impair the personal exchange with the guests. Every service staff member should be able to remember at least four orders without typing them straight away while standing by a customer's table, as typing on a device is impersonal and eye contact with the guest must not be lost."*

The interviewed FLEs emphasize that personal interactions with customers are very important to them. Elmer states: *"You have to establish contact with the customer. Whether with or without technology. Personal contact with people is still the most important thing in the job. [...] The customer should feel comfortable and is happy for a personal conversation."* These conversations motivate FLEs in their jobs, because *"it's fun to communicate"* (Evan). Elinor, Elsa, and Emily agree that personal interaction is the main reason *"why I do the job"* (Emily). While the majority of interviewed full-time FLEs are passionate about communicating with customers, Marc increasingly observes inhibitions among temporary staff: *"It's getting harder and harder to find young people working as waiters or waitresses on an hourly basis. As they are used to screen communication instead of talking to anyone on the phone or in person, they often feel really uncomfortable about approaching customers personally. Consequently, they prefer earning money behind the scenes."*

Regarding the relevance of personal touch, the interviewed customers are divided by disagreement. Customers like Christina highly appreciate personal conversations: *"In spite of the tablet, the contact with the staff should still be maintained, because that is also an important factor. For instance, I went to a Greek restaurant with my family and the owner was just super funny and you want to go there again just because of the people because they can entertain you."* Carla shares the same opinion: *"I think tablets are partly good, but partly not so good. It's just that this person-to-person contact is really missing. [...] I'd rather place my order with a human."* Charles says that prior experience with the service is his most important reason to choose one restaurant over another because *"the personal interaction is very important to me."* As Carlos points out, excellent personal service is *"an important component that sometimes lets me connive at things that are not ideal."*

Contrarily, the second group of interviewed customers seems to be unconcerned about personal conversations with FLEs, as Claudia puts it: *"Well, I don't think it's really important. I'm just satisfied when the right food is brought. I don't have to make small talk with anyone."* Chrystal agrees: *"For me, the personal contact is not really important. I must honestly say that I am satisfied with a restaurant visit when the food is good."* Charlotte expresses this more drastically: *"So you are actually there in the restaurant to eat and not to talk to the waiter."* The taste and quality of the dish are Cedric's main focus as well: *"I think there is no connection between me and the service staff. It doesn't change the quality of the food. [...] I've been to a restaurant where the service was a bit unfriendly, but the food was still good."*

## 5.5 Discussion

A recent literature review by Moreno and Tejada (2019) highlights that the adoption and implementation of technology in the restaurant industry remains a largely underexploited research area. Even though scattered research has examined restaurants' return on investment in technology (Creamer, 2018; Lee *et al.*, 2015), barriers for technology adoption in independent restaurants (Ashcroft *et al.*, 2019; Demen-Meier *et al.*, 2018), and customer acceptance of restaurant technology (Kimes and Kies, 2012), a comprehensive view is still lacking. Such a comprehensive view is of importance because the restaurant industry is highly competitive and it seems crucial to understand the reasons for the typically low technology adoption rates, particularly among independent restaurants (Ashcroft *et al.*, 2019). Against this backdrop, this qualitative study aimed at providing a 360-degree view of the idiosyncrasies of technology deployment in full-service restaurants.

### 5.5.1 Implications for Theory

Study B contributes to a better understanding of how FLEs observe the use of technology in their daily work. Bakker and Demerouti's (2007) JD-R model seems to be well suited to explain that—depending on technology characteristics, situational factors, and an individual's predisposition—technology can either be perceived as a demand or resource. As such, role overload can be regarded as one of the most prevalent job demands evoking technology-induced stress. In the context of Study B, role overload is primarily triggered through the required familiarization with—sometimes unintuitive—system interfaces and system downtime. Additionally, system downtime or even complete breakdowns may evoke role ambiguity when FLEs are uncertain whether it is their responsibility to resolve a technological issue rather than focusing on serving customers. Such considerations hinder FLEs from performing their tasks.

In line with this, establishing role clarity is one key prerequisite for technology to enhance FLEs. Additionally, supervisors who are strongly committed to technology pass their enthusiasm on to their employees. Thereby, managerial commitment can be perceived as a job resource by FLEs that instigates motivational processes. At the same time, FLEs' personal resources are of importance when handling technology and potential unexpected issues at work. The findings of Study B demonstrate that FLEs' general optimism toward technology interrelates with how they talk about and operate technology at work.

From a customer perspective, using Oliver and DeSarbo's (1988) expectancy-disconfirmation paradigm fostered the exploration of customer attitudes toward restaurant technology. On this basis, it would be of great use to further investigate negative customer evaluations regarding the time until food is served at their table. Combined with results from a quantitative study by Ahn and Seo (2018), the findings of Study B could serve as a promising starting point to explore the underlying patterns. Blame attribution theory may be an appropriate theoretical concept to differ between technology and personal service as a cause of dissatisfaction. This would be in line with a proposition of Rodríguez-López *et al.* (2020) to focus future restaurant research on exploring how to achieve the maximum benefit of technology.

### 5.5.2 Implications for Practice

Restaurant managers often have little financial leeway to allow investments in digital technology. However, the findings of Study B should encourage management to look consciously at the diverse options to digitize their business. Even relatively minor investments in platform-based technologies—such as online reservation systems—can increase efficiency and free FLEs' time to focus on core tasks. Yet, the decision for or against a digital solution requires a full overview of organizational processes and a firm's cost structure. Thus, restaurant managers must know their operating costs in detail to be able to estimate a digital solution's return on investment. Of course, information seeking, selecting a provider, and deploying technology arouse costs and also take time. Yet, this time needs to be invested for firms to benefit from efficiency gains.

Similarly, money needs to be invested to ensure a functioning IS infrastructure. The latter is a prerequisite to prevent FLEs from technostress. Moreover, it is indispensable to meet customer expectations. When ordering via a tableside device, long waiting times until the food is served lead to greater dissatisfaction compared to slow personal service. Thus, digital processes and a restaurant's capacities both in the kitchen and in the frontline must be brought in accordance to ensure efficient workflows. In line with findings from Ahn and Seo (2018), Study B demonstrates that customers weigh utilitarian aspects like functionality and speed higher than the hedonic stimuli of digital devices. These customer expectations need to be integrated into a restaurant's technology strategy.

Especially for young customers of the age group below 30 years, digital interfaces have long become an integral part of their lives (McMillan and Morrison, 2006; Öze, 2017). As becomes prevalent in the findings of Study B, some young customers even prefer technology over personal service as long as it speeds up the ordering process. Nonetheless, the majority of participating customers in Study B state that personal service is important to them. After all, it is one means to differentiate a restaurant from the competition. Thus, when restaurants let customers choose between using technology and interacting personally with an employee, for instance, to reserve a table or place orders, they remain attractive for customers with different attitudes toward technology.

### 5.5.3 Limitations and Avenues for Further Research

The fact that the sample of Study B focuses on three technology providers may be seen as a limitation. Yet, the digital solutions offered by these three providers represent a broad range of restaurant technology, and all three providers granted detailed insights into their business and their customers' experiences with the deployment of the respective technology. Moreover, while the sample of restaurant managers and FLEs can be considered as being sufficiently diverse with regard to age and restaurant type, the customer sample is relatively homogeneous. This results from the aim to conduct the semi-structured customer interviews primarily in restaurants where customers themselves operate technology during service provision.

Due to the backlog in digitizing customer-facing processes, full-service restaurants using tableside order technology are still rare in the German restaurant industry. After all, tablets represent a considerable investment regarding hardware and the digitization of the menu. In fact, tablets are most commonly deployed in sushi or burger restaurants[3] in Germany, and some of them have already gone bankrupt and closed locations.[4] Thus, thirteen out of fifteen customer interviews were conducted in a sushi restaurant to still be able to obtain multiple opinions on the deployed interactive tableside tablets. The age within this subgroup ranged from 16 to 28, reflecting the typically young target group of this particular sushi restaurant. However, attitudes toward technology and usage patterns yet varied among these young customers, indicating that the customer sample encompasses sufficiently diverse interviewees.

A further limitation refers to the possibility that the findings might be affected by a rather conservative mindset toward technology that is prevalent in large groups of the German population. Technology penetration in full-service restaurants differs substantially between different cultural areas. While restaurant chains in the U.S. have started to implement self-service tablets in 2013 (Puzder, 2016), tableside technologies are still rare in full-service restaurants in Central and Western Europe. On the one hand, there are fewer full-service restaurant chains that push technology in countries like Spain, France, Italy, or Germany. On the other hand, culture influences people's technology acceptance and thus customer demand for technology (Meng, Elliott, and Hall, 2009). While some cultures are even relatively reserved toward well-established restaurant technology, diners in Japan, China, and the U.S. are yet served by robots in particular restaurants (Tuomi, Tussyadiah, and Stienmetz, 2020). Accordingly, the findings of this research design may vary in cross-cultural settings with different attitudes toward technology and digital maturity levels.

[3] https://www.metro-gruenderstudie.de/custom-burger-per-tablet [17.10.2019]

[4] https://www.koeln.de/koeln/essen_und_trinken/burgerlaeden/burgerlich_838133.html [17.10.2019]

Finally, some interviewees' responses diverged substantially within the different groups. For instance, while most FLEs only experience technostress in case of system downtime, few FLEs generally feel uncomfortable using technology because they perceive it as diminishing the personal touch of their work. From the customer perspective, the majority of interviewees state that valuable personal interactions enrich their restaurant experience. Opposing, several customers hardly care about personal service as long as their food and drinks are served timely and in proper quality. To obtain a more complete picture of how technology affects FLE behaviors and customer responses, a quantitative survey seems reasonable to further elaborate on the findings of Study B. Accordingly, Study C considers these findings to develop a research model that is tested through a dyadic field survey among restaurant FLEs and corresponding customers.

# Study C: A Dyadic Study on Employees' Technostress and Customer Responses

6

## 6.1 Context, Aim, and Design of Study C

The increasing adoption of digital technology is fundamentally transforming the nature of services (Rust and Huang, 2012; van Doorn *et al.*, 2017). Researchers such as Larivière *et al.* (2017) consider service encounters nowadays to be comprised of interrelated technologies, processes, and human actors like customers and employees. Indeed, service encounters that once consisted of intense social interactions increasingly involve technology interfaces, such as tablets, kiosks, or point-of-sale terminals (Giebelhausen et al. 2014). These technological advancements are changing service delivery and the experiences of both frontline employees (FLEs) and customers (de Keyser *et al.*, 2019).

From the perspective of FLEs, technology infusion in personnel-intense service settings is a two-sided phenomenon. On the one hand, technology has the potential to enhance FLEs' role performance by helping them focus on core activities and customer-oriented behaviors (de Keyser *et al.*, 2019; Larivière *et al.*, 2017). On the other hand, FLEs face several challenges when their operations are complemented by digital technologies that require changes in organizational processes (Rafaeli *et al.*, 2017). This is because technology components increase the

A version of Study C with a narrower focus has been published in the Journal of Business Research: Christ-Brendemühl, S. and Schaarschmidt, M. (2020), "The impact of service employees' technostress on customer satisfaction and delight: A dyadic analysis", Journal of Business Research, Vol. 117, pp. 378–388.

**Supplementary Information** The online version contains supplementary material available at https://doi.org/10.1007/978-3-658-37885-1_6.





S. Christ-Brendemühl, *Digital Technology in Service Encounters*, Innovation, Entrepreneurship und Digitalisierung,
https://doi.org/10.1007/978-3-658-37885-1_6

complexity of services and frequently confront FLEs with additional demands (Gustafsson, 2009; Subramony *et al.*, 2017). Such demands involve trusting processes in which technology partly replaces human interaction, dealing with increased efficiency expectations, and coping with new and often unreliable technological equipment (Ayyagari *et al.*, 2011). For instance, when a digital interface freezes or a system breaks down while entering customer data or orders, FLEs are interrupted in their work, lose time, and may have to start their entries all over again.

From the perspective of customers, unreliable technology impairs the service experience. Although technology may be perceived as convenient because it potentially speeds up service delivery (Kokkinoua and Cranage, 2013), unreliable technology can arouse the opposite effect (see Section 5.4.5 of Study B for findings of the semi-structured customer interviews). Moreover, even when technology functions properly, it requires FLEs' and/or customers' attention and thereby distracts from rapport-building behaviors such as eye contact or smiling (Giebelhausen *et al.*, 2014). Despite the advances of technology, customers still seek for the human touch in their interactions with a firm because the way FLEs serve them differentiates one service from another (Bowen, 2016). Thus, technology may limit the value created through personal interactions between FLEs and customers (Solnet *et al.*, 2019).

Similarly, when FLEs are confronted with technology-induced job demands, technology may cause technostress which is expected to be perceptible for the customer. Technostress is defined as an individual's experience of stress when using technologies (Ragu-Nathan *et al.*, 2008). When an FLE feels stressed, this may negatively affect customer satisfaction and delight with the FLE and interrelated customer responses such as tipping behavior and intentions to engage in word-of-mouth (WOM). However, the extent to which FLEs perceive technostress may depend on an individual's optimism toward technology (Parasuraman and Colby, 2015). Moreover, when job and personal resources compensate for technology-induced job demands, FLEs using technology are expected to be better able to display customer-oriented behaviors. The latter should then increase customer satisfaction and delight with the FLE.

Against this backdrop, it is important to study how FLEs perceive the demands from technology in personnel-intensive service encounters and to determine how such demands, as well as job and personal resources, affect customer interactions. In this context, Study C consists of a quantitative dyadic field survey to address three main **research questions**:

| | |
|---|---|
| RQ$_C$-1 | How do technology-induced job demands and resources affect frontline employee technostress and customer orientation? |
| RQ$_C$-2 | To what degree do frontline employee technostress and customer orientation affect customer satisfaction and delight with the frontline employee? |
| RQ$_C$-3 | To what degree do tipping behavior and customer intentions to engage in (electronic) word-of-mouth (WOM) depend on customer satisfaction and delight with the frontline employee? |

To answer these questions, Study C empirically investigates service encounters augmented by technology. In their conceptual paper, de Keyser *et al.* (2019) refer to frontline service technology as augmenting if it facilitates the interaction between FLEs and customers by freeing FLE time. Within this spectrum, the focus of Study C lies on technology operated by FLEs either to assist their core tasks or to complement interactions with customers. Hypotheses according to the FLE perspective are developed in line with Bakker and Demerouti's (2007) job demands–resources (JD-R) model and Hobfoll's (1989) conservation of resources (COR) theory. Next, using a dyadic approach, FLE technostress and customer orientation are brought together with customer satisfaction and delight with the FLE. Finally, the effects of customer satisfaction and delight with the FLE on tipping behavior and customer intentions to engage in positive word-of-mouth (WOM) are investigated. To do so, a field survey generated an effective sample of 147 FLEs and 373 matching customers in 73 full-service restaurants. The data sets were analyzed using structural equation modeling.

With its dyadic empirical research design, Study C offers important theoretical, empirical, and practical contributions. Theoretically, it tests COR theory and its ability to predict forms of strain in technology-induced service encounters. Empirically, it matches dyadic data sets and uses them to explore relationships among FLEs' sentiments and technology-induced behaviors and determine their impact on customer satisfaction and delight with the FLE. By doing so, Study C provides initial empirical evidence on customer responses to FLE technostress. Practically, Study C, as one of the first to examine digitization in the service sector from both the employee and the customer perspective, helps to identify technology-induced job demands and resources as well as their effect on FLE technostress and customer orientation. Thus, service managers might find these results useful in preparing their workforce for the increasing use of digital technology in service encounters.

## 6.2 Theoretical Framework

### 6.2.1 Conceptual Model

Bakker and Demerouti's (2007) JD-R model serves as the framework for developing a research model and hypotheses on the effects of technology on frontline employees (FLEs) in service encounters. Originally used to explain employee burnout, the JD-R model is now recognized as an appropriate framework for explaining various facets of job stress and employee well-being. Researchers have applied the model successfully to service employees in different contexts and cultures (Salanova *et al.*, 2005; Walsh *et al.*, 2015; e.g., Yoo and Arnold, 2016). According to the model, all types of job characteristics can be classified as either job demand or job resource. As further elaborated in Section 3.1.3 of this thesis, job demands have the potential to evoke health-impairment processes and thereby hinder personal and organizational outcomes, whereas job resources instigate motivational processes that have positive effects on FLEs' job performance (Bakker and Demerouti, 2017).

The mechanisms that underlie the JD-R model are consistent with Hobfoll's (1989) COR theory. This theory is introduced in Section 3.1.2 and has been applied broadly to challenging occupational settings (Halbesleben and Bowler, 2007; Ito and Brotheridge, 2003; e.g., Rod and Ashill, 2009). It assumes that "people strive to retain, protect and build resources" (Hobfoll, 1989, p. 513), including health, well-being, and a positive sense of self. People must invest resources to gain new ones and avoid the loss of existing resources. A central principle of COR theory is that those individuals with greater resources are more resilient to the loss of resources and more capable of gaining new resources, which results in a gain cycle.

In contrast, in a loss cycle, those with few resources are more vulnerable to resource loss and less capable of gaining new ones (Hobfoll, 2011). Transferred to organizational settings, job resources can contribute to resource gains, because they allow employees to save their personal resources (Stock *et al.*, 2017). Conversely, job demands tend to evoke resource losses, which can lead to strain and negative job performance (Salanova, Llorens, and Cifre, 2013; Wallgren and Hanse, 2007).

Surprisingly, neither Hobfoll *et al.*'s (2018) review of the application of COR theory in organizational behavior research nor Bakker and Demerouti's (2017) retrospective on JD-R theory explicitly addresses the subject of technology. In those authors' recently published articles, none of the keywords "digit*," "ICT," or "techno*" appear. This basic assessment illustrates the research gap in the application of COR theory and the JD-R model to organizational settings that involve technology. Salanova *et al.* (2013) provide one of the few studies to consider information and communication technology (ICT) obstacles and facilitators as job demands and resources.

As demonstrated in Figure 6.1, the research model of Study C recognizes the technology-induced job demands role overload and role ambiguity as central drivers of technostress. FLE optimism toward technology is expected to buffer the latter relationships. Managerial commitment as a job resource and self-efficacy as a personal resource are conceptualized as predictors of FLE customer orientation. From a customer perspective, the model predicts that technostress will result in lower levels of customer satisfaction and delight with the FLE. In contrast, customer orientation will result in higher levels of customer satisfaction and delight with the FLE, thereby favoring tipping behavior and strengthening customer intention to engage in positive (electronic) word-of-mouth (WOM). The relationships among customer satisfaction and delight and electronic word-of-mouth intention are expected to be enhanced by customer optimism toward technology.

### 6.2.2 Hypotheses Regarding the Employee Perspective

***Job demands and technostress***

Although productivity gains represent one of the presumptions of increased technology use, such use can have unintended and counterproductive consequences for employees and service firms. When FLEs appraise the demands of technology to be incompatible with their abilities and values, this results in technology-related stressors (Ragu-Nathan *et al.*, 2008; Ayyagari *et al.*, 2011). In contrast with other forms of work stress triggered by career issues or work-family conflicts (Elloy and Smith, 2003; e.g., Karatepe and Karadas, 2016), the dominant technology-related stressors in service encounters are determined by the characteristics of FLEs' tasks and roles.

Among these stressors, Ayyagari *et al.* (2011) find that work overload and role ambiguity are the most dominant predictors of *technostrain*. The latter is conceptualized as "the individual's psychological response" (Ayyagari *et al.*, 2011, p. 834) to demands that are perceived as stressful, whereas *technostress* refers to the transactional process while using technology (Maier *et al.*, 2019). Hereafter, the term technostress—rather than technostrain—is used to capture the overall process that FLEs go through when their work involves operating digital technology. It is predicted that job demands that arise from technology use—specifically,

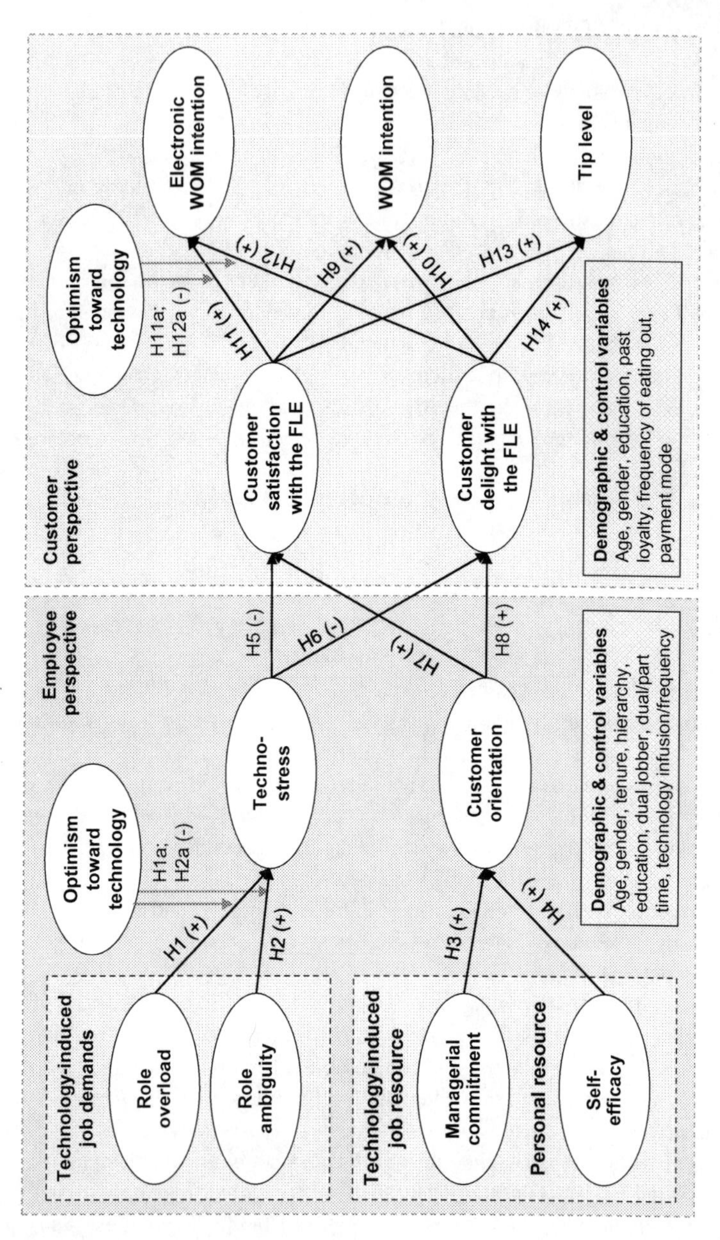


**Figure 6.1** Conceptual model of Study C

technology-induced role overload and role ambiguity—relate positively to FLEs' level of technostress.

Role overload "has considerable overlap with work overload" (Ayyagari *et al.*, 2011, p. 835). It occurs when employees face too many work requirements in relation to the time available (Beehr, Walsh, and Taber, 1976). Technology forces employees to work more and adapt their routines (Thatcher *et al.*, 2002). They must invest more working time in learning how to operate new technologies and integrate them into their daily routines. This requirement often results in an excess of tasks (Król, 2017), thereby creating or intensifying role overload. The latter may also occur if unreliable technology forces employees to repeat digital inputs or to restart a system. Similarly, role overload can even arise when FLEs solely perceive the technology as unreliable and thus take time-consuming precautions against possible breakdowns (Ayyagari *et al.*, 2011).

Furthermore, technology may induce role ambiguity, in the form of uncertainty about expected work behaviors (Beehr *et al.*, 1976). Typically, role ambiguity is caused by a lack of available information about certain organizational roles (Rizzo *et al.*, 1970), but it also might result from the increasing technology penetration in service encounters (Larivière *et al.*, 2017). For instance, when there are few guidelines to help FLEs work with deployed technologies, they lack information to carry out their job. Furthermore, role ambiguity will arise if customer requests are incompatible with processes underlying the deployed technology (see Study A) or if customers complain about digital processes (Zhang, Z. *et al.*, 2010). The lack of clarity about whether and to what extent employees should deal with technology-related issues, rather than with the core activities of their specific roles, is referred to as *technology-induced role ambiguity* (Ayyagari *et al.*, 2011; Maier *et al.*, 2015).

Both role overload and role ambiguity can be classified as *hindrance* job demands involving undesirable constraints that impede the achievement of valued goals (LePine *et al.*, 2005). According to COR theory, employees perceive these job demands as threatening to their valued resources and therefore as antecedents of job-related stress (Bakker, Demerouti, and Euwema, 2005; Ebbers and Wijnberg, 2017; Jackson and Schuler, 1985; Narayanan, Menon, and Spector, 1999). When job-related stress results from the use of technologies and the speed with which digitization changes employee requirements, it is known as technostress (Ayyagari, 2007; Salanova *et al.*, 2013). Accordingly, it is hypothesized:

*$H_1$: Frontline employees' technology-induced role overload relates positively to their level of technostress.*

*$H_2$: Frontline employees' technology-induced role ambiguity relates positively to their levels of technostress.*

***Moderating effect of FLE optimism toward technology***

Job demands deriving from the use of technology are perceived differently by individuals. Thus, the effects of technology-induced role overload and role ambiguity on technostress are likely to be mitigated by FLEs' predisposition toward technology. As Section 3.2 demonstrates, several well-established concepts in academic literature capture such predispositions and the likelihood to adopt digital technology. On the contrary, frontline employees seldom have the choice to use digital technology provided by their employers. Of course, employers cannot force employees to install mobile applications for digital shift planning or internal communication on their private smartphones. In contrast, FLEs working in service encounters basically must operate digital technology provided by the firm, for instance, to keep up with pre-defined ordering or payment processes.

Since Study C examines to which extent demands deriving from technology arouse FLE technostress, the concept of technology readiness seems viable as a moderator of the effects of technology-induced job demands on technostress. Technology readiness goes beyond the decision process before using technology. Particularly, it includes an individual's propensity "to embrace and effectively use new technologies" (Parasuraman, 2000, p. 309). According to the Oxford dictionary, one meaning of the verb 'embrace' is to "accept (a belief, theory, or change) willingly and enthusiastically"[1]. Thus, technology readiness considers how willingly, enthusiastically, and effectively individuals handle technology that they have adopted.

Technology readiness is conceptualized as a multidimensional construct including optimism, innovativeness, discomfort, and insecurity. The first two

[1] https://www.lexico.com/definition/embrace [17.03.2020]

dimensions are regarded as motivators that contribute to an individual's technology readiness (see Figure 3.7 in Section 3.2.3). Innovativeness focuses on a person's tendency to be among the first to use new technologies and thus emphasizes actual behavioral patterns (Parasuraman and Colby, 2015). Yet, behavioral patterns are regarded as less stable than attitudes and beliefs (Jones and Harris, 1967). Accordingly, optimism is defined as "a positive view of technology and a belief that it offers people increased control, flexibility, and efficiency in their lives" (Parasuraman and Colby, 2015, p. 60). Therefore, it measures attitudinal patterns that are of high relevance when coping with demands deriving from technology.

Furthermore, Bakker and Demerouti (2017) consider a general level of optimism to serve as a personal resource when employees are confronted with job demands. The JD-R model proposes that personal resources can play a similar role as job resources and that the latter can buffer the impact of job demands on stress (Bakker and Demerouti, 2017). Accordingly, optimism toward technology strengthens an individual's belief that technology-induced job demands will be manageable and might thus mitigate the influence of job demands on technostress. Additionally, FLEs could build upon resources that result from their readiness to use technology in their private lives (Lam, Chiang, and Parasuraman, 2008). More specifically, a general optimism toward technology affects work environments by increasing employees' perceived ease of technology use at work (Walczuch *et al.*, 2007). Accordingly, it is hypothesized:

$H_{1a}$: *Frontline employees' optimism toward technology mitigates the effect of technology-induced role overload on their level of technostress.*

$H_{2a}$: *Frontline employees' optimism toward technology mitigates the effect of technology-induced role ambiguity on their level of technostress.*

***Job and personal resources and customer orientation***

Customers' impressions of service firms tend to be shaped by their interactions with FLEs (Hartline *et al.*, 2000; Zeithaml *et al.*, 2017). Therefore, the development and enhancement of FLE customer orientation are critical for service management success (Hogreve *et al.*, 2017; Kelley, 1992). At the individual level, customer orientation traditionally refers to employees' abilities to satisfy customers' needs (Saxe and Weitz, 1982). These abilities encompass technical as well as social skills (Hennig-Thurau and Thurau, 2003). However, having the necessary abilities does not automatically lead to customer-oriented behaviors. Rather, employees intrinsically need to place importance on meeting customer needs and expectations (Liao and Subramony, 2008; Nguyen *et al.*, 2014). Similarly, Brown *et al.* (2002) postulate that an employee's disposition or motivation to meet customer needs is mainly determined by personality traits—namely emotional stability, agreeability, and need for activity.

Thus, customer orientation is considered as a multidimensional construct encompassing an employee's motivation to display customer-oriented behaviors as well as the actual abilities to do so. Complementary to these two dimensions, Hennig-Thurau and Thurau (2003) propose self-perceived decision-making authority as the third dimension of customer-orientation. Employees will only behave in customer-oriented ways when they feel authorized to make decisions in service encounters—particularly when unexpected issues occur during the interaction with customers (Hennig-Thurau and Thurau, 2003). Similarly, Donavan, Brown, and Mowen (2004) regard customer orientation to result from the interplay of environmental and individual factors. In line with this proposition, managerial commitment (as an environmental factor and job resource) and self-efficacy (as an individual factor and personal resource) are hereafter conceptualized as potential antecedents of FLE customer orientation.

First, the motivation of FLEs is a key prerequisite of customer-oriented behaviors (Hennig-Thurau and Thurau, 2003). According to the JD-R model, job resources can instigate motivational processes (Bakker and Demerouti, 2017). Study C investigates the job resource of *managerial commitment* to technology, which refers to the degree to which managers acknowledge the use of technology and enable their employees to adopt it (Ramaseshan *et al.*, 2015). Managerial commitment is one form of organizational support that can motivate employees and have a positive impact on their attitudes and behaviors when they interact with customers (Yoo and Arnold, 2016; Zablah *et al.*, 2012). It is an important job resource because employees need supervisory and organizational support to cope with the demands of technology and free up the resources needed to deliver customer-oriented service (Chan and Wan, 2012). Accordingly, it is hypothesized:

> *$H_3$: Managerial commitment toward technology relates positively to frontline employees' customer orientation.*

Second, a central proposition of the JD-R model is that personal resources such as self-efficacy play a role similar to job resources (Bakker and Demerouti, 2017). Self-efficacy is a person's expectation of "how well one can execute courses of action required to deal with prospective situations" (Bandura, 1982, p. 122). This expectation is formed by past experiences as well as by an individual's belief whether success derives from external factors, own skills, or fortune (Bandura, 1977). Consequently, individuals differ in their level of self-efficacy and resultant attitudes and behaviors (Sherer and Adams, 1983).

Employees who report high levels of work-related self-efficacy cope better with challenges and stressful jobs (Jex and Bliese, 1999). In a recent study, Kim and Byon (2018) presume that self-efficacious employees are better able to address challenges and demands at work, including customer needs. Thus, self-efficacy can be conceptualized as a personal resource that allows FLEs to effectively focus on customer needs; those FLEs with high levels of work-related self-efficacy act more confident in service encounters and are able to display a higher level of customer orientation. Accordingly, it is hypothesized:

> *$H_4$: Frontline employees' work-related self-efficacy relates positively to their customer orientation.*

### 6.2.3 Hypotheses Regarding the Customer Perspective

***Effects of FLE technostress on customer satisfaction and delight***

As Table 3.1 in Section 3.2.3 demonstrates, prior empirical studies have shown that technostress in the workplace bears the potential to decrease organizational commitment, employee engagement, and job satisfaction (e.g., Maier *et al.*, 2015). Likewise, the positive effects of the aforementioned concepts on customer satisfaction have been extensively studied. For instance, Hogreve *et al.* (2017) provide a meta-analysis on the service-profit chain that links job satisfaction and employee productivity to customer satisfaction. Similarly, Stock *et al.* (2017) find that employee job engagement and job satisfaction affect customer delight with the FLE through FLE innovative service behaviors. Yet, to the best of the author's knowledge, FLE technostress has never been empirically investigated as a direct antecedent of customer satisfaction and delight.

Although customer satisfaction is widely researched in academic literature, there is no generally accepted definition of the construct (Oliver, 2014). In line with Oliver and DeSarbo's (1988) expectancy-disconfirmation paradigm depicted in Section 3.3.1, customers are dissatisfied with a product or service if their expectations remain unmet. A customer's expectations derive from individual needs, prior experiences, a firm's marketing activities, and information from one's network, media, or online review platforms (Voorhees *et al.*, 2017). Fulfillment of expectations leads to customer satisfaction, whereas exceeding expectations leads to customer delight (Kotler and Keller, 2016).

Similarly, researchers have not yet agreed on a common conceptualization of delight (Finn, 2012). One of the two predominant research perspectives presumes that delight represents an extraordinarily high level of satisfaction, referred to as 'zone of delight' (e.g., Anderson and Mittal, 2000). According to insights from emotion psychology, the second research perspective conceives customer delight as an affective customer response involving positive emotions such as joy, surprise, or excitement (Collier *et al.*, 2018; Finn, 2012; Oliver *et al.*, 1997; Plutchik, 1980). Following this conceptualization, delight arises as a result of surprisingly positive customer experiences (Oliver *et al.*, 1997). Instead, Kumar, Olshavsky, and King (2001) propose that there may be two different kinds of delight—one involving surprise and the other one not necessitating it. Still, researchers widely recognize that elements that positively surprise customers strengthen their delight experience (e.g., Ludwig *et al.*, 2017).

However, stress withdraws FLEs' resources from interacting with customers. Thus, FLEs' reactions to stressful working conditions negatively affect customer satisfaction and delight (Dormann and Kaiser, 2002). This is because employees' capacity for self-regulation in stressful job situations is a limited resource (Muraven, Tice, and Baumeister, 1998). In particular, as customers are well versed in detecting employees' emotions and non-verbal cues (Groth, Hennig-Thurau, and Walsh, 2009), they are likely to sense FLE technostress-induced symptoms.

For instance, technostress is accompanied by higher levels of the stress hormone cortisol (Riedl *et al.*, 2012), and cognitive symptoms such as poor concentration (Arnetz and Wiholm, 1997; La Torre *et al.*, 2019). In service encounters, customers presumably detect FLEs' stress in cases where it manifests in carelessness, inhospitable looks, or the inability to provide quality customer interactions (Netemeyer *et al.*, 2005). It is thus expected that customers' detection of these technostress-induced symptoms results in reduced evaluations of satisfaction and delight with the FLE. Accordingly, it is hypothesized:

> *H5: Frontline employees' level of technostress relates negatively to customer satisfaction with the frontline employee.*

> *H6: Frontline employees' level of technostress relates negatively to customer delight with the frontline employee.*

***Effects of FLE customer orientation on customer satisfaction and delight***

The relationship between FLE customer orientation and customer satisfaction is yet reflected in Saxe and Weitz's (1982) conceptualization of customer orientation as an employee's ability to satisfy customers' needs. Highly customer-oriented FLEs are expected to "engage in behaviors that lead to long-term customer satisfaction" (Hoffman and Ingram, 1992, p. 69). In service encounters, customer satisfaction highly depends on employee behaviors because customers' impressions of service firms are shaped by their interactions with FLEs (Hartline *et al.*, 2000). Rust *et al.* (1996) state that personal interactions between FLEs and customers often are the primary determinants of customer satisfaction.

It has been found that meeting customers' expectations and needs positively influences customer satisfaction (Hennig-Thurau, 2004). When employees have internalized the importance of this relationship, they are more willing to behave in customer-oriented ways (Nguyen *et al.*, 2014). While customer orientation strongly relates to a customer's overall satisfaction with a service (Susskind, Kacmar, and Borchgrevink, 2003), it also shapes the satisfaction with the employee. When customers perceive that employees demonstrate empathy and sincere concern during a service encounter, customer evaluations of the frontline employee's service is expected to be more positive (Sharma, 1999). Accordingly, it is hypothesized:

*H*$_7$: *Frontline employees' customer orientation relates positively to customer satisfaction with the frontline employee.*

With regard to customer delight with the FLE, Barnes *et al.* (2011) find that employee affect (e.g., being caring and friendly) and effort (e.g., being attentive and helpful) have the strongest impact on arousing customer delight. Thus, when FLE behavior exceeds customer expectations, it can even arouse customer delight (Keiningham and Vavra, 2001; Torres and Kline, 2013). A recent conceptualization by Parasuraman *et al.* (2021) associates customer delight with six different properties of a service encounter, namely positive emotions, interactions with others, successful problem-solving, engaging customer's senses, the timing of actions, and sense of control. The group of authors has found that the majority of delightful experiences reported by customers contain the first three properties listed above (Parasuraman *et al.*, 2021).

Hence, customer delight is expected to most likely occur when service encounters encompass the trinity of positively valenced emotions, valued personal interactions, and customers' perception that their need has been met or a problem has successfully been solved (Parasuraman *et al.*, 2021). As FLEs affect all of these properties, their sentiments and customer-oriented behaviors are crucial in determining customer delight (Bowen, 2016; Delcourt *et al.*, 2016). For instance, Parasuraman *et al.* (2021) propose that FLEs valuing customers or making them feel special arouse positive emotions. Moreover, customer delight may arouse in service encounters in which FLEs are particularly patient, helpful, attentive, and enjoy interacting with the customer. Finally, customer delight emerges when FLEs make sure that customers get exactly what they need or when they anticipate customer problems and solve them right away (Parasuraman *et al.*, 2021). Accordingly, it is hypothesized:

*H*$_8$: *Frontline employees' customer orientation relates positively to customer delight with the frontline employee.*

***Satisfaction and delight as antecedents of WOM***

Word-of-mouth (WOM) is regarded as one of the eldest mechanisms of exchanging information between humans (Dellarocas, 2003). It refers to informal communications directed at other customers or potential customers about the characteristics and user experience of certain products or services (Anderson, 1998; Westbrook, 1987). Although the impact of WOM depends on various personal and situational factors like the sender's trustworthiness or the richness of the message (Sweeney, Soutar, and Mazzarol, 2008), it is regarded as considerably more effective than marketing activities initiated by a firm (Martin and Lueg, 2013). This is particularly true for services that are difficult to assess before their consumption, for instance, in the hospitality industry (Litvin, Goldsmith, and Pan, 2008). As customers increasingly base their purchase decisions on others' evaluations, it has become crucial for service firms to understand the antecedents of WOM (King, Racherla, and Bush, 2014).

Over decades, studies have indicated that customer satisfaction increases the probability of engaging in positive WOM (Bitner, 1990; Bradley *et al.*, 2010; Cronin, Brady, and Hult, 2000; Oliver, 1980). This is because satisfied customers are expected to engage in behaviors or indicate behavioral intentions that are beneficial to the firm (e.g., Szymanski and Henard, 2001). The same positive relationship seems to apply to the effect of customer delight on positive WOM intentions (Arnold *et al.*, 2005; Barnes, Beauchamp, and Webster, 2010). However, in academic research, there is a disagreement concerning antecedents, underlying mechanisms, and the effects of customer satisfaction and delight. While some studies suggest that delighted customers achieve even higher levels of loyalty and recommend intentions than satisfied ones (Bartl, Gouthier, and Lenker, 2013), others show that both satisfaction and delight have significant effects on customers' behavioral intentions (Finn, 2005).

The links between customer satisfaction, delight, and WOM intention can be explained by drawing on Adams' (1965) work on the inequity of social exchange. As depicted in Section 3.3.2, equity theory suggests that individuals will perceive an exchange as fair if the perceived outcome equals their input (Adams, 1965). In service encounters, such exchanges involve the customer being served by the FLE and the firm receiving an agreed-on payment for the service (Homburg, Koschate, and Hoyer, 2005). When customers are satisfied or even delighted with the FLE, they might feel that the payment they make to the firm is insufficient to value the FLE's effort. This perceived inequity can, for instance, release a commitment toward the service firm that is reflected in the provision of positive WOM to friends and relatives (Beatty *et al.*, 2012).

Research in the restaurant industry emphasizes the effect of customer satisfaction on WOM intentions (Tripathi, 2017). Besides positive cognitions such as satisfaction, Nyer (1997) acknowledges positive emotions like joy as determinants of the intention to engage in positive WOM. Since delight is conceptualized as the feeling of joy and surprise (Plutchik, 1980), customer delight is equally expected to arouse intentions to spread positive WOM. Accordingly, it is hypothesized:

*H₉:* *Customer satisfaction with the frontline employee relates positively to customer intention to engage in positive word-of-mouth.*

*H₁₀:* *Customer delight with the frontline employee relates positively to customer intention to engage in positive word-of-mouth.*

***Satisfaction and delight as antecedents of eWOM***

Along with the advent of social media and the rising popularity of review sites, electronic word-of-mouth—eWOM—has become a significant research stream (Bradley, Sparks, and Weber, 2016). Yet, eWOM is more than an electronic version of WOM. It substantially differs from WOM with regard to the credibility, privacy, accessibility, and diffusion speed of the shared information (Huete-Alcocer, 2017). This is because any potential, actual, or former customer can make personal experiences and advice about a firm's product or services available to a multitude of other potential customers via the internet (Hennig-Thurau *et al.*, 2004). Thus, the anonymous and large-scale nature of the internet enables new ways of influencing others in their purchasing decisions (Litvin *et al.*, 2008). Particularly in service industries like hospitality, eWOM that is shared via review sites today belongs to the key drivers of firm performance (Zhang, Gao, and Zheng, 2020).

Based on equity theory, Hennig-Thurau *et al.* (2004b) propose that satisfied customers engage in eWOM to return the favor of having good experiences with firms. Similarly, Belarmino and Koh (2018) emphasize that customer motivation to engage in eWOM derives from the strive to rebalance inequitable relationships. Litvin *et al.* (2008) suggest that positive customer–employee relationships result in higher probabilities that customers will engage in positive eWOM. Findings by Jeong and Jang (2011) confirm that customer satisfaction with FLEs triggers positive eWOM. Interestingly, to the best of the author's knowledge, no empirical research has yet been conducted on the relationship between customer delight and the propensity to engage in positive eWOM. However, following the line of argument of hypothesis $H_{10}$, customer delight that arises from joyful interactions with FLEs is expected to enhance eWOM intentions. Accordingly, it is hypothesized:

*$H_{11}$: Customer satisfaction with the frontline employee relates positively to customer intention to engage in positive electronic word-of-mouth.*

*$H_{12}$: Customer delight with the frontline employee relates positively to customer intention to engage in positive electronic word-of-mouth.*

***Moderating effect of customers' optimism toward technology***

As recommending a service online requires both the usage of an online device and a positive attitude about sharing information online, it is hypothesized that the effects of customer satisfaction and delight on eWOM intention are mitigated by customer's optimism toward technology. Following the line of argument of hypotheses $H_{1a}$ and $H_{2a}$, optimism toward technology as conceptualized by Parasuraman and Colby (2015) seems to be an appropriate moderator since it measures attitudinal patterns. Among others, individuals' attitudes are shaped by the socio-economic influences and experiences that they grew up with (Zhang, Omran, and Cobanoglu, 2017). Typically, individuals who belong to Generation Y (born between 1982 and 1995) or younger generations are regarded as digital natives (Bento, Martinez, and Martinez, 2018). They have spent their entire lives in an increasingly digital world and might thus render interaction through social media natural and intuitive (Bento *et al.*, 2018; Zhang *et al.*, 2017).

Strutton, Taylor, and Thompson (2011) find that members of Generation Y engage stronger in spreading eWOM via social media networks while members of Generation X (born between 1965 and 1981) rely on forwarding eWOM via emails more often. Bento *et al.* (2018) propose that age groups who consume more content on social media platforms report higher intentions to engage in eWOM than other age groups. Zhang *et al.* (2017) find that the propensity of Generation Y members to engage in positive eWOM significantly increases with their self-reported technology sophistication. In spite of this, Zhang *et al.* (2017) also acknowledge that individuals of all ages might embrace technology. Thus, rather than customer age, customer optimism toward technology is expected to mitigate the relationship between customer satisfaction and delight on eWOM intentions. Accordingly, it is hypothesized:

> *$H_{11a}$: Customer optimism toward technology strengthens the effect of customer satisfaction with the frontline employee on electronic word-of-mouth intention.*

> *$H_{12a}$: Customer optimism toward technology strengthens the effect of customer delight with the frontline employee on electronic word-of-mouth intention.*

***Satisfaction and delight as antecedents of tipping behavior***

In many service industries such as hospitality, hairstyling salons, or the taxi industry, customers typically grant service employees voluntary extra compensation, also known as tips (Lynn, 2019). The terminology 'tip' is considered to originate from the 18$^{th}$ century when customers in British pubs would give the waiter extra coins 'to insure promptness' ('tip') of the service (Lynn and Latane, 1984). Tipping is of high economic importance for service employees since they derive a considerable proportion of their income from tips (Azar, 2003). From the customer perspective, social norms are the primary reason for the decision to leave a tip (Lynn, 2019). However, apart from this basic decision of whether to tip at all, a customer's consideration on the tip level depends on manifold factors.

A substantial number of studies have examined such determinants of the tip level in the past. For instance, Conlin, Lynn, and O'Donoghue (2003) show that the tip level is positively influenced by service quality and, more specifically, by the knowledge, friendliness, and speed of the FLE. Accordingly, Parrett (2006) proposes that the relationship between service quality and tip size is positive. Moreover, Bradley *et al.* (2010) propose that tipping is one behavioral consequence of customer need satisfaction. In turn, tipping behavior is regarded as a valid indicator of customer satisfaction with the service (Lynn and Latane, 1984; Seiter, 2007). Accordingly, it is hypothesized:

> *$H_{13}$: Customer satisfaction with the frontline employee relates positively to the tip level.*

Contrarily, research on the relationship between customer delight and tipping behavior is scarce. Relying on Oliver and DeSarbo's (1988) expectancy-disconfirmation paradigm, delighted customers perceive that their expectations have been exceeded, thus they have received more than they had anticipated for the agreed-on price. According to Adams' (1965) equity theory, individuals strive for equity and are therefore motivated to variate their input if they perceive inequity in an exchange (Homburg *et al.*, 2005). Such inequity can, for instance, be counterbalanced by tipping the FLE that delivered the service (Lynn and McCall, 2000). Accordingly, it is hypothesized:

> *$H_{14}$: Customer delight with the frontline employee relates positively to the tip level.*

## 6.3 Methodology

### 6.3.1 Data Collection and Sample

A dyadic research design was used to study the perspectives of both frontline employees and customers on the effects of digital technology in service encounters. One dyad consisted of one FLE serving customers in a full-service restaurant and two to three corresponding customers matched by a numerical code on the questionnaires. The author of this thesis and ten Master students who received interviewer training in advance conducted a paper-and-pencil field survey. To underscore the seriousness of the survey, the questionnaires contained corporate logos of the University of Koblenz-Landau and the regional chamber of commerce. The regional chamber of commerce had agreed to support the survey by informing its members about the research project via online channels[2]. In addition, interviewers handed out business cards of the author of this thesis so that participants could reach out to the author in case of questions or remarks.

Restaurants were chosen randomly and were visited unannounced during a period of nine weeks. When the interviewers entered a restaurant, they first approached FLEs using a standardized, trained procedure. In principle, restaurant managers were not asked for permission beforehand or informed about the survey. In spite of this, when supervisors were present and noticed the questionnaires, interviewers described that the survey was about digital technology in service encounters, that it would only take ten minutes for FLEs to fill out the questionnaire, and that customers would only be approached shortly before leaving the restaurant to avoid any interruption of their restaurant experience. Depending on the current busyness in the restaurant, supervisors then let their FLEs decide whether they wanted to participate.

Interviewers then handed out a single-paged information sheet to each participant. As shown in Appendix C.I (FLEs) and Appendix C.II (customers) in the Electronic Supplementary Material, this information sheet contained a descriptive overview of the scale design. After introducing the scale design to FLEs, the interviewers assured that the survey was anonymous and that the data would be used only for research purposes and not shared with their employers. They told FLEs that the research aimed at interviewing both FLEs and customers. However, to avoid influencing FLEs' behavior, they did not specify that they would approach only customers served by participating FLEs. To minimize the interruption of workflows in the respective restaurants, the interviewers focused on off-peak hours, for instance, shortly after opening for lunch when hardly any customers had been seated yet.

Next, the interviewers waited until any customer served by the participating FLEs had paid the check. Customers were chosen randomly. Still, only those who were in charge of paying the bill were approached since the questionnaire contained questions on the payment method, check size, and tip level. Paying guests were asked to take part in an anonymous survey, either at their table or outside the restaurant. As an incentive, both participating FLEs and customers received a small bag of sweets and had the chance to take part in a raffle for eleven shopping gift cards worth €350 in total. To increase motivation, these gift cards could be used for a stationary or online shop of their choice[3]. Out of all

[2] https://rlp.tourismusnetzwerk.info/2018/11/08/befragung-der-universitaet-koblenz-landau-zur-digitalisierung-in-der-gastronomie/ [20.10.2019]

[3] https://www.cadooz.com/en/products/bestchoice-shoppinggiftcard/ [13.07.2020]

participants, 212 FLEs and customers decided to leave their e-mail address for the raffle. These addresses were collected on separate lists to ensure that they could not be connected to the anonymous survey responses.

In total, the survey team approached 155 full-service restaurants that use frontline service technologies. These technologies included both well-established systems such as digital cash registers or handheld ordering devices, as well as more advanced ordering tablets. A total of 163 FLEs in 85 restaurants filled out the questionnaire, resulting in a participation rate of 54.8 percent at the firm level. Among those FLEs that negated to participate, 34.3 percent stated they were not interested in the study and 27.1 percent indicated to have no time. Further 21.4 percent of FLEs said their German was insufficient to clearly understand the questions, particularly in Asian or Italian-style restaurants. For 17.1 percent, the supervisor interdicted the participation when FLEs wished to ask for permission.

Out of the 163 participating FLEs, eight had to be excluded because either none or only one customer served by them agreed to participate. As outlined in the data analysis section, eight more FLEs were excluded due to low interrater agreements among the participating customers. Finally, data sets of 147 FLEs and 373 corresponding customers in 73 restaurants in 14 cities qualified for data analysis. Of the 147 FLEs, 18.4 percent worked in a restaurant belonging to a chain and 81.6 percent were employed in privately owned restaurants.

As depicted in Table 6.1, the FLEs included 36.7 percent men and 63.3 percent women, with ages ranging from 17 to 67 years (mean [M] = 31.5 years, standard deviation [SD] = 10.4). Accordingly, a considerable proportion of participating FLEs were female. This is consistent with data from the German federal employment agency showing that women represent the majority of employees in the hospitality industry (Bundesagentur für Arbeit, 2019). In 2012, 61.8 percent of all employees and 66.0 percent of all those who were temporarily employed in the hospitality industry were women (Maack *et al.*, 2013). Thus, the proportion of women among the participating FLEs can be considered as characteristic for the restaurant industry.

Among the FLEs, 10.9 percent held a University degree and 39.5 had finished high school with an A-Level ('Abitur'). Further 32.7 percent had completed an apprenticeship and 12.9 percent had completed middle school. The average organizational tenure of FLEs was five years and five months, with 20.4 percent working in this restaurant for at least ten years. The average size of restaurants they worked in was 144 indoor seats. Regarding technology, 57.8 percent indicated they spent at least 30 percent of their working time on tasks involving the use of technology; and almost every third employee (30.6%) specified that at least 50 percent of their working time was devoted to tasks that involved the use of digital technology.

In the customer sample, the ratio between men and women was balanced. As demonstrated in Table 6.1, 48.3 percent of customers were male and 51.7 percent female. Customers' age ranged from 16 to 86 years (M = 42.1 years, SD = 16.8); and 18.2 percent were 60 years or older. Thus, all age groups are represented in the customer sample. The educational level can be regarded as considerably high as 37.5 percent of customers held a University degree. Most customers indicated they dined out in a full-service restaurant once or twice a month (42.4%) or at least once a week (43.6%). Moreover, 22.5 percent specified that they visited the approached restaurant for the first time when interviewed, and approximately one third (33.2%) were regular guests, having made ten or more visits to this specific restaurant.

**Table 6.1** Sample characteristics of Study C

| | **FLEs** (% of N = 147) | **Customers** (% of N = 373) |
|---|---|---|
| *Gender* | | |
| Male | 36.7 | 46.4 |
| Female | 63.3 | 53.6 |
| *Age* | *Ø 31.5 years* | *Ø 42.1 years* |
| < 25 years | 27.9 | 15.5 |
| 25–29 years | 23.8 | 15.3 |
| 30–39 years | 29.3 | 21.2 |
| 40–49 years | 11.6 | 13.7 |
| 50–59 years | 6.1 | 16.1 |
| ≥ 60 years | 1.4 | 18.2 |
| *Education* | | |
| No degree (yet) | 4.1 | 0.5 |
| Middle school | 12.9 | 6.7 |
| Apprenticeship | 32.7 | 32.4 |
| A-Level | 39.5 | 22.8 |
| University degree | 10.9 | 37.5 |
| *Employers' type of business* | | |
| Chain | 18.4 | |

(continued)

**Table 6.1** (continued)

| | **FLEs** (% of N = 147) | **Customers** (% of N = 373) |
|---|---|---|
| Privately owned | 81.6 | |
| *Employers' size (indoor) Ø 144 seats* | | |
| 0–49 seats | 12.9 | |
| 50–99 seats | 39.4 | |
| 100–149 seats | 17.0 | |
| 150–199 seats | 12.9 | |
| 200–2999 seats | 5.4 | |
| ≥ 300 seats | 12.2 | |

Of the questionnaires, 7.8 percent were filled out after breakfast or brunch, 41.0 percent at lunchtime, and 51.2 percent in the evening. The average check size per person was €16.48 (SD = 14.44). The majority of customers (52.3%) had paid only for themselves, 34.6 percent had paid for themselves and one accompanying person, and 13.1 percent for themselves and at least two accompanying persons.

## 6.3.2 Measures

Unless stated otherwise, a 7-point Likert scale was used, anchored at "fully disagree" and "fully agree", to measure each construct. The FLE questionnaire included several specifications in which the items referred to situations involving digital technology. Three items by Beehr *et al.* (1976) measured role overload and a three-item scale, inspired by Kohli and Jaworski (1994), assessed FLEs' technology-induced role ambiguity. Based on a pre-test with N = 57 students, four items of the 'Technology Readiness Index 2.0' by Parasuraman and Colby (2015) were selected to assess FLE optimism toward technology. The updated and streamlined technology readiness index (TRI 2.0) reflects the significant evolution of the technological landscape since the beginning of the twenty-first century and thus represents a timely instrument to measure the four dimensions of technology readiness.

Four items developed by Ramaseshan *et al.* (2015) were used to assess managerial commitment and a four-item scale adapted from Schwarzer and Jerusalem (1995) to operationalize general self-efficacy to the occupational context. Five items of Ayyagari (2007), on Likert-type scales with "never" and "daily" as the anchors, were used to measure technostress, and a four-item scale inspired by Korschun, Bhattacharya, and Swain (2014) was adopted to assess FLEs' customer-oriented behavior. The latter scale contained well-established items developed by Brown *et al.* (2002) and Saxe and Weitz (1982). Appendix C.III in the Electronic Supplementary Material contains the measures and items of the FLE questionnaire.

In addition to the main constructs of the research model, numerous control variables were assessed to support the validity of the results of the regression analysis; these included FLEs' age, gender, organizational tenure, hierarchy level, education, type of contract, and percentage of working time that involves the use of frontline service technology. To assess firm characteristics, the researchers asked FLEs to indicate the number of seats (indoor) in their restaurants, whether their restaurants belonged to a chain, and the types of technology in use at their restaurants. Among these technologies were back-office systems (e.g., digital shift planning, time recording), frontline service technologies (e.g., handheld ordering devices or tablets, digital cash register systems, devices to process card or smartphone payments), and solutions aimed at increasing customer convenience (e.g., online reservation systems, free Wi-Fi, self-ordering devices).

The customer questionnaire included three items of customer satisfaction with the FLE and customer delight with the FLE, taken from Stock *et al.* (2017). All measures and items of the customer questionnaire are included in Appendix C.IV in the Electronic Supplementary Material. One item to measure customer intention to engage in positive WOM toward friends and colleagues stemmed from Keiningham *et al.* (2007). Similarly, a second item by Keiningham et al. (2007) was used to assess customer's propensity to engage in positive eWOM and thus recommend the restaurant in a rating portal on the web.

Inspired by Conlin *et al.* (2003), tip level was measured by comparing today's tip in relation to the check size with prior restaurant experiences on a seven-point Likert scale, anchored at "significantly lower" and "significantly higher". Customers' optimism toward technology as one dimension of technology readiness was operationalized with the same four items by Parasuraman and Colby's (2015) TRI 2.0 as in the FLE questionnaire. Customer age, gender, education, check size per person, tip size, loyalty to the restaurant, frequency of dining out, and payment method were gathered as control variables.

A pre-test of the clarity of scale design, items used, and references to frontline service technology in the FLE questionnaire among six servers of a full-service restaurant resulted in some wording adaptations of the scales' introductory remarks (e.g., working time spent on technology). Pre-testing of the customer questionnaire among ten students led to minor alterations in the control variables (e.g., adding gift vouchers as a payment method, explicitly excluding self-service restaurants when assessing the frequency of dining out). All items and scales were rated as comprehensible and adequate to assess service encounters in a restaurant.

### 6.3.3 Quantitative Data Analysis

In the first step, customer data was aggregated to the employee level by calculating the customer mean of each item per FLE. This procedure allowed analyzing the data at the individual FLE level, in line with previous research (Evanschitzky *et al.*, 2011; Homburg and Stock, 2004; Stock and Bednarek, 2014). Using the $r_{wg}$ index by James, Demaree, and Wolf (1993), the within-group interrater agreement was estimated to determine whether customers' evaluations were interchangeable in terms of their absolute values (LeBreton and Senter, 2008). This test revealed a high interrater agreement for customer satisfaction with the FLE, but the mean $r_{wg}$ index for customer delight with the FLE ranged below .70, i.e., the most commonly proposed threshold value of high interrater agreements (Lance, Butts, and Michels, 2006).

Consequently, eight FLEs that had been matched with two customers each were excluded from the sample because of opposing ratings. Analyzing the IRA of dyads of one FLE and three customers led to an exclusion of 24 customers whose ratings were inconsistent with the remaining two customers. This procedure led to an effective sample of 147 FLEs and 373 customers, corresponding to an average of 2.5 customers per FLE. Within this sample, the mean $r_{wg}$ index for customer delight with the FLE ranges as 70.4 percent (Median of 82.6), indicating strong agreement (LeBreton and Senter, 2008). The mean $r_{wg}$ index for customer satisfaction with the FLE attains 89.0 percent (Median of 95.3), demonstrating an even stronger agreement among customers who were served by the same FLE.

Following Anderson and Gerbing (1988), the measurement model's validity and reliability were assessed prior to analyzing the proposed structural effects. From a principal component analysis for all multi-item constructs within the FLE and the customer questionnaire with Varimax rotation, ten discrete factors emerged. Yet, it was necessary to drop one item of customer orientation, due to its factor loading of only .51 and cross-loading of .42 with the self-efficacy factor. The Cronbach's alpha of each construct ranged from .69 to .92. Among these, solely the role ambiguity scale's alpha (.69) scored slightly below the most commonly used threshold of .70.

A confirmatory factor analysis was conducted, using IBM SPSS AMOS 25, to evaluate the psychometric properties of the model. The analysis revealed that the factor loading of one role ambiguity item was .59, which is acceptable (Hair *et al.*, 2014). Otherwise, the factor loadings were at least .63, and the vast majority of the 36 items scored above .70. Fornell and Larcker's (1981) criterion to ensure discriminant validity affirmed that all correlations between the constructs were lower than the square root of the average variance extracted (AVE) for each construct. Table 6.2 summarizes the means, standard deviations, Cronbach's alpha, correlations, and square roots of the AVE on the diagonal.

Structural equation modeling was used to assess the hypothesized model; the comparative fit index (CFI), incremental fit index (IFI), Tucker-Lewis index (TLI), and root mean square error of approximation (RMSEA) measured model fit. A common latent factor test was conducted to assess the possibility of common method variance, though this risk is low because the survey data was derived from more than one source (Podsakoff *et al.*, 2003).

The common latent factor technique introduces a new latent variable, related to all manifest variables. When comparing factor loadings with or without this common latent factor, substantial differences would indicate a common method bias (Lindell and Whitney, 2001). However, after the introduction of the common latent factor for this sample, all changes in factor loadings were less than .20, so common method bias was not a concern for Study C. Finally, the computational tool PROCESS (Hayes, 2012) was used to calculate the hypothesized moderating effects. Several t-tests were conducted with regard to the socio-demographic variables of both FLEs and customers.

## 6.4 Results

### 6.4.1 Validation of the Research Model

***Main effects***

According to the results of the structural equation model without control variables, the hypothesized model fits the data well ($\chi^2$/df = 1.526; IFI = .919; TLI = .908; CFI = .917; RMSEA = .060). In line with hypotheses $H_1$ and $H_2$, role overload ($\beta$ = .225; $p < .05$) and role ambiguity ($\beta$ = .326; $p < .01$) positively influence FLEs' level of technostress. Taken together, these two technology-induced job demands account for 16 percent of the variance explained in technostress.

The job resource of managerial commitment toward technology relates positively to FLEs' customer orientation ($\beta$ = .211; $p < .05$), supporting hypothesis $H_3$. Furthermore, FLEs' work-related self-efficacy strengthens their customer

**Table 6.2** Correlations and psychometric properties of Study C

| | (1) | (2) | (3) | (4) | (5) | (6) | (7) | (8) | (9) | (10) | (11) | (12) | (13) |
|---|---|---|---|---|---|---|---|---|---|---|---|---|---|
| (1) RO | **.77** | | | | | | | | | | | | |
| (2) RA | .16* | **.66** | | | | | | | | | | | |
| (3) MC | .02 | .01 | **.84** | | | | | | | | | | |
| (4) SE | – .18* | – .08 | .05 | **.82** | | | | | | | | | |
| (5) FT | – .04 | – .10 | .13 | .18* | **.70** | | | | | | | | |
| (6) TS | .29** | .30** | .05 | – .26** | – .23** | **.74** | | | | | | | |
| (7) CO | – .21* | – .03 | .19* | .44** | .13 | – .14 | **.74** | | | | | | |
| (8) CS | – .03 | – .12 | .07 | .24** | .02 | – .32** | .24** | **.88** | | | | | |
| (9) CD | – .06 | – .04 | .12 | .28** | .10 | – .23** | .30** | .61** | **.86** | | | | |
| (10) CT | .01 | – .06 | – .01 | .10 | – .10 | – .01 | .16 | .15 | .27** | **.79** | | | |
| (11) WOM | – .11 | .00 | .07 | .05 | .16 | – .29** | .20* | .43** | .48** | .03 | n/a | | |
| (12) eWOM | .03 | .00 | .03 | – .03 | .00 | – .15 | .17* | .31** | .48** | .18* | .45** | n/a | |
| (13) Tip | – .05 | – .04 | .09 | – .03 | – .01 | .04 | .08 | .08 | .25** | .09 | .25** | .17* | n/a |
| Mean | 2.79 | 2.18 | 4.05 | 5.92 | 4.66 | 2.09 | 5.62 | 6.17 | 4.69 | 4.38 | 6.06 | 3.48 | 4.26 |
| SD | 1.41 | 1.26 | 1.68 | 1.09 | 1.25 | 1.11 | 1.21 | .76 | 1.27 | 1.01 | .91 | 1.77 | .64 |
| CR | .82 | .69 | .92 | .89 | .79 | .86 | .79 | .91 | .90 | .87 | n/a | n/a | n/a |

Notes: N = 147; * p< .05; ** p < .01; n/a = not applicable; RO = Role overload; RA = Role ambiguity; MC = Managerial commitment; SE = Self-efficacy; FT = FLE optimism toward technology; TS = Technostress; CO = Customer orientation; CS = Customer satisfaction with the FLE; CD = Customer delight with the FLE; CT = Customer optimism toward technology; WOM = WOM intention; eWOM = eWOM intention; Tip = Tip level; SD = Standard deviation; CR = Composite reliability; diagonal elements in bold indicate the square roots of the average variance extracted for constructs measured with multiple items.

orientation ($\beta = .445$; $p < .001$). Accordingly, hypothesis $H_4$ is supported; managerial commitment and FLEs' personal resource self-efficacy explain 24 percent of the variance in customer orientation. Table 6.3 summarizes the results of structural equation modeling.

**Table 6.3** Results of structural equation modeling

| | | β | S.E. | C.R. | Hypothesis supported? |
|---|---|---|---|---|---|
| H1 | Role overload → technostress | .225* | .070 | 2.282 | Yes |
| H2 | Role ambiguity → technostress | .326** | .108 | 2.811 | Yes |
| H3 | Managerial commitment → customer orientation | .211* | .068 | 2.375 | Yes |
| H4 | Self-efficacy → customer orientation | .445*** | .100 | 4.494 | Yes |
| H5 | Technostress → customer satisfaction | – .230** | .058 | – 2.774 | Yes |
| H6 | Technostress → customer delight | – .203* | .145 | – 2.242 | Yes |
| H7 | Customer orientation → customer satisfaction | .195* | .044 | 2.311 | Yes |
| H8 | Customer orientation → customer delight | .318*** | .117 | 3.286 | Yes |
| H9 | Customer satisfaction → positive WOM intention | .238* | .143 | 2.541 | Yes |
| H10 | Customer delight → positive WOM intention | .354*** | .062 | 3.803 | Yes |
| H11 | Customer satisfaction → positive eWOM intention | .034n.s. | .278 | .367 | No |

(continued)

In addition to Table 6.3, Figure 6.2 illustrates the regression weights of the main effects. In support of hypotheses $H_5$ and $H_6$, technostress influences both

**Table 6.3** (continued)

| | | β | S.E. | C.R. | Hypothesis supported? |
|---|---|---|---|---|---|
| H12 | Customer delight → positive eWOM intention | .503*** | .122 | 5.315 | Yes |
| H13 | Customer satisfaction → tip level | – .087n.s. | .113 | – .840 | No |
| H14 | Customer delight → tip level | .322** | .049 | 3.088 | Yes |

Notes: N = 147; β = Standardized regression weight; S.E. = Standard Error; C.R. = Critical Ratio; eWOM = electronic word-of-mouth; $^{*}p < .05$; $^{**}p < .01$; $^{***}p < .001$; n.s. = not significant.

customer satisfaction (β = – .230; $p < .01$) and delight with the FLE (β = – .203; $p < .05$) negatively. In contrast, FLEs' customer orientation relates positively to customer satisfaction (β = .195; $p < .05$) and delight with the FLE (β = .318; $p = .001$), supporting $H_7$ and $H_8$. Technostress and customer orientation account for 9 percent of the variance explained of customer satisfaction with the FLE and 14 percent of customer delight.

As predicted by hypotheses $H_9$ and $H_{10}$, customer satisfaction (β = .238; $p < .05$) and delight (β = .354; $p < .001$) with the FLE both relate positively to customer intention to engage in positive WOM, explaining 28 percent of the variance. Customer eWOM intention is positively influenced by customer delight with the FLE (β = .492; $p < .001$), but there is no significant effect of customer satisfaction (β = .034; $p = .714$). Thus, hypothesis $H_{11}$ is rejected, but the results support hypothesis $H_{12}$. Customer satisfaction and delight account for 27 percent of the eWOM variance explained.

Similarly, customer satisfaction with the FLE does not significantly influence the tip level (β = – .087; $p = .401$). However, customer delight with the FLE influences the tip level significantly positive (β = .322; $p < .01$). Hence, hypothesis $H_{13}$ must be rejected, while hypothesis $H_{14}$ is supported. Customer satisfaction and delight with the FLE explain 8 percent of the variance of tip level. In contrast to customer intentions to engage in positive WOM or electronic WOM, the tip level captures the actual tip customers granted the FLE prior to filling out the questionnaire.

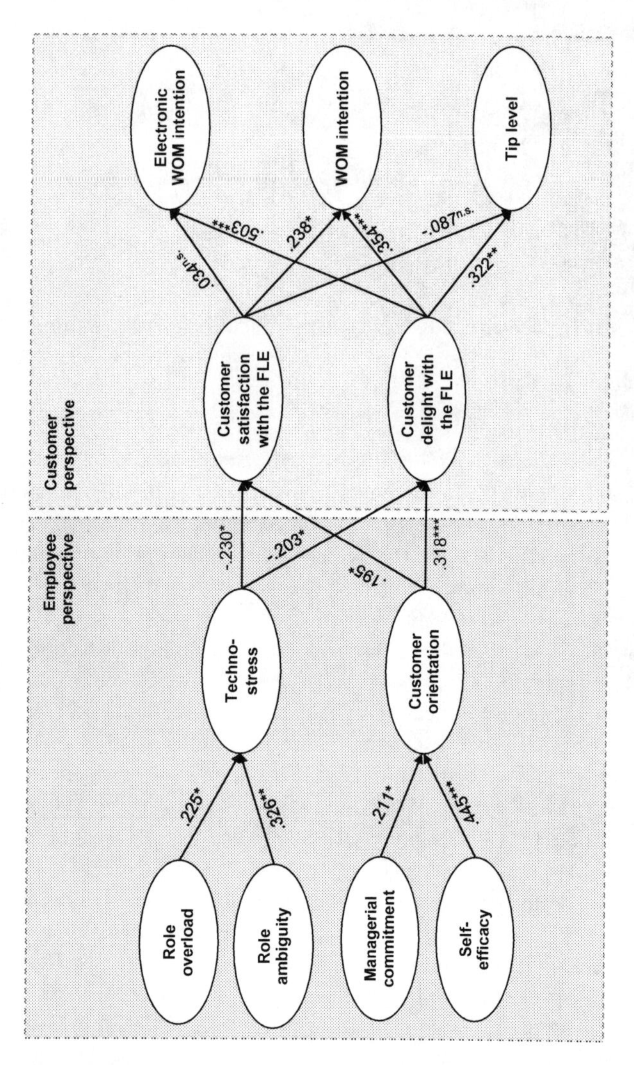


**Figure 6.2** Structural model of Study C including the main effects. (Notes: Standardized regression weights; $^{*}p < .05$; $^{**}p < .01$; $^{***}p < .001$; n.s. = not significant)

***Moderating effects***

Evaluating the moderating effects proposed in hypotheses $H_{1a}$ and $H_{2a}$ showed that the relationship between role overload and technostress is not significantly influenced by FLE optimism toward technology ($b = -.07$; $p = .22$). Thus, hypothesis $H_{1a}$ must be rejected. In contrast, FLE optimism toward technology buffers the relationship between technology-induced role ambiguity and technostress ($b = -.14$; $p < .05$), in support of hypothesis $H_{2a}$. The variance explained of technostress increases by 2.4 percent. Figure 6.3 visualizes the moderating effect.

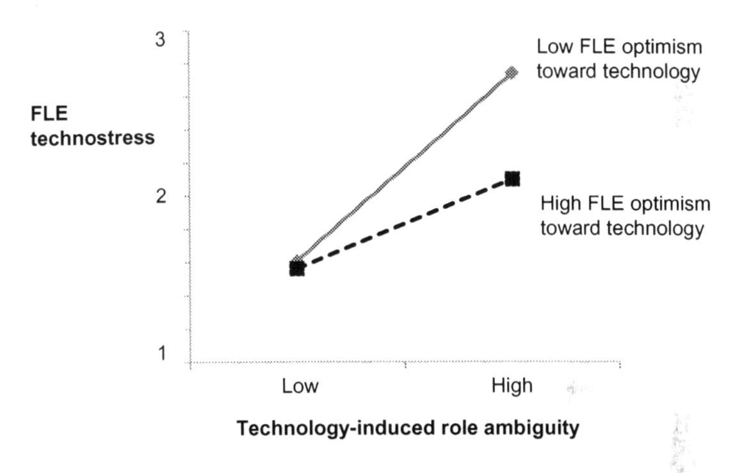


**Figure 6.3** Moderating effect of FLE optimism toward technology

To evaluate the moderating effect of customer optimism toward technology on the relationship between customer satisfaction with the FLE and customer eWOM intentions, the non-aggregated data of $N = 373$ customers were used. In line with hypothesis $H_{11a}$, customer optimism toward technology strengthens the effect of customer satisfaction with the FLE on eWOM intention ($b = .28$; $p < .05$). Figure 6.4 illustrates this effect. In contrast, customer optimism toward technology does not significantly influence the effect of customer delight with the FLE on eWOM intention ($b = .11$; $p = .09$). Hypothesis $H_{12a}$ must, therefore, be rejected.

**Figure 6.4** Moderating effect of customer optimism toward technology

### 6.4.2 Demographic and Control Variables

Including the demographic variables age, gender, and education of both FLEs and customers as controls slightly changed the model fit indices ($\chi^2$/df = 1.496; IFI = .898; TLI = .879; CFI = .894; RMSEA = .057). FLE age, gender, and education neither effect FLE technostress and customer orientation nor any of the assessed customer responses significantly. Still concerning the antecedents of technostress, a t-test revealed that FLEs of the age 30 or above report significantly higher levels of technology-induced role overload (N = 71; $M_{Load}$ = 3.08) than FLEs younger than 30 (N = 76, $M_{Load}$ = 2.52) (F (1,145) = 4.540, p < .05).

Customer age does not trigger any significant effects. In contrast, higher levels of customer education reduce the intention to engage in positive eWOM (β = − .256; *p* < .001). Moreover, customer gender affects customer delight significantly (β = .222; *p* < .01), suggesting that men (coded as 2) indicate higher levels of delight than women (coded as 1). Subsequently, a t-test with the non-aggregated customer data confirmed that the mean ratings of delight with the FLE significantly differs between male (N = 180; $M_{Del}$ = 4.96) and female (N = 193; $M_{Del}$ = 4.57) customers (F (1,371) = 7.988, p < .01).

A closer look at this phenomenon was taken to examine whether men might report higher levels of delight when they are served by women—who made up

63.3 percent of the FLE sample. However, no significant effects of gender congruency have been found. Reported levels of customer satisfaction and delight with the FLE were not significantly higher for male customers served by a waitress (N = 111; $M_{Sat}$ = 6.24; $M_{Del}$ = 4.99) than for male customers served by a waiter (N = 69; $M_{SAT}$ = 6.31; $M_{Del}$ = 4.93) ($F_{Sat}$ (1,178) = .226, p = .615; $F_{Del}$ (1,178) = .002, p = .758). For female customers, reported levels of customer satisfaction and delight with the FLE were not significantly higher when served by a waitress (N = 127; $M_{Sat}$ = 6.13; $M_{Del}$ = 4.60) than for female customers served by a waiter (N = 66; $M_{Sat}$ = 6.26; $M_{Del}$ = 4.52) ($F_{Sat}$ (1,191) = 1.102, p = .508; $F_{Del}$ (1,191) = .793, p = .722).

Including all control variables in the model revealed solely one more significant effect on FLE variables; firm size buffers the level of FLE technostress (β = − .212; $p < .05$), indicating that FLEs working in larger restaurants report lower levels of technostress. This result appears to be independent of the circumstance of whether the restaurant belongs to a chain or is privately owned. Indeed, both the restaurant with the least number of indoor seats (20) as well as the largest one (800 seats) within the sample were both privately owned. The number of indoor seats in participating chain restaurants ranged from 30 to 300. A further t-test revealed no significant mean difference of technostress between FLEs working in privately owned restaurants (N = 120; $M_{Tech}$ = 2.15) as compared to those working in chain restaurants ($M_{Tech}$ = 1.83; N = 27) (F (1,145) = 3.072, p = .082).

Regarding customer outcomes, several further significant effects emerged when considering all control variables. With proceeding daytime, intention to engage in WOM (β = .222; p < .01) and tip level (β = .222; p < .01) decreased, indicating that customers consuming breakfast or brunch were more willing to recommend a restaurant to their family and friends and more likely to leave a higher tip than usual as compared to customers that visited restaurants for lunch or dinner. Customer frequency of eating out negatively influenced intention to engage in positive WOM (β = − .149; p < .05) and positively influenced customer delight with the FLE (β = .193; p < .05). Customer past loyalty to the particular restaurant effected WOM (β = .357; p < .001) and eWOM (β = 231; p < .001) intentions positively and tip level negatively (β = − .151; p < .05). The number of accompanying customers that the participating customer paid for positively effected customer delight with the FLE (β = .168; p < .05) and intention to engage in positive eWOM (β = − .128; p < .05). All significance levels for main effects remain.

### 6.4.3 Alternative Models

Models such as the one in Study C suggest alternative paths might explain significant proportions of variance in the dependent variables. For instance, prior research on the JD-R model has investigated interaction effects between job demands and resources, implying that job resources have the potential to reduce the impact of job demands on stress (Bakker and Demerouti, 2017). Similarly, job demands may have direct but negative effects on customer orientation. Moreover, job resources may mitigate technostress. These alternative theoretical considerations were tested using IBM SPSS AMOS 25 to calculate a model with additional direct paths from job demands to customer orientation and from job resources to technostress. This analysis revealed a direct and significantly negative effect of self-efficacy on technostress ($ß = -.20$; $p < .05$). However, none of the other new paths was significant.

In a further step, the SPSS macro PROCESS was used, together with the Johnson-Neyman technique, to test for moderating effects (Hayes, Montoya, and Rockwood, 2017). Although regions of significance for the interaction of self-efficacy and role overload can be observed (indicating that with increasing self-efficacy, the effect of role overload on technostress is buffered), the actual interaction effect was non-significant. No other interactions between job demands and resources yielded significance.

In addition to potential moderating effects, the conceptual model of Study C depicted in Figure 6.1 calls for an investigation of mediation effects (Iacobucci, Saldanha, and Deng, 2007). In particular, job demands and resources may have direct, as well as indirect, effects on customer satisfaction and delight with the FLE. A model with both direct and indirect paths from job demands, job and personal resources to customer satisfaction and delight revealed a good fit with the data ($\chi^2/df = 1.582$; IFI = .922; TLI = .909; CFI = .920; RMSEA = .063). However, all results remained stable, and no significant indirect effect emerged.

With regard to the interactions between FLEs and customers, FLE customer orientation could be regarded as a potential mediator of the hypothesized relationships among technostress and customer satisfaction and delight with the FLE. Thus, structural equation modeling in AMOS was used to test this alternative model. AMOS allows bootstrapping to test indirect effects, following the approach of Preacher and Hayes (2004). The model with both direct and indirect paths from FLE technostress to customer satisfaction and delight with the FLE revealed a good fit with the data ($\chi^2/df = 1.591$; IFI = .917; TLI = .903; CFI = .915; RMSEA = .064). As shown in Table 6.4, both total effects and direct effects are significant. Contrarily, neither of the indirect effects is significant. According to this result, no mediation effect for customer orientation exists (Zhao, Lynch, and Chen, 2010).

**Table 6.4** Results of mediation analysis for customer orientation as a mediator

| | ß | p | [LLCI; ULCI] |
|---|---|---|---|
| Technostress → Customer satisfaction with the FLE | | | |
| Direct effect | $-.211^{*}$ | .018 | [−.371; −.049] |
| Indirect effect | $-.022^{n.s.}$ | .069 | [−.072; .002] |
| Total | $-.242^{**}$ | .002 | [−.397; −.079] |
| Technostress → Customer delight with the FLE | | | |
| Direct effect | $-.194^{*}$ | .046 | [−.359; −.008] |
| Indirect effect | $-.077^{n.s.}$ | .055 | [−.239; .004] |
| Total | $-.241^{**}$ | .003 | [−.402; −.043] |

Notes: Standardized regression weights; LLCI = Lower Level for Confidence Interval; ULCI = Upper Level for Confidence Interval; $^{*}$ $p < .05$; $^{**}$ $p < .01$; n.s. = not significant.

## 6.5 Discussion

Study C demonstrates that the job demands of technology-induced role overload and role ambiguity can instigate technostress among FLEs whose tasks involve the use of technology. Yet, FLEs exhibiting optimism toward technology seem to be better able to cope with role ambiguity and report technostress less frequently. In contrast, if technology induces role overload, optimism toward technology does not buffer the impact on technostress. Optimism toward technology can be seen as a personal resource of FLEs. At the same time, managerial commitment to technology and FLE self-efficacy act as job and personal resources for FLEs that improve their customer orientation. Employees who are confident of their abilities to solve problems or cope with unexpected situations seem better able to focus their attention on customers.

The results of Study C further show that FLEs' self-reported technostress reduces customer satisfaction and delight with the FLE, whilst customer orientation results in higher levels of the latter two. Customer intention to engage in positive WOM is positively influenced by both customer satisfaction and delight with the FLE, whereas solely customer delight with the FLE significantly increases eWOM intentions and tip level. However, customer optimism toward technology can strengthen the effect of customer satisfaction with the FLE to eWOM intentions.

### 6.5.1 Implications for Theory

The research conducted in Study C offers four central theoretical contributions. First, it contributes to the investigation of employee-related impacts of new technologies in service encounters. Hobfoll's (1989) COR theory and Bakker and Demerouti's (2007) JD-R model offer appropriate theoretical frameworks to deepen the understanding of the mechanisms that cause stress in occupational settings and those mechanisms that allow FLEs to conserve their resources and focus on customers. More particularly, the results of Study C support the prediction that technology-induced role overload and role ambiguity are stressors that increase FLE self-reported technostress. Out of the four dimensions of Parasuraman and Colby's (2015)'s technology readiness index 2.0, optimism toward technology turns out to be a buffer of role ambiguity. While role ambiguity can be partly intercepted by optimistic FLEs, role overload seems to be perceived as unalterable by FLEs. Thus, even optimism toward technology cannot dampen the impact of technology-induced role overload on technostress.

Second, the results support the prediction that FLE technostress negatively affects customer satisfaction and delight with the FLE. According to pertinent literature, stress withdraws FLEs' resources from customer interaction, resulting in potentially unsatisfying service encounters (Netemeyer et al., 2005). Even when FLEs attribute technostress either to the device itself or their employer, they seem to let it affect their interactions with customers. As research on technostress so far was limited to outcomes within organizations rather than the examination of effects on customers, this phenomenon deserves supplementary theoretical and empirical investigation.

Third, Study C provides several indications that the concept of delight considerably differs from satisfaction. As such, Table 6.2 demonstrates that customer satisfaction ratings achieve a mean of 6.17 on a 7-point Likert-type scale and a very moderate SD of .76; this implies that customers' aspirations about the way service is provided by FLEs are relatively easy to fulfill. In contrast, customer delight with the FLE attains a mean of only 4.69 and displays a high SD of 1.27. Therefore, the feeling of joy expressed in customer delight varies intensely among participants. Upon the return of completed questionnaires, several customers felt obliged to justify their low ratings of customer delight. These customers explicitly told the interviewers they did not expect FLEs to delight them, and that a low rating of these items did not mean they were not satisfied. These results support the conceptualization of customer delight as an emotion of joy or excitement rather than a cognitive mechanism (Parasuraman *et al.*, 2021).

One further indication for the proposition that delight is conceptually different from satisfaction is that in Study C, customers paying for accompanying friends or family reported higher levels of delight than those customers paying only for themselves. This is in line with the assumption that delight has an interpersonal nature and is a function of shared experience (Parasuraman *et al.*, 2021). At the same time, customer delight ratings increased with an increasing frequency of eating out and with past loyalty toward a specific restaurant. This supports the notion that surprise is not a prerequisite of delight (Kumar *et al.*, 2001; Ludwig *et al.*, 2017).

Fourth, the examination of customer intention to engage in positive eWOM shows that customer delight with the FLE—in contrast to mere satisfaction—has a strong effect on customers' eWOM intentions. Delight seems to arouse customers' needs to share their positive experiences with others and/or return the favor to FLEs who represent the service firm in customers' eyes. The same seems to apply to the tip level that is significantly positively influenced by customer delight. As with recommending a service online, granting a tip that exceeds habits is one way of returning the favor of a delightful experience. Taken together, Study C sheds more light on the mechanisms that lead to and result from technostress as a central construct from the FLE perspective and customer delight as the most idiosyncratic construct from the customer perspective.

### 6.5.2 Implications for Practice

This research provides various impulses for practitioners to reflect their approach of engaging and relieving employees during the deployment of new technologies. The results of the field survey imply that one prerequisite for avoiding FLE technostress and its negative consequences is to grant FLEs the support necessary to cope with technology-induced demands. When introducing new technologies, managers should aim at reducing technology-induced role ambiguity by clarifying role expectations for their FLEs. Following the items assessed in the FLE questionnaire that are listed in Appendix C.III in the Electronic Supplementary Material, this encompasses guidelines or policies to support FLEs' work with the deployed technology as well as information on the responsibilities of each team member.

Moreover, managers should ensure that the technological prerequisites (e.g., IS infrastructure) for adopting technologies are completely met. Otherwise, such technological requirements intensify role ambiguity since employees often lack information on what to do in case of unreliable hardware. The same applies to deficiencies of the wireless internet connection that cause the disconnection of mobile devices that FLEs are currently working with. Concomitant, unreliable technology forces employees to work more because it interrupts their workflows and frequently forces them to repeat entries (e.g., ordering) or to start tasks all over again.

Concerning cashless payment in full-service restaurants, malfunctioning technology is particularly demanding for FLEs. When the money transfer takes extraordinary long or does not work at all, FLEs have to ask customers for patience, or customers even muss leave their table and accompany FLEs to the stationary cash register to settle the invoice. This is dissatisfying for customers and intensifies FLE role overload and technostress. Thus, service firms need to invest in a reliable IS infrastructure and support FLEs in operating digital technologies. As the results of Study C imply that the level of self-reported technostress decreases with firm size, larger firms seem to have more efficient structures in place to prevent FLEs from technostress.

The analysis of moderating effects demonstrates that the negative effect of technology-induced role ambiguity on technostress is buffered by FLE optimism toward technology. Hence, for service firms, it is advisable to assess applicants' general attitude toward technology when recruiting new employees. After all, optimism toward technology helps FLEs to cope with role ambiguity. Moreover, a firm that largely counts on the use of frontline service technology can integrate this philosophy into job advertisements to specifically appeal to those applicants with a high optimism toward technology. However, it is important to note that optimism does not prevent FLEs to feel strained if they experience technology-induced role overload, for instance, because technological requirements result in an excess of tasks (Król, 2017).

Besides counteracting role overload, managers need to grant FLEs the resources necessary to cope with demands deriving from technology. The results of Study C demonstrate that managerial commitment to technology reinforces FLEs to embrace technology and focus their attention on customers. FLEs who perceive that the firm management proactively responds to a constantly changing technological environment and is open to suggestions related to technology report higher levels of customer orientation. This implies that managerial commitment acts as a job resource that helps FLEs save on their personal resources.

One important personal resource is self-efficacy. Naturally, individuals differ in their level of self-efficacy as the latter is primarily predetermined by past experiences as well as by an individual's belief whether success derives from external factors, own skills, or fortune (Bandura, 1977). Like an individual's optimism toward technology, an applicant's self-efficacy can partly be assessed in job interviews. At the same time, self-efficacy should not be the focal criterion when recruiting new employees. In times of skills shortage, managers seldom have a choice between multiple appropriate candidates. Rather, they can strengthen their existing employees' self-efficacy by precisely training their skills, supporting them in challenging situations, and by simply praising them for good work. Honest positive feedback will strengthen FLEs' belief in their abilities to cope with demands at work.

A further managerial implication relates to the outcomes of technostress. The negative effect technostress has on customer satisfaction and delight with the FLE is only one reason why managers should counteract technostress. Moreover, technostress should be reduced to prevent the health-impairment effects of strain and avoid negative organizational outcomes such as burn-out and employee turnover (Bakker *et al.*, 2005; Schaufeli and Taris, 2014). In turn, effective management of service employees and their job demands can drive customer-related outcomes (Subramony *et al.*, 2017).

Finally, as demonstrated by the theoretical implications, the results emphasize that exceptional customer orientation can lead to customer delight, which increases customer intention to engage in positive eWOM. Moreover, FLEs in service industries that commonly involve tipping benefit from increased customer delight through higher tip levels. Thus, both the firm and FLEs would benefit from training tip-enhancing behaviors that arouse customer delight with the FLE (Fernandez *et al.*, 2020). At the same time, prior research has proven further positive internal effects of customer delight. For instance, perceived customer delight leads to employee positive affect and, in turn, to increased commitment and job satisfaction (Barnes *et al.*, 2015). Accordingly, it is imperative for service firms to try to delight their customers by delivering unexpected and extraordinary service.

### 6.5.3 Limitations and Avenues for Further Research

This research aimed to apply the JD-R model to service encounters that are induced by technology. Despite its valuable implications, limitations of this research need to be addressed. Due to the intense timely effort of personally visiting service firms to collect data from both FLEs and corresponding customers, the field survey focused on one single service industry. This might be seen as a limitation. On the other hand, this approach enabled the interviewers to collect a large data set while simultaneously precluding industry effects. Future research might apply the research model to different service settings, either including or excluding tipping behavior. A supplementary avenue for further research could integrate supervisor perspectives by connecting supervisors' evaluations of job demands and resources to FLEs' perceptions. Moreover, Study C could be replicated in cross-cultural settings with differing digital maturity levels.

All restaurants approached have deployed several forms of technology that affect FLEs' workflows and routines. Yet, most of these technologies are extant and established. More forward-looking technologies such as service robots were disregarded for two reasons. First, the actual dispersion of service robots in the restaurant industry is so minor that accessibility to restaurants that deploy service robots is low. Second—and perhaps more important—FLEs' sentiments, attitudes, and behaviors in technology-induced service encounters are the focus of Study C, as are technologies that are meant to augment the relationship between FLEs and customers instead of replacing these interactions (Keating *et al.*, 2018). Nevertheless, researchers could investigate the differences between customer satisfaction and customer delight in service encounters that involve interactions with service robots in the future.

The constructs of Study C are promising starting points for further investigation of technology-induced job demands and resources as antecedents of technostress and customer orientation. However, while the conceptual model does assess FLE self-efficacy, it precludes personality traits that may affect FLEs' exposure to stressors or their customer orientations. Similarly, the conceptual model investigates the effect of technostress on customer-related outcomes but does neglects individual outcomes for the FLE (e.g., burnout, turnover intentions) or organizational ones (e.g., efficiency, financial performance). Prior research with the JD-R model identifies such potentially negative consequences of FLE strain (Bakker and Demerouti, 2017). These findings could be applied to the construct of technostress in the future. Moreover, it might be of interest to examine whether customer satisfaction and delight with the FLE are always directly impacted by FLE technostress or rather by FLE behaviors resulting from technostress.

A further avenue for future research lies in integrating aspects about service that go beyond an FLE's responsibility. For instance, an exceptional ambiance or unexpected discounts might as well influence customer delight with the FLE. Such aspects could explain a further proportion of the variance in customer delight. So far, customer delight is still an underexploited concept. Concomitant, in academic literature there is no definite explanation for the phenomenon that male customers in Study C report significantly higher levels of customer delight with the FLE than female ones. In general, women tend to be more emotional than men and are expected to experience positive affect like joy more intensely than their male counterparts (Loureiro and Ribeiro, 2014). Concerning customer delight in personal service encounters, Torres, Fu, and Lehto (2014) propose that employee friendliness and professionalism are the primary drivers of delight among female customers. Meanwhile, male customers primarily report delight when their needs are met, and when a service is delivered timely and efficiently (Torres *et al.*, 2014). The gender differences in arousing delight deserve supplementary investigation.

# 7 Study D: Fairness Perceptions of Customer Participation in Online Services

## 7.1 Context, Aim, and Design of Study D

Nowadays, customers are primarily in control of where the interaction with a service firm takes place. They can choose between multiple ways of service delivery (Sands *et al.*, 2020), the spectrum ranging from face-to-face interactions to complete online environments (Larivière *et al.*, 2017). In retail, online stores offer an extended assortment of goods (Pantano *et al.*, 2017), and make customers' purchase highly convenient (Hilken *et al.*, 2017). However, firms distributing high-involvement goods such as fashion apparel have long lagged behind in online retailing because it is challenging to transfer branch store experiences to the online store (Blázquez, 2014). The absence of opportunities to touch, smell, feel, and try on fashion items frequently arouses customer dissatisfaction with the purchase experience (Heller *et al.*, 2019b). Moreover, sensory deficiencies increase the complexity of online purchase decisions for customers (Merle, Senecal, and St-Onge, 2012).

This complexity frequently results in virtual shopping cart abandonment or additional costs for online retailers as return rates of products purchased online continuously increase (Janakiraman, Syrdal, and Freling, 2016). Hence, online

---

A different version of Study D has been published in the Journal of Service Management: Christ-Brendemühl, S. and Schaarschmidt, M. (2022). "Customer fairness perceptions in augmented reality-based online services", Journal of Service Management, Vol. 33, No. 1, pp. 9–32.

---

**Supplementary Information** The online version contains supplementary material available at https://doi.org/10.1007/978-3-658-37885-1_7.



S. Christ-Brendemühl, *Digital Technology in Service Encounters*, Innovation, Entrepreneurship und Digitalisierung,
https://doi.org/10.1007/978-3-658-37885-1_7

retailers attempt to find means to support customers in their decision-making process by introducing advanced technologies in the online shopping experience (Pantano *et al.*, 2017). Among these, virtual try-on for fashion items represents a product visualization technology that has been among the first to be adopted in online retail (Kim and Forsythe, 2008). With the progress of technology, virtual try-on has evolved toward the integration of more advanced augmented reality (AR) features. As outlined in Section 2.2.3, such features offer customers even better possibilities to try out and evaluate products before buying them (Beck and Crié, 2018; Heller *et al.*, 2019b).

Several empirical studies have investigated which characteristics of AR applications in online retail influence customer acceptance and perceived benefits. For instance, Poushneh and Vasquez-Parraga (2017a) identify the quality of augmentation, informative value, interactivity, search features, connectivity, and entertaining attributes to determine satisfaction (Poushneh and Vasquez-Parraga, 2017a). The results of an experimental study by Hilken *et al.* (2017) demonstrate that privacy concerns mitigate the positive effect of interactive AR technology on customer decision comfort. Furthermore, Huang, Mathews, and Chou (2019) demonstrate that perceived ownership control, modality, as well as re-processability of virtual try-on technology, enhance customers' rapport experience.

Hence, there seems to be a consensus in the academic literature that interactivity and perceived control maximize positive customer evaluations of augmented reality (AR) features. In spite of this, research presents contradictory findings on whether this leads to increased purchases. In an empirical study, Poushneh and Vasquez-Parraga (2017b) compare traditional online shopping, virtual model, and video try-on. Their results suggest that AR enhances the user experience which, in turn, increases customer satisfaction and willingness to buy (Poushneh and Vasquez-Parraga, 2017b). Beck and Crié (2018) propose that the presence of a virtual fitting room significantly increases customer curiosity, patronage intention, and purchase intention.

Rese *et al.* (2017) demonstrate that, compared to marker-based applications, markerless ones achieve consistently higher ratings of perceived usefulness, perceived ease of use, positive attitude toward using, and intention to use (see section 2.2.3 for a differentiation between marker-based and markerless AR). Riedel and Mulcahy (2019) find that in addition to visual and aural senses, engaging customers through haptic touch enhances the interactivity of AR technology and is perceived as more enjoyable and entertaining. Nevertheless, increased satisfaction with the service provider does not automatically lead to significantly higher purchase intentions across the experimental groups (Riedel and Mulcahy, 2019).

Given the uncertainty of whether AR technology will generate additional purchases and profit, investments into it represent a considerable financial risk for retailers (Bonetti, Warnaby, and Quinn, 2018). Addressing the threat that customers might not value AR features, Hilken *et al.* (2017) claim that service management requires a better understanding of how AR is appraised by customers. Even though the above-summarized research tackles customer acceptance and appraisal of different AR technology variations compared to traditional online shopping, it remains largely under-investigated whether advanced AR technology can replace branch store experiences.

Accordingly, based on the results of an experimental study among students in Germany and Italy, Pantano *et al.* (2017) postulate that trying on eyewear with an interactive AR technology of high aesthetic quality would be accepted as an equal substitution of a physical try-on in a store. However, customers' trial of a product does not necessarily result in their engagement with it or the service provider. Indeed, customer engagement with AR has often been seen to fall short of service firms' expectations (Heller *et al.*, 2021). Moreover, in their study, Pantano *et al.* (2017) disregard the potential effects of purchase advisory service on in-store experiences.

As outlined in Section 2.1.2, FLEs assist customers with their purchase decision by recognizing, addressing, and resolving customer needs (Homburg *et al.*, 2009). In contrast, when customers try something online, they cannot rely on this kind of personal interaction with FLEs. Consequently, technology-based services require a higher level of customer participation than in-store experiences (Heidenreich and Handrich, 2015). While substantial research exists concerning customer participation in services as such, fairness perceptions and their outcomes have not been linked to different levels of customer participation. Table 7.1 provides an overview of the scarce research on fairness perceptions with regard to customer participation. Against this background, Study D aims at answering the following **research questions**:

RQ$_D$-1 Do AR-enabled online services achieve equal levels of perceived fairness and engagement intention as offline service encounters with frontline employees?

RQ$_D$-2 How does cross-channel price comparison affect fairness perceptions, engagement intentions, negative word-of-mouth, and silent endurance for online and offline customers?

To answer the research questions of Study D, a 2 × 2 scenario-based online experiment was conducted involving customer participation (high (virtual video try-on) versus low (branch store)) and next-day cross-channel price comparison (same versus lower price). The effective sample comprises of N = 215 persons that had been assigned to the four different scenarios randomly. Analysis of variance (ANOVA) and multivariate analysis of variance (MANOVA) are performed to assess potential between-group differences in mean values and their significance.

With its experimental research design, Study D contributes to the persistent discussion on the value of AR-enabled online services for customers and thus for firms. Theoretically, it tests whether increased levels of customer participation due to the usage of AR are reflected in fairness perceptions, engagement intention, negative word-of-mouth, and silent endurance. Practically, it demonstrates the chances and limitations of AR-enabled online services with regard to intended customer responses. Simultaneously, it emphasizes the value of FLEs guiding and helping customers make a purchase decision that best meets their needs. Thus, service managers can integrate these findings into their strategy regarding the channel(s) used to offer their services or goods as well as regarding cross-channel price differentiation.

## 7.2 Theoretical Framework

### 7.2.1 Conceptual Framework

The offerings of online retailers are considered as a technology-based service experience (Dabholkar and Bagozzi, 2002). For these technology-based services, it is essential that customers actively participate in the service provision (Heidenreich and Handrich, 2015). The following section combines research on customer participation with fairness concepts. The aim is to derive hypotheses regarding customer responses when service either requires a high or low level of customer participation. In Study D, a high level of customer participation is represented by using a markerless augmented reality (AR) application that offers web-based video try-on. Opposing, a low level of customer participation is anticipated for

**Table 7.1** Research on fairness perceptions in customer participation settings

| Study | Analysis | Theoretical Framework | Term used | Stage of integration | Outcomes considered | Key propositions regarding fairness |
|---|---|---|---|---|---|---|
| Auh et al. (2007) | Survey (N = 1,197 financial services customers and N = 100 patients) | Social exchange theory | Co-production | SD → **SP** → SR | Customer loyalty | Interactional fairness perceptions increase customer willingness to co-produce financial services, but there is no such effect for medical services. |
| Roggeveen, Tsiros, and Grewal (2012) | Four scenario-based experiments (N = 79;111;87;168 students) | Equity theory | Co-creation | SD → SP → **SR** | Customer satisfaction with recovery efforts | Co-creation during service recovery only leads customers to view the overall encounter as fairer (distributive, procedural, and interactional fairness) when customers rate co-creation positively. In contrast, co-creation can harm evaluations if it is perceived as an effort. |

(continued)

**Table 7.1** (continued)

| Study | Analysis | Theoretical Framework | Term used | Stage of integration | Outcomes considered | Key propositions regarding fairness |
|---|---|---|---|---|---|---|
| Franke, Keinz, and Klausberger (2013) | Two scenario-based experiments (N = 711 design students; N = 182 internet users) | Theory of organizatio-nal fairness | Customer integration | **SD** → SP → SR | Willingness to contribute in innovation | Expectations regarding both distributive fairness and procedural fairness impact the likelihood of submitting a design to the crowdsourcing for those who have not yet participated in crowdsourcing before. |
| Dong et al. (2015) | Conceptual paper | Process-output framework | Customer participation | SD → **SP** → SR | Service satisfaction and efficiency | When customers perceive greater fairness from a structured participation process, they are more motivated to participate. |

(continued)

**Table 7.1** (continued)

| Study | Analysis | Theoretical Framework | Term used | Stage of integration | Outcomes considered | Key propositions regarding fairness |
|---|---|---|---|---|---|---|
| Cheung and To (2016) | Survey (N = 594 customers) | Social exchange theory | Co-creation | SD → SP → **SR** | Perceived justice of, satisfaction with service recovery | Co-creation of service recovery is positively related to customer-perceived distributive, procedural, and interactional justice of service recovery. |
| van Vaerenbergh, Hazée, and Costers (2018) | Meta-analysis of 30 samples in 21 studies (N = 7,872) | n/a | Customer participation | SD → SP → **SR** | Satisfaction with service recovery, overall satisfaction | Customers consider their participation in service recovery as a fair procedure (procedural fairness) and as a sign of fair interpersonal treatment (interactional fairness), and fair redress (distributive fairness). |

(continued)

**Table 7.1** (continued)

| Study | Analysis | Theoretical Framework | Term used | Stage of integration | Outcomes considered | Key propositions regarding fairness |
|---|---|---|---|---|---|---|
| Study D of this thesis | One scenario-based experiment (N = 215) | Fairness theory | Customer participation | SD → **SP** → SR | Customer fairness perceptions and behavioral intentions | Customers perceive AR-enhanced services that require more customer participation as less fair than personal service encounters that involve purchase advisory service. |

Note. n/a = not applicable; SD = Service development; SP = Service provision; SR = Service recovery

customers receiving purchase advisory service by a frontline employee in a branch store. Figure 7.1 depicts the conceptual framework of Study D.

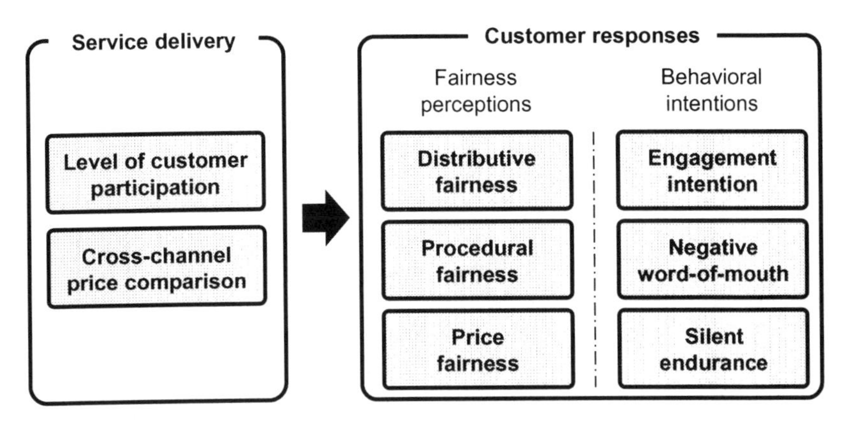


**Figure 7.1** Conceptual framework of Study D

The following section will use equity theory (see Section 3.3.2) and the concept of service fairness (see Section 3.3.3) as a theoretical framework to discuss how the perceived intensity of customer participation in service delivery might be reflected in customer responses. It is assumed that the level of customer participation varies across the different channels of service delivery. Thus, distributive fairness, procedural fairness, price fairness, and engagement intention are expected to vary as well. The latter four are also expected to be affected by cross-channel price comparisons. When customers purchase a product and then find out that they would have paid less using a different channel for service delivery, this might result in more unfavorable fairness perceptions and weaker engagement intentions. Moreover, cross-channel price comparison is likely to affect negative word-of-mouth or silent endurance.

### 7.2.2 Hypotheses on Customer Fairness Perceptions

***Distributive fairness***

As outlined in Section 2.1.3, there are three different levels of customer participation, depending on which and how many resources customers contribute to a service (Bitner *et al.*, 1997). Besides monetary resources such as the price paid for a purchased product, non-monetary resources have to be considered in the context of customer participation (Haumann *et al.*, 2015). For customers, using a technology-based service to purchase a product online is generally associated with "a minimum of effort" (Perea y Monsuwé, Dellaert, and de Ruyter, 2004, p. 108). Indeed, online purchasing can save time and effort. After all, it enables customers to complete transactions in their preferred environment and at any time they want (Perea y Monsuwé *et al.*, 2004). Mobile devices such as smartphones further facilitate customers' engagement in technology-based services (Heidenreich and Handrich, 2015).

However, due to the concomitant home delivery, there is a delay between purchase and value derivation that incurs costs of waiting for customers (Lieber and Syverson, 2012). Moreover, online purchasing contexts may require a higher cognitive effort from customers than offline ones (Mosteller, Donthu, and Eroglu, 2014). This is because online environments offer more choices to customers (Dou and Ghose, 2006). The perceived time, effort, and complexity of comparing such choices are subsumed as 'costs of thinking' (Shugan, 1980). These non-monetary costs incur because customers strive to reduce perceived risk and uncertainty of purchase decisions by gathering and processing available information (Wang, 2017). Besides the mere quantity of choices in online purchasing contexts, it is particularly difficult to evaluate the alternative products that customers would normally like to touch, smell, or try on before purchase (Pantano *et al.*, 2017).

Some online retailers try to compensate for the lack of possibilities to try on products with markerless AR features (Pantano *et al.*, 2017). Yet, markerless AR additionally increases the level of customer participation because customers need to display their face (for eyewear and cosmetics), feet (for footwear), or private rooms (for furniture or decoration) to the camera. First, this increases the visual attention effort for users (Mosteller *et al.*, 2014). Second, a general understanding of how to use AR features properly is fundamental (Bonetti *et al.*, 2018). Third, and perhaps most importantly, customers need to provide sensitive data when using markerless AR (Poushneh, 2018). Data privacy and data security issues are among the major factors that online customers are concerned with (Huseynov and Yıldırım, 2016). Therefore, an additional cognitive effort is needed to cope with these concerns.

Taken together, using markerless AR for online purchasing represents a high level of customer participation in which customers actively co-create a service (Heidenreich *et al.*, 2015). Hence, customers' perceived input (i.e., cognitive effort, costs of waiting, provision of sensitive data) is assumed to be higher than for branch store visits. At the same time, the physical outcome received (purchased product at a certain price) remains equal across different distribution channels (Vogel and Paul, 2015). The overall outcome of AR-enabled online purchasing might even be perceived as lower than in branch stores. This is because online customers receive computer-generated purchase recommendations instead of personal purchase advisory service by a frontline employee.

The perceived (in)equity of the allocation of outcomes in relation to the respective inputs is reflected in customer evaluations of distributive fairness (Franke *et al.*, 2013). According to equity theory (see Section 3.3.2), individuals weigh the ratio of their inputs as compared to their outcomes to the perceived ratio of a comparable reference person, group, or institution (Adams, 1963). While customer inputs are higher for AR-enabled online purchases, the input of the service provider in terms of costs and effort is perceived as being lower for online retail than for services delivered in physical branch stores (Lieber and Syverson, 2012). Accordingly, it is hypothesized:

> $H_1$: *Customers' distributive fairness evaluations are lower after an AR-enabled online purchase than after a frontline employee-assisted branch store purchase when a cross-channel price comparison reveals the same price for the same product.*

The same rationale applies to situations in which customers receive information about cross-channel price differentiation to their disadvantage. This is because individuals firstly compare their ratio of input and outcome against that of the exchange partner. Secondly, they might as well use a reference person or group not directly involved in the exchange (Adams, 1963). When customers find out that the same outcome would have required less monetary input (i.e., lower price) using a different distribution channel, they perceive their input as too high compared to other customers (Vogel and Paul, 2015). This inequity in distributive fairness is assumed to be particularly high for customers using AR-enabled online service since they additionally invest higher non-monetary input than customers in branch stores. Accordingly, it is hypothesized:

> $H_2$: *Customers' distributive fairness evaluations are lower after an AR-enabled online purchase than after a frontline employee-assisted branch store purchase when a cross-channel price comparison reveals a lower price in the alternative channel.*

***Procedural fairness***

Besides distributive fairness, overall fairness perceptions are determined by the degree of procedural fairness during service delivery. Based on the judgment of whether the processes applied are consistent with general norms and all exchange partners' interests, customers form evaluations about procedural fairness (Ferguson *et al.*, 2014). These evaluations are based on procedural aspects like service efficiency, the time needed, or the degree of service personalization (Han *et al.*, 2019). Again, customers using an online service face comparatively high information-seeking costs. Regarding AR-enabled video try-on features, they need to contribute considerable procedural knowledge to complete the transaction (Wu *et al.*, 2014). Thereby, perceived service efficiency may decrease compared to customers that receive purchase advisory service in a branch store.

Moreover, the time needed to complete a service transaction might be perceived differently in online and offline environments. Judgments of how slow time seems to pass in a particular situation are considered to be shaped by feelings of boredom or frustration (Jones, 2019). In contrast, positive emotions such as enjoying an experience make an individual feel that time passes faster (Gable and Poole, 2012). When interacting with customers, frontline employees can arouse positive emotions like joy or delight through exceptional service delivery or emotional contagion (Liu, Chi, and Gremler, 2019). Additionally, time spent interacting with someone can be assumed to be more versatile and thus passing by faster than time spent in front of a screen during an online service.

The third procedural aspect, personalization, is an important component of service quality both for personal service encounters and services delivered through a website (Zeithaml, Parasuraman, and Malhotra, 2002). For online services, interpersonal interactions are replaced by information exchanges, enabling a system to personalize product recommendations based on the customer's preferences (Glushko and Nomorosa, 2013). However, highly personalized online offerings arise the awareness that personal data is processed and collected while many customers refuse to be profiled online (Awad and Krishnan, 2006).

In contrast, preferences that the customer indicates while personally interacting with a frontline employee are neither collected nor are purchases assigned to personal data unless the customer is a loyalty program member (Bruneau, Swaen, and Zidda, 2018). Moreover, service encounters in branch stores can be personalized even without the provision of personal data when personalization is based on the customer type (Glushko and Nomorosa, 2013). Especially for fashion, make-up, or eyewear, frontline employees can recommend products based on their expertise on what matches the customer type best (Baron, Harris, and Davies, 1996). Thus, purchase advisory service is typically perceived as offering better personal advice than online services (Verhoef, Neslin, and Vroomen, 2007). This is particularly the case for service encounters without preexisting relationships (i.e., without an existing database of personal preferences and purchase history).

Summarizing, service efficiency, invested time, and personalization might be evaluated as less favorable for an AR-enabled online purchase than for purchase advisory service in branch stores. These procedural aspects are weighed against the service outcome and the price paid. Accordingly, it is hypothesized:

*$H_3$: Customers' procedural fairness evaluations are lower after an AR-enabled online purchase than after a frontline employee-assisted branch store purchase when a cross-channel price comparison reveals the same price for the same product.*

*$H_4$: Customers' procedural fairness evaluations are lower after an AR-enabled online purchase than after a frontline employee-assisted branch store purchase when a cross-channel price comparison reveals a lower price in the alternative channel.*

***Price fairness***

One further aspect of procedural fairness from a customer's perspective is the evaluation of the procedures a service provider applies to set a price (Bolton *et al.*, 2003). Likewise, the effective price paid for a product or service is an important monetary input when evaluating distributive fairness (Chiu *et al.*, 2009). Accordingly, perceptions of distributive and procedural fairness represent the basis for price fairness evaluations (Ferguson et al., 2014). The latter relationship is illustrated in Figure 3.11. Based on comparisons with a particular reference point, customers evaluate whether the price offered to them is acceptable, reasonable, and just (Xia et al., 2004). The price offered in the service provider's alternative distribution channel can be such a reference point.

As the vast majority of retailers pursue a multichannel strategy and offer their goods in physical stores as well as online (Zhang, J. *et al.*, 2010), it is relevant how customers react to cross-channel price comparisons between offline and online environments (Homburg, Lauer, and Vomberg, 2019). Given that AR-enabled online services require a higher level of customer participation, online customers have to actively perform service production tasks to benefit from this kind of online service (van Birgelen *et al.*, 2012). At the same time, customers anticipate that online retailers save costs for store rent and on-site staff when they offer their products and services online (Rodrigue, 2020). Indeed, given the example of a high-end fashion item, Rodrigue (2020) states that the lean cost structure of online retail enables profit margins of around 30 percent that approximately double that of branch stores item (see Appendix D.I in the Electronic Supplementary Material for an exemplary comparison).

Because of the different cost structures, firms theoretically need to charge higher offline prices to maintain their reference profit (Homburg *et al.*, 2019). Consequently, online retailers have a greater leeway to offer discounts or lower prices, leveraging a competitive advantage toward branch stores (Rodrigue, 2020). Following the dual entitlement principle, consumers find it fair when firms price their products or services asymmetrically when offline costs exceed online costs (Chen *et al.*, 2018). Reversely, customers often expect firms to consistently pass on cost advantages of online channels to them in the form of reduced prices (Bertrandie and Zielke, 2019). Thus, customers are likely to expect lower online than offline prices (Brynjolfsson and Smith, 2000). Accordingly, it is hypothesized:

> *$H_5$: Customers' price fairness evaluations are lower after an AR-enabled online purchase than after a frontline employee-assisted branch store purchase when a cross-channel price comparison reveals the same price for the same product.*

The hypothesized discrepancy in price fairness evaluations is as well expected to occur if prices differ across channels. Given the high transparency of online prices, deviations from uniform prices across channels are likely to arise unfairness perceptions (Li, Gordon, and Netzer, 2018). When transparency about cross-channel price differences is only generated after purchase, customers engage in 'counterfactual reasoning' (McColl-Kennedy and Sparks, 2003). Hence, they are made aware that they could have saved money when using the alternative distribution channel. Concomitant, a higher price paid compared to other customers is expected to trigger negative price fairness perceptions (Haws and Bearden, 2006). However, fairness theory suggests that offerings accompanying branch store visits (e.g., purchase advisory service) increase customers' willingness to pay higher offline prices (Homburg *et al.*, 2019). Accordingly, it is hypothesized:

> $H_6$: *Customers' price fairness evaluations are lower after an AR-enabled online purchase than after a frontline employee-assisted branch store purchase when a cross-channel price comparison reveals a lower price in the alternative channel.*

### 7.2.3 Hypotheses on Customer Behavioral Intentions

***Engagement intention***

Augmented reality features enable customers to virtually try on or try out various goods before purchase and thereby aim at facilitating the decision-making process (Pantano *et al.*, 2017). Yet, this level of customer participation in service provision requires customers to actively perform tasks that require monetary or non-monetary resources (van Birgelen *et al.*, 2012). Accordingly, customers will only participate in co-creating technology-based services if the potential benefits outweigh their required contribution (Heidenreich and Handrich, 2015).

In this thesis, customer co-creation is conceptualized as a particularly high level of customer participation that is iteratively connected to **customer engagement** (see Figure 2.5 in Section 2.1.3). On the one hand, customer engagement behaviors affect the co-creation process by virtue of customers' resource contribution (Jaakkola and Alexander, 2014). On the other hand, customer engagement can be seen as a psychological state resulting from co-created customer experiences (Brodie *et al.*, 2011).

Customer engagement reflects an individual's willingness to interact with a firm beyond purchase and to engage with their network to engender positive effects for the service provider (Groeger, Moroko, and Hollebeek, 2016). The aforementioned willingness to interact with a firm beyond purchase is reflected in **loyalty intentions** toward a service provider (Bowden, 2009). Loyalty occurs when favorable customer attitudes toward a brand or service provider are reflected in repeat purchasing behavior (Keller, 1993). The service-profit chain proposes that a service provider's financial performance can be improved through customer loyalty (Homburg *et al.*, 2009). The same rational applies to loyalty toward online service providers (Anderson and Srinivasan, 2003).

However, the focus on generated revenue through repeat purchase transactions limits the concept of loyalty to a rather narrow perspective (Pansari and Kumar, 2018). Besides loyalty as a direct effect, the concept of customer engagement comprises aspects that indirectly effect a service provider, namely **referral, influence, and feedback behaviors** of customers (Pansari and Kumar, 2017). These customer engagement behaviors or behavioral intentions go beyond transactions and reflect customers' motivational drivers (van Doorn *et al.*, 2010). The motivational drivers that determine customer engagement depend on the degree to which a customer feels connected to a service provider based on the experienced intensity and quality of exchange (Vivek *et al.*, 2012).

The level of customer participation is assumed to be higher for AR-enabled online services than for branch store purchases. Nevertheless, the intensity and quality of exchange are expected to be perceived as lower for customers interacting with an AR-enabled online interface than for those receiving purchase advisory service. That is because frontline employees can engage in rapport-building behaviors that favor positive service encounter evaluations (Giebelhausen *et al.*, 2014).

Thus, it is assumed that customers experiencing an online service at the same price as branch store customers will report less engagement regarding their referral intentions or their intentions to use the service in the future. When experiences diminish the expected value of future usage, customers seek to restore equity by refusing to use this service again (Bolton and Lemon, 1999). Accordingly, it is hypothesized:

> *$H_7$: Customers' engagement intention is lower after an AR-enabled online purchase than after a frontline employee-assisted branch store purchase when a cross-channel price comparison reveals the same price for the same product.*

Consistent with the hypotheses on fairness perceptions, the discrepancy in customer engagement intentions between online and offline customers is also expected to exist when customers are confronted with cross-channel price comparisons to their disadvantage. When customers find out that other customers paid less money for the same product or service, this perceived inequity results in anger or feelings of being upset (Shehryar and Hunt, 2005). In turn, these adverse feelings are reflected in decreased loyalty intentions toward the service provider (Kumar and Mokhtar, 2017). Accordingly, it is hypothesized:

$H_8$: *Customers' engagement intention is lower after an AR-enabled online purchase than after a frontline employee-assisted branch store purchase when a cross-channel price comparison reveals a lower price in the alternative channel.*

***Negative word-of-mouth***

Whereas most research emphasizes that customer engagement creates value for firms either directly or indirectly (see Pansari and Kumar, 2017 for an overview), it is important to consider that customer engagement may bear negative consequences for firms as well. For instance, when customer interactions with a firm arouse affective states like regret or anger, customers might proactively engage in **negative word-of-mouth** (negative WOM) to express their adverse experiences or to warn others (van Doorn *et al.*, 2010).

Negative word-of-mouth is one form of customer response to a service provider but differs fundamentally from complaining (Singh and Wilkes, 1996). The latter is directed toward the causer and is driven by a customer's intention to get a problem solved or to recover a service failure (Richins, 1983). In contrast, negative WOM "involves simply telling others (e.g., friends, family, etc.) about the unsatisfactory experience with little or no attempt to remedy the situation" (Ferguson *et al.*, 2014, p. 220). Thereby, negative WOM represents an assertive form of customer response that requires little customer resources (Reinartz and Berkmann, 2018).

Negative WOM can be regarded as a "low-cost action" (Xia *et al.*, 2004, p. 8) that is thought to prevent others from being exploited. At the same time, it helps customers cope with disappointment or regret. One cause of such negative feelings can be the belief of being treated unfairly (Bougie, Pieters, and Zeelenberg, 2003). In the context of Study D, distributive and procedural fairness perceptions are expected to be lower for customers that actively participate in service delivery by contributing their resources to an AR-enabled video try-on. Accordingly, it is hypothesized:

*H*$_9$: *Customers' intention to spread negative word-of-mouth is higher after an AR-enabled online purchase than after a frontline employee-assisted branch store purchase when a cross-channel price comparison reveals the same price for the same product.*

Besides distributive and procedural fairness, customers aim at maintaining price fairness in their exchange with service providers. Ferguson *et al.* (2014) propose that customers who assess a price to be unfair may want to get even with or even punish the service provider by engaging in negative WOM. This is in line with the assumption that overall price unfairness arouses strong intentions to spread negative WOM (Xia *et al.*, 2004). When customers use an external reference price to evaluate whether a price is reasonable and just, they might be particularly sensitive when price discrimination exists (Bolton *et al.*, 2003). However, according to fairness theory, quality offerings like purchase advisory service are expected to increase customers' willingness to pay a higher price on-site (Homburg *et al.*, 2019). Concomitantly, it is assumed that price discrimination arouses less anger and disappointment and thus weaker intentions to spread negative WOM for branch store than for online customers. Accordingly, it is hypothesized:

*H*$_{10}$: *Customers' intention to spread negative word-of-mouth is higher after an AR-enabled online purchase than after a frontline employee-assisted branch store purchase when a cross-channel price comparison reveals a lower price in the alternative channel.*

***Silent endurance***

Davidow (2003) proposes that customer complaints can prevent negative word-of-mouth when service firms have policies and procedures in place that facilitate complaint handling. Yet, a "necessary condition for effective complaint management is that customers actually do voice their frustration and dissatisfaction to the firm" (Andreassen and Streukens, 2013, p. 4). Yet, the vast majority of dissatisfied customers do not complain to service firms (Chebat, Davidow, and Codjovi, 2005). The reasons why customers do not voice their complaints remain largely under-investigated (Kwok, 2019; Voorhees, 2006). Still, there is a consensus in the academic literature about Richins' (1983) proposition that different complaint responses result from separate processes. More precisely, even when different complaint responses are rooted in the same variables, they are influenced in different ways (Singh and Wilkes, 1996).

Complaint responses are most commonly differentiated as follows: Customers that are willing to complain either voice their dissatisfaction directly to the firm, to an independent third party, or engage in negative WOM (Singh and Wilkes, 1996). Customers who are not willing to complain are expected to either exit the encounter or stay while silently bearing their frustration (Chebat *et al.*, 2005). In his theory of exit, voice, and loyalty, Hirschman (1970, p. 38) remarks that dissatisfied customers may "suffer in silence, confident that things will soon get better." Beatty *et al.* (2012) entitle this type of complaint response **silent endurance**. They suggest that customers endure a situation when they feel unable to exit or to effectively voice their concerns or complaints (Beatty *et al.*, 2012).

Three factors hindering customers from effectively expressing concerns or complaints seem particularly relevant when comparing AR-enabled online services with branch store encounters: First, the perception that it is hopeless or too late to complain or that the service provider wouldn't do anything about the problem anyways hinders customers from complaining (Snellman and Vihtkari, 2003). This is especially the case for service experiences that are retrospectively evaluated as unfair based on downstream comparisons. Second, a customer does not necessarily know where, to whom, or how to complain in an online setting (Snellman and Vihtkari, 2003). Customers using AR-enabled online services usually seldom talk to or chat with an employee as part of the core service delivery. They would need to contact the customer support actively via phone, chat, or mail in case of complaints. Thus, a representative of the service provider is not automatically available—a circumstance that Voorhees (2006) determines as one explanation for noncomplaining behavior in the service industry.

Third, the time and effort needed to address a complaint may induce a customer to rather endure frustration in silence instead of investing additional resources (Voorhees, 2006). Concomitant with the lack of direct availability of a point of contact for customers using AR-enabled online services, time and effort to complain are higher than for branch store customers that directly interact with a frontline employee as part of their service experience. Even when a reason to complain occurs after the purchase, customers who were served in a branch store have a reference person or location they could turn to instead of silently enduring the situation. Accordingly, it is hypothesized:

*$H_{11}$: Customers' silent endurance is higher after an AR-enabled online purchase than after a frontline employee-assisted branch store purchase when a cross-channel price comparison reveals the same price for the same product.*

*$H_{12}$: Customers' silent endurance is higher after an AR-enabled online purchase than after a frontline employee-assisted branch store purchase when a cross-channel price comparison reveals a lower price in the alternative channel.*

## 7.3 Methodology

### 7.3.1 Data Collection and Sample

To test the hypothesized effects, a scenario-based 2 (service delivery: in-store versus virtual video try-on) × 2 (next-day price in the alternative channel: same versus 20 percent lower) between-subjects experiment setting was chosen. Given their hypothetical nature, scenario-based studies are well-suited to investigate responses to different procedures (Lind and Tyler, 1988). Available information can be manipulated across different scenarios while simultaneously controlling for potential disruptive factors. Thus, experimental scenarios are an appropriate means to investigate how individuals respond to fairness-related information (Collie *et al.*, 2002). Figure 7.2 depicts the experimental design of Study D. Moreover, Appendix D.I in the Electronic Supplementary Material contains the exact wording of the four scenarios.

In all four scenarios, participants read a brief text stating that they wanted to buy a pair of high-quality sunglasses (without a prescription) with a black frame for a maximum of 100 EUR. In the online shop scenarios (1 and 2), customers were told they used the video try-on function to virtually test which sunglasses suits them best. The screenshot in Figure 7.3 supported participants in putting themselves in the position of the customer.

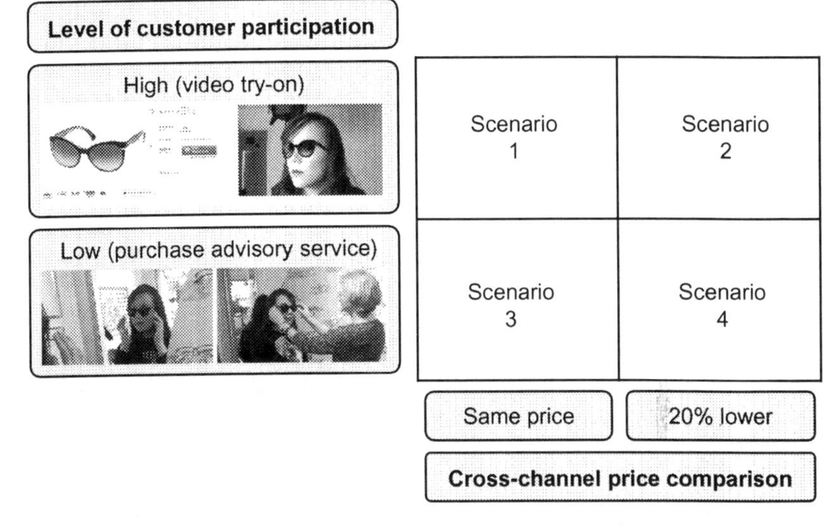


**Figure 7.2** Design of the 2×2 between-subjects experiment. (Source: Own illustration)

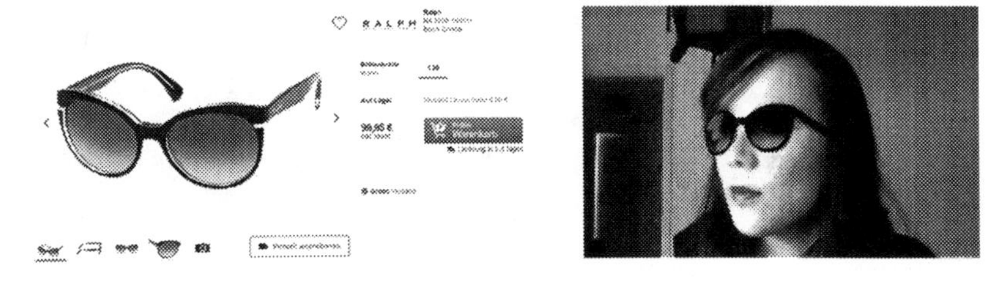

**Figure 7.3** Screenshots of the online shop scenario. (Source: Screenshots of the website 'Mister Spex'[1] taken by Master students of the University of Koblenz-Landau)

In the branch store scenarios (3 and 4), participants were told they received purchase advisory service by a frontline employee. This description was supplemented by the two photos shown in Figure 7.4. Each of the four scenarios contained the information that after 20 minutes of comparing models that match with their requirements, the participant purchased a pair of sunglasses for

[1] https://www.misterspex.de/sonnenbrillen/ralph-ra-5238-169511_f6696550.html [31.12.2019]

99,95 EUR. At the end of each scenario, participants were informed that on the next day, they would see that the exact same pair of sunglasses either costs the same (scenarios 1 and 3) or 20,00 EUR less (scenarios 2 and 4) in the alternative distribution channel of this service provider. The price difference of 20 percent was inspired by Haws and Bearden's (2006) research on dynamic pricing and customer fairness perceptions.

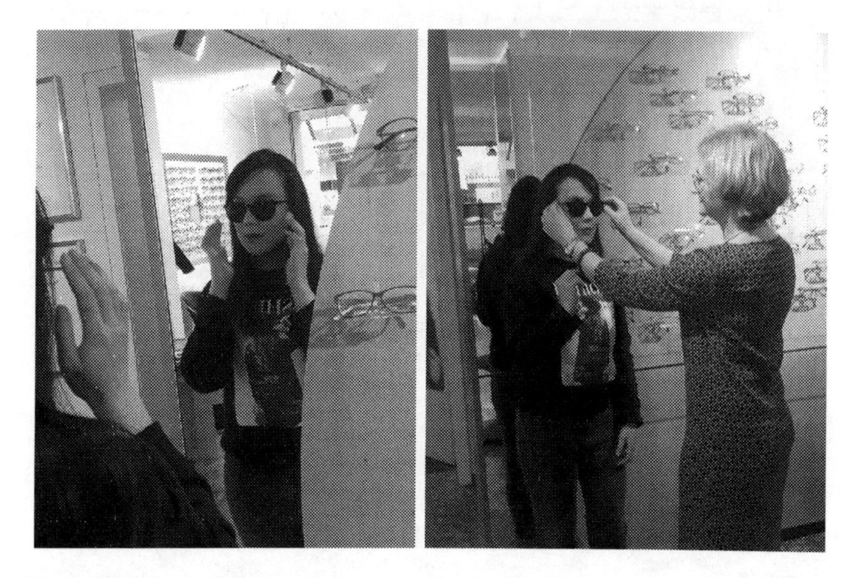

**Figure 7.4** Photos of the branch store scenario. (Source: Photos taken by Master students of the University of Koblenz-Landau)

The scenarios were embedded into an online survey. The author and five Master students distributed a call for participation via personal emails, social media, instant messaging, blog posts, and email newsletters, stating that participants are needed for an online survey about purchasing sunglasses. The call contained a hyperlink leading to an online survey that was hosted on the platform *Unipark*[2]. Upon retrieving the link, participants were assured that the gathered data would

[2] https://www.unipark.com/ [23.03.2020]

be analyzed anonymously. Then, an algorithm randomly allocated each participant to one of the four scenarios. Participants were asked to read the scenario carefully and to answer the subsequent questions.

The survey included a logo of the *University of Koblenz-Landau* to underline the integrity of the study. As an incentive, each participant had the possibility to take part in a raffle of three online shopping vouchers with a total value of 150 EUR upon completion of the survey. The email addresses needed to draw the three winners were collected on a separate platform to assure that survey data did not contain any personal data. After a period of four weeks, 246 participants had completed the survey.

Overall, 31 (12.6%) participants did not pass each of the three attention checks included in the questionnaire and were thus excluded from further analysis. This led to an effective sample of N = 215 participants. Table 7.2 summarizes the sample characteristics with regard to the size of each group, gender, age, education, occupation, and whether participants wear glasses with a prescription. The different group sizes reflect the fact that out of the 31 participants that were excluded from data analysis, eleven had priory belonged to the second group. Within the effective sample of N = 215, the mean age ranged at 34.6 years (SD = 15.4). 90 participants (41.9%) were male, 125 (58.1%) were female. Any potential effects of the partly dissimilar distribution of age groups among the four groups will be addressed in Section 7.4.

### 7.3.2 Measures

In academic literature on customer-firm interactions, various scales exist to measure the different dimensions of fairness (or justice). For instance, distributive and procedural fairness scales have been applied to customer service in online shopping (Chiu *et al.*, 2009) or service fairness in retail banking (Han *et al.*, 2019). Fairness scales have also been used to determine customer responses to complaint handling after a firm-created service failure (Crisafulli and Singh, 2016; Maxham and Netemeyer, 2002) or a service failure co-created by the customer (Wei, Ang, and Anaza, 2019). Moreover, fairness perceptions of customers that actively participate in the service recovery process have been measured (Balaji *et al.*, 2018).

**Table 7.2** Sample characteristics of Study D listed by experimental group

| | Group 1 | Group 2 | Group 3 | Group 4 |
|---|---|---|---|---|
| *Group size* | N = 56 | N = 47 | N = 53 | N = 59 |
| *Mean age [SD]* | 33.0 [14.1] | 31.7 [15.4] | 37.0 [14.9] | 36.4 [16.5] |
| *Gender* | | | | |
| Male | 44.6% | 42.6% | 41.5% | 37.3% |
| Female | 55.4% | 57.4% | 58.5% | 62.7% |
| *Education* | | | | |
| No degree (yet) | 0.0% | 0.0% | 0.0% | 1.7% |
| Middle school | 7.1% | 6.4% | 7.5% | 6.8% |
| Apprentice-ship | 12.5% | 14.9% | 13.2% | 16.9% |
| A-Level | 35.7% | 36.2% | 30.2% | 28.8% |
| University degree | 44.6% | 42.6% | 49.1% | 45.8% |
| *Occupation* | | | | |
| Student | 55.4% | 48.9% | 39.6% | 44.1% |
| Employed | 39.3% | 42.6% | 47.2% | 42.4% |
| Seeking work | 1.8% | 0.0% | 1.9% | 1.7% |
| Retired | 3.6% | 8.5% | 11.3% | 11.9% |
| *Wearer of glasses* | | | | |
| No | 37.5% | 44.7% | 39.6% | 27.1% |
| Yes, but sunglasses without prescription | 23.2% | 27.7% | 24.5% | 35.6% |
| Yes, and sunglasses with prescription as well | 33.9% | 40.4% | 35.8% | 37.3% |

However, a comprehensive literature review by the author of this thesis revealed no established scales to measure distributive and procedural fairness in the context of customer participation in the service delivery stage. More specifically, existing scales turned out to be hardly applicable to both the AR-enabled video try-on scenario (without any service employee interaction) and the branch store scenario (with purchase advisory service by a frontline employee). Thus, two scales by Franke *et al.* (2013) assessing distributive and procedural fairness perceptions of customers who participate in firm innovation were adapted for the purpose of Study D.

Within the questionnaire, participants rated their perceptions of the scenario along 7-point Likert scales, anchored at "fully disagree" and "fully agree". For distributive fairness, three items were used to weigh participants' inputs against the derived value. For procedural fairness, three items captured how participants evaluated their involvement and time needed to choose a pair of sunglasses. Three items by Ferguson *et al.* (2014) reflected price fairness perceptions. Furthermore, the online questionnaire included three items adapted from Kumar and Mokhtar (2017) to measure the following three aspects of customer engagement intentions: willingness to use the service in the future, willingness to recommend, and willingness to defend the service when others speak poorly about it. Negative word-of-mouth was assessed with three items that Beatty *et al.* (2012) had adapted from Jones *et al.* (2007). Silent endurance was captured with a three-item scale developed by Beatty *et al.* (2012).

All items of the aforementioned scales are listed in Appendix D.IV in the Electronic Supplementary Material. To validate whether participants had read the scenario carefully, the online questionnaire included three attention check questions. Participants were asked (i) how much money they had spent on the pair of sunglasses, (ii) whether the price had dropped, remained stable, or increased on the next day, and (iii) in which distribution channel they had bought the sunglasses.

The questionnaire finished off with several control variables to support the validity of the results. These were measured with a single item each to keep the questionnaire as brief as possible. Control variables included (online) shopping habits and expenditures for fashion items per month and whether participants possess glasses or sunglasses with a prescription. Moreover, the questionnaire assessed the preferred distribution channel and maximum budget for purchasing sunglasses, the distance to the next branch store of an optician, and prior experience with virtual try-on applications.

### 7.3.3 Quantitative Data Analysis

In a preliminary analysis, the reliability and validity of the measures were assessed. For each latent variable, composite reliability and item-total correlation were analyzed. Composite reliability ranged between .83 and .94. Except for the first item of silent endurance (ITC = .60), the item-total correlation ranged above .70 for all remaining items. Appendix D.IV in the Electronic Supplementary Material depicts the mean, standard deviation, item-total correlation, and standardized factor loading for each item.

For all multi-item constructs, confirmatory factor analysis was conducted using IBM SPSS 25. All loadings were significant with only the first item of silent endurance ranging below .70 (standardized estimate = .65). All other items reached standardized estimates of at least .73, proving convergent validity. To verify discriminant validity, Fornell and Larcker's (1981) criterion was applied. The analysis revealed that the correlations between any of the constructs were lower than the square root of the average variance extracted (AVE) for each construct. Table 7.3 displays the means, standard deviations, composite reliabilities, correlations, and the square root of AVE on the diagonal.

Despite the fulfillment of Fornell and Larcker's (1981) criterion, there are significant correlations between the respective fairness dimensions, intentions to use, and negative word-of-mouth (WOM). Due to the conceptual interrelatedness of the fairness dimensions, significant correlations between distributive and procedural fairness are regarded as common in empirical studies on organizational fairness (Cohen-Charash and Spector, 2001; Franke *et al.*, 2013). However, to avert any concern about these and the remaining correlations, the data were tested for multicollinearity. Collinearity "exists if there is a high multiple correlation when one of the variates is regressed on the others" (Belsley, Kuh, and Welsch, 2005, p. 86). This is referred to as multicollinearity when there are more than two variates (Craney and Surles, 2002).

Kaplan (1994) proposes five ad hoc methods to identify multicollinearity. Out of these five methods, the calculation of the variance inflation factor (VIF) is one of the widest applied measures (Salmerón, García, and García, 2018). The VIF estimates to which degree the variance of a coefficient is 'inflated' by the linear dependence with other variates (Craney and Surles, 2002). Although ten is the most commonly used threshold value associated with VIF, such high values are partly regarded as a sign of multicollinearity (O'Brien, 2007). Thus, more recent recommendations refer to a more stringent threshold value of three (Zuur, Ieno, and Elphick, 2010). To calculate the VIF, six linear regression analyses were conducted in SPSS. Each multi-item construct was treated as a dependent variable

**Table 7.3** Correlations and psychometric properties of Study D

| | (1) | (2) | (3) | (4) | (5) | (6) | (7) | (8) | (9) |
|---|---|---|---|---|---|---|---|---|---|
| (1) Procedural fairness | **.87** | | | | | | | | |
| (2) Distributive fairness | .59** | **.83** | | | | | | | |
| (3) Price fairness | .64** | .75** | **.91** | | | | | | |
| (4) Engagement intention | .62** | .57** | .53** | **.88** | | | | | |
| (5) Negative WOM | – .44** | – .51** | – .52** | – .52** | **.92** | | | | |
| (6) Silent endurance | – .27** | – .33** | – .24** | – .32** | .23** | **.79** | | | |
| (7) Age | .07 | .19** | .10 | .08 | – .15* | – .23** | n/a | | |
| (8) Gender | .00 | – .05 | – .04 | – .08 | .11 | .06 | .06 | n/a | |
| (9) Education | .06 | .00 | .08 | – .05 | – .05 | .04 | – .22** | .14* | n/a |
| Mean | 5.18 | 4.73 | 4.52 | 4.89 | 2.49 | 4.15 | 34.95 | 1.43 | 4.16 |
| Standard deviation | 1.41 | 1.57 | 1.84 | 1.61 | 1.63 | 1.71 | 15.41 | .51 | .95 |
| Composite reliability | .90 | .87 | .94 | .91 | .94 | .83 | n/a | n/a | n/a |

Notes: N = 215; $^{*}p < .05$; $^{**}p < .01$; n/a = not applicable; diagonal elements in bold indicate the square roots of the average variance extracted for constructs measured with multiple items.

and the remaining five multi-item constructs served as independent variables. The calculated values ranged between 1.13 and 2.79, indicating an acceptable level of multicollinearity.

Following the preliminary analysis, the hypotheses derived in Section 7.2 were tested. Neyman and Pearson (1933) identified two types of errors that can be made when testing hypotheses. These two types are illustrated in Table 7.4. Type I error occurs when a true null hypothesis ($H_0$) is rejected based on conclusions from statistical analysis (Field, 2013). In contrast, type II error refers to "failing to declare a statistically significant difference" (Ross and Willson, 2018, p. 21) when it should have been declared. Thus, a type II error occurs when a false null hypothesis is accepted.

**Table 7.4** Type I and Type II error in hypothesis testing. (Source: Adapted from Casella and Berger, 2002)

| | | **Conclusion from statistical analysis** | |
|---|---|---|---|
| | | Accept $H_0$ | Reject $H_0$ |
| **The real state of nature** | $H_0$ is true | Correct conclusion | **Type I error** Reject a true null hypothesis |
| | $H_0$ is false | **Type II error** Accept a false null hypothesis | Correct conclusion |

Two analyses of variance (ANOVA) were conducted with SPSS to compare the mean values for each of the experimental variables. For this purpose, the sample was first split into video try-on (N = 103) and branch store (N = 112) groups. For a second analysis, the sample was split into two groups that were either opposed to the same cross-channel price on the next day (N = 109) or a price 20 percent below (N = 106). While such comparison does not require equal group sizes, a sample size of at least 30 per group reduces the risk of a type II error (Ross and Willson, 2018).

As an extension of the ANOVA, a multivariate analysis of variance (MANOVA) was conducted to be able to compare the mean values for each of the four experimental groups. By contrast with several independent ANOVA, a MANOVA reduces the type I error that is likely to occur from multiple separate comparisons within one data set (Howell, 2013). Moreover, MANOVA considers multiple dependent and independent variables simultaneously and allows to draw conclusions on interactions between independent variables (Field, 2013).

## 7.4 Results

The results of the first ANOVA indicate that participants opposed to the video try-on scenarios report significantly lower levels of distributive fairness, procedural fairness, and price fairness than those in the branch store scenarios. The low fairness ratings are reflected in significantly lower engagement intentions of the video try-on and higher intentions to spread negative word-of-mouth. Moreover, participants experiencing the video try-on report significantly higher levels of silent endurance toward the service provider.

Despite the random allocation of participants to the different experimental groups, the age difference between the two groups in the first ANOVA is remarkable ($\Delta M = -3.63$), yet only marginally significant ($p < .10$). Furthermore, the correlation analysis (see Table 7.3) reveals that the distributive fairness dimension is the only one that correlates significantly positive with participants' age ($r = .19$; $p < .01$). Accordingly, age differences are not expected to limit the validity of the results of the group comparisons. Table 7.5 presents the results of the first ANOVA.

**Table 7.5** Means after ANOVA divided by the level of customer participation

| | Video try-on | | | Branch store | | | | |
|---|---|---|---|---|---|---|---|---|
| | M | SD | N | M | SD | N | ΔM | p |
| Distributive fairness | 4.15 | 1.56 | 103 | 5.26 | 1.39 | 112 | – 1.12 | .000 |
| Procedural fairness | 4.68 | 1.52 | 103 | 5.64 | 1.12 | 112 | – .96 | .000 |
| Price fairness | 3.98 | 1.87 | 103 | 5.02 | 1.67 | 112 | – 1.04 | .000 |
| Engagement intention | 4.05 | 1.60 | 103 | 5.67 | 1.17 | 112 | 1.61 | .000 |
| Neg. word-of-mouth | 3.07 | 1.71 | 103 | 1.95 | 1.35 | 112 | 1.12 | .000 |
| Silent endurance | 4.44 | 1.62 | 103 | 3.88 | 1.75 | 112 | .56 | .016 |
| Age | 33.1 | 14.8 | 103 | 36.7 | 15.8 | 112 | −3.63 | .084 |

Notes: M = Mean; SD = Standard Deviation; N = Subsample size.

The results of the second ANOVA show that the mean age is almost even within the two groups when divided by cross-channel price comparison. As expected, the groups opposed to a lower price in the alternative distribution channel on the next day reported significantly lower levels of procedural fairness, distributive fairness, and price fairness. Furthermore, the engagement intention is significantly lower for participants opposed to a lower price in the alternative distribution channel on the day after the purchase. Similarly, the intention to spread negative word-of-mouth is significantly higher. However, there is no significant difference regarding the mean of silent endurance. Table 7.6 summarizes these results.

**Table 7.6** Means after ANOVA divided by cross-channel price comparison

| | Same price | | | 20% lower price | | | | |
|---|---|---|---|---|---|---|---|---|
| | M | SD | N | M | SD | N | ΔM | p |
| Distributive fairness | 5.36 | 1.45 | 109 | 4.08 | 1.43 | 106 | 1.29 | .000 |
| Procedural fairness | 5.53 | 1.37 | 109 | 4.83 | 1.36 | 106 | .70 | .000 |
| Price fairness | 5.21 | 1.73 | 109 | 3.82 | 1.68 | 106 | 1.39 | .000 |
| Engagement intention | 5.28 | 1.55 | 109 | 4.50 | 1.57 | 106 | .78 | .000 |
| Neg. word-of-mouth | 2.00 | 1.49 | 109 | 2.99 | 1.62 | 106 | − .99 | .000 |
| Silent endurance | 4.04 | 1.76 | 109 | 4.26 | 1.66 | 106 | − .22 | .344 |
| Age | 35.0 | 14.7 | 109 | 34.9 | 16.2 | 106 | .03 | .989 |

Notes: M = Mean; SD = Standard Deviation; N = Subsample size.

For the subsequent MANOVA, procedural fairness, distributive fairness, price fairness, engagement intention, negative word-of-mouth, and silent endurance served as dependent variables. The level of customer participation (video try-on versus branch store) and cross-channel price comparison (same price versus 20 percent less on the day after purchase) were assumed independent variables. This analysis revealed significant main effects (level of customer participation: Wilks' Lamda $= .668$, $F_{(6,206)} = 17.039$, $p < .001$ / cross-channel price comparison: Wilks' Lamda $= .743$, $F_{(6,206)} = 11.883$, $p < .001$).

Table 7.7 contains the results of the MANOVA. The results demonstrate that customers' distributive fairness evaluations are lower after an AR-enabled online purchase than after a frontline employee-assisted branch store purchase, regardless of whether a cross-channel price comparison reveals the same price for the same product on the next day or a price 20 percent below. Thus, hypotheses $H_1$ and $H_2$ are supported. The same inference applies to procedural fairness and price fairness as perceived by the customer, supporting hypotheses $H_3$, $H_4$, $H_5$, and $H_6$.

Consistent with hypotheses $H_7$ and $H_8$, customers' engagement intentions are lower after an AR-enabled online purchase than after receiving purchase advisory service in a branch store. The mean differences are significant regardless of whether the price remained stable or decreased by 20 percent in the opposing distribution channel on the next day. In line with hypotheses $H_9$ and $H_{10}$, the means

**Table 7.7** Means and standard deviations after MANOVA

| | | | Video try-on | | | Branch store | | | Levene test | | | Hyp. supp[1] |
|---|---|---|---|---|---|---|---|---|---|---|---|---|
| | | | M | SD | N | M | SD | N | ΔM | $F_{(3,211)}$ | p | |
| Distributive fairness | $H_1$ | Same price | 4.63 | 1.42 | 56 | 6.14 | 1.02 | 53 | − 1.52 | 40.774 | .000 | Yes |
| | $H_2$ | 20% less | 3.58 | 1.54 | 47 | 4.47 | 1.20 | 59 | − .89 | 11.279 | .001 | Yes |
| Procedural fairness | $H_3$ | Same price | 5.04 | 1.41 | 56 | 6.04 | 1.12 | 53 | − 1.01 | 16.901 | .000 | Yes |
| | $H_4$ | 20% less | 4.26 | 1.54 | 47 | 5.28 | .99 | 59 | − 1.02 | 16.969 | .000 | Yes |
| Price fairness | $H_5$ | Same price | 4.72 | 1.77 | 56 | 5.72 | 1.55 | 53 | − 1.00 | 9.862 | .002 | Yes |
| | $H_6$ | 20% less | 3.11 | 1.61 | 47 | 4.39 | 1.53 | 59 | − 1.28 | 17.579 | .000 | Yes |
| Engagement intention | $H_7$ | Same price | 4.30 | 1.51 | 56 | 6.30 | .70 | 53 | − 2.00 | 76.819 | .000 | Yes |
| | $H_8$ | 20% less | 3.75 | 1.66 | 47 | 5.10 | 1.22 | 59 | − 1.34 | 23.130 | .000 | Yes |
| Negative WOM | $H_9$ | Same price | 2.61 | 1.65 | 56 | 1.36 | .98 | 53 | 1.24 | 22.576 | .000 | Yes |
| | $H_{10}$ | 20% less | 3.63 | 1.64 | 47 | 2.48 | 1.43 | 59 | 1.15 | 14.928 | .000 | Yes |
| Silent endurance | $H_{11}$ | Same price | 4.40 | 1.57 | 56 | 3.65 | 1.89 | 53 | .74 | 5.045 | .027 | Yes |
| | $H_{12}$ | 20% less | 4.48 | 1.70 | 47 | 4.08 | 1.62 | 59 | .40 | 1.558 | .215 | No |

Notes: M = Mean; SD = Standard Deviation; N = Subsample size; [1]Hypothesis supported?

of customers' intention to spread negative WOM differed significantly among participants of the video try-on and the branch store scenario. For silent endurance, there is solely a significant mean difference for those customers opposed to the same price on the next day ($\Delta M = .74$; $p < .05$). Thus, hypothesis $H_{11}$ is supported while hypothesis $H_{12}$ must be rejected. Figure 7.5 visualizes the mean comparisons of each dependent variable with six diagrams.

Despite the predominantly significant mean differences, however, the multivariate interaction effect was found only marginally significant (Wilks' Lamda = .942, $F_{(6,206)} = 2.105$, $p = .054$). Although not formally hypothesized, it could have been expected that customers benefitting from purchase advisory service in a branch store display a greater resilience toward cross-channel price differences than online customers. The results will be discussed in the following section.

## 7.5 Discussion

The results of Study D reveal that the degree of customer participation in services affects individuals' fairness perceptions and behavioral intentions. Generally, customers weigh their monetary and non-monetary inputs to a service against the received outcome. For online services including video try-on, the monetary input is primarily determined by the price paid for the purchased item including shipping costs. Non-monetary inputs encompass searching costs, the effort to operate the digital interface, waiting costs, and sensitive personal data. Therefore, customer participation is considered high for AR-enhanced online services.

However, for the increased input, online customers essentially receive the same core outcome as customers in a branch store (i.e., the purchased item). In spite of this, online customers experience a different kind of service. As Study D's results show, the weighing price and effort against the received service outcome results in lower fairness perceptions for participants in the video try-on scenarios compared to participants receiving purchase advisory service. Along with lower perceptions of distributive, procedural, and price fairness, the video try-on aroused lower engagement intentions and higher intentions to spread negative word-of-mouth.

Similar results emerge from the comparison of participants who were informed that the sunglasses cost exactly the same the following day compared to those who read that the sunglasses cost 20 percent less in the opposing distribution channel the following day. Yet, the interaction effect for distribution channel and price was found only marginally significant. Apparently, online and offline customers display similar reactions to cross-channel price differentiation. Moreover, the assessment of silent endurance revealed mixed results.

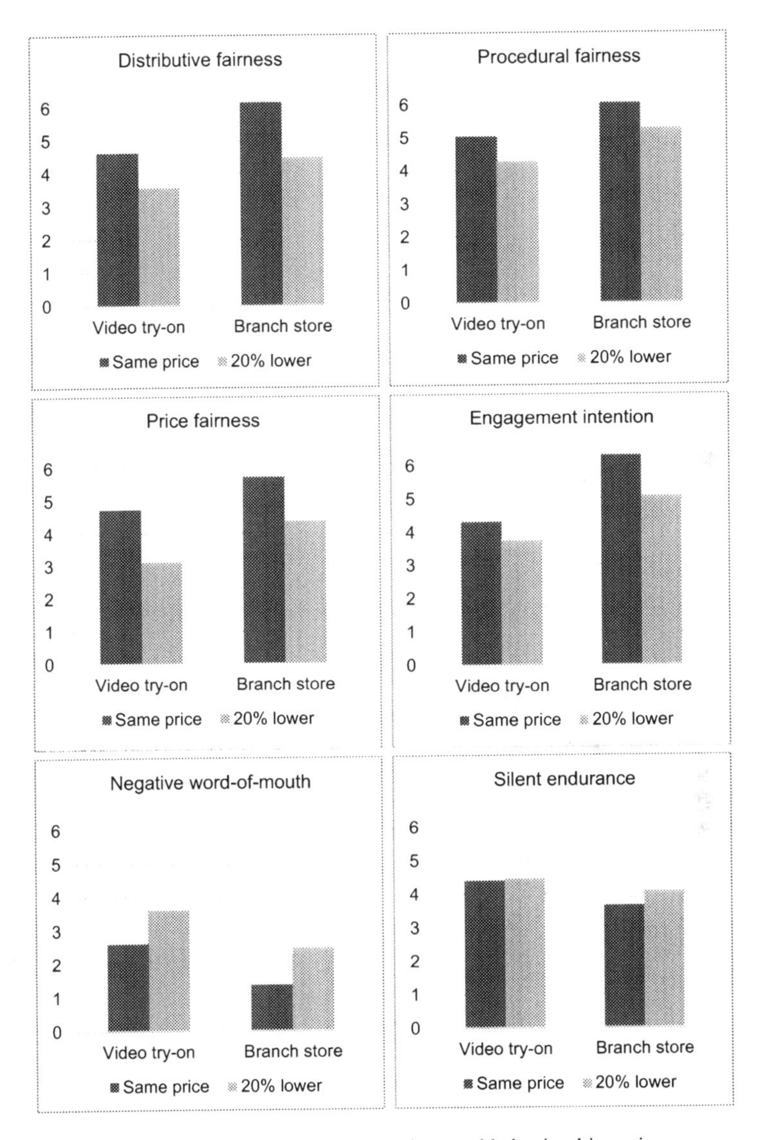


**Figure 7.5** Means of customer fairness perceptions and behavioral intentions

### 7.5.1 Implications for Theory

Augmented reality (AR) incorporates computer-generated objects into physical environments in real time (Hilken *et al.*, 2017). Research suggests that the more interactivity and control customers perceive when using AR, the more positive is their evaluation of the AR features (Huang *et al.*, 2019). However, the extent to which AR features can compensate for the lack of possibilities to touch, smell, feel, and physically try on objects that appear virtually remains unclear. Moreover, prior research has disregarded customer evaluations for online services enhanced with AR compared to service encounters in branch stores involving personal interactions between customers and frontline employees (FLEs).

Therefore, Study D represents an initial approach to address this research gap. The results demonstrate that AR-enhanced online services achieve significantly lower levels of perceived fairness than service encounters involving purchase advisory service in a branch store. Regarding distributive fairness, customers using a video try-on feature perceive the allocation of outcomes in relation to their inputs less fair than branch store customers. This supports the assumption that video try-on requires higher inputs and thus a high level of customer participation. Simultaneously, these customer inputs are apparently not compensated by higher outcomes in the form of enjoyment or fun through AR-enhanced online services. This agrees with the proposition that hedonic aspects are relatively less important than utilitarian ones when using AR in the retail context (Rese *et al.*, 2017).

Furthermore, participants in video try-on scenarios indicate lower levels of procedural fairness than those in branch store scenarios. Procedural fairness comprises aspects such as the time required and the manner in which customers are involved in a service. Indeed, AR is meant to actively involve customers and enable them to create their unique, individual service experience (Rafaeli *et al.*, 2017). In spite of this, some customers might perceive such involvement as a burden rather than as convenience. In fact, the differences in procedural fairness evaluations in Study D challenge the assumption that online services are convenient per se. Apparently, customers perceive high levels of participation in the service as less fair than being served by a frontline employee in a branch store.

In line with the dual entitlement principle, the results of Study D suggest that participants' price fairness evaluations are higher after an FLE-assisted branch store purchase compared to an AR-enabled online purchase. This implies that customers associate online services with lower costs and expect to benefit from lower prices in turn. However, when participants are confronted with a lower price in the opposing distribution channel after their purchase, ratings of price fairness decrease both for participants in the video try-on and in the branch store scenario. While theory suggests that branch store customers receiving additional services are more willing to pay higher offline prices (Homburg et al., 2019), the results of Study D demonstrate that this kind of resilience is limited.

Eventually, branch store customers become upset about higher offline prices because it would have been comparatively easy for them to check online prices before their purchase. This wide-spread phenomenon is entitled 'showrooming'. It refers to customers gathering information in a branch store but purchasing online at lower prices (Gensler, Neslin, and Verhoef, 2017). Moreover, customers that received purchase advisory service might be personally disappointed if they believe that the frontline employee advised them to purchase an item that would have cost less online. Such cognitive mechanisms referred to as 'counterfactual reasoning' represent a component of fairness theory (McColl-Kennedy and Sparks, 2003).

### 7.5.2 Implications for Practice

The results of Study D support the claims by Hilken *et al.* (2017) and Heller *et al.* (2021) that service managers need to build a conceptual understanding of how AR is appraised by customers and how it can add value. As demonstrated in this paper, AR-enhanced video try-on achieves lower customer fairness ratings than purchase advisory service in a branch store. To balance perceptions of distributive fairness, service managers should design AR-enhanced applications in a manner that involves minimum customer input. For instance, an effective video try-on does not require additional software installation, is intuitive to handle and reliable, and ensures that customers' input to the service exchange is more proportional to the outcome.

Furthermore, computer-generated recommendations that are tailored to customer preferences and assist their choices can reduce the time needed to complete an online purchase, thereby contributing to a better sense of procedural fairness. With regard to price fairness, a more progressive communication of components that drive costs in online retail could contribute to a greater appreciation of complex AR features. After all, the development and integration of such features entail considerable financial investments for firms. The same implication applies to a more progressive communication of shipping policies that frequently favor customers. Numerous online retailers do not charge shipping costs at all or when customers meet a certain minimum order value (Ma, 2017). Consequently, many customers consider free shipping as a matter of course.

To enhance the perceived price fairness of both online and branch store customers, omni-channel retailers could pursue a uniform pricing strategy. Nonetheless, retailers can still be undercut by competitors. Therefore, service firms can try to mitigate branch store customers' temptation to engage in online price comparisons. For instance, Gensler *et al.* (2017) find that waiting for purchase advisory service evokes showrooming. In contrast, FLEs who welcome customers upon entering the branch store and proactively offer support when needed contribute to positive customer experiences and can prevent customers from looking up online prices.

A further managerial implication refers to the differences in behavioral intentions between customers using video try-on and purchase advisory service. When the cross-channel price comparison reveals equal prices on the next day, customers using video try-on report higher levels of silent endurance. Silent endurance captures customers' propensity to not complain or make suggestions for improvement to the firm despite having a reason to do so. Instead of addressing the firm, customers who silently endure such a situation tend to engage in negative word-of-mouth with friends, family, an independent third party, or via review sites (Beatty *et al.*, 2012).

Thus, service managers should encourage customers to report potential discomfort directly to the service firm. One means to do so is the integration of a customer satisfaction survey directly after purchase. For instance, one single question about their satisfaction could be displayed to online customers directly upon completing their orders. Furthermore, branch stores can be equipped with small touch screens that enable customers to indicate their satisfaction by clicking on a smiling, neutral, or sad face. The mere act of participating in such a survey can increase customer engagement with the firm and positively affect customer fairness perceptions (Borle *et al.*, 2007; van Doorn *et al.*, 2010). However, service managers should also implement and promote feedback channels that customers can easily access even after the purchase. This entails easily visible contact forms or chat options on websites as well as contact details of branch stores including the option to reach out to someone via phone.

### 7.5.3 Limitations and Avenues for Further Research

Given the opportunity to manipulate information while simultaneously controlling for potential disruptive factors, scenario-based experiments are well-suited to investigate responses to different conditions (Lind and Tyler, 1988). Nonetheless, the screenshots displayed in the video try-on scenarios can hardly replace real experiences and might thus less capably engage customers than the actual use of an AR feature. Yet, the branch store scenarios were also complemented with photos. Therefore, the possibility to put oneself in the customer's position can be considered comparable between the scenarios. One avenue for further research could be to investigate differences between offline and AR-enhanced online service encounters through a laboratory experiment or even a field survey.

A second potential limitation refers to the price difference of 20 percent about which the participants in two of the four scenarios were informed. This amount was inspired by Haws and Bearden's (2006) research on dynamic pricing. While it can be considered realistic that cross-channel prices vary to this extent due to discounts or special offers, further research could specify which price threshold elicits negative fairness perceptions and behavioral intentions. As Homburg *et al.* (2019) state, the acceptance of cross-channel price differentiation varies by product category or service and its price level. Accordingly, this phenomenon deserves further investigation.

Moreover, aspects determining customer fairness perceptions regarding the use of AR-enhanced online services should be further specified. Regarding distributive fairness, the results of Study D demonstrate that participants in the video try-on scenarios weigh their input-outcome ratio as less fair than branch store customers. However, it remains unclear whether this ratio is primarily outbalanced by increased monetary and non-monetary inputs or by decreased outputs (i.e., no personal service). Empirical evidence on the underlying mechanisms would contribute to evolving the fairness theory. Moreover, service managers could adapt their firms' offerings according to such findings.

Finally, while Study D further sheds light on silent endurance, the concept remains under-investigated regarding its antecedents and consequences. The absence of customer voice and complaints is significant in service management because it hinders firms from improving their service. As firms are increasingly shifting service delivery to technology-based environments, customers are increasingly taking over tasks that were earlier performed by, or at least in the presence of, FLEs. Despite the potential to increase firm efficiency, customer participation can arouse perceptions of unfairness and lead to silent endurance when technology represents a barrier to provide direct feedback to the firm.

# 8 Summary and Outlook

## 8.1 Summary and Contributions

The implementation of digital technology is transforming the nature of service encounters tremendously (Larivière *et al.*, 2017; Singh *et al.*, 2017). Consequently, the roles and experiences of both frontline employees (FLEs) and customers are undergoing substantial changes (de Keyser *et al.*, 2019; Rust and Huang, 2012; van Doorn *et al.*, 2017). This reasoning particularly applies to service encounters that are traditionally characterized by intense personal interactions between human actors. Hence, the overall **objective** of this dissertation thesis was to further examine the impact of digital technology on FLEs and customer responses in such service encounters.

To approach this objective and locate it within academic research, this thesis first outlined the evolution of service management and the roles of FLEs and customers in service encounters. Derived from this, the technology-induced transformation of service encounters was discussed. The subsequent **theoretical part** began with illustrating theories on stress and strain in the occupational context. These theories are comparatively extensive and have seldom been applied to investigate the potential impact of technology on FLEs. Therefore, the theoretical foundations were complemented with a section on concepts exploring individual predisposition toward technology and appraisals of the latter. Finally, the customer perspective was considered by describing mechanisms of how customers form their evaluation of service encounters.

These theoretical foundations provided the basis for the **empirical part** of this thesis. Four empirical studies were conducted to address the research question of how FLEs and customers respond to digital technology in service encounters.



S. Christ-Brendemühl, *Digital Technology in Service Encounters*, Innovation, Entrepreneurship und Digitalisierung,
https://doi.org/10.1007/978-3-658-37885-1_8

Moreover, the studies aimed at providing implications for service firms and technology providers. To this end, the perspectives of FLEs, customers, managers, and technology providers were reflected in the quadripartite set of studies. Moreover, the technology considered differed regarding its intended role in service encounters. The spectrum covered by this thesis ranged from digital technology that mediates personal interactions between FLEs and customers to augmented reality-enabled online services that completely substitute personal interaction.

Within this spectrum, **Study A** focused on online reservation systems. These are meant to substitute remote interactions between FLEs and customers that would normally occur before the core service encounter. Study A involved an online survey among N = 123 FLEs in restaurants. The results have demonstrated that customer demands and processes that accompany the implementation of online reservation systems can arouse FLE role ambiguity. Considering the principles of Lazarus and Folkman's (1984) transactional theory of stress and coping, it has further been found that FLEs who feel ambiguous about their role tend to display both constructive and destructive process deviance as coping behaviors. Such deviant behaviors harm service firms, hindering them from effectively managing digital technology and achieving the intended productivity gains.

Inspired by the results of Study A, **Study B** used a qualitative approach to gain a 360-degree view on technology deployment in full-service restaurants. For this purpose, a total of 36 semi-structured interviews with FLEs, customers, restaurant managers, and technology providers was conducted. While FLEs primarily appreciated the digital devices and systems facilitating their tasks, several respondents reported role overload due to unreliable technology. Similarly, customers predominantly emphasized the advantages of technology that enhances service delivery and convenience. Yet, technology-mediated service encounters can evoke customer dissatisfaction when technology is inadequately effective. Moreover, the interviews revealed a differentiated picture regarding the significance of personal interactions. FLEs indicated that interrelating with customers is essential and motivating in their job. In contrast, some customers admitted that they would willingly prefer using self-service technologies over communicating with FLEs. However, the vast majority of customers seemed to value personal interactions as they differentiate one service from another.

Accordingly, **Study C** examined the impact of digital technology on the aforementioned interactions. Based on Hobfoll's (1989) conservation of resources (COR) theory and Bakker and Demerouti's (2007) job demand–resources (JD-R) model, hypotheses regarding the impact of technology on FLEs were developed. Furthermore, Oliver's (1980) expectancy-disconfirmation paradigm and Adams'

(1965) equity theory were used to investigate customer responses to technology-mediated service encounters. In a dyadic field survey, answers of 147 FLEs and 373 customers served by these FLEs were collected in 79 full-service restaurants. The results demonstrated that technology-induced role ambiguity and role overload can be classified as hindrance job demands that evoke FLE technostress. In contrast, managerial commitment to technology and FLE self-efficacy fostered customer orientation. While FLE customer orientation related positively to customer satisfaction and delight with the FLE, technostress mitigated both these customer responses. As opposed to customer satisfaction, customer delight with the FLE had a stronger impact on the tip level and customer intentions to engage in word-of-mouth (WOM) and electronic WOM.

While studies A, B, and C encompassed digital technology that does not completely substitute FLEs, **Study D** was dedicated to technology-based services that customers can use without interacting with FLEs at all. Hence, Study D solely addressed the customer perspective to determine how customers evaluate video try-on features based on augmented reality (AR) technology. Eventually, service firms must understand the extent to which customers value the benefits of such digital technology to make profound investment decisions. Accordingly, a 2×2 between-subject online experiment was conducted and data of N = 215 participants were analyzed. The results indicated that participants in the video try-on scenarios reported lower levels of fairness perceptions and engagement intentions than those in the branch store scenarios.

To summarize, the four empirical studies integrated the perspectives of four stakeholder groups, namely FLEs, customers, service managers, and technology providers. Different theoretical concepts were applied to investigate the effects of digital technology in service encounters. Two service industries in which technology is rapidly transforming the way service firms interact with customers were selected. However, the human touch of service encounters remains vital in the restaurant industry and stationary retail of high-involvement goods. Both quantitative and qualitative research methods were applied to investigate the relevance of personal interactions as well as the impact of technology on FLEs and customer responses. Therefore, this dissertation thesis provides important **contributions** theoretically, empirically, and practically.

**Theoretically**, two leading stress theories and their capabilities to predict technology-induced forms of stress were tested. Thereby, this thesis contributes to investigating employee-related impacts of digital technology in service encounters. Most research in service management still focuses on customer-related outcomes of digital technology. Subramony *et al.* (2017) assume that the under-exploited potential of employee-related research results from a lack of awareness that employees are the key to recognizing and resolving predominant service-related issues. Moreover, studies A, B, and C indicated that technology-induced role ambiguity, role overload, and technostress can distract FLEs from recognizing such issues and engaging in quality interactions with customers. Finally, Study D demonstrated that personal interactions achieve more favorable customer evaluations than technology-based services that supposedly offer higher convenience to customers.

**Empirically**, different approaches were used to explore the relationships among the relevant constructs and to test the developed hypotheses. Study A used a quantitative online survey to only address FLEs experienced with online reservation systems. Study B applied a qualitative approach to acquire insights into how technology providers, service managers, FLEs and customers perceive and evaluate technology in the restaurant industry. Study C was conceptualized as a quantitative field survey among FLEs in restaurants and customers served by these FLEs. This dyadic approach intended to match FLEs' sentiments and technology-induced behaviors with customer responses. Finally, Study D was based on a scenario-based online experiment to compare customer responses to personal encounters with AR-enabled online services.

**Practically**, to the author's knowledge, this is the first research examining digitization in more traditional service sectors from both the FLE and the customer perspective. The findings revealed important implications for practice concerning FLE and customer responses to digital technology. Technology meant to facilitate and augment personal interactions between FLEs and customers might impair the personal touch of service encounters, thereby reducing the satisfaction of the involved parties. Accordingly, the findings emphasize the challenge of effectively managing frontline employees and balancing technology and human touch in service encounters. Overall, this dissertation thesis contributes to service management by investigating the interrelated roles of technology, FLEs, and customers' in personnel-intensive service industries.

## 8.2 Implications for Theory and Management

### 8.2.1 Implications for Theory

Most conceptualizations of technology in service encounters differ between technologies that either augment or substitute FLEs (de Keyser *et al.*, 2019; Larivière *et al.*, 2017). However, these conceptualizations essentially neglect that digital technology meant to support FLEs might also overstrain them or distract from interacting with customers. Accordingly, the potential negative effects of technology on FLEs and their impact on customer responses and service firms' performance remain insufficiently explored in academic research. In this context, Study A used Lazarus and Folkman's (1984) transactional theory of stress and coping to investigate technology-induced role ambiguity as a component of role stress. When FLEs are torn between technological restrictions and customer requests, role ambiguity can occur. The results of Study A suggest that individual resistance to change fosters role ambiguity, while self-efficacy mitigates the same.

Furthermore, Study A provides initial empirical evidence for the influence of technology-induced role ambiguity on FLE behaviors that deviate from prescribed organizational processes. Therefore, the findings validate the existence of two distinct types of process deviance, classified as constructive and destructive. Thus, this thesis expands previous research on workplace deviance to organizational processes characterized by increasing technology penetration. As technology-induced role ambiguity seems to equally evoke constructive and destructive process deviance, both forms should henceforth be analyzed in conjunction instead of isolated. These deviant behaviors can be classified as problem-focused coping strategies, thus implying that the transactional theory of stress and coping is well suited to explaining certain employee-related outcomes of digitization.

While transactional theory conceptualizes stress as individual perception, the conservation of resources theory (COR) theory assumes external events to have a common level of impact on individuals (Hobfoll *et al.*, 2018). Along with COR theory, the deduced job demands-resources (JD-R) model by Bakker and Demerouti (2007) serves as the theoretical framework for Study B and Study C. These studies demonstrate that personal resources such as self-efficacy can play a similar role in instigating motivational processes as job resources. Furthermore, Study C highlights that the JD-R model is appropriate to explain the effects of technology-induced job demands on FLE technostress. Particularly, technology-induced role ambiguity and role overload increase self-reported technostress among FLEs.

While there is considerable empirical evidence for these antecedents of technostress (e.g., Ayyagari *et al.*, 2011), no empirical research has yet considered how FLE technostress actually affects customer responses (see Table 3.1). Study C addresses this research gap with dyadic data sets from FLEs and corresponding customers. The results demonstrate that FLE technostress is reflected in less favorable ratings of customer satisfaction and delight with the FLE. In turn, customer satisfaction and delight with the FLE relate to customer intention to engage in positive word-of-mouth (WOM). Therefore, technostress significantly influences customer responses.

Regarding customer evaluations of technology-induced service encounters, the results of Study B and particularly those of Study C provide further empirical evidence that customer delight refers to more than high customer satisfaction as proposed by the 'zone of delight' (e.g., Anderson and Mittal, 2000). While satisfaction is most commonly conceptualized as the result of a cognitive comparison between expectations and actual perceptions, delight rather seems to stem from affective components such as excitement or joy (Oliver *et al.*, 1997; Plutchik, 1980). Furthermore, high delight ratings of regular customers in Study C imply that surprise might not be a necessary prerequisite for delight. Although the feeling of surprise can contribute to delightful experiences, delight foremost has an interpersonal nature (Parasuraman *et al.*, 2021). Moments of surprise become scarce as interpersonal connections evolve. In contrast, shared experiences continue to constitute a breeding ground for delight over time.

According to the findings of Study C, customer delight—in contrast to satisfaction—translates to a higher intention to engage in positive electronic WOM and to higher tip levels. This further supports the assumption that "customer delight is something more than a nonlinear effect of satisfaction" (Finn, 2005, p. 103). In line with the equity theory, delight seems to produce higher perceived 'outcomes' for customers than satisfaction. Accordingly, delight induces stronger perceptions of inequity when customers compare their ratio of inputs and outcomes to that of a reference person or group. Therefore, delight evokes a higher motivation to return the favor of a positive experience to the FLE and/or the firm providing the service. Equity theory thus seems adequate to explain the varying effects of satisfaction and delight on customer behavior and behavioral intentions.

Moreover, Study D implies that equity theory can be applied when comparing personal service encounters with technology-based services. The results of the scenario-based experiment in Study D imply that customers perceive video try-on features to require a high level of participation. Therefore, when weighing their ratio of inputs and outcomes against that of the firm and/or that of customers in branch stores, customers using technology-based services perceive inequity. This inequity is reflected in lower ratings of distributive, procedural, and price fairness. Moreover, Study D indicates that lower fairness perceptions are accompanied by lower engagement intentions and a higher propensity to engage in negative word-of-mouth. These results are vital because prior research has only focused on examining which functionalities of augmented reality (AR) technology maximize customer evaluations. However, a comparison of AR-enabled online services with personal service encounters has not been drawn prior to this thesis.

### 8.2.2 Implications for Practice

Service firms that introduce new digital technology predominantly aim to optimize their processes and increase productivity. The empirical studies of this dissertation thesis provide further proof that a prerequisite for achieving this aim is to actively involve FLEs and win their commitment to effectively using the aforementioned technologies. Otherwise, FLEs might deviate from the redesigned processes and harm organizational effectiveness. Study A identified technology-induced role ambiguity as a trigger of constructive and destructive process deviance. Technology-induced role ambiguity refers to the perceived lack of clarity about whether and to which extent an employee should deal with technology-related issues instead of core activities (Ayyagari *et al.*, 2011; Maier *et al.*, 2015).

Demands leading to technology-induced role ambiguity frequently exceed mere technical aspects of operating digital interfaces. Through redesigned processes and more sophisticated customer expectations, digital technology considerably impacts FLEs' workflows, daily routines, and their interaction with customers. Despite the recognition that the role ambiguity of frontline employees arouses negative outcomes, insight into how this can be prevented is scarce (Selzer *et al.*, 2021). In spite of this, Selzer *et al.* (2021) find that supervisor support is a helpful resource to cope with role ambiguity. Accordingly, Study B and Study C propose that managerial commitment toward technology is vital to FLEs. Moreover, managers must clarify role expectations to reduce role ambiguity and thereby prevent FLEs from the negative impacts of this prevailing technology-induced job demand.

Fortunately, FLEs participating in Study A, Study B, and Study C reported moderate absolute levels of technology-induced role ambiguity. This is an encouraging finding for service managers who are concerned about whether the deployment of new digital technology would overburden their employees. Yet, most service firms will continue or rather intensify investments in digital technology in the future. Along with a higher penetration of technology in the workplace, technology-induced job demands will further increase. This will require managers to systematically assess and reduce technology-induced role ambiguity to mitigate constructive and destructive process deviance (Study A), and technostress (Study C).

All three aforementioned consequences of role ambiguity harm service firms. However, while destructive process deviance affects inward-looking aspects of service delivery, constructive process deviance captures FLE behaviors that break organizational rules for the benefit of customers. In contrast, FLE technostress can have a detrimental impact on customer interactions. As Study C demonstrates, technostress negatively affects both customer satisfaction and delight with the FLE. Since FLEs are crucial in driving successful service encounters (Giebelhausen *et al.*, 2014), customer satisfaction and delight with the FLE considerably determine the overall satisfaction with the service provider. For service managers, this emphasizes the importance of effectively managing job demands that might elicit technostress.

Furthermore, it might be fruitful for service managers to integrate the findings of this thesis into their human resources strategy. Service firms that already rely on an extensive range of digital technology in service encounters or plan to do so in the future can assess their applicants' attitudes toward technology in job interviews. While the results of Study A suggest that individuals who seek routines and generally react emotionally toward changes are susceptible to perceive technology-induced role ambiguity, self-efficacy helps reduce the same. Additionally, Study C shows that self-efficacious FLEs seem to better respond to customer needs and thereby deliver service in a remarkably customer-oriented manner. Service managers can contribute to strengthening their employees' self-efficacy by properly preparing them for operating frontline service technology and giving positive feedback when they have successfully handled technology-related issues.

Similarly, a general optimism toward technology mitigates the effect of role ambiguity on technostress (Study C) and increases FLE appreciation of the support of technology (Study B). When recruiting, these findings could be used to specifically address individuals that are optimistic toward technology through job advertisements that explicitly mention the service firm's digital affinity. In this manner, digital technology that facilitates work routines can be one means to attract employees who value being supported by modern devices and systems. Furthermore, to retain employees and to ensure enhanced effects of digital technology, service managers should take FLEs' potential concerns about usability features seriously. Moreover, service firms need to invest in stable network connections and reliable devices to avoid system downtime and thereby circumvent the most prevalent hassle of digital technology in service encounters.

In fact, reliable devices also represent a fundamental prerequisite for customer satisfaction with technology-mediated service encounters. As Study B demonstrates, customers presuppose that digital technology operated either by themselves or by FLEs while interacting with them works properly and quickens service delivery. When their expectations regarding the effectiveness of digital technology are not met, customers will likely evaluate such service encounters more negatively than those in which slow service could be attributed to FLEs being occupied with too many tasks at the same time. Thus, ensuring system reliability and aligning digital technology with service processes is key to supporting FLEs and satisfy customers.

To meet the diverse customer preferences regarding the ratio of technology use and personal touch in service encounters, it is advisable for service firms to pair digital devices with value-creating personal service—if technically possible and financially feasible. This will allow them to increase efficiency and consistency in service delivery while maintaining the human touch through personal interactions that complement technology (Solnet *et al.*, 2019). As demonstrated in Study B, customers of age groups below 30 partly indicated that personal interactions with FLEs in service encounters are comparatively unimportant to them. Thus, a service firm's digitization strategy depends on knowing and accurately addressing individual target groups.

While digital technology in the restaurant industry is predominantly used to complement personal service, a sizeable proportion of transactions in retail has been transferred to online shops (Verhoef *et al.*, 2021). To compensate for the lack of possibilities to touch or try on items online, retailers are attempting to enhance customers' online experience with augmented reality (AR) features. Essentially, retailers aim to address customers who are seeking the convenience of service delivery independently from opening hours and without having to go to a branch store. However, the fairness ratings of Study D imply that such convenience does not seem to compensate for the lack of purchase advisory service provided by FLEs in branch stores.

Moreover, online services such as the video try-on feature presented in Study D require a certain level of customer participation. Consequently, customers expect increased outcomes for their increased inputs. Otherwise, a comparison with customers benefitting from purchase advisory service in a branch store might evoke inequity. Service providers need to integrate these equity considerations when designing technology-based services and when pricing their services in online and offline environments. Finally, customers often take technological solutions for granted. They consider service firms to have minimal costs for technology-based service delivery and perceive it as unfair to pay the same price as customers who are personally advised in branch stores. Thus, it is recommended to reinforce the customer-directed communication about the advantages of technology-based services and the effort service firms invest in it.

## 8.3 Outlook and Conclusion

Leveraging technology to advance services is a cross-cutting priority in service management (Ostrom *et al.*, 2010). An increasing number of tasks in service encounters will be complemented or even substituted by technology in the near future (Bolton *et al.*, 2018; Marinova *et al.*, 2017). This will significantly change the roles of and expectations toward FLEs (Singh *et al.*, 2017). To fully exploit the potential enhancing effects of newly implemented digital tools, service firms need to align technology and FLE behaviors with the redesigned processes (Rafaeli *et al.*, 2017). Thus, research in service management should focus more on the impact of digital technology and its underlying processes on FLE sentiments, attitudes, and customer-facing behaviors.

According to Subramony *et al.* (2017), the underexploiting of employee-related research in service management results from a lack of awareness that employees are the key to recognizing and resolving customer issues. Issue resolution is one facet of customer orientation that—according to the dyadic data of the field survey—strengthens customer satisfaction and delight. On the other hand, customer satisfaction and delight with the FLE are mitigated by FLE technostress. Therefore, it is highly relevant for service research to examine the mechanisms that allow FLEs to effectively cope with technology and focus their attention on customer interactions.

The degree to which service encounters still depend on personal interactions today has become evident during the COVID-19 crisis that hit the global economy in early 2020. The economic lockdown imposed by numerous governments due to increasing infection rates has highly impacted people-intense service industries as they completely lost their basis of business (Zeng, Chen, and Lew, 2020). Even when businesses were allowed to gradually reopen, they needed to stick to strict health and safety regulations to ensure physical distancing (Dube, Nhamo, and Chikodzi, 2021). In light of these restrictions, service firms are expected to accelerate the adoption of technology in service encounters in the near future (Jiang and Wen, 2020).

Digital technology can help decrease or even avoid close contact between FLEs and customers. As an example, service firms can offer customers to place their order via company-owned digital devices such as kiosks or tablets instead of personally interacting with FLEs. Moreover, elicited through the COVID-19 crisis, several service firms have passed over to asking customers to use their smartphones in service encounters. For instance, by capturing a QR code upon entering a restaurant, customers can provide their contact details to the firm as required by the German government to retrace potential infection chains. Moreover, customers can use QR codes to pull up a restaurant's menu or even place orders on their own digital device (Drescher and Engelking, 2020). Thus, digital technology can facilitate the provision of services under the restrictions imposed on service firms due to the COVID-19 pandemic, particularly when it requires minor investments as in the case of using QR codes.

However, apart from the technical feasibility of executing health and safety regulations, the lockdown of innumerable service industries during the COVID-19 pandemic has demonstrated that humans are first and foremost social beings that naturally long for personal interactions (Donthu and Gustafsson, 2020). Even advanced technologies can hardly replace the intuitive and empathetic skills that enable FLEs to provide extraordinary customer service (Huang and Rust, 2018). Accordingly, the requirements of a 'low touch' economy pose numerous challenges on 'high touch' service industries. One of these challenges is finding the perfect equilibrium between efficiency, comfort, hospitableness, and safety for both customers and FLEs. Certainly, this reasoning will equally apply to service management after the COVID-19 crisis.

In many service industries, FLEs are still considered an organization's most important asset (Wirtz *et al.*, 2018). As demonstrated in the empirical studies of this thesis, most customers appreciate valuable personal interactions with FLEs. Moreover, the results show that service firms can help FLEs focus on personal interactions by thoughtfully adopting digital technology and effectively managing the continuous demands arising from technology. Service firms need a thorough understanding of these demands, the potential benefits of digital technology, and the degree to which their target customers value human interactions. This is crucial to effectively integrate the roles of FLEs, customers, and technology and to build a competitive advantage. This dissertation thesis aimed to contribute to an improved understanding of the impact of digital technology on frontline employees and customer responses in service encounters.

# Bibliography


Abramis, D.J. (1994), "Work role ambiguity, job satisfaction, and job performance: Meta-analyses and review", *Psychological Reports*, Vol. 75 No. 3, pp. 1411–1433.

Adams, S.J. (1963), "Toward an understanding of inequity", *Journal of Abnormal Psychology*, Vol. 67 No. 5, pp. 422–436.

Adams, S.J. (1965), "Inequity in social exchange", in Berkowitz, L. (Ed.), *Advances in Experimental Social Psychology*, Vol. 2, Elsevier, New York, pp. 267–299.

Ahn, J.A. and Seo, S. (2018), "Consumer responses to interactive restaurant self-service technology: The role of gadget-loving propensity", *International Journal of Contemporary Hospitality Management*, Vol. 74 No. 7, pp. 109–121.

Akingbola, K., Rogers, S.E., and Baluch, A. (2019), "Organizational change", in Akingbola, K., Baluch, A.M. and Rogers, S.E. (Eds.), *Change management in nonprofit organizations: Theory and practice*, Springer International Publishing, Cham, pp. 1–35.

Albrecht, C.-M., Hattula, S., Bornemann, T., and Hoyer, W. D. (2016), "Customer response to interactional service experience", *Journal of Service Management*, Vol. 27 No. 5, pp. 704–729.

Albrecht, K. (1988), *At America's service: How corporations can revolutionize the way they treat their customers*, Dow Jones-Irwin, Homewood.

Anderson, E.W. (1998), "Customer satisfaction and word of mouth", *Journal of Service Research*, Vol. 1 No. 1, pp. 5–17.

Anderson, E.W. and Mittal, V. (2000), "Strengthening the satisfaction-profit chain", *Journal of Service Research*, Vol. 3 No. 2, pp. 107–120.

Anderson, J.C. and Gerbing, D.W. (1988), "Structural equation modeling in practice: A review and recommended two-step approach", *Psychological Bulletin*, Vol. 3 No. 103, pp. 411–423.

Anderson, R.E. (1973), "Consumer dissatisfaction: The effect of disconfirmed expectancy on perceived product performance", *Journal of Marketing Research*, Vol. 10 No. 1, pp. 38–44.

Anderson, R.E. and Srinivasan, S.S. (2003), "E-satisfaction and e-loyalty: A contingency framework", *Psychology and Marketing*, Vol. 20 No. 2, pp. 123–138.

Andreassen, T.W. and Streukens, S. (2013), "Online complaining", *Managing Service Quality*, Vol. 23 No. 1, pp. 4–24.





S. Christ-Brendemühl, *Digital Technology in Service Encounters*, Innovation, Entrepreneurship und Digitalisierung, https://doi.org/10.1007/978-3-658-37885-1

Anitsal, I. and Schumann, D.W. (2007), "Toward a conceptualization of customer productivity: The customer's perspective on transforming customer labor into customer outcomes using technology-based self-service options", *Journal of Marketing Theory and Practice*, Vol. 15 No. 4, pp. 349–363.

Appelbaum, S.H., Degbe, M.C., MacDonald, O., and Nguyen-Quang, T.-S. (2015), "Organizational outcomes of leadership style and resistance to change (part one)", *Industrial and Commercial Training*, Vol. 47 No. 2, pp. 73–80.

Arnetz, B.B. and Wiholm, C. (1997), "Technological stress: Psychophysiological symptoms in modern offices", *Journal of Psychosomatic Research*, Vol. 43 No. 1, pp. 35–42.

Arnold, M.J., Reynolds, K.E., Ponder, N., and Lueg, J.E. (2005), "Customer delight in a retail context: Investigating delightful and terrible shopping experiences", *Journal of Business Research*, Vol. 58 No. 8, pp. 1132–1145.

Ashcroft, E., Tuomi, A., Wang, M., and Solnet, D. (2019), "Resistance to the adoption of ICTs in independent restaurants: Insights from China & the UK", *e-Review of Tourism Research*, Vol. 16 No. 2/3, pp. 105–114.

Ashforth, B.E. (2001), *Role transitions in organizational life: An identity-based perspective, LEA's organization and management series*, Lawrence Erlbaum Associates, Mahwah, N.J.

Awad, N.F. and Krishnan, M.S. (2006), "The personalization privacy paradox: An empirical evaluation of information transparency and the willingness to be profiled online for personalization", *MIS Quarterly*, Vol. 30 No. 1, pp. 13–28.

Ayyagari, R. (2007), "What and why of technostress: Technology antecedents and implications", Dissertation, Clemson University, 2007.

Ayyagari, R., Grover, V., and Purvis, R. (2011), "Technostress: Technological antecedents and implications", *MIS Quarterly*, Vol. 35 No. 4, pp. 831–858.

Azar, O.H. (2003), "The implications of tipping for economics and management", *International Journal of Social Economics*, Vol. 30 No. 10, pp. 1084–1094.

Azuma, R., Baillot, Y., Behringer, R., Feiner, S., Julier, S., and MacIntyre, B. (2001), "Recent advances in augmented reality", *IEEE Computer Graphics and Applications*, Vol. 21 No. 6, pp. 34–47.

Babakus, E., Yavas, U., and Karatepe, O.M. (2017), "Work engagement and turnover intentions", *International Journal of Contemporary Hospitality Management*, Vol. 29 No. 6, pp. 1580–1598.

Bagozzi, R.P. and Yi, Y. (1991), "Multitrait-multimethod matrices in consumer research", *Journal of Consumer Research*, Vol. 17 No. 4, pp. 426–439.

Bakker, A.B. and Costa, P.L. (2014), "Chronic job burnout and daily functioning: A theoretical analysis", *Burnout Research*, Vol. 1 No. 3, pp. 112–119.

Bakker, A.B. and Demerouti, E. (2007), "The job demands-resources model: State of the art", *Journal of Managerial Psychology*, Vol. 22 No. 3, pp. 309–328.

Bakker, A.B. and Demerouti, E. (2017), "Job demands-resources theory: Taking stock and looking forward", *Journal of Occupational Health Psychology*, Vol. 22 No. 3, pp. 273–285.

Bakker, A.B., Demerouti, E., and Euwema, M.C. (2005), "Job resources buffer the impact of job demands on burnout", *Journal of Occupational Health Psychology*, Vol. 10 No. 2, pp. 170–180.

Bakker, A.B., Demerouti, E., and Verbeke, W. (2004), "Using the job demands-resources model to predict burnout and performance", *Human Resource Management*, Vol. 43 No. 1, pp. 83–104.

Bakker, A.B., van Emmerik, H., and van Riet, P. (2008), "How job demands, resources, and burnout predict objective performance: A constructive replication", *Anxiety, Stress & Coping*, Vol. 21 No. 3, pp. 309–324.

Balaji, M.S., Jha, S., Sengupta, A.S., and Krishnan, B.C. (2018), "Are cynical customers satisfied differently? Role of negative inferred motive and customer participation in service recovery", *Journal of Business Research*, Vol. 86 No. 5, pp. 109–118.

Bandura, A. (1977), "Self-efficacy: Toward a unifying theory of behavioral change", *Psychological Review*, Vol. 84 No. 2, pp. 191–215.

Bandura, A. (1982), "Self-efficacy mechanism in human agency", *The American Psychologist*, Vol. 37 No. 2, pp. 122–147.

Barnes, D.C., Beauchamp, M.B., and Webster, C. (2010), "To delight, or not to delight? This is the question service firms must address", *Journal of Marketing Theory and Practice*, Vol. 18 No. 3, pp. 275–284.

Barnes, D.C., Collier, J.E., Howe, V., and Douglas Hoffman, K. (2016), "Multiple paths to customer delight: The impact of effort, expertise and tangibles on joy and surprise", *Journal of Services Marketing*, Vol. 30 No. 3, pp. 277–289.

Barnes, D.C., Ponder, N., and Dugar, K. (2011), "Investigating the key routes to customer delight", *Journal of Marketing Theory and Practice*, Vol. 19 No. 4, pp. 359–376.

Barnes, D.C., Ponder, N., and Hopkins, C.D. (2015), "The impact of perceived customer delight on the frontline employee", *Journal of Business Research*, Vol. 68 No. 2, pp. 433–441.

Baron, S., Harris, K., and Davies, B.J. (1996), "Oral participation in retail service delivery: A comparison of the roles of contact personnel and customers", *European Journal of Marketing*, Vol. 30 No. 9, pp. 75–90.

Bartl, C., Gouthier, M.H.J., and Lenker, M. (2013), "Delighting consumers click by click", *Journal of Service Research*, Vol. 16 No. 3, pp. 386–399.

Beatty, S.E., Ogilvie, J., Northington, W.M., Harrison, M.P., Holloway, B.B., and Wang, S. (2016), "Frontline service employee compliance with customer special requests", *Journal of Service Research*, Vol. 19 No. 2, pp. 158–173.

Beatty, S.E., Reynolds, K.E., Noble, S.M., and Harrison, M.P. (2012), "Understanding the relationships between commitment and voice: Hypotheses, empirical evidence, and directions for future research", *Journal of Service Research*, Vol. 15 No. 3, pp. 296–315.

Beck, M. and Crié, D. (2018), "I virtually try it… I want it! Virtual fitting room: A tool to increase on-line and off-line exploratory behavior, patronage and purchase intentions", *Journal of Retailing and Consumer Services*, Vol. 40 No. 1, pp. 279–286.

Beehr, T.A., Walsh, J.T., and Taber, T.D. (1976), "Relationships of stress to individually and organizationally valued states: Higher order needs as a moderator", *Journal of Applied Psychology*, Vol. 61 No. 1, pp. 41–47.

Belarmino, A.M. and Koh, Y. (2018), "How e-WOM motivations vary by hotel review website", *International Journal of Contemporary Hospitality Management*, Vol. 30 No. 8, pp. 2730–2751.

Belsley, D.A., Kuh, E., and Welsch, R.E. (2005), *Regression diagnostics: Identifying influential data and sources of collinearity, Wiley Series in Probability and Statistics*, Vol. 571, John Wiley & Sons.

Bennett, R.J. and Robinson, S.L. (2000), "Development of a measure of workplace deviance", *Journal of Applied Psychology*, Vol. 85 No. 3, pp. 349–360.

Bennett, R.J. and Robinson, S.L. (2003), "The past, present, and future of workplace deviance research", in Greenberg, J. (Ed.), *Organizational behavior: The state of the science (2nd ed)*, Lawrence Erlbaum Associates Publishers, Mahwah, NJ, US, pp. 247–281.

Bento, M., Martinez, L.M., and Martinez, L.F. (2018), "Brand engagement and search for brands on social media: Comparing generations X and Y in Portugal", *Journal of Retailing and Consumer Services*, Vol. 43 No. 4, pp. 234–241.

Berry, C.M., Carpenter, N.C., and Barratt, C.L. (2012), "Do other-reports of counterproductive work behavior provide an incremental contribution over self-reports? A meta-analytic comparison", *Journal of Applied Psychology*, Vol. 97 No. 3, pp. 613–636.

Berry, L.L. (1981), "The employee as customer", *Journal of Retail Banking*, Vol. 3 No. 1, pp. 33–40.

Berry, L.L. (1995), *On great service: A framework for action*, 3. print, Simon & Schuster, New York.

Berry, L.L. (2009), "Competing with quality service in good times and bad", *Business Horizons*, Vol. 52 No. 4, pp. 309–317.

Berry, L.L. and Parasuraman, A. (1993), "Building a new academic field—the case of services marketing", *Journal of Retailing*, Vol. 69 No. 1, pp. 13–60.

Berry, L.L., Parasuraman, A., and Zeithaml, V.A. (1994), "Improving service quality in America: Lessons learned", *Academy of Management Perspectives*, Vol. 8 No. 2, pp. 32–45.

Bertrandie, L. and Zielke, S. (2019), "The influence of multi-channel pricing strategy on price fairness and customer confusion", *The International Review of Retail, Distribution and Consumer Research*, Vol. 29 No. 5, pp. 504–517.

Bettencourt, L.A., Ostrom, A.L., Brown, S.W., and Roundtree, R.I. (2002), "Client co-production in knowledge-intensive business services", *California Management Review*, Vol. 44 No. 4, pp. 100–128.

Bhattacherjee, A. and Hikmet, N. (2007), "Physicians' resistance toward healthcare information technology: A theoretical model and empirical test", *European Journal of Information Systems*, Vol. 16 No. 6, pp. 725–737.

Bitner, M.J. (1990), "Evaluating service encounters: The effects of physical surroundings and employee responses", *Journal of Marketing*, Vol. 54 No. 2, pp. 69–82.

Bitner, M.J. (1992), "Servicescapes: The impact of physical surroundings on customers and employees", *Journal of Marketing*, Vol. 56 No. 2, pp. 57–71.

Bitner, M.J. (1995), "Building service relationships: It's all about promises", *Journal of the Academy of Marketing Science*, Vol. 23 No. 4, pp. 246–251.

Bitner, M.J. (2001), "Service and technology: Opportunities and paradoxes", *Managing Service Quality*, Vol. 11 No. 6, pp. 375–379.

Bitner, M.J., Booms, B.H., and Tetreault, M.S. (1990), "The service encounter: Diagnosing favorable and unfavorable incidents", *Journal of Marketing*, Vol. 54 No. 1, pp. 71–84.

Bitner, M.J., Brown, S.W., and Meuter, M.L. (2000), "Technology infusion in service encounters", *Journal of the Academy of Marketing Science*, Vol. 28 No. 1, pp. 138–149.

Bitner, M.J., Faranda, W.T., Hubbert, A.R., and Zeithaml, V.A. (1997), "Customer contributions and roles in service delivery", *International Journal of Service Industry Management*, Vol. 8 No. 3, pp. 193–205.

Bitner, M.J. and Hubbert, A.R. (1994), "Encounter satisfaction versus overall satisfaction versus quality", in Rust, R.T. (Ed.), *Service quality: New directions in theory and practice*, Vol. 34, SAGE Publications, Thousand Oaks, Calif., pp. 72–94.

Bitner, M.J. and Wang, H.S. (2014), "Service encounters in service marketing research", in Huang, M.-H. and Rust, R.T. (Eds.), *Handbook of service marketing research*, Edward Elgar Publishing, Cheltenham, pp. 221–243.

Black, J.M. and Ford, G.B. (1963), *Front-line management: A guide to effective supervisory action*, McGraw-Hill.

Blázquez, M. (2014), "Fashion shopping in multichannel retail: The role of technology in enhancing the customer experience", *International Journal of Electronic Commerce*, Vol. 18 No. 4, pp. 97–116.

Bliese, P.D., Edwards, J.R., and Sonnentag, S. (2017), "Stress and well-being at work: A century of empirical trends reflecting theoretical and societal influences", *The Journal of Applied Psychology*, Vol. 102 No. 3, pp. 389–402.

Bloemer, J. and de Ruyter, K. (1998), "On the relationship between store image, store satisfaction and store loyalty", *European Journal of Marketing*, Vol. 32 No. 5/6, pp. 499–513.

Blut, M., Wang, C., and Schoefer, K. (2016), "Factors influencing the acceptance of self-service technologies", *Journal of Service Research*, Vol. 19 No. 4, pp. 396–416.

Bolton, L.E., Warlop, L., and Alba, J.W. (2003), "Consumer perceptions of price (un)fairness", *Journal of Consumer Research*, Vol. 29 No. 4, pp. 474–491.

Bolton, R.N. and Lemon, K.N. (1999), "A dynamic model of customers' usage of services: Usage as an antecedent and consequence of satisfaction", *Journal of Marketing Research*, Vol. 36 No. 2, pp. 171–186.

Bolton, R.N., McColl-Kennedy, J.R., Cheung, L., Gallan, A., Orsingher, C., Witell, L., and Zaki, M. (2018), "Customer experience challenges: Bringing together digital, physical and social realms", *Journal of Service Management*, Vol. 29 No. 5, pp. 776–808.

Bonetti, F., Warnaby, G., and Quinn, L. (2018), "Augmented reality and virtual reality in physical and online retailing: A review, synthesis and research agenda", in Jung, T. and tom Dieck, C.M. (Eds.), *Augmented reality and virtual reality: Empowering human, place and business*, Springer International Publishing, Cham, pp. 119–132.

Bordia, P., Hunt, E., Paulsen, N., Tourish, D., and DiFonzo, N. (2004), "Uncertainty during organizational change: Is it all about control?", *European Journal of Work and Organizational Psychology*, Vol. 13 No. 3, pp. 345–365.

Borle, S., Dholakia, U.M., Singh, S.S., and Westbrook, R.A. (2007), "The impact of survey participation on subsequent customer behavior: An empirical investigation", *Marketing Science*, Vol. 26 No. 5, pp. 711–726.

Bott, G. and Tourish, D. (2016), "The critical incident technique reappraised: Using critical incidents to illuminate organizational practices and build theory", *Qualitative Research in Organizations and Management: An International Journal*, Vol. 11 No. 4, pp. 276–300.

Bougie, R., Pieters, R., and Zeelenberg, M. (2003), "Angry customers don't come back, they get back: The experience and behavioral implications of anger and dissatisfaction in services", *The Marketing Review*, Vol. 31 No. 4, pp. 377–393.

Bove, L.L. and Johnson, L.W. (2001), "Customer relationships with service personnel: Do we measure closeness, quality or strength?", *Journal of Business Research*, Vol. 54 No. 3, pp. 189–197.

Bowden, J.L.-H. (2009), "The process of customer engagement: A conceptual framework", *Journal of Marketing Theory and Practice*, Vol. 17 No. 1, pp. 63–74.

Bowen, D.E. (2016), "The changing role of employees in service theory and practice: An interdisciplinary view", *Human Resource Management Review*, Vol. 26 No. 1, pp. 4–13.

Bowen, D.E. and Jones, G.R. (1986), "Transaction cost analysis of service organization-customer exchange", *Academy of Management Review*, Vol. 11 No. 2, pp. 428–441.

Bowling, N.A. and Eschleman, K.J. (2010), "Employee personality as a moderator of the relationships between work stressors and counterproductive work behavior", *Journal of Occupational Health Psychology*, Vol. 15 No. 1, pp. 91–103.

Boyd, D.E. and Koles, B. (2019), "An introduction to the special issue "Virtual reality in marketing": Definition, theory and practice", *Journal of Business Research*, Vol. 100 No. 7, pp. 441–444.

Brach, S., Walsh, G., Hennig-Thurau, T., and Groth, M. (2015), "A dyadic model of customer orientation: Mediation and moderation effects", *British Journal of Management*, Vol. 26 No. 2, pp. 292–309.

Bradley, G.L., McColl-Kennedy, J.R., Sparks, B.A., Jimmieson, N.L., and Zapf, D. (2010), "Service encounter needs theory: A dyadic, psychosocial approach to understanding service encounters", in Zerbe, W.J., Härtel, C.E.J. and Ashkanasy, N.M. (Eds.), *Emotions and organizational dynamism, Research on emotion in organizations*, Vol. 6, Emerald, Bingley, UK, pp. 221–258.

Bradley, G.L., Sparks, B.A., and Weber, K. (2016), "Perceived prevalence and personal impact of negative online reviews", *Journal of Service Management*, Vol. 27 No. 4, pp. 507–533.

Brady, M.K. (2019), *Interdisciplinary service research: Lessons from an editor's chair, Let's Talk About Service Conference*, New York.

Brady, M.K. and Cronin, J.J. (2001), "Some new thoughts on conceptualizing perceived service quality: A hierarchical approach", *Journal of Marketing*, Vol. 65 No. 3, pp. 34–49.

Brady, M.K., Voorhees, C.M., and Brusco, M.J. (2012), "Service sweethearting: Its antecedents and customer consequences", *Journal of Marketing*, Vol. 76 No. 2, pp. 81–98.

Breidbach, C.F., Antons, D., and Salge, T.O. (2016), "Seamless service? On the role and impact of service orchestrators in human-centered service systems", *Journal of Service Research*, Vol. 19 No. 4, pp. 458–476.

Brito, P.Q. and Stoyanova, J. (2018), "Marker versus markerless augmented reality. Which has more impact on users?", *International Journal of Human-Computer Interaction*, Vol. 34 No. 9, pp. 819–833.

Brock, G.W. (1998), *Telecommunication policy for the information age: From monopoly to competition*, Harvard University Press.

Brod, C. (1984), *Technostress: The human cost of the computer revolution*, Addison-Wesley, Reading, Mass.

Brodie, R.J., Hollebeek, L.D., Jurić, B., and Ilić, A. (2011), "Customer engagement: Conceptual domain, fundamental propositions, and implications for research", *Journal of Service Research*, Vol. 14 No. 3, pp. 252–271.

Brown, S.P., Ganesan, S., and Challagalla, G. (2001), "Self-efficacy as a moderator of information-seeking effectiveness", *Journal of Applied Psychology*, Vol. 86 No. 5, pp. 1043–1051.

Brown, S.P. and Lam, S.K. (2008), "A meta-analysis of relationships linking employee satisfaction to customer responses", *Journal of Retailing*, Vol. 84 No. 3, pp. 243–255.

Brown, T.J., Mowen, J.C., Donavan, D.T., and Licata, J.W. (2002), "The customer orientation of service workers: Personality trait effects on self-and supervisor performance ratings", *Journal of Marketing Research*, Vol. 39 No. 1, pp. 110–119.

Bruneau, V., Swaen, V., and Zidda, P. (2018), "Are loyalty program members really engaged? Measuring customer engagement with loyalty programs", *Journal of Business Research*, Vol. 91 No. 10, pp. 144–158.

Brynjolfsson, E., Hu, Y.J., and Rahman, M.S. (2013), *Competing in the age of omnichannel retailing*, MIT Cambridge.

Brynjolfsson, E. and Smith, M.D. (2000), "Frictionless commerce? A comparison of internet and conventional retailers", *Management Science*, Vol. 46 No. 4, pp. 563–585.

Buhalis, D., Harwood, T., Bogicevic, V., Viglia, G., Beldona, S., and Hofacker, C. (2019), "Technological disruptions in services: Lessons from tourism and hospitality", *Journal of Service Management*, Vol. 30 No. 4, pp. 484–506.

Buhrmester, M., Kwang, T., and Gosling, S.D. (2011), "Amazon's Mechanical Turk: A new source of inexpensive, yet high-quality, data?", *Perspectives on Psychological Science*, Vol. 6 No. 1, pp. 3–5.

Bundesagentur für Arbeit (2019), "Die Arbeitsmarktsituation von Frauen und Männern 2018", available at: https://statistik.arbeitsagentur.de/Statischer-Content/Arbeitsmarktberichte/Personengruppen/generische-Publikationen/Frauen-Maenner-Arbeitsmarkt.pdf (accessed 13 July 2020).

Cadwallader, S., Jarvis, C.B., Bitner, M.J., and Ostrom, A.L. (2010), "Frontline employee motivation to participate in service innovation implementation", *Journal of the Academy of Marketing Science*, Vol. 38 No. 2, pp. 219–239.

Califf, C.B., Sarker, S., Sarker, S., and Fitzgerald, C. (2015), "The bright and dark sides of technostress: An empirical study of healthcare workers", in Carte, T., Heinzl, A. and Urquhart, C. (Eds.), *Proceedings of the International Conference on Information Systems (ICIS) - Exploring the Information Frontier, Fort Worth, Texas, USA, December 13–16, 2015*, Association for Information Systems.

Campbell, J.L., Quincy, C., Osserman, J., and Pedersen, O.K. (2013), "Coding in-depth semistructured interviews", *Sociological Methods and Research*, Vol. 42 No. 3, pp. 294–320.

Cardozo, R.N. (1965), "An experimental study of customer effort, expectation, and satisfaction", *Journal of Marketing Research*, Vol. 2 No. 3, pp. 244–249.

Carlborg, P., Kindström, D., and Kowalkowski, C. (2014), "The evolution of service innovation research: A critical review and synthesis", *The Service Industries Journal*, Vol. 34 No. 5, pp. 373–398.

Cartwright, S. (2018), "Workplace well-being: Responsibilities, challenges and future directions", in Sparrow, P.R. and Cooper, C.L. (Eds.), *A research agenda for human resource management, Elgar research agendas*, paperback edition, Edgar Elgar Publishing, Cheltenham, UK, Northampton, MA, USA, pp. 114–129.

Casella, G. and Berger, R.L. (2002), *Statistical inference, Duxbury advanced series*, 2. ed., Duxbury/Thomson Learning, Pacific Grove, Calif.

Cavanaugh, M.A., Boswell, W.R., Roehling, M.V., and Boudreau, J.W. (2000), "An empirical examination of self-reported work stress among U.S. managers", *Journal of Applied Psychology*, Vol. 85 No. 1, pp. 65–74.

Chan, K.W. and Wan, E.W. (2012), "How can stressed employees deliver better customer service? The underlying self-regulation depletion mechanism", *Journal of Marketing*, Vol. 76 No. 1, pp. 119–137.

Chang, W. and Taylor, S.A. (2016), "The effectiveness of customer participation in new product development: A meta-analysis", *Journal of Marketing*, Vol. 80 No. 1, pp. 47–64.

Chase, R.B. (1978), "Where does the customer fit in a service operation", *Harvard Business Review*, Vol. 56 No. 6, pp. 137–142.

Chebat, J.-C., Davidow, M., and Codjovi, I. (2005), "Silent voices. why some dissatisfied consumers fail to complain", *Journal of Service Research*, Vol. 7 No. 4, pp. 328–342.

Chebat, J.-C. and Kollias, P. (2000), "The impact of empowerment on customer contact employees' roles in service organizations", *Journal of Service Research*, Vol. 3 No. 1, pp. 66–81.

Chen, H., Bolton, L.E., Ng, S., Lee, D., and Wang, D. (2018), "Culture, relationship norms, and dual entitlement", *Journal of Consumer Research*, Vol. 45 No. 1, pp. 1–20.

Chiu, C.-M., Lin, H.-Y., Sun, S.-Y., and Hsu, M.-H. (2009), "Understanding customers' loyalty intentions towards online shopping: An integration of technology acceptance model and fairness theory", *Behaviour & Information Technology*, Vol. 28 No. 4, pp. 347–360.

Christ-Brendemühl, S. (2022), "Bridging the gap: An interview study on frontline employee responses to restaurant technology", *International Journal of Hospitality Management*, Vol. 102, p. 103183.

Christ-Brendemühl, S. and Schaarschmidt, M. (2019), "Frontline backlash: Service employees' deviance from digital processes", *Journal of Services Marketing*, Vol. 31 No. 7, pp. 936–945.

Christ-Brendemühl, S. and Schaarschmidt, M. (2020), "The impact of service employees' technostress on customer satisfaction and delight: A dyadic analysis", *Journal of Business Research*, Vol. 117, pp. 378–388.

Christ-Brendemühl, S. and Schaarschmidt, M. (2022), "Customer fairness perceptions in augmented reality-based online services", *Journal of Service Management*, Vol. 33 No. 1, pp. 9–32.

Cohen-Charash, Y. and Spector, P.E. (2001), "The role of justice in organizations: A meta-analysis", *Organizational Behavior and Human Decision Processes*, Vol. 86 No. 2, pp. 278–321.

Colby, C.L. and Parasuraman, A. (2001), *Techno-ready marketing: How and why customers adopt technology*, Simon and Schuster.

Collie, T., Bradley, G., and Sparks, B.A. (2002), "Fair process revisited: Differential effects of interactional and procedural justice in the presence of social comparison information", *Journal of Experimental Social Psychology*, Vol. 38 No. 6, pp. 545–555.

Collier, J.E., Barnes, D.C., Abney, A.K., and Pelletier, M.J. (2018), "Idiosyncratic service experiences: When customers desire the extraordinary in a service encounter", *Journal of Business Research*, Vol. 84 No. 3, pp. 150–161.

Conlin, M., Lynn, M., and O'Donoghue, T. (2003), "The norm of restaurant tipping", *Journal of Economic Behavior & Organization*, Vol. 52 No. 3, pp. 297–321.

Conner, D.R. (1993), *Managing at the speed of change: How resilient managers succeed and prosper where others fail*, Villard Books, New York, NY.

Cook, L.S., Bowen, D.E., Chase, R.B., Dasu, S., Stewart, D.M., and Tansik, D.A. (2002), "Human issues in service design", *Journal of Operations Management*, Vol. 20 No. 2, pp. 159–174.

Coombs, R. and Miles, I. (2000), "Innovation, measurement and services: The new problematique", in Metcalfe, J.S. and Miles, I. (Eds.), *Innovation systems in the service economy: Measurement and case study analysis, Economics of Science, Technology and Innovation*, Vol. 18, Springer, Boston, MA, pp. 85–103.

Cooper, C.L. and Dewe, P. (2005), *Stress: A brief history, Blackwell brief histories of psychology*, Vol. 1, 1. ed., Blackwell Pub, Oxford, U.K.

Corbin, J.M. and Strauss, A.L. (2015), *Basics of qualitative research: Techniques and procedures for developing grounded theory*, Fourth edition, SAGE Publications, Los Angeles.

Cowles, D. and Crosby, L.A. (1990), "Consumer acceptance of interactive media in service marketing encounters", *The Service Industries Journal*, Vol. 10 No. 3, pp. 521–540.

Cox, T. and Ferguson, E. (1991), "Individual differences, stress and coping", in Cooper, C.L. and Payne, R. (Eds.), *Personality and stress: Individual differences in the stress process, Wiley series on studies in occupational stress*, John Wiley & Sons, Oxford, England, pp. 7–30.

Craney, T.A. and Surles, J.G. (2002), "Model-dependent variance inflation factor cutoff values", *Quality Engineering*, Vol. 14 No. 3, pp. 391–403.

Creamer, D. (2018), "2018 restaurant technology study. insight enabled innovation", available at: https://hospitalitytech.com/2018-restaurant-technology-study-insight-enabled-innovation (accessed 17 May 2018).

Creswell, J.W. and Poth, C.N. (2017), *Qualitative inquiry and research design: Choosing among five approaches*, SAGE Publications, Los Angeles.

Crisafulli, B. and Singh, J. (2016), "Service guarantee as a recovery strategy", *Journal of Service Management*, Vol. 27 No. 2, pp. 117–143.

Cronin, J.J., Brady, M.K., and Hult, T.M. (2000), "Assessing the effects of quality, value, and customer satisfaction on consumer behavioral intentions in service environments", *Journal of Retailing*, Vol. 76 No. 2, pp. 193–218.

Cropanzano, R., Byrne, Z.S., Bobocel, D., and Rupp, D.E. (2001), "Moral virtues, fairness heuristics, social entities, and other denizens of organizational justice", *Journal of Vocational Behavior*, Vol. 58 No. 2, pp. 164–209.

Cullen, M.J. and Sackett, P.R. (2003), "Personality and counterproductive behavior", in Barrick, M.R. and Ryan, A.M. (Eds.), *Personality and work: Reconsidering the role of personality in organizations, The organizational frontiers series*, 1. ed., Jossey-Bass, San Francisco, Calif., pp. 150–182.

Czepiel, J.A., Solomon, M.R., and Surprenant, C.F. (Eds.) (1985), *The service encounter: Managing employee customer interaction in service businesses, The advances in retailing series,* 2. print, Lexington Books, Lexington, Mass.

Dabholkar, P.A. (1996), “Consumer evaluations of new technology-based self-service options: An investigation of alternative models of service quality”, *International Journal of Research in Marketing*, Vol. 13 No. 1, pp. 29–51.

Dabholkar, P.A. and Bagozzi, R.P. (2002), “An attitudinal model of technology-based self-service: Moderating effects of consumer traits and situational factors”, *Journal of the Academy of Marketing Science*, Vol. 30 No. 3, pp. 184–201.

Dacko, S.G. (2017), “Enabling smart retail settings via mobile augmented reality shopping apps”, *Technological Forecasting and Social Change*, Vol. 124 No. 11, pp. 243–256.

Danna, K. (1999), “Health and well-being in the workplace: A review and synthesis of the literature”, *Journal of Management*, Vol. 25 No. 3, pp. 357–384.

Darling, J.R. and Taylor, R.E. (1989), “A model for reducing internal resistance to change in a firm's international marketing strategy”, *European Journal of Marketing*, Vol. 23 No. 7, pp. 34–41.

Davidow, M. (2003), “Organizational responses to customer complaints: What works and what doesn't”, *Journal of Service Research*, Vol. 5 No. 3, pp. 225–250.

Davis, F.D. (1986), “Technology acceptance model for empirically testing new end-user information systems: Theory and results”, Disseration, MIT Sloan School of Management, Cambridge, MA, 1986.

Davis, F.D. (1989), “Perceived usefulness, perceived ease of use, and user acceptance of information technology”, *MIS Quarterly*, Vol. 13 No. 3, p. 319.

Dawes, R.M., Singer, D., and Lemons, F. (1972), “An experimental analysis of the contrast effect and its implications for intergroup communication and the indirect assessment of attitude”, *Journal of Personality and Social Psychology*, Vol. 21 No. 3, pp. 281–295.

de Cuyper, N., Mäkikangas, A., Kinnunen, U., Mauno, S., and de Witte, H. (2012), “Cross-lagged associations between perceived external employability, job insecurity, and exhaustion: Testing gain and loss spirals according to the conservation of resources theory”, *Journal of Organizational Behavior*, Vol. 33 No. 6, pp. 770–788.

de Keyser, A., Köcher, S., Alkire, L., Verbeeck, C., and Kandampully, J. (2019), “Frontline service technology infusion: Conceptual archetypes and future research directions”, *Journal of Service Management*, Vol. 30 No. 1, pp. 156–183.

DEHOGA (2020a), “DEHOGA-Zahlenspiegel IV/2019”, available at: https://www.dehoga-bundesverband.de/fileadmin/Startseite/04_Zahlen___Fakten/07_Zahlenspiegel___Branchenberichte/Zahlenspiegel/Zahlenspiegel_4._Quartal_2019.pdf (accessed 2 March 2020).

DEHOGA (2020b), “Umsätze und Umsatzenwicklung im Gaststättengewerbe”, available at: https://www.dehoga-bundesverband.de/zahlen-fakten/umsatz/gaststaettengewerbe/ (accessed 2 March 2020).

Delcourt, C., Gremler, D.D., van Riel, A.C.R., and van Birgelen, M.J.H. (2016), “Employee emotional competence”, *Journal of Service Research*, Vol. 19 No. 1, pp. 72–87.

Dellarocas, C. (2003), “The digitization of word of mouth: Promise and challenges of online feedback mechanisms”, *Management Science*, Vol. 49 No. 10, pp. 1407–1424.

Deloitte Insights (2018), "The services powerhouse. increasingly vital to world economic growth", available at: https://www2.deloitte.com/us/en/insights/economy/issues-by-the-numbers/trade-in-services-economy-growth.html (accessed 4 June 2020).
DeLongis, A. and Holtzman, S. (2005), "Coping in context: The role of stress, social support, and personality in coping", *Journal of Personality*, Vol. 73 No. 6, pp. 1633–1656.
Demen-Meier, C., Guigou, C., Vetterli, I., and Millar, I. (2018), "Independent restaurateurs and technology, what is the future? technology use and implementation barriers among European and Japanese independent restaurateurs", available at: https://innovationchair.com/wp-content/uploads/2017/06/METRO-Chair_Booklet_2017_EN.pdf (accessed 28 March 2019).
Demerouti, E., Bakker, A.B., Nachreiner, F., and Schaufeli, W.B. (2001), "The job demands-resources model of burnout", *Journal of Applied Psychology*, Vol. 86 No. 3, p. 499.
den Hertog, P. (2000), "Knowledge-intensive business services as co-producers of innovation", *International Journal of Innovation Management*, Vol. 4 No. 4, pp. 491–528.
den Hertog, P., van der Aa, W., and de Jong, M.W. (2010), "Capabilities for managing service innovation: Towards a conceptual framework", *Journal of Service Management*, Vol. 21 No. 4, pp. 490–514.
Devlin, J.F., Roy, S.K., and Sekhon, H. (2014), "Perceptions of fair treatment in financial services", *European Journal of Marketing*, Vol. 48 No. 7/8, pp. 1315–1332.
Dewe, P.J. (1989), "Examining the nature of work stress: Individual evaluations of stressful experiences and coping", *Human Relations*, Vol. 42 No. 11, pp. 993–1013.
Dewe, P.J., Cox, T., and Ferguson, E. (1993), "Individual strategies for coping with stress at work: A review", *Work & Stress*, Vol. 7 No. 1, pp. 5–15.
Donavan, D.T., Brown, T.J., and Mowen, J.C. (2004), "Internal benefits of service-worker customer orientation: Job satisfaction, commitment, and organizational citizenship behaviors", *Journal of Marketing*, Vol. 68 No. 1, pp. 128–146.
Dong, B. and Sivakumar, K. (2017), "Customer participation in services: Domain, scope, and boundaries", *Journal of the Academy of Marketing Science*, Vol. 45 No. 6, pp. 944–965.
Dong, B., Sivakumar, K., Evans, K.R., and Zou, S. (2015), "Effect of customer participation on service outcomes", *Journal of Service Research*, Vol. 18 No. 2, pp. 160–176.
Donthu, N. and Gustafsson, A. (2020), "Effects of COVID-19 on business and research", *Journal of Business Research*, Vol. 117 No. 12, pp. 284–289.
Dormann, C. and Kaiser, D.M. (2002), "Job conditions and customer satisfaction", *European Journal of Work and Organizational Psychology*, Vol. 11 No. 3, pp. 257–283.
Dotzel, T., Shankar, V., and Berry, L.L. (2013), "Service innovativeness and firm value", *Journal of Marketing Research*, Vol. 50 No. 2, pp. 259–276.
Dou, W. and Ghose, S. (2006), "A dynamic nonlinear model of online retail competition using cusp catastrophe theory", *Journal of Business Research*, Vol. 59 No. 7, pp. 838–848.
Drescher, N. and Engelking, N. (2020), "COVID-19: QR code use cases in the fight against coronavirus", *QR Code Generator Blog*, 15 July, available at: https://www.qr-code-generator.com/blog/qr-code-use-cases-coronavirus/ (accessed 10 September 2020).
Dube, K., Nhamo, G., and Chikodzi, D. (2021), "COVID-19 cripples global restaurant and hospitality industry", *Current Issues in Tourism*, Vol. 24 No. 11, pp. 1487–1490.
Dvorak, N. and Robison, J. (2020), "How to deliver on your brand promise, even during disruption", *Gallup Blog*, 18 August, available at: https://www.gallup.com/workplace/317084/deliver-brand-promise-even-during-disruption.aspx (accessed 3 September 2020).

Ebbers, J.J. and Wijnberg, N.M. (2017), "Betwixt and between: Role conflict, role ambiguity and role definition in project-based dual-leadership structures", *Human Relations*, Vol. 70 No. 11, pp. 1342–1365.

Edvardsson, B., Gustafsson, A., Kristensson, P., and Witell, L. (2011), "Customer integration in service innovation", in Gallouj, F. and Djellal, F. (Eds.), *The handbook of innovation and services: A multi-disciplinary perspective*, Edward Elgar Publishing, pp. 301–317.

Edvardsson, B., Gustafsson, A., and Roos, I. (2005), "Service portraits in service research: A critical review", *International Journal of Service Industry Management*, Vol. 16 No. 1, pp. 107–121.

Edwards, J.R. (2008), "Person–environment fit in organizations: An assessment of theoretical progress", *Academy of Management Annals*, Vol. 2 No. 1, pp. 167–230.

Ellinger, A.E., Elmadağ, A.B., and Ellinger, A.D. (2007), "An examination of organizations' frontline service employee development practices", *Human Resource Development Quarterly*, Vol. 18 No. 3, pp. 293–314.

Elloy, D.F. and Smith, C.R. (2003), "Patterns of stress, work-family conflict, role conflict, role ambiguity and overload among dual-career and single-career couples: An Australian study", *Cross Cultural Management: An International Journal*, Vol. 10 No. 1, pp. 55–66.

Elmadağ, A.B., Ellinger, A.E., and Franke, G.R. (2008), "Antecedents and consequences of frontline service employee commitment to service quality", *Journal of Marketing Theory and Practice*, Vol. 16 No. 2, pp. 95–110.

Enz, C.A. (2012), "Strategies for the implementation of service innovations", *Cornell Hospitality Quarterly*, Vol. 53 No. 3, pp. 187–195.

Etgar, M. (2008), "A descriptive model of the consumer co-production process", *Journal of the Academy of Marketing Science*, Vol. 36 No. 1, pp. 97–108.

Evans, F.B. (1963), "Selling as a dyadic relationship–a new approach", *American Behavioral Scientist*, Vol. 6 No. 9, pp. 76–79.

Evans, T. (2013), "Organisational rules and discretion in adult social work", *British Journal of Social Work*, Vol. 43 No. 4, pp. 739–758.

Evanschitzky, H., Groening, C., Mittal, V., and Wunderlich, M. (2011), "How employer and employee satisfaction affect customer satisfaction: An application to franchise services", *Journal of Service Research*, Vol. 14 No. 2, pp. 136–148.

Feldman, R.S. (2019), *Essentials of understanding psychology,* Thirteenth edition, McGraw-Hill Education, New York, NY.

Feldmann, N., Fromm, H., Satzger, G., and Schüritz, R. (2019), "Using employees' collective intelligence for service innovation: Theory and instruments", in Maglio, P.P. (Ed.), *Handbook of service science. Vol. II, Service Science: Research and Innovations in the Service Economy*, Vol. 14, Springer Nature, Cham, Switzerland, pp. 249–284.

Felin, T., Foss, N.J., Heimeriks, K.H., and Madsen, T.L. (2012), "Microfoundations of routines and capabilities: Individuals, processes, and structure", *Journal of Management Studies*, Vol. 49 No. 8, pp. 1351–1374.

Ferguson, J.L., Ellen, P.S., and Bearden, W.O. (2014), "Procedural and distributive fairness: Determinants of overall price fairness", *Journal of Business Ethics*, Vol. 121 No. 2, pp. 217–231.

Fernandez, S., Dufour, F., Costa, V., de Boer, C., Terrier, L., and Golay, P. (2020), "Increasing tips in less than two hours: Impact of a training intervention on the amount of tips received by restaurant employees", *Cornell Hospitality Quarterly*, Vol. 61 No. 1, pp. 98–107.

Festinger, L. (1957), *A theory of cognitive dissonance*, Stanford University Press, Stanford.

Fida, R., Paciello, M., Tramontano, C., Barbaranelli, C., and Farnese, M.L. (2015), ""Yes, I can": The protective role of personal self-efficacy in hindering counterproductive work behavior under stressful conditions", *Anxiety, Stress, and Coping*, Vol. 28 No. 5, pp. 479–499.

Field, A. (2013), *Discovering statistics using IBM SPSS statistics, MobileStudy*, 4th edition, SAGE Publications, Los Angeles, London, New Delhi, Singapore, Washington DC.

Finn, A. (2005), "Reassessing the foundations of customer delight", *Journal of Service Research*, Vol. 8 No. 2, pp. 103–116.

Finn, A. (2012), "Customer delight", *Journal of Service Research*, Vol. 15 No. 1, pp. 99–110.

Fitzsimmons, J.A. (1985), "Consumer participation and productivity in service operations", *Interfaces*, Vol. 15 No. 3, pp. 60–67.

Fitzsimmons, J.A. and Fitzsimmons, M.J. (2011), *Service management: Operations, strategy, information technology, The McGraw-Hill/Irwin series operations and decision sciences*, 7th ed., McGraw-Hill, New York.

Flanagan, J.C. (1954), "The critical incident technique", *International Journal of Public Opinion Research*, Vol. 51 No. 4, pp. 327–358.

Fliess, S., Dyck, S., and Schmelter, M. (2014), "Mirror, mirror on the wall – how customers perceive their contribution to service provision", *Journal of Service Management*, Vol. 25 No. 4, pp. 433–469.

Fliess, S. and Kleinaltenkamp, M. (2004), "Blueprinting the service company", *Journal of Business Research*, Vol. 57 No. 4, pp. 392–404.

Flikkema, M., Jansen, P., and van der Sluis, L. (2007), "Identifying neo-Schumpeterian innovation in service firms: A conceptual essay with a novel classification", *Economics of Innovation and New Technology*, Vol. 16 No. 7, pp. 541–558.

Folger, R. and Cropanzano, R. (2001), "Fairness theory: Justice as accountability", in Greenberg, J. and Cropanzano, R. (Eds.), *Advances in organizational justice*, Vol. 1, Stanford University Press, Stanford, Calif, pp. 1–55.

Folger, R.G. and Cropanzano, R. (1998), *Organizational justice and human resource management*, SAGE Publications.

Folkman, S., Lazarus, R.S., Dunkel-Schetter, C., DeLongis, A., and Gruen, R.J. (1986), "Dynamics of a stressful encounter: Cognitive appraisal, coping, and encounter outcomes", *Journal of Personality and Social Psychology*, Vol. 50 No. 5, pp. 992–1003.

Folkman, S., Lazarus, R.S., Gruen, R.J., and DeLongis, A. (1986), "Appraisal, coping, health status, and psychological symptoms", *Journal of Personality and Social Psychology*, Vol. 50 No. 3, pp. 571–579.

Fornell, C. and Larcker, D.F. (1981), "Evaluating structural equation models with unobservable variables and measurement error", *Journal of Marketing Research*, Vol. 18 No. 1, pp. 39–50.

Fox, S., Spector, P.E., and Miles, D. (2001), "Counterproductive work behavior (CWB) in response to job stressors and organizational justice: Some mediator and moderator tests for autonomy and emotions", *Journal of Vocational Behavior*, Vol. 59 No. 3, pp. 291–309.

Franke, N., Keinz, P., and Klausberger, K. (2013), ""Does this sound like a fair deal?": Antecedents and consequences of fairness expectations in the individual's decision to participate in firm innovation", *Organization Science*, Vol. 24 No. 5, pp. 1495–1516.

French, J.R.P. and Kahn, R.L. (1962), "A programmatic approach to studying the industrial environment and mental health", *Journal of Social Issues*, Vol. 18 No. 3, pp. 1–47.

Frey, C.B. and Osborne, M.A. (2017), "The future of employment: How susceptible are jobs to computerisation?", *Technological Forecasting and Social Change*, Vol. 114 No. 1, pp. 254–280.

Fuglseth, A.M. and Sørebø, Ø. (2014), "The effects of technostress within the context of employee use of ICT", *Computers in Human Behavior*, Vol. 40, pp. 161–170.

Fuller, J.B., Marler, L.E., and Hester, K. (2006), "Promoting felt responsibility for constructive change and proactive behavior: Exploring aspects of an elaborated model of work design", *Journal of Organizational Behavior*, Vol. 27 No. 8, pp. 1089–1120.

Gable, P.A. and Poole, B.D. (2012), "Time flies when you're having approach-motivated fun: Effects of motivational intensity on time perception", *Psychological science*, Vol. 23 No. 8, pp. 879–886.

Gallouj, F. and Savona, M. (2009), "Innovation in services: A review of the debate and a research agenda", *Journal of Evolutionary Economics*, Vol. 19 No. 2, pp. 149–172.

Gallup (2014), "State of the American consumer: Insights for business leaders", available at: https://www.gallup.com/services/176282/state-american-consumer.aspx (accessed 16 September 2019).

Galperin, B.L. (2012), "Exploring the nomological network of workplace deviance: Developing and validating a measure of constructive deviance", *Journal of Applied Social Psychology*, Vol. 42 No. 12, pp. 2988–3025.

Gandhi, P., Khanna, S., and Ramaswamy, S. (2016), "Which industries are the most digital (and why)?", available at: https://hbr.org/2016/04/a-chart-that-shows-which-industries-are-the-most-digital-and-why (accessed 17 May 2018).

Gemmel, P., van Looy, B., and van Dierdonck, R. (Eds.) (2013), *Service management: An integrated approach,* 3. ed., Pearson, Harlow.

Gensler, S., Neslin, S.A., and Verhoef, P.C. (2017), "The showrooming phenomenon: It's more than just about price", *Journal of Interactive Marketing*, Vol. 38 No. 2, pp. 29–43.

Giannopoulou, E., Gryszkiewicz, L., and Barlatier, P.-J. (2014), "Creativity for service innovation: A practice-based perspective", *Managing Service Quality*, Vol. 24 No. 1, pp. 23–44.

Giebelhausen, M., Robinson, S.G., Sirianni, N.J., and Brady, M.K. (2014), "Touch versus tech: When technology functions as a barrier or a benefit to service encounters", *Journal of Marketing*, Vol. 78 No. 4, pp. 113–124.

Glushko, R.J. and Nomorosa, K.J. (2013), "Substituting information for interaction", *Journal of Service Research*, Vol. 16 No. 1, pp. 21–38.

Goodhue, D.L. and Thompson, R.L. (1995), "Task-technology fit and individual performance", *MIS Quarterly*, Vol. 19 No. 2, p. 213.

Goodman, J.K., Cryder, C.E., and Cheema, A. (2013), "Data collection in a flat world: The strengths and weaknesses of Mechanical Turk samples", *Journal of Behavioral Decision Making*, Vol. 26 No. 3, pp. 213–224.

Gregoire, M.B. (2017), *Foodservice organizations: A managerial and systems approach,* Ninth edition, Pearson, Boston.

Gremler, D.D. (2004), "The critical incident technique in service research", *Journal of Service Research*, Vol. 7 No. 1, pp. 65–89.

Gremler, D.D. and Gwinner, K.P. (2000), "Customer-employee rapport in service relationships", *Journal of Service Research*, Vol. 3 No. 1, pp. 82–104.

Gremler, D.D. and Gwinner, K.P. (2008), "Rapport-building behaviors used by retail employees", *Journal of Retailing*, Vol. 84 No. 3, pp. 308–324.

Griffin, R.W., O'Leary-Kelly, A., and Collins, J.M. (Eds.) (1998), *Dysfunctional behavior in organizations, Monographs in organizational behavior and industrial relations*, Vol. 23, JAI Press, Greenwich, Conn.

Grimm, P. (2011), "Social desirability bias", in Sheth, J.N. and Malhotra, N.K. (Eds.), *Wiley international encyclopedia of marketing*, Vol. 50, Wiley Interscience, Hoboken, NJ, p. 537.

Groeger, L., Moroko, L., and Hollebeek, L.D. (2016), "Capturing value from non-paying consumers' engagement behaviours: Field evidence and development of a theoretical model", *Journal of Strategic Marketing*, Vol. 24 No. 3-4, pp. 190–209.

Grönroos, C. (1984), "A service quality model and its marketing implications", *European Journal of Marketing*, Vol. 18 No. 4, pp. 36–44.

Grönroos, C. (1990a), *Service management and marketing: Managing the moments of truth in service competition, Maxwell Macmillan international editions in business & economics*, 1. print, Lexington Books, Lexington, Mass.

Grönroos, C. (1990b), "Service management: A management focus for service competition", *International Journal of Service Industry Management*, Vol. 1 No. 1, pp. 6–14.

Grönroos, C. (1994), "From scientific management to service management", *International Journal of Service Industry Management*, Vol. 5 No. 1, pp. 5–20.

Grönroos, C. (2020), "Viewpoint: Service marketing research priorities", *Journal of Services Marketing*, Vol. 34 No. 3, pp. 291–298.

Grönroos, C. and Voima, P. (2012), "Critical service logic: Making sense of value creation and co-creation", *Journal of the Academy of Marketing Science*, Vol. 41 No. 2, pp. 133–150.

Groth, M., Hennig-Thurau, T., and Walsh, G. (2009), "Customer reactions to emotional labor: The roles of employee acting strategies and customer detection accuracy", *Academy of Management Journal*, Vol. 52 No. 5, pp. 958–974.

Groth, M., Wu, Y., Nguyen, H., and Johnson, A. (2019), "The moment of truth: A review, synthesis, and research agenda for the customer service experience", *Annual Review of Organizational Psychology and Organizational Behavior*, Vol. 6 No. 1, pp. 89–113.

Guest, G., Bunce, A., and Johnson, L. (2006), "How many interviews are enough? An experiment with data saturation and variability", *Field Methods*, Vol. 18 No. 1, pp. 59–82.

Gustafsson, A. (2009), "Customer satisfaction with service recovery", *Journal of Business Research*, Vol. 62 No. 11, pp. 1220–1222.

Gustafsson, A., Kristensson, P., and Witell, L. (2012), "Customer co-creation in service innovation: A matter of communication?", *Journal of Service Management*, Vol. 23 No. 3, pp. 311–327.

Gustafsson, A., Snyder, H., and Witell, L. (2020), "Service innovation: A new conceptualization and path forward", *Journal of Service Research*, Vol. 23 No. 2, pp. 111–115.

Gwinner, K.P., Bitner, M.J., Brown, S.W., and Kumar, A. (2005), "Service customization through employee adaptiveness", *Journal of Service Research*, Vol. 8 No. 2, pp. 131–148.

Hair, J.F., Babin, B.J., Anderson, R.E., and Black, W.C. (2014), *Multivariate data analysis, Pearson custom library*, Seventh edition, Pearson, Harlow, Essex.

Halbesleben, J.R.B. and Bowler, W.M. (2007), "Emotional exhaustion and job performance: The mediating role of motivation", *Journal of Applied Psychology*, Vol. 92 No. 1, pp. 93–106.

Halbesleben, J.R.B., Harvey, J., and Bolino, M.C. (2009), "Too engaged? A conservation of resources view of the relationship between work engagement and work interference with family", *Journal of Applied Psychology*, Vol. 94 No. 6, pp. 1452–1465.

Halbesleben, J.R.B., Neveu, J.-P., Paustian-Underdahl, S.C., and Westman, M. (2014), "Getting to the "COR"", *Journal of Management*, Vol. 40 No. 5, pp. 1334–1364.

Hamborg, K.-C. and Greif, S. (2015), "New technologies and stress", in Cooper, C.L., Quick, J.C. and Schabracq, M. (Eds.), *International handbook of work and health psychology*, 3rd ed., Wiley-Blackwell, Chichester, pp. 221–250.

Hammes, E.K. and Walsh, G. (2017), "Service employees' job demands and two types of deviance: The moderating role of organizational resources", *Marketing ZFP*, Vol. 39 No. 1, pp. 15–26.

Han, X., Fang, S., Xie, L., and Yang, J. (2019), "Service fairness and customer satisfaction", *Journal of Contemporary Marketing Science*, Vol. 2 No. 1, pp. 50–62.

Hanks, L., Line, N., and Kim, W.G. (2017), "The impact of the social servicescape, density, and restaurant type on perceptions of interpersonal service quality", *International Journal of Hospitality Management*, Vol. 61 No. 2, pp. 35–44.

Hansen, K.V., Jensen, Ø., and Gustafsson, I.-B. (2005), "The meal experiences of á la carte restaurant customers", *Scandinavian Journal of Hospitality and Tourism*, Vol. 5 No. 2, pp. 135–151.

Harris, E.G. and Fleming, D.E. (2017), "The productive service employee: Personality, stress, satisfaction and performance", *Journal of Services Marketing*, Vol. 31 No. 6, pp. 499–511.

Harris, L.C. and Ogbonna, E. (2002), "Exploring service sabotage. the antecedents, types and consequences of frontline, deviant, antiservice behaviors", *Journal of Service Research*, Vol. 4 No. 3, pp. 163–183.

Harris, L.C. and Ogbonna, E. (2006), "Service sabotage: A study of antecedents and consequences", *Journal of the Academy of Marketing Science*, Vol. 34 No. 4, pp. 543–558.

Hartline, M.D., Maxham, J.G., and McKee, D.O. (2000), "Corridors of influence in the dissemination of customer-oriented strategy to customer contact service employees", *Journal of Marketing*, Vol. 64 No. 2, pp. 35–50.

Harvard Business School (2018), "Can Opentable survive, or is it losing popularity?", available at: https://digit.hbs.org/submission/can-opentable-survive-or-is-it-losing-popularity/ (accessed 10 May 2019).

Haumann, T., Güntürkün, P., Schons, L.M., and Wieseke, J. (2015), "Engaging customers in coproduction processes: How value-enhancing and intensity-reducing communication strategies mitigate the negative effects of coproduction intensity", *Journal of Marketing*, Vol. 79 No. 6, pp. 17–33.

Haws, K.L. and Bearden, W.O. (2006), "Dynamic pricing and consumer fairness perceptions", *Journal of Consumer Research*, Vol. 33 No. 3, pp. 304–311.

Hayes, A.F. (2012), *PROCESS. A versatile computational tool for observed variable mediation, moderation, and conditional process modeling*, available at: http://www.afhayes.com/public/process2012.pdf (accessed 1 July 2021).

Hayes, A.F., Montoya, A.K., and Rockwood, N.J. (2017), "The analysis of mechanisms and their contingencies: PROCESS versus structural equation modeling", *Australasian Marketing Journal*, Vol. 25 No. 1, pp. 76–81.

Heerwegh, D. (2009), "Mode differences between face-to-face and web surveys: An experimental investigation of data quality and social desirability effects", *International Journal of Public Opinion Research*, Vol. 21 No. 1, pp. 111–121.

Heidenreich, S. and Handrich, M. (2015), "Adoption of technology-based services: The role of customers' willingness to co-create", *Journal of Service Management*, Vol. 26 No. 1, pp. 44–71.

Heidenreich, S. and Spieth, P. (2013), "Why innovations fail – the case of passive and active innovation resistance", *International Journal of Innovation Management*, Vol. 17 No. 5, p. 1350021.

Heidenreich, S. and Talke, K. (2020), "Consequences of mandated usage of innovations in organizations: Developing an innovation decision model of symbolic and forced adoption", *AMS Review*, Vol. 10 No. 3, pp. 279–298.

Heidenreich, S., Wittkowski, K., Handrich, M., and Falk, T. (2015), "The dark side of customer co-creation: Exploring the consequences of failed co-created services", *Journal of the Academy of Marketing Science*, Vol. 43 No. 3, pp. 279–296.

Heller, J., Chylinski, M., de Ruyter, K., Keeling, D.I., Hilken, T., and Mahr, D. (2021), "Tangible service automation: Decomposing the technology-enabled engagement process (TEEP) for augmented reality", *Journal of Service Research*, Vol. 24 No. 1, 84-103.

Heller, J., Chylinski, M., de Ruyter, K., Mahr, D., and Keeling, D.I. (2019a), "Let me imagine that for you: Transforming the retail frontline through augmenting customer mental imagery ability", *Journal of Retailing*, Vol. 95 No. 2, pp. 94–114.

Heller, J., Chylinski, M., de Ruyter, K., Mahr, D., and Keeling, D.I. (2019b), "Touching the untouchable: Exploring multi-sensory augmented reality in the context of online retailing", *Journal of Retailing*, Vol. 95 No. 4, pp. 219–234.

Hennig-Thurau, T. (2004), "Customer orientation of service employees. Its impact on customer satisfaction, commitment, and retention", *International Journal of Service Industry Management*, Vol. 15 No. 5, pp. 460–478.

Hennig-Thurau, T., Gwinner, K.P., Walsh, G., and Gremler, D.D. (2004), "Electronic word-of-mouth via consumer-opinion platforms: What motivates consumers to articulate themselves on the internet?", *Journal of Interactive Marketing*, Vol. 18 No. 1, pp. 38–52.

Hennig-Thurau, T. and Thurau, C. (2003), "Customer orientation of service employees – toward a conceptual framework of a key relationship marketing construct", *Journal of Relationship Marketing*, Vol. 2 No. 1-2, pp. 23–41.

Heskett, J.L., Jones, T.O., Loveman, G.W., Sasser, W.E., and Schlesinger, L.A. (1994), "Putting the service-profit chain to work", *Harvard Business Review*, Vol. 72 No. 2, pp. 164–174.

Heskett, J.L., Sasser, W.E., and Schlesinger, L.A. (2015), *What great service leaders know and do: Creating breakthroughs in service firms*, Berrett-Koehler Publishers, Oakland, United States.

Hibbert, S., Winklhofer, H., and Temerak, M.S. (2012), "Customers as resource integrators", *Journal of Service Research*, Vol. 15 No. 3, pp. 247–261.

Hilken, T., de Ruyter, K., Chylinski, M., Mahr, D., and Keeling, D.I. (2017), "Augmenting the eye of the beholder: Exploring the strategic potential of augmented reality to enhance online service experiences", *Journal of the Academy of Marketing Science*, Vol. 45 No. 6, pp. 884–905.

Hilton, T., Hughes, T., Little, E., and Marandi, E. (2013), "Adopting self-service technology to do more with less", *Journal of Services Marketing*, Vol. 27 No. 1, pp. 3–12.

Hipp, C. and Grupp, H. (2005), "Innovation in the service sector: The demand for service-specific innovation measurement concepts and typologies", *Research Policy*, Vol. 34 No. 4, pp. 517–535.

Hirschman, A.O. (1970), *Exit, voice, and loyalty: Responses to decline in firms, organizations, and states*, Harvard Univ. Press, Cambridge, Mass.

Hobfoll, S.E. (1989), "Conservation of resources. A new attempt at conceptualizing stress", *The American Psychologist*, Vol. 44 No. 3, pp. 513–524.

Hobfoll, S.E. (2001), "The influence of culture, community, and the nested-self in the stress process: Advancing conservation of resources theory", *Applied Psychology*, Vol. 50 No. 3, pp. 337–421.

Hobfoll, S.E. (2011), "Conservation of resource caravans and engaged settings", *Journal of Occupational and Organizational Psychology*, Vol. 84 No. 1, pp. 116–122.

Hobfoll, S.E., Halbesleben, J.R.B., Neveu, J.-P., and Westman, M. (2018), "Conservation of resources in the organizational context: The reality of resources and their consequences", *Annual Review of Organizational Psychology and Organizational Behavior*, Vol. 5 No. 1, pp. 103–128.

Hoffman, K.D. and Ingram, T.N. (1992), "Service provider job satisfaction and customer-oriented performance", *Journal of Services Marketing*, Vol. 6 No. 2, pp. 68–78.

Hogreve, J., Iseke, A., Derfuss, K., and Eller, T. (2017), "The service–profit chain: A meta-analytic test of a comprehensive theoretical framework", *Journal of Marketing*, Vol. 81 No. 3, pp. 41–61.

Holbrook, A.L., Green, M.C., and Krosnick, J.A. (2003), "Telephone versus face-to-face interviewing of national probability samples with long questionnaires", *Public Opinion Quarterly*, Vol. 67 No. 1, pp. 79–125.

Hollebeek, L. (2011), "Exploring customer brand engagement: Definition and themes", *Journal of Strategic Marketing*, Vol. 19 No. 7, pp. 555–573.

Holmes, T.H. and Rahe, R.H. (1967), "The social readjustment rating scale", *Journal of Psychosomatic Research*, Vol. 11 No. 2, pp. 213–218.

Homburg, C., Koschate, N., and Hoyer, W. D. (2005), "Do satisfied customers really pay more? A study of the relationship between customer satisfaction and willingness to pay", *Journal of Marketing*, Vol. 69 No. 2, pp. 84–96.

Homburg, C., Lauer, K., and Vomberg, A. (2019), "The multichannel pricing dilemma: Do consumers accept higher offline than online prices?", *International Journal of Research in Marketing*, Vol. 36 No. 4, pp. 597–612.

Homburg, C. and Stock, R.M. (2004), "The link between salespeople's job satisfaction and customer satisfaction in a business-to-business context: A dyadic analysis", *Journal of the Academy of Marketing Science*, Vol. 32 No. 2, pp. 144–158.

Homburg, C., Wieseke, J., and Bornemann, T. (2009), "Implementing the marketing concept at the employee—customer interface: The role of customer need knowledge", *Journal of Marketing*, Vol. 73 No. 4, pp. 64–81.

Hopstaken, J.F., van der Linden, D., Bakker, A.B., Kompier, M.A.J., and Leung, Y.K. (2016), "Shifts in attention during mental fatigue: Evidence from subjective, behavioral, physiological, and eye-tracking data", *Journal of Experimental Psychology. Human perception and performance*, Vol. 42 No. 6, pp. 878–889.

Hovland, C.I., Harvey, O.J., and Sherif, M. (1957), "Assimilation and contrast effects in reactions to communication and attitude change", *Journal of Abnormal Psychology*, Vol. 55 No. 2, pp. 244–252.

Howard, M.C. and Rose, J.C. (2019), "Refining and extending task–technology fit theory: Creation of two task–technology fit scales and empirical clarification of the construct", *Information & Management*, Vol. 56 No. 6, pp. 103–134.

Howell, D.C. (2013), *Statistical methods for psychology*, Eighth edition, Wadsworth Cengage Learning, Belmont, Calif.

Hoyer, W. D., Chandy, R., Dorotic, M., Krafft, M., and Singh, S.S. (2010), "Consumer cocreation in new product development", *Journal of Service Research*, Vol. 13 No. 3, pp. 283–296.

Huang, M.-H. and Rust, R.T. (2017), "Technology-driven service strategy", *Journal of the Academy of Marketing Science*, Vol. 45 No. 6, pp. 906–924.

Huang, M.-H. and Rust, R.T. (2018), "Artificial intelligence in service", *Journal of Service Research*, Vol. 21 No. 2, pp. 155–172.

Huang, T.-L., Mathews, S., and Chou, C.Y. (2019), "Enhancing online rapport experience via augmented reality", *Journal of Services Marketing*, Vol. 33 No. 7, pp. 851–865.

Hubert, M., Blut, M., Brock, C., Zhang, R.W., Koch, V., and Riedl, R. (2019), "The influence of acceptance and adoption drivers on smart home usage", *European Journal of Marketing*, Vol. 53 No. 6, pp. 1073–1098.

Huete-Alcocer, N. (2017), "A literature review of word of mouth and electronic word of mouth: Implications for consumer behavior", *Frontiers in psychology*, Vol. 8 No. 1, pp. 78–81.

Hulland, J. (1999), "Use of partial least squares (PLS) in strategic management research: A review of four recent studies", *Strategic Management Journal*, Vol. 20 No. 2, pp. 195–204.

Huppertz, J.W., Arenson, S.J., and Evans, R.H. (1978), "An application of equity theory to buyer-seller exchange situations", *Journal of Marketing Research*, Vol. 15 No. 2, pp. 250–260.

Huseynov, F. and Yıldırım, S.Ö. (2016), "Internet users' attitudes toward business-to-consumer online shopping", *Information Development*, Vol. 32 No. 3, pp. 452–465.

Hüttel, B.A., Ates, Z., Schumann, J.H., Büttgen, M., Haager, S., Komor, M., and Volz, J. (2019), "The influence of customer characteristics on frontline employees' customer need knowledge", *Journal of Services Marketing*, Vol. 33 No. 2, pp. 220–232.

Iacobucci, D., Saldanha, N., and Deng, X. (2007), "A meditation on mediation: Evidence that structural equations models perform better than regressions", *Journal of Consumer Psychology*, Vol. 17 No. 2, pp. 139–153.

Im, J. and Qu, H. (2017), "Drivers and resources of customer co-creation: A scenario-based case in the restaurant industry", *International Journal of Hospitality Management*, Vol. 64 No. 5, pp. 31–40.

International Labour Office (2019), "World employment and social outlook", available at: https://www.ilo.org/global/research/global-reports/weso/2019/lang--en/index.htm (accessed 4 June 2020).

Ito, J.K. and Brotheridge, C.M. (2003), "Resources, coping strategies, and emotional exhaustion: A conservation of resources perspective", *Journal of Vocational Behavior*, Vol. 63 No. 3, pp. 490–509.

Jaakkola, E. and Alexander, M. (2014), "The role of customer engagement behavior in value co-creation", *Journal of Service Research*, Vol. 17 No. 3, pp. 247–261.

Jackson, S.E. and Schuler, R.S. (1985), "A meta-analysis and conceptual critique of research on role ambiguity and role conflict in work settings", *Organizational Behavior and Human Decision Processes*, Vol. 36 No. 1, pp. 16–78.

Jalilvand, M.R., Salimipour, S., Elyasi, M., and Mohammadi, M. (2017), "Factors influencing word of mouth behaviour in the restaurant industry", *Marketing Intelligence and Planning*, Vol. 35 No. 1, pp. 81–110.

James, L.R., Demaree, R.G., and Wolf, G. (1993), "Rwg: An assessment of within-group interrater agreement", *Journal of Applied Psychology*, Vol. 78 No. 2, pp. 306–309.

Janakiraman, N., Syrdal, H.A., and Freling, R. (2016), "The effect of return policy leniency on consumer purchase and return decisions: A meta-analytic review", *Journal of Retailing*, Vol. 92 No. 2, pp. 226–235.

Jasmand, C., Blazevic, V., and de Ruyter, K. (2012), "Generating sales while providing service: A study of customer service representatives' ambidextrous behavior", *Journal of Marketing*, Vol. 76 No. 1, pp. 20–37.

Jaworski, B.J. and MacInnis, D.J. (1989), "Marketing jobs and management controls: Toward a framework", *Journal of Marketing Research*, Vol. 25 No. 4, pp. 406–419.

Jeong, E. and Jang, S. (2011), "Restaurant experiences triggering positive electronic word-of-mouth motivations", *International Journal of Contemporary Hospitality Management*, Vol. 30 No. 2, pp. 356–366.

Jex, S.M., Beehr, T.A., and Roberts, C.K. (1992), "The meaning of occupational stress items to survey respondents", *Journal of Applied Psychology*, Vol. 77 No. 5, 623-628.

Jex, S.M. and Bliese, P.D. (1999), "Efficacy beliefs as a moderator of the impact of work-related stressors: A multilevel study", *Journal of Applied Psychology*, Vol. 84 No. 3, pp. 349–361.

Jiang, Y. and Wen, J. (2020), "Effects of COVID-19 on hotel marketing and management: A perspective article", *International Journal of Contemporary Hospitality Management*, Vol. 32 No. 8, pp. 2563–2573.

Johnstone, M. and Feeney, J.A. (2015), "Individual differences in responses to workplace stress: The contribution of attachment theory", *Journal of Applied Social Psychology*, Vol. 45 No. 7, pp. 412–424.

Jones, E.E. and Harris, V.A. (1967), "The attribution of attitudes", *Journal of Experimental Social Psychology*, Vol. 3 No. 1, pp. 1–24.

Jones, L.A. (2019), "The perception of duration and the judgment of the passage of time", in Arstila, V., Bardon, A., Power, S.E. and Vatakis, A. (Eds.), *Illusions of time: Philosophical and psychological essays on timing and time*, Springer Nature, Heidelberg, pp. 53–67.

Jones, M.A., Reynolds, K.E., Mothersbaugh, D.L., and Beatty, S.E. (2007), "The positive and negative effects of switching costs on relational outcomes", *Journal of Service Research*, Vol. 9 No. 4, pp. 335–355.

Kahn, R.L., Wolfre, D.M., Quinn, R.P., Scnoek, J.D., and Rosenthal, R.A. (1964), *Organizational stress: Studies in role conflict and ambiguity*, Wiley, New York.

Kaplan, D. (1994), "Estimator conditioning diagnostics for covariance structure models", *Sociological Methods and Research*, Vol. 23 No. 2, pp. 200–229.

Karatepe, O.M. and Karadas, G. (2016), "Service employees' fit, work-family conflict, and work engagement", *Journal of Services Marketing*, Vol. 30 No. 5, pp. 554–566.

Katiyar, A., Kalra, K., and Garg, C. (2015), "Marker based augmented reality", *Advances in Computer Science and Information Technology (ACSIT)*, Vol. 2 No. 5, pp. 441–445.

Keating, B.W., McColl-Kennedy, J.R., and Solnet, D. (2018), "Theorizing beyond the horizon: Service research in 2050", *Journal of Service Management*, Vol. 29 No. 5, pp. 766–775.

Keiningham, T.L., Cooil, B., Aksoy, L., Andreassen, T.W., and Weiner, J. (2007), "The value of different customer satisfaction and loyalty metrics in predicting customer retention, recommendation, and share-of-wallet", *Managing Service Quality*, Vol. 17 No. 4, pp. 361–384.

Keiningham, T.L. and Vavra, T. (2001), *The customer delight principle: Exceeding customers' expectations for bottom-line success*, McGraw Hill Professional, New York, NY.

Keller, K.L. (1993), "Conceptualizing, measuring, and managing customer-based brand equity", *Journal of Marketing*, Vol. 57 No. 1, pp. 1–22.

Kelley, S.W. (1992), "Developing customer orientation among service employees", *Journal of the Academy of Marketing Science*, Vol. 20 No. 1, pp. 27–36.

Khedhaouria, A. and Cucchi, A. (2019), "Technostress creators, personality traits, and job burnout: A fuzzy-set configurational analysis", *Journal of Business Research*, Vol. 101, pp. 349–361.

Kim and Kankanhalli (2009), "Investigating user resistance to information systems implementation: A status quo bias perspective", *MIS Quarterly*, Vol. 33 No. 3, pp. 567–582.

Kim, H. (2019), "Service science: Past, present, and future", *Journal of Service Science Research*, Vol. 11 No. 2, pp. 117–132.

Kim, J. and Forsythe, S. (2008), "Adoption of virtual try-on technology for online apparel shopping", *Journal of Interactive Marketing*, Vol. 22 No. 2, pp. 45–59.

Kim, K.A. and Byon, K.K. (2018), "Examining relationships among consumer participative behavior, employee role ambiguity, and employee citizenship behavior: The moderating role of employee self-efficacy", *European Sport Management Quarterly*, Vol. 56 No. 5, pp. 1–19.

Kimes, S.E. (2008), "The role of technology in restaurant revenue management", *Cornell Hospitality Quarterly*, Vol. 49 No. 3, pp. 297–309.

Kimes, S.E. (2009), "How restaurant customers view on-line reservations", Cornell Hospitality Report, Center for Hospitality Research, Cornell University, 2009.

Kimes, S.E. and Chase, R.B. (1998), "The strategic levers of yield management", *Journal of Service Research*, Vol. 1 No. 2, pp. 156–166.

Kimes, S.E. and Kies, K. (2012), "The role of multi-restaurant reservation sites in restaurant distribution management", *Cornell Hospitality Report*, Vol. 12 No. 3, pp. 6–13.

Kimes, S.E. and Wirtz, J. (2007), "Customer satisfaction with seating policies in casual-dining restaurants", *Cornell Hospitality Report*, Vol. 7 No. 16, pp. 6–17.

King, R.A., Racherla, P., and Bush, V.D. (2014), "What we know and don't know about online word-of-mouth: A review and synthesis of the literature", *Journal of Interactive Marketing*, Vol. 28 No. 3, pp. 167–183.

Kirton, M. (1980), "Adaptors and innovators in organizations", *Human Relations*, Vol. 33 No. 4, pp. 213–224.

Kivijärvi, H. (2020), "Theorizing IT Project success", *International Journal of Information Technology Project Management*, Vol. 11 No. 1, pp. 71–98.

Kohli, A.K. and Jaworski, B.J. (1994), "The influence of coworker feedback on salespeople", *Journal of Marketing*, Vol. 58 No. 4, pp. 82–94.

Kokkinoua, A. and Cranage, D.A. (2013), "Using self-service technology to reduce customer waiting times", *International Journal of Hospitality Management*, Vol. 33 No. 2, pp. 435–445.

Korschun, D., Bhattacharya, C.B., and Swain, S.D. (2014), "Corporate social responsibility, customer orientation, and the job performance of frontline employees", *Journal of Marketing*, Vol. 78 No. 3, pp. 20–37.

Kotler, P. and Keller, K.L. (2016), *Marketing management,* 15. global edition, Pearson, Boston.

Koutroumanis, D.A. (2011), "Technology's effect on hotels and restaurants: Building a strategic competitive advantage", *Journal of Applied Business and Economics*, Vol. 12 No. 1, pp. 72–80.

Król, G. (2017), "Individual differences in dealing with overflow", *European Management Journal*, Vol. 35 No. 6, pp. 794–802.

Krüger, F. (2016), *The influence of culture and personality on customer satisfaction: An empirical analysis across countries, International Management Studies,* 1st ed. 2016, Springer Fachmedien, Wiesbaden.

Krumpal, I. (2013), "Determinants of social desirability bias in sensitive surveys: A literature review", *Quality & Quantity*, Vol. 47 No. 4, pp. 2025–2047.

Kumar, A., Olshavsky, R.W., and King, M.F. (2001), "Exploring alternative antecedents of customer delight", *Journal of Consumer Satisfaction, Dissatisfaction & Complaining Behavior*, Vol. 14 No. 1, pp. 14–26.

Kumar, P. and Mokhtar, S.S.M. (2017), "Female shoppers' outlook of firms' fairness in marketing communications and distribution channels", *Management & Marketing Journal*, Vol. 15 No. 1, pp. 40–60.

Kumar, V., Aksoy, L., Donkers, B., Venkatesan, R., Wiesel, T., and Tillmanns, S. (2010), "Undervalued or overvalued customers: Capturing total customer engagement value", *Journal of Service Research*, Vol. 13 No. 3, pp. 297–310.

Kumar, V., Dixit, A., Javalgi, R.G., and Dass, M. (2016), "Research framework, strategies, and applications of intelligent agent technologies in marketing", *Journal of the Academy of Marketing Science*, Vol. 44 No. 1, pp. 24–45.

Kumar, V. and Pansari, A. (2016), "Competitive advantage through engagement", *Journal of Marketing Research*, Vol. 53 No. 4, pp. 497–514.

Kunz, W., Heinonen, K., and Lemmink, J. (2019), "Future service technologies – is service research on track with business reality?", *Journal of Services Marketing*, Vol. 33 No. 4, pp. 479–487.

Kwok, S. (2019), "Can't complain? Factors influencing dissatisfied customers' non-complaining behaviour", *New Vistas*, Vol. 5 No. 2, pp. 4–7.

La Torre, G., Esposito, A., Sciarra, I., and Chiappetta, M. (2019), "Definition, symptoms and risk of techno-stress: A systematic review", *International Archives of Occupational and Environmental Health*, Vol. 92 No. 1, pp. 13–35.

Lahman, M.K.E., Rodriguez, K.L., Moses, L., Griffin, K.M., Mendoza, B.M., and Yacoub, W. (2015), "A rose by any other name is still a rose? Problematizing pseudonyms in research", *Qualitative Inquiry*, Vol. 21 No. 5, pp. 445–453.

Lam, S.Y., Chiang, J., and Parasuraman, A. (2008), "The effects of the dimensions of technology readiness on technology acceptance: An empirical analysis", *Journal of Interactive Marketing*, Vol. 22 No. 4, pp. 19–39.

Lance, C.E., Butts, M.M., and Michels, L.C. (2006), "The sources of four commonly reported cutoff criteria", *Organizational Research Methods*, Vol. 9 No. 2, pp. 202–220.

Lapidus, R.S. and Pinkerton, L. (1995), "Customer complaint situations: An equity theory perspective", *Psychology and Marketing*, Vol. 12 No. 2, pp. 105–122.

Larivière, B., Bowen, D.E., Andreassen, T.W., Kunz, W., Sirianni, N.J., Voss, C.A., Wünderlich, N.V., and de Keyser, A. (2017), ""Service encounter 2.0": An investigation into the roles of technology, employees and customers", *Journal of Business Research*, Vol. 79 No. 10, pp. 238–246.

Laumer, S. and Eckhardt, A. (2012), "Why do people reject technologies: A review of user resistance theories", in Dwivedi, Y., Wade, M.R. and Schneberger, S.L. (Eds.), *Information systems theory: Explaining and predicting our digital society, Integrated series in information systems*, 1st ed., Springer Science & Business Media, New York, NY, pp. 63–86.

Laumer, S., Maier, C., Eckhardt, A., and Weitzel, T. (2016), "User personality and resistance to mandatory information systems in organizations: A theoretical model and empirical test of dispositional resistance to change", *Journal of Information Technology*, Vol. 31 No. 1, pp. 67–82.

Lazarus, R.S. (1966), *Psychological stress and the coping process*, McGraw-Hill, New York, NY.

Lazarus, R.S. and Folkman, S. (1984), *Stress, appraisal, and coping*, Springer, New York.

Lazarus, R.S. and Folkman, S. (1987), "Transactional theory and research on emotions and coping", *European Journal of Personality*, Vol. 1 No. 3, pp. 141–169.

LeBreton, J.M. and Senter, J.L. (2008), "Answers to 20 questions about interrater reliability and interrater agreement", *Organizational Research Methods*, Vol. 11 No. 4, pp. 815–852.

Lee, J. and Ok, C.M. (2014), "Understanding hotel employees' service sabotage: Emotional labor perspective based on conservation of resources theory", *International Journal of Contemporary Hospitality Management*, Vol. 36 No. 1, pp. 176–187.

Lee, J.S., Keil, M., and Shalev, E. (2019), "Seeing the trees or the forest? The effect of IT project managers' mental construal on IT project risk management activities", *Information Systems Research*, Vol. 30 No. 3, pp. 1051–1072.

Lee, M.K., Verma, R., and Roth, A. (2015), "Understanding customer value in technology-enabled services: A numerical taxonomy based on usage and utility", *Service Science*, Vol. 7 No. 3, pp. 227–248.

Lee-Baggley, D., Preece, M., and DeLongis, A. (2005), "Coping with interpersonal stress: Role of big five traits", *Journal of Personality*, Vol. 73 No. 5, pp. 1141–1180.

Lemon, K.N., Rust, R.T., and Zeithaml, V.A. (2001), "What drives customer equity?", *Marketing Management*, Vol. 10 No. 1, pp. 20–25.

LePine, J.A., Podsakoff, N.P., and LePine, M.A. (2005), "A meta-analytic test of the challenge stressor–hindrance stressor framework: An explanation for inconsistent relationships among stressors and performance", *Academy of Management Journal*, Vol. 48 No. 5, pp. 764–775.

Leventhal, G.S. (1980), "What should be done with equity theory?", in Gergen, K., Greenberg, M. and Willis, R. (Eds.), *Social exchange: Advances in theory and research*, Plenum Press, New York, pp. 27–55.

Li, Y., Gordon, B.R., and Netzer, O. (2018), "An empirical study of national versus local pricing by chain stores under competition", *Marketing Science*, Vol. 37 No. 5, pp. 812–837.

Liao, H. and Subramony, M. (2008), "Employee customer orientation in manufacturing organizations: Joint influences of customer proximity and the senior leadership team", *Journal of Applied Psychology*, Vol. 93 No. 2, pp. 317–328.

Lichtblau, K., Bertenrath, R., Kleissner, A., Kempermann, H., Millack, A., and Ewald, J. (2017), "Die Bedeutung des Hotel- und Gaststättengewerbes", available at: https://www.dehoga-bayern.de/fileadmin/news_import/Studie_IW_Consult_2017_Bedeutung_des_Gastgewerbes_final.pdf (accessed 2 March 2020).

Lieber, E. and Syverson, C. (2012), "Online versus offline competition", in Peitz, M. and Waldfogel, J. (Eds.), *The oxford handbook of the digital economy*, Oxford Univ. Press, Oxford, pp. 189–223.

Liljander, V., Gillberg, F., Gummerus, J., and van Riel, A. (2006), "Technology readiness and the evaluation and adoption of self-service technologies", *Journal of Retailing and Consumer Services*, Vol. 13 No. 3, pp. 177–191.

Lin, C.-H., Shih, H.-Y., and Sher, P.J. (2007), "Integrating technology readiness into technology acceptance: The TRAM model", *Psychology and Marketing*, Vol. 24 No. 7, pp. 641–657.

Lin, J.-S.C. and Hsieh, P.-L. (2012), "Refinement of the technology readiness index scale", *Journal of Service Management*, Vol. 23 No. 1, pp. 34–53.

Lind, E.A., Kulik, C.T., Ambrose, M., and de Vera Park, M.V. (1993), "Individual and corporate dispute resolution: Using procedural fairness as a decision heuristic", *Administrative Science Quarterly*, Vol. 38 No. 2, pp. 224–251.

Lind, E.A. and Tyler, T.R. (1988), *The social psychology of procedural justice, Critical issues in social justice*, Plenum Pr, New York, NY.

Lindell, M.K. and Whitney, D.J. (2001), "Accounting for common method variance in cross-sectional research designs", *Journal of Applied Psychology*, Vol. 86 No. 1, pp. 114–121.

Litvin, S.W., Goldsmith, R.E., and Pan, B. (2008), "Electronic word-of-mouth in hospitality and tourism management", *Tourism Management*, Vol. 29 No. 3, pp. 458–468.

Liu, X.-Y., Chi, N.-W., and Gremler, D.D. (2019), "Emotion cycles in services: Emotional contagion and emotional labor effects", *Journal of Service Research*, Vol. 22 No. 3, pp. 285–300.

Loureiro, S.M.C. and Ribeiro, L. (2014), "Virtual atmosphere: The effect of pleasure, arousal, and delight on word-of-mouth", *Journal of Promotion Management*, Vol. 20 No. 4, pp. 452–469.

Lovelock, C.H. (1983), "Classifying services to gain strategic marketing insights", *Journal of Marketing*, Vol. 47 No. 3, pp. 9–20.

Lovelock, C.H. and Gummesson, E. (2004), "Whither services marketing?", *Journal of Service Research*, Vol. 7 No. 1, pp. 20–41.

Lovelock, C.H. and Young, R.F. (1979), "Look to consumers to increase productivity", *Harvard Business Review*, Vol. 57 No. 3, pp. 168–178.

Loveman, G.W. (1998), "Employee satisfaction, customer loyalty, and financial performance", *Journal of Service Research*, Vol. 1 No. 1, pp. 18–31.

Luca, M., Mohan, K., and Rooney, P. (2016), "Launching Yelp reservations", Teaching Note, Harvard Business School, July 2016.

Ludwig, N.L., Heidenreich, S., Kraemer, T., and Gouthier, M.H.J. (2017), "Customer delight: Universal remedy or a double-edged sword?", *Journal of Service Theory and Practice*, Vol. 27 No. 1, pp. 22–45.

Luria, G., Gal, I., and Yagil, D. (2009), "Employees' willingness to report service complaints", *Journal of Service Research*, Vol. 12 No. 2, pp. 156–174.

Lusch, R.F. and Vargo, S.L. (2006), "Service-dominant logic: Reactions, reflections and refinements", *Marketing Theory*, Vol. 6 No. 3, pp. 281–288.

Lusch, R.F., Vargo, S.L., and O'Brien, M. (2007), "Competing through service: Insights from service-dominant logic", *Journal of Retailing*, Vol. 83 No. 1, pp. 5–18.

Lynn, M. (2019), "Predictors of occupational differences in tipping", *International Journal of Contemporary Hospitality Management*, Vol. 81 No. 6, pp. 221–228.

Lynn, M. and Latane, B. (1984), "The psychology of restaurant tipping", *Journal of Applied Social Psychology*, Vol. 14 No. 6, pp. 549–561.

Lynn, M. and McCall, M. (2000), "Gratitude and gratuity: A meta-analysis of research on the service-tipping relationship", *The Journal of Socio-Economics*, Vol. 29 No. 2, pp. 203–214.

Ma, S. (2017), "Fast or free shipping options in online and omni-channel retail? The mediating role of uncertainty on satisfaction and purchase intentions", *The International Journal of Logistics Management*, Vol. 28 No. 4, pp. 1099–1122.

Maack, K., Haves, J., Homann, B., and Schmid, K. (2013), *Die Zukunft des Gastgewerbes: Beschäftigungsperspektiven im deutschen Gastgewerbe*, Düsseldorf, available at: https://www.boeckler.de/pdf/p_edition_hbs_188.pdf (accessed 13 July 2020).

Maglio, P.P. and Spohrer, J. (2008), "Fundamentals of service science", *Journal of the Academy of Marketing Science*, Vol. 36 No. 1, pp. 18–20.

Maier, C., Laumer, S., and Eckhardt, A. (2015), "Information technology as daily stressor: Pinning down the causes of burnout", *Journal of Business Economics*, Vol. 85 No. 4, pp. 349–387.

Maier, C., Laumer, S., Wirth, J., and Weitzel, T. (2019), "Technostress and the hierarchical levels of personality: A two-wave study with multiple data samples", *Eur. J. Inf. Syst.*, Vol. 28 No. 5, pp. 496–522.

Mani, Z. and Chouk, I. (2017), "Drivers of consumers' resistance to smart products", *Journal of Marketing Management*, Vol. 33 No. 1-2, pp. 76–97.

Marinova, D., de Ruyter, K., Huang, M.-H., Meuter, M.L., and Challagalla, G. (2017), "Getting smart", *Journal of Service Research*, Vol. 20 No. 1, pp. 29–42.

Markus, M.L. and Robey, D. (1988), "Information technology and organizational change: Causal structure in theory and research", *Management Science*, Vol. 34 No. 5, pp. 583–598.

Marshall, B., Cardon, P., Poddar, A., and Fontenot, R. (2013), "Does sample size matter in qualitative research? A review of qualitative interviews in is research", *Journal of Computer Information Systems*, Vol. 54 No. 1, pp. 11–22.

Martin, W.C. and Lueg, J.E. (2013), "Modeling word-of-mouth usage", *Journal of Business Research*, Vol. 66 No. 7, pp. 801–808.

Matud, M. (2004), "Gender differences in stress and coping styles", *Personality and Individual Differences*, Vol. 37 No. 7, pp. 1401–1415.

Maxham, J.G. and Netemeyer, R.G. (2002), "Modeling customer perceptions of complaint handling over time: The effects of perceived justice on satisfaction and intent", *Journal of Retailing*, Vol. 78 No. 4, pp. 239–252.

Maxham, J.G., Netemeyer, R.G., and Lichtenstein, D.R. (2008), "The retail value chain: Linking employee perceptions to employee performance, customer evaluations, and store performance", *Marketing Science*, Vol. 27 No. 2, pp. 147–167.

McCallum, R.J. and Harrison, W. (1985), "Interdependence in the service encounter", in Czepiel, J.A., Solomon, M.R. and Surprenant, C.F. (Eds.), *The service encounter: Managing employee customer interaction in service businesses, The advances in retailing series*, 2. print, Lexington Books, Lexington, Mass., pp. 35–48.

McColl-Kennedy, J.R. and Sparks, B.A. (2003), "Application of fairness theory to service failures and service recovery", *Journal of Service Research*, Vol. 5 No. 3, pp. 251–266.

McGrath, J.E. (Ed.) (1970), *Social and psychological factors in stress*, Holt, Rinehart and Winston, New York.

McLean Parks, J., Ma, L., and Gallagher, D.G. (2010), "Elasticity in the 'rules' of the game: Exploring organizational expedience", *Human Relations*, Vol. 63 No. 5, pp. 701–730.

McMillan, S.J. and Morrison, M. (2006), "Coming of age with the internet", *New Media & Society*, Vol. 8 No. 1, pp. 73–95.

Melton, H.L. and Hartline, M.D. (2010), "Customer and frontline employee influence on new service development performance", *Journal of Service Research*, Vol. 13 No. 4, pp. 411–425.

Meng, J., Elliott, K.M., and Hall, M.C. (2009), "Technology readiness index: Assessing cross-cultural validity", *Journal of International Consumer Marketing*, Vol. 22 No. 1, pp. 19–31.

Merle, A., Senecal, S., and St-Onge, A. (2012), "Whether and how virtual try-on influences consumer responses to an apparel web site", *International Journal of Electronic Commerce*, Vol. 16 No. 3, pp. 41–64.

Meuter, M.L., Ostrom, A.L., Bitner, M.J., and Roundtree, R.I. (2003), "The influence of technology anxiety on consumer use and experiences with self-service technologies", *Journal of Business Research*, Vol. 56 No. 11, pp. 899–906.

Meyer, P., Jonas, J.M., and Roth, A. (2020), "Frontline employees' acceptance of and resistance to service robots in stationary retail – an exploratory interview study", *Journal of Service Management Research*, Vol. 4 No. 1, pp. 21–34.

Mick, D.G. and Fournier, S. (1998), "Paradoxes of technology: Consumer cognizance, emotions, and coping strategies", *Journal of Consumer Research*, Vol. 25 No. 2, pp. 123–143.

Miles, I. (2007), "Research and development (R&D) beyond manufacturing: The strange case of services R&D", *R&D Management*, Vol. 37 No. 3, pp. 249–268.

Milgram, P. and Kishino, F. (1994), "A taxonomy of mixed reality visual displays", *IEICE Transactions on Information and Systems*, No. E77-D, pp. 1321–1329.

Mills, P.K. and Morris, J.H. (1986), "Clients as 'partial' employees of service organizations: Role development in client participation", *Academy of Management Review*, Vol. 11 No. 4, pp. 726–735.

Moeller, S. (2008), "Customer integration—a key to an implementation perspective of service provision", *Journal of Service Research*, Vol. 11 No. 2, pp. 197–210.

Montargot, N. and Ben Lahouel, B. (2018), "The acceptance of technological change in the hospitality industry from the perspective of front-line employees", *Journal of Organizational Change Management*, Vol. 31 No. 3, pp. 637–655.

Moreno, P. and Tejada, P. (2019), "Reviewing the progress of information and communication technology in the restaurant industry", *Journal of Hospitality and Tourism Technology*, Vol. 10 No. 4, pp. 673–688.

Mosteller, J., Donthu, N., and Eroglu, S. (2014), "The fluent online shopping experience", *Journal of Business Research*, Vol. 67 No. 11, pp. 2486–2493.

Mulki, J.P., Jaramillo, F., Malhotra, S., and Locander, W.B. (2012), "Reluctant employees and felt stress: The moderating impact of manager decisiveness", *Journal of Business Research*, Vol. 65 No. 1, pp. 77–83.

Mun, S.G. and Jang, S. (2018), "Restaurant operating expenses and their effects on profitability enhancement", *International Journal of Hospitality Management*, Vol. 71, pp. 68–76.

Muraven, M., Tice, D.M., and Baumeister, R.F. (1998), "Self-control as a limited resource: Regulatory depletion patterns", *Journal of Personality and Social Psychology*, Vol. 74 No. 3, pp. 774–789.

Mustak, M., Jaakkola, E., and Halinen, A. (2013), "Customer participation and value creation: A systematic review and research implications", *Managing Service Quality*, Vol. 23 No. 4, pp. 341–359.

Nambisan, S. (2013), "Information technology and product/service innovation: A brief assessment and some suggestions for future research", *Journal of the Association for Information Systems*, Vol. 14 No. 4, pp. 215–226.

Narayanan, L., Menon, S., and Spector, P.E. (1999), "Stress in the workplace: A comparison of gender and occupations", *Journal of Organizational Behavior*, Vol. 20 No. 1, pp. 63–73.

National Restaurant Association (2017), "Restaurant industry pocket factbook", available at: https://www.restaurant.org/Downloads/PDFs/News-Research/Pocket_Factbook_FEB_2017-FINAL.pdf (accessed 29 June 2018).

National Restaurant Association (2018), "Restaurant technology survey 2016: Mapping the restaurant technology landscape in 2016", available at: https://www.restaurant.org/Downloads/PDFs/News-Research/TechResearch_Show2016-web.pdf (accessed 9 August 2018).

National Restaurant Association (2019), "Restaurant industry pocket factbook", available at: https://restaurant.org/Downloads/PDFs/Research/SOI/restaurant_industry_fact_sheet_2019.pdf (accessed 10 May 2019).

Nayyar, A., Mahapatra, B., Le, D., and Suseendran, G. (2018), "Virtual reality (VR) & augmented reality (AR) technologies for tourism and hospitality industry", *International Journal of Engineering & Technology*, Vol. 7 No. 2.21, pp. 156–160.

Netemeyer, R.G., Johnston, M.W., and Burton, S. (1990), "Analysis of role conflict and role ambiguity in a structural equations framework", *Journal of Applied Psychology*, Vol. 75 No. 2, pp. 148–157.

Netemeyer, R.G., Maxham, J.G., and Pullig, C. (2005), "Conflicts in the work-family interface: Links to job stress, customer service employee performance, and customer purchase intent", *Journal of Marketing*, Vol. 69 No. 2, pp. 130–143.

Neves, P. and Champion, S. (2015), "Core self-evaluations and workplace deviance: The role of resources and self-regulation", *European Management Journal*, Vol. 33 No. 5, pp. 381–391.

Neyman, J. and Pearson, E.S. (1933), "On the problem of the most efficient tests of statistical hypotheses", *Philosophical Transactions of the Royal Society of London. Series A, Containing Papers of a Mathematical or Physical Character*, Vol. 231, pp. 289–337.

Nguyen, B. and Klaus, P. (2013), "Retail fairness: Exploring consumer perceptions of fairness towards retailers' marketing tactics", *Journal of Retailing and Consumer Services*, Vol. 20 No. 3, pp. 311–324.

Nguyen, H., Groth, M., Walsh, G., and Hennig-Thurau, T. (2014), "The impact of service scripts on customer citizenship behavior and the moderating role of employee customer orientation", *Psychology & Marketing*, Vol. 31 No. 12, pp. 1096–1109.

Nielsen, K., Nielsen, M.B., Ogbonnaya, C., Känsälä, M., Saari, E., and Isaksson, K. (2017), "Workplace resources to improve both employee well-being and performance: A systematic review and meta-analysis", *Work & Stress*, Vol. 31 No. 2, pp. 101–120.

Noone, B.M. (2008), "Customer perceived control and the moderating effect of restaurant type on evaluations of restaurant employee performance", *International Journal of Hospitality Management*, Vol. 27 No. 1, pp. 23–29.

Normann, R. (1984), *Service management: strategy and leadership in service businesses*, Wiley, New York, NY.

Nov, O. and Ye, C. (2009), "Resistance to change and the adoption of digital libraries: An integrative model", *Journal of the American Society for Information Science and Technology*, Vol. 60 No. 8, pp. 1702–1708.

Nyer, P.U. (1997), "A study of the relationships between cognitive appraisals and consumption emotions", *Journal of the Academy of Marketing Science*, Vol. 25 No. 4, pp. 296–304.

O'Brien, R.M. (2007), "A caution regarding rules of thumb for variance inflation factors", *Quality & Quantity*, Vol. 41 No. 5, pp. 673–690.

OECD (2017), "The rise of services in the global economy", in OECD (Ed.), *Services Trade Policies and the Global Economy*, OECD Publishing, Paris, pp. 11–33.

Oertzen, A.-S., Odekerken-Schröder, G., Brax, S.A., and Mager, B. (2018), "Co-creating services—conceptual clarification, forms and outcomes", *Journal of Service Management*, Vol. 29 No. 4, pp. 641–679.

Oertzen, A.-S., Odekerken-Schröder, G., and Mager, B. (2020), "Driving users' behaviours and engagement in co-creating services", *Journal of Services Marketing*, Vol. 34 No. 4, pp. 549–573.

Oliver, R.L. (1980), "A cognitive model of the antecedents and consequences of satisfaction decisions", *Journal of Marketing Research*, Vol. 17 No. 4, pp. 460–469.

Oliver, R.L. (2014), *Satisfaction: A behavioral perspective on the consumer*, 2nd ed., Taylor and Francis, Hoboken.

Oliver, R.L. and DeSarbo, W.S. (1988), "Response determinants in satisfaction judgments", *Journal of Consumer Research*, Vol. 14 No. 4, pp. 495–507.

Oliver, R.L., Rust, R.T., and Varki, S. (1997), "Customer delight: Foundations, findings, and managerial insight", *Journal of Retailing*, Vol. 73 No. 3, pp. 311–336.

Oliver, R.L. and Swan, J.E. (1989), "Consumer perceptions of interpersonal equity and satisfaction in transactions: A field survey approach", *Journal of Marketing*, Vol. 53 No. 2, pp. 21–35.

Olson, J.C. and Dover, P.A. (1979), "Disconfirmation of consumer expectations through product trial", *Journal of Applied Psychology*, Vol. 64 No. 2, pp. 179–189.

Ordanini, A. and Parasuraman, A. (2011), "Service innovation viewed through a service-dominant logic lens: A conceptual framework and empirical analysis", *Journal of Service Research*, Vol. 14 No. 1, pp. 3–23.

Oreg, S. (2003), "Resistance to change: Developing an individual differences measure", *Journal of Applied Psychology*, Vol. 88 No. 4, pp. 680–693.

Oreg, S. (2006), "Personality, context, and resistance to organizational change", *European Journal of Work and Organizational Psychology*, Vol. 15 No. 1, pp. 73–101.

Oronsky, C.R. and Chathoth, P.K. (2007), "An exploratory study examining information technology adoption and implementation in full-service restaurant firms", *International Journal of Contemporary Hospitality Management*, Vol. 26 No. 4, pp. 941–956.

Ostrom, A.L., Bitner, M.J., Brown, S.W., Burkhard, K.A., Goul, M., Smith-Daniels, V., Demirkan, H., and Rabinovich, E. (2010), "Moving forward and making a difference: Research priorities for the science of service", *Journal of Service Research*, Vol. 13 No. 1, pp. 4–36.

Ostrom, A.L., Fotheringham, D., and Bitner, M.J. (2019), "Customer acceptance of AI in service encounters: Understanding antecedents and consequences", in Maglio, P.P. (Ed.), *Handbook of service science. Vol. II, Service Science: Research and Innovations in the Service Economy*, Vol. 24, Springer Nature, Cham, Switzerland, pp. 77–103.

Ostrom, A.L., Parasuraman, A., Bowen, D.E., Patrício, L., and Voss, C.A. (2015), "Service research priorities in a rapidly changing context", *Journal of Service Research*, Vol. 18 No. 2, pp. 127–159.

Öze, N. (2017), "Communication and devices: Face to face communication versus communication with mobile technologies", *World Academy of Science, Engineering and Technology International Journal of Social, Behavioral, Educational, Economic, Business and Industrial Engineering*, Vol. 11 No. 4, pp. 974–987.

Pansari, A. and Kumar, V. (2017), "Customer engagement: The construct, antecedents, and consequences", *Journal of the Academy of Marketing Science*, Vol. 45 No. 3, pp. 294–311.

Pansari, A. and Kumar, V. (2018), "Customer engagement marketing", in Palmatier, R.W., Kumar, V. and Harmeling, C.M. (Eds.), *Customer Engagement Marketing*, Springer International Publishing, Cham, pp. 1–27.

Pantano, E. (2014), "Innovation drivers in retail industry", *International Journal of Information Management*, Vol. 34 No. 3, pp. 344–350.

Pantano, E., Rese, A., and Baier, D. (2017), "Enhancing the online decision-making process by using augmented reality: A two country comparison of youth markets", *Journal of Retailing and Consumer Services*, Vol. 38 No. 5, pp. 81–95.

Paolacci, G., Chandler, J., and Ipeirotis, P.G. (2010), "Running experiments on Amazon Mechanical Turk", *Judgment and Decision Making*, Vol. 5 No. 5, pp. 411–419.

Parasuraman, A. (2000), "Technology readiness index: A multiple-item scale to measure readiness to embrace new technologies", *Journal of Service Research*, Vol. 2 No. 4, pp. 307–320.

Parasuraman, A., Ball, J., Aksoy, L., Keiningham, T.L., and Zaki, M. (2021), "More than a feeling? Toward a theory of customer delight", *Journal of Service Management*, Vol. 32 No. 1, pp. 1–26.

Parasuraman, A. and Colby, C.L. (2015), "An updated and streamlined technology readiness index", *Journal of Service Research*, Vol. 18 No. 1, pp. 59–74.

Parasuraman, A., Zeithaml, V.A., and Berry, L.L. (1985), "A conceptual model of service quality and its implications for future research", *Journal of Marketing*, Vol. 49 No. 4, pp. 41–50.

Parasuraman, A., Zeithaml, V.A., and Berry, L.L. (1988), "SERVQUAL: A multiple-item scale for measuring consumer perceptions of service quality", *Journal of Retailing*, Vol. 64 No. 1, pp. 12–40.

Parasuraman, A., Zeithaml, V.A., and Malhotra, A. (2005), "E-S-QUAL", *Journal of Service Research*, Vol. 7 No. 3, pp. 213–233.

Park, H.I., Jacob, A.C., Wagner, S.H., and Baiden, M. (2014), "Job control and burnout: A meta-analytic test of the conservation of resources model", *Applied Psychology*, Vol. 63 No. 4, pp. 607–642.

Parrett, M. (2006), "An analysis of the determinants of tipping behavior: A laboratory experiment and evidence from restaurant tipping", *Southern Economic Journal*, Vol. 73 No. 2, pp. 489–514.

Patrício, L., Fisk, R.P., Falcão e Cunha, J., and Constantine, L. (2011), "Multilevel service design: From customer value constellation to service experience blueprinting", *Journal of Service Research*, Vol. 14 No. 2, pp. 180–200.

Perea y Monsuwé, T., Dellaert, B.G., and de Ruyter, K. (2004), "What drives consumers to shop online? A literature review", *International Journal of Service Industry Management*, Vol. 15 No. 1, pp. 102–121.

Peterson, D.K. (2002), "Deviant workplace behavior and the organization's ethical climate", *Journal of Business and Psychology*, Vol. 17 No. 1, pp. 47–61.

Piderit, S.K. (2000), "Rethinking resistance and recognizing ambivalence: A multidimensional view of attitudes toward an organizational change", *Academy of Management Review*, Vol. 25 No. 4, pp. 783–794.

Pilat, D. (1996), "Competition, productivity and efficiency", *OECD Economic Studies*, Vol. 27 No. 2, pp. 107–146.

Pina e Cunha, M., Campos e Cunha, R., and Rego, A. (2009), "Exploring the role of leader—subordinate interactions in the construction of organizational positivity", *Leadership*, Vol. 5 No. 1, pp. 81–101.

Ployhart, R.E., Nyberg, A.J., Reilly, G., and Maltarich, M.A. (2014), "Human capital is dead; long live human capital resources!", *Journal of Management*, Vol. 40 No. 2, pp. 371–398.

Plutchik, R. (1980), *Emotion, a psychoevolutionary synthesis*, Harper & Row, New York.

Podsakoff, N.P., LePine, J.A., and LePine, M.A. (2007), "Differential challenge stressor-hindrance stressor relationships with job attitudes, turnover intentions, turnover, and withdrawal behavior: A meta-analysis", *Journal of Applied Psychology*, Vol. 92 No. 2, pp. 438–454.

Podsakoff, P.M., MacKenzie, S.B., Lee, J.-Y., and Podsakoff, N.P. (2003), "Common method biases in behavioral research: A critical review of the literature and recommended remedies", *Journal of Applied Psychology*, Vol. 88 No. 5, pp. 879–903.

Poushneh, A. (2018), "Augmented reality in retail: A trade-off between user's control of access to personal information and augmentation quality", *Journal of Retailing and Consumer Services*, Vol. 41 No. 2, pp. 169–176.

Poushneh, A. and Vasquez-Parraga, A.Z. (2017a), "Customer dissatisfaction and satisfaction with augmented reality in shopping and entertainment", *Journal of Consumer Satisfaction, Dissatisfaction & Complaining Behavior*, Vol. 30 No. 1, pp. 97–118.

Poushneh, A. and Vasquez-Parraga, A.Z. (2017b), "Discernible impact of augmented reality on retail customer's experience, satisfaction and willingness to buy", *Journal of Retailing and Consumer Services*, Vol. 34 No. 1, pp. 229–234.

Prahalad, C.K. and Ramaswamy, V. (2004), "Co-creation experiences: The next practice in value creation", *Journal of Interactive Marketing*, Vol. 18 No. 3, pp. 5–14.

Preacher, K.J. and Hayes, A.F. (2004), "SPSS and SAS procedures for estimating indirect effects in simple mediation models", *Behavior Research Methods, Instruments, & Computers*, Vol. 36 No. 4, pp. 717–731.

Price, L.L., Arnould, E.J., and Deibler, S.L. (1995), "Consumers' emotional responses to service encounters", *International Journal of Service Industry Management*, Vol. 6 No. 3, pp. 34–63.

Puzder, A. (2016), "Why restaurant automation is on the menu", available at: https://www.wsj.com/articles/why-restaurant-automation-is-on-the-menu-1458857730?mg=id-wsj (accessed 15 December 2019).

Qiu, H., Li, M., Shu, B., and Bai, B. (2019), "Enhancing hospitality experience with service robots: The mediating role of rapport building", *Journal of Hospitality Marketing & Management*, Vol. 29 No. 3, pp. 1–22.

Qiu, R. (2013), "Editorial—we must rethink service encounters", *Service Science*, Vol. 5 No. 1, pp. 1–3.

Raddats, C., Kowalkowski, C., Benedettini, O., Burton, J., and Gebauer, H. (2019), "Servitization: A contemporary thematic review of four major research streams", *Industrial Marketing Management*, Vol. 83 No. 8, pp. 207–223.

Rafaeli, A., Altman, D., Gremler, D.D., Huang, M.-H., Grewal, D., Iyer, B., Parasuraman, A., and de Ruyter, K. (2017), "The future of frontline research", *Journal of Service Research*, Vol. 20 No. 1, pp. 91–99.

Rafaeli, A., Ziklik, L., and Doucet, L. (2008), "The impact of call center employees' customer orientation behaviors on service quality", *Journal of Service Research*, Vol. 10 No. 3, pp. 239–255.

Ragu-Nathan, T.S., Tarafdar, M., Ragu-Nathan, B.S., and Tu, Q. (2008), "The consequences of technostress for end users in organizations: Conceptual development and empirical validation", *Information Systems Research*, Vol. 19 No. 4, pp. 417–433.

Ramaseshan, B., Kingshott, R.P., and Stein, A. (2015), "Firm self-service technology readiness", *Journal of Service Management*, Vol. 26 No. 5, pp. 751–776.

Rathmell, J.M. (1974), *Marketing in the service sector*, Winthrop Publ, Cambridge, Mass.

Reinartz, W.J. and Berkmann, M. (2018), "From customer to partner engagement: A conceptualization and typology of engagement in B2B", in Palmatier, R.W., Kumar, V. and Harmeling, C.M. (Eds.), *Customer Engagement Marketing*, Springer International Publishing, Cham, pp. 243–268.

Reinders, M.J., Dabholkar, P.A., and Frambach, R.T. (2008), "Consequences of forcing consumers to use technology-based self-service", *Journal of Service Research*, Vol. 11 No. 2, pp. 107–123.

Rese, A., Baier, D., Geyer-Schulz, A., and Schreiber, S. (2017), "How augmented reality apps are accepted by consumers: A comparative analysis using scales and opinions", *Technological Forecasting and Social Change*, Vol. 124 No. 11, pp. 306–319.

Richins, M.L. (1983), "Negative word-of-mouth by dissatisfied consumers: A pilot study", *Journal of Marketing*, Vol. 47 No. 1, pp. 68–78.

Riedel, A. and Mulcahy, R.F. (2019), "Does more sense make sense? An empirical test of high and low interactive retail technology", *Journal of Services Marketing*, Vol. 33 No. 3, pp. 331–343.

Riedl, R., Kindermann, H., Auinger, A., and Javor, A. (2012), "Technostress from a neurobiological perspective: System breakdown increases the stress hormone cortisol in computer users", *Business & Information Systems Engineering*, Vol. 4 No. 2, pp. 61–69.

Rizzo, J.R., House, R.J., and Lirtzman, S.I. (1970), "Role conflict and ambiguity in complex organizations", *Administrative Science Quarterly*, Vol. 15 No. 2, pp. 150–163.

Robinson, S., Orsingher, C., Alkire, L., de Keyser, A., Giebelhausen, M., Papamichail, K.N., Shams, P., and Temerak, M.S. (2020), "Frontline encounters of the AI kind: An evolved service encounter framework", *Journal of Business Research*, Vol. 116 No. 11, pp. 366–376.

Rod, M. and Ashill, N.J. (2009), "Symptoms of burnout and service recovery performance", *Managing Service Quality*, Vol. 19 No. 1, pp. 60–84.

Rodrigue, J.-P. (2020), *The geography of transport systems,* 5th edition, Routledge.

Rodríguez-López, M.E., Alcántara-Pilar, J.M., Del Barrio-García, S., and Muñoz-Leiva, F. (2020), "A review of restaurant research in the last two decades: A bibliometric analysis", *International Journal of Hospitality Management*, Vol. 87 No. 4.

Ross, A. and Willson, V.L. (2018), "One-way ANOVA", in Ross, A. and Willson, V.L. (Eds.), *Basic and advanced statistical tests: writing results sections and creating tables and figures*, Sense Publishers, Rotterdam, pp. 21–24.

Roy, P.K., Mahmud, I., Jahan, N., and Sadia, F. (2017), "An investigation on exhaustion of SAP ERP users: Influence of pace of change and technostress", *Annals of Emerging Technologies in Computing*, Vol. 1 No. 1, pp. 19–25.

Roy, S.K., Shekhar, V., Lassar, W.M., and Chen, T. (2018), "Customer engagement behaviors: The role of service convenience, fairness and quality", *Journal of Retailing and Consumer Services*, Vol. 44 No. 5, pp. 293–304.

Rust, R.T. and Huang, M.-H. (2012), "Optimizing service productivity", *Journal of Marketing*, Vol. 76 No. 2, pp. 47–66.

Rust, R.T. and Huang, M.-H. (2014), "The service revolution and the transformation of marketing science", *Marketing Science*, Vol. 33 No. 2, pp. 206–221.

Rust, R.T., Zahorik, A.J., and Keiningham, T.L. (1995), "Return on quality: Making service quality financially accountable", *Journal of Marketing*, Vol. 59 No. 2, pp. 58–70.

Rust, R.T., Zahorik, A.J., and Keiningham, T.L. (1996), *Service marketing*, HarperCollins College Publishers, New York, NY.

Ryu, H.-S. and Lee, J.-N. (2018), "Understanding the role of technology in service innovation: Comparison of three theoretical perspectives", *Information & Management*, Vol. 55 No. 3, pp. 294–307.

Salanova, M., Agut, S., and Peiró, J.M. (2005), "Linking organizational resources and work engagement to employee performance and customer loyalty: The mediation of service climate", *Journal of Applied Psychology*, Vol. 90 No. 6, pp. 1217–1227.

Salanova, M., Llorens, S., and Cifre, E. (2013), "The dark side of technologies: Technostress among users of information and communication technologies", *International Journal of Psychology*, Vol. 48 No. 3, pp. 422–436.

Saldaña, J. (2016), *The coding manual for qualitative researchers*, 3. edition, SAGE Publications, Los Angeles.

Salmerón, R., García, C.B., and García, J. (2018), "Variance inflation factor and condition number in multiple linear regression", *Journal of Statistical Computation and Simulation*, Vol. 88 No. 12, pp. 2365–2384.

Sands, S., Ferraro, C., Campbell, C., and Tsao, H.-Y. (2020), "Managing the human–chatbot divide: How service scripts influence service experience", *Journal of Service Management*, Vol. 32 No. 2, pp. 246–264.

Sangiorgi, D., Lima, F., Patrício, L., Joly, M.P., and Favini, C. (2019), "A human-centred, multidisciplinary, and transformative approach to service science: A service design perspective", in Maglio, P.P. (Ed.), *Handbook of service science. Vol. II, Service Science: Research and Innovations in the Service Economy*, Vol. 18, Springer Nature, Cham, Switzerland, pp. 147–181.

Saxe, R. and Weitz, B.A. (1982), "The SOCO scale: A measure of the customer orientation of salespeople", *Journal of Marketing Research*, Vol. 19 No. 3, pp. 343–351.

Schaarschmidt, M. (2016), "Frontline employees' participation in service innovation implementation: The role of perceived external reputation", *European Management Journal*, Vol. 34 No. 5, pp. 540–549.

Schaarschmidt, M. and Hoeber, B. (2017), "Digital booking services: Comparing online with phone reservation services", *Journal of Services Marketing*, Vol. 31 No. 7, pp. 704–719.

Schaufeli, W.B. and Taris, T.W. (2014), "A critical review of the job demands-resources model: Implications for improving work and health", in Bauer, G.F. and Hämmig, O. (Eds.), *Bridging occupational, organizational and public health: A transdisciplinary approach*, Springer, Dordrecht, pp. 43–68.

Schepers, J. and van der Borgh, M. (2020), "A meta-analysis of frontline employees' role behavior and the moderating effects of national culture", *Journal of Service Research*, Vol. 23 No. 3, 255-280.

Scherer, A., Wünderlich, N.V., and von Wangenheim, F. (2015), "The value of self-service: Long-term effects of technology-based self-service usage on customer retention", *MIS Quarterly*, Vol. 39 No. 1, pp. 177–200.

Schneider, B. and Bowen, D.E. (1999), "Understanding customer delight and outrage", *Sloan management review*, Vol. 41 No. 1, pp. 35–45.

Scholz, J. and Duffy, K. (2018), "We ARe at home: How augmented reality reshapes mobile marketing and consumer-brand relationships", *Journal of Retailing and Consumer Services*, Vol. 44 No. 5, pp. 11–23.

Schwartz, K. (2019), "The latest in translation devices", available at: https://www.nytimes.com/2019/11/07/travel/the-latest-in-translation-devices.html (accessed 15 January 2020).

Schwarzer, R. and Jerusalem, M. (1995), "Generalized self-efficacy scale", in Johnston, M., Wright, S. and Weinman, J. (Eds.), *Measures in health psychology: A user's portfolio. Causal and control beliefs*, Vol. 1, NFER Nelson Publishing, Windsor, pp. 35–37.

Seiders, K. and Berry, L.L. (1998), "Service fairness: What it is and why it matters", *Academy of Management Perspectives*, Vol. 12 No. 2, pp. 8–20.

Seiter, J.S. (2007), "Ingratiation and gratuity: The effect of complimenting customers on tipping behavior in restaurants", *Journal of Applied Social Psychology*, Vol. 37 No. 3, pp. 478–485.

Selzer, V.L., Schumann, J.H., Büttgen, M., Ates, Z., Komor, M., and Volz, J. (2021), "Effective coping strategies for stressed frontline employees in service occupations: Outcomes and drivers", *The Service Industries Journal*, Vol. 41 No. 5-6, pp. 382–399.

Sharma, A. (1999), "Does the salesperson like customers? A conceptual and empirical examination of the persuasive effect of perceptions of the salesperson's affect toward customers", *Psychology and Marketing*, Vol. 16 No. 2, pp. 141–162.

Shehryar, O. and Hunt, D.M. (2005), "Buyer behavior and procedural fairness in pricing: Exploring the moderating role of product familiarity", *Journal of Product & Brand Management*, Vol. 14 No. 4, pp. 271–276.

Sherer, M. and Adams, C.H. (1983), "Construct validation of the self-efficacy scale", *Psychological Reports*, Vol. 53 No. 3, pp. 899–902.

Shin, J., Taylor, M.S., and Seo, M.-G. (2012), "Resources for change: The relationships of organizational inducements and psychological resilience to employees' attitudes and behaviors toward organizational change", *Academy of Management Journal*, Vol. 55 No. 3, pp. 727–748.

Shoemaker, M.E. (1999), "Leadership practices in sales managers associated with the self-efficacy, role clarity, and job satisfaction of individual industrial salespeople", *The Journal of Personal Selling and Sales Management*, Vol. 19 No. 4, pp. 1–19.

Shugan, S.M. (1980), "The cost of thinking", *Journal of Consumer Research*, Vol. 7 No. 2, pp. 99–111.

Silpakit, P. and Fisk, R.P. (1985), "Participatizing' the service encounter: A theoretical framework", in Block, T.M., Upah, G.D. and Zeithaml, V.A. (Eds.), *Services marketing in a changing environment*, Chicago, IL, pp. 117–121.

Singh, J., Brady, M.K., Arnold, T.J., and Brown, T.J. (2017), "The emergent field of organizational frontlines", *Journal of Service Research*, Vol. 20 No. 1, pp. 3–11.

Singh, J. and Wilkes, R.E. (1996), "When consumers complain: A path analysis of the key antecedents of consumer complaint response estimates", *Journal of the Academy of Marketing Science*, Vol. 24 No. 4, pp. 350–365.

Sirianni, N.J., Bitner, M.J., Brown, S.W., and Mandel, N. (2013), "Branded service encounters: Strategically aligning employee behavior with the brand positioning", *Journal of Marketing*, Vol. 77 No. 6, pp. 108–123.

Sirianni, N.J., Castro-Nelson, I., Morales, A.C., and Fitzsimons, G.J. (2009), "The influence of service employee characteristics on customer choice and post-choice satisfaction", paper presented at Northern America - Advances in Consumer Research Conference, 2009, Duluth, Minnesota.

Smith, D.E. (1965), "Front-line organization of the state mental hospital", *Administrative Science Quarterly*, Vol. 10 No. 3, pp. 381–399.

Snellman, K. and Vihtkari, T. (2003), "Customer complaining behaviour in technology-based service encounters", *International Journal of Service Industry Management*, Vol. 14 No. 2, pp. 217–231.

Söderlund, M., Liljander, V., Gummerus, J., Hellman, P., Lipkin, M., Oikarinen, E.-L., Sepp, M., and T. Liljedal, K. (2014), "Preferential treatment in the service encounter", *Journal of Service Management*, Vol. 25 No. 4, pp. 512–530.

Sok, P., Sok, K.M., Danaher, T.S., and Danaher, P.J. (2018), "The complementarity of front-line service employee creativity and attention to detail in service delivery", *Journal of Service Research*, Vol. 21 No. 3, 365-378.

Solnet, D., Subramony, M., Ford, R.C., Golubovskaya, M., Kang, H.J., and Hancer, M. (2019), "Leveraging human touch in service interactions: Lessons from hospitality", *Journal of Service Management*, Vol. 30 No. 3, pp. 392–409.

Solomon, M.R., Surprenant, C., Czepiel, J.A., and Gutman, E.G. (1985), "A role theory perspective on dyadic interactions: The service encounter", *Journal of Marketing*, Vol. 49 No. 1, pp. 99–111.

Sparks, K., Faragher, B., and Cooper, C.L. (2001), "Well-being and occupational health in the 21st century workplace", *Journal of Occupational and Organizational Psychology*, Vol. 74 No. 4, pp. 489–509.

Spector, P.E., Chen, P.Y., and O'Connell, B.J. (2000), "A longitudinal study of relations between job stressors and job strains while controlling for prior negative affectivity and strains", *Journal of Applied Psychology*, Vol. 85 No. 2, pp. 211–218.

Spector, P.E. and Jex, S.M. (1998), "Development of four self-report measures of job stressors and strain: Interpersonal conflict at work scale, organizational constraints scale, quantitative workload inventory, and physical symptoms inventory", *Journal of Occupational Health Psychology*, Vol. 3 No. 4, pp. 356–367.

Spohrer, J., Kwan, S.K., and Fisk, R.P. (2014), "Marketing: A service science and arts perspective", in Huang, M.-H. and Rust, R.T. (Eds.), *Handbook of service marketing research*, Edward Elgar Publishing, Cheltenham, pp. 489–526.

Srivastava, S.C., Chandra, S., and Shirish, A. (2015), "Technostress creators and job outcomes: Theorising the moderating influence of personality traits", *Information Systems Journal*, Vol. 25 No. 4, pp. 355–401.

Steuer, J. (1992), "Defining virtual reality: Dimensions determining telepresence", *Journal of Communication*, Vol. 42 No. 4, pp. 73–93.

Stock, R.M. and Bednarek, M. (2014), "As they sow, so shall they reap: Customers' influence on customer satisfaction at the customer interface", *Journal of the Academy of Marketing Science*, Vol. 42 No. 4, pp. 400–414.

Stock, R.M., de Jong, A., and Zacharias, N.A. (2017), "Frontline employees' innovative service behavior as key to customer loyalty: Insights into FLEs' resource gain spiral", *Journal of Product Innovation Management*, Vol. 34 No. 2, pp. 223–245.

Storey, C., Cankurtaran, P., Papastathopoulou, P., and Hultink, E.J. (2016), "Success factors for service innovation: A meta-analysis", *Journal of Product Innovation Management*, Vol. 33 No. 5, pp. 527–548.

Stritch, J.M., Pedersen, M.J., and Taggart, G. (2017), "The opportunities and limitations of using Mechanical Turk (MTurk) in public administration and management scholarship", *International Public Management Journal*, Vol. 20 No. 3, pp. 489–511.

Strutton, D., Taylor, D.G., and Thompson, K. (2011), "Investigating generational differences in e-WOM behaviours", *International Journal of Advertising*, Vol. 30 No. 4, pp. 559–586.

Subramaniam, M., Iyer, B., and Venkatraman, V. (2019), "Competing in digital ecosystems", *Business Horizons*, Vol. 62 No. 1, pp. 83–94.

Subramony, M., Ehrhart, K., Groth, M., Holtom, B.C., van Jaarsveld, D.D., Yagil, D., Darabi, T., Walker, D., Bowen, D.E., Fisk, R.P., Grönroos, C., and Wirtz, J. (2017), "Accelerating employee-related scholarship in service management", *Journal of Service Management*, Vol. 28 No. 5, pp. 837–865.

Subramony, M. and Pugh, S.D. (2015), "Services management research", *Journal of Management*, Vol. 41 No. 1, pp. 349–373.

Surprenant, C.F. and Solomon, M.R. (1987), "Predictability and personalization in the service encounter", *Journal of Marketing*, Vol. 51 No. 2, pp. 86–96.

Susskind, A.M., Kacmar, K.M., and Borchgrevink, C.P. (2003), "Customer service providers' attitudes relating to customer service and customer satisfaction in the customer-server exchange", *Journal of Applied Psychology*, Vol. 88 No. 1, pp. 179–187.

Sweeney, J.C., Soutar, G.N., and Mazzarol, T. (2008), "Factors influencing word of mouth effectiveness: Receiver perspectives", *European Journal of Marketing*, Vol. 42 No. 3/4, pp. 344–364.

Szymanski, D.M. and Henard, D.H. (2001), "Customer satisfaction: A meta-analysis of the empirical evidence", *Journal of the Academy of Marketing Science*, Vol. 29 No. 1, pp. 16–35.

Tan, T.F. and Netessine, S. (2020), "At your service on the table: Impact of tabletop technology on restaurant performance", *Management Science*, Vol. 66 No. 10, 4496-4515.

Tarafdar, M., Cooper, C.L., and Stich, J.-F. (2019), "The technostress trifecta - techno eustress, techno distress and design: Theoretical directions and an agenda for research", *Information Systems Journal*, Vol. 29 No. 1, pp. 6–42.

Tarafdar, M., Pullins, E.B., and Ragu-Nathan, T.S. (2015), "Technostress: Negative effect on performance and possible mitigations", *Information Systems Journal*, Vol. 25 No. 2, pp. 103–132.

Tarafdar, M., Tu, Q., Ragu-Nathan, B.S., and Ragu-Nathan, T.S. (2007), "The impact of technostress on role stress and productivity", *Journal of Management Information Systems*, Vol. 24 No. 1, pp. 301–328.

Tarafdar, M., Tu, Q., and Ragu-Nathan, T.S. (2010), "Impact of technostress on end-user satisfaction and performance", *Journal of Management Information Systems*, Vol. 27 No. 3, pp. 303–334.

Teas, R.K., Wacker, J.G., and Hughes, R.E. (1979), "A path analysis of causes and consequences of salespeople's perceptions of role clarity", *Journal of Marketing Research*, Vol. 16 No. 3, pp. 355–369.

ten Brummelhuis, L.L., ter Hoeven, C.L., Bakker, A.B., and Peper, B. (2011), "Breaking through the loss cycle of burnout: The role of motivation", *Journal of Occupational and Organizational Psychology*, Vol. 84 No. 2, pp. 268–287.

Tether, B.S. (2005), "Do services innovate (differently)? Insights from the European Innobarometer survey", *Industry & Innovation*, Vol. 12 No. 2, pp. 153–184.

Thatcher, J.B., Stepina, L.P., and Boyle, R.J. (2002), "Turnover of information technology workers: Examining empirically the influence of attitudes, job characteristics, and external markets", *Journal of Management Information Systems*, Vol. 19 No. 3, pp. 231–261.

The World Bank (2020), "Employment in services", available at: https://data.worldbank.org/indicator/SL.SRV.EMPL.ZS (accessed 3 July 2020).

Tims, M., Bakker, A.B., and Derks, D. (2012), "Development and validation of the job crafting scale", *Journal of Vocational Behavior*, Vol. 80 No. 1, pp. 173–186.

Ting, S.-C. (2013), "Service fairness scale: Development, validation, and structure", *International Journal of Marketing Studies*, Vol. 5 No. 6, pp. 25–36.

Toast Inc. (2017), "Restaurant technology in 2017. industry report", available at: https://pos.toasttab.com/resources/restaurant-technology-industry-report (accessed 5 June 2019).

Toivonen, M. and Tuominen, T. (2009), "Emergence of innovations in services", *The Service Industries Journal*, Vol. 29 No. 7, pp. 887–902.

tom Dieck, M.C. and Jung, T.H. (2017), "Value of augmented reality at cultural heritage sites: A stakeholder approach", *Journal of Destination Marketing & Management*, Vol. 6 No. 2, pp. 110–117.

Torres, E.N., Fu, X., and Lehto, X. (2014), "Are there gender differences in what drives customer delight?", *Tourism Review*, Vol. 69 No. 4, pp. 297–309.

Torres, E.N. and Kline, S. (2013), "From customer satisfaction to customer delight", *International Journal of Contemporary Hospitality Management*, Vol. 25 No. 5, pp. 642–659.

Tripathi, G. (2017), "Customer satisfaction and word of mouth intentions: Testing the mediating effect of customer loyalty", *Journal of Service Research*, Vol. 17 No. 2, pp. 1–16.

Trougakos, J.P., Hideg, I., Cheng, B.H., and Beal, D.J. (2014), "Lunch breaks unpacked: The role of autonomy as a moderator of recovery during lunch", *Academy of Management Journal*, Vol. 57 No. 2, pp. 405–421.

Tsikriktsis, N. (2004), "A technology readiness-based taxonomy of customers: A replication and extension", *Journal of Service Research*, Vol. 7 No. 1, pp. 42–52.

Tu, Q., Wang, K., and Shu, Q. (2005), "Computer-related technostress in China", *Communications of the ACM*, Vol. 48 No. 4, p. 77.

Tuomi, A., Tussyadiah, I., and Stienmetz, J. (2020), "Service robots and the changing roles of employees in restaurants: A cross cultural study", *e-Review of Tourism Research*, Vol. 5 No. 17, pp. 662–673.

Turner-Cobb, J.M. and Hawken, T. (2019), "Stress and coping assessment", in Llewellyn, C.D., McManus, C., Weinman, J., Petrie, K.J., Newman, S., Ayers, S. and Revenson, T.A. (Eds.), *Cambridge Handbook of Psychology, Health and Medicine, Cambridge handbooks in psychology*, 3rd ed., Cambridge University Press, Cambridge, pp. 229–236.

van Birgelen, M., Dellaert, B.G., and de Ruyter, K. (2012), "Communication channel consideration for in-home services", *Journal of Service Management*, Vol. 23 No. 2, pp. 216–252.

van den Bos, K., Lind, E.A., Vermunt, R., and Wilke, H.A.M. (1997), "How do I judge my outcome when I do not know the outcome of others? The psychology of the fair process effect", *Journal of Personality and Social Psychology*, Vol. 72 No. 5, pp. 1034–1046.

van Doorn, J., Lemon, K.N., Mittal, V., Nass, S., Pick, D., Pirner, P., and Verhoef, P.C. (2010), "Customer engagement behavior: Theoretical foundations and research directions", *Journal of Service Research*, Vol. 13 No. 3, pp. 253–266.

van Doorn, J., Mende, M., Noble, S.M., Hulland, J., Ostrom, A.L., Grewal, D., and Petersen, J.A. (2017), "Domo arigato Mr. Roboto", *Journal of Service Research*, Vol. 20 No. 1, pp. 43–58.

van Woerkom, M., Bakker, A.B., and Nishii, L.H. (2016), "Accumulative job demands and support for strength use: Fine-tuning the job demands-resources model using conservation of resources theory", *Journal of Applied Psychology*, Vol. 101 No. 1, pp. 141–150.

Vargo, S.L. and Lusch, R.F. (2004a), "Evolving to a new dominant logic for marketing", *Journal of Marketing*, Vol. 68 No. 1, pp. 1–17.

Vargo, S.L. and Lusch, R.F. (2004b), "The four service marketing myths", *Journal of Service Research*, Vol. 6 No. 4, pp. 324–335.

Vargo, S.L. and Lusch, R.F. (2016), "Institutions and axioms: An extension and update of service-dominant logic", *Journal of the Academy of Marketing Science*, Vol. 44 No. 1, pp. 5–23.

Vella, P.J., Gountas, J., and Walker, R. (2009), "Employee perspectives of service quality in the supermarket sector", *Journal of Services Marketing*, Vol. 23 No. 6, pp. 407–421.

Venkatesh, V. and Brown, S.A. (2001), "A longitudinal investigation of personal computers in homes: Adoption determinants and emerging challenges", *MIS Quarterly*, Vol. 25 No. 1, pp. 71–102.

Venkatesh, V., Morris, M.G., Davis, G.B., and Davis, F.D. (2003), "User acceptance of information technology: Toward a unified view", *MIS Quarterly*, Vol. 27 No. 3, pp. 425–478.

Verhoef, P.C., Broekhuizen, T., Bart, Y., Bhattacharya, A., Qi Dong, J., Fabian, N., and Haenlein, M. (2021), "Digital transformation: A multidisciplinary reflection and research agenda", *Journal of Business Research*, No. 122, pp. 889–901.

Verhoef, P.C., Neslin, S.A., and Vroomen, B. (2007), "Multichannel customer management: Understanding the research-shopper phenomenon", *International Journal of Research in Marketing*, Vol. 24 No. 2, pp. 129–148.

Vivek, S.D., Beatty, S.E., and Morgan, R.M. (2012), "Customer engagement: Exploring customer relationships beyond purchase", *Journal of Marketing Theory and Practice*, Vol. 20 No. 2, pp. 122–146.

Vogel, J. and Paul, M. (2015), "One firm, one product, two prices: Channel-based price differentiation and customer retention", *Journal of Retailing and Consumer Services*, Vol. 27 No. 6, pp. 126–139.

Vogel, V., Evanschitzky, H., and Ramaseshan, B. (2008), "Customer equity drivers and future sales", *Journal of Marketing*, Vol. 72 No. 6, pp. 98–108.

Voorhees, C.M. (2006), "A voice from the silent masses: An exploratory and comparative analysis of noncomplainers", *Journal of the Academy of Marketing Science*, Vol. 34 No. 4, pp. 514–527.

Voorhees, C.M., Fombelle, P.W., Gregoire, Y., Bone, S., Gustafsson, A., Sousa, R., and Walkowiak, T. (2017), "Service encounters, experiences and the customer journey: Defining the field and a call to expand our lens", *Journal of Business Research*, Vol. 79 No. 10, pp. 269–280.

Vos, J.F. and Rupert, J. (2018), "Change agent's contribution to recipients' resistance to change: A two-sided story", *European Management Journal*, Vol. 36 No. 4, pp. 453–462.

Walczuch, R., Lemmink, J., and Streukens, S. (2007), "The effect of service employees' technology readiness on technology acceptance", *Information & Management*, Vol. 44 No. 2, pp. 206–215.

Wallgren, L.G. and Hanse, J.J. (2007), "Job characteristics, motivators and stress among information technology consultants: A structural equation modeling approach", *International Journal of Industrial Ergonomics*, Vol. 37 No. 1, pp. 51–59.

Walsh, G. and Hammes, E.K. (2017), "Do service scripts exacerbate job demand-induced customer perceived discrimination?", *Journal of Services Marketing*, Vol. 31 No. 4/5, pp. 471–479.

Walsh, G., Yang, Z., Dose, D., and Hille, P. (2015), "The effect of job-related demands and resources on service employees' willingness to report complaints", *Journal of Service Research*, Vol. 18 No. 2, pp. 193–209.

Walster, E., Berscheid, E., and Walster, G.W. (1973), "New directions in equity research", *Journal of Personality and Social Psychology*, Vol. 25 No. 2, pp. 151–176.

Wang, H.-J. (2017), "Determinants of consumers' purchase behaviour towards green brands", *The Service Industries Journal*, Vol. 37 No. 13-14, pp. 896–918.

Wei, S., Ang, T., and Anaza, N.A. (2019), "Recovering co-created service failures: The missing link of perceived justice and ethicalness", *Journal of Services Marketing*, Vol. 33 No. 7, pp. 921–935.

Weil, M.M. and Rosen, L.D. (1997), *Technostress. Coping with technology @work @home @play*, Wiley, New York.

Westbrook, R.A. (1987), "Product/consumption-based affective responses and postpurchase processes", *Journal of Marketing Research*, Vol. 24 No. 3, pp. 258–270.

Whiting, A. and Donthu, N. (2006), "Managing voice-to-voice encounters", *Journal of Service Research*, Vol. 8 No. 3, pp. 234–244.

Wilder, K.M., Collier, J.E., and Barnes, D.C. (2014), "Tailoring to customers' needs", *Journal of Service Research*, Vol. 17 No. 4, pp. 446–459.

Williams, M.D., Dwivedi, Y.K., Lal, B., and Schwarz, A. (2009), "Contemporary trends and issues in IT adoption and diffusion research", *Journal of Information Technology*, Vol. 24 No. 1, pp. 1–10.

Wilson, A. (1972), *The marketing of professional services*, McGraw-Hill, London.

Winston, C. (1993), "Economic deregulation: Days of reckoning for microeconomists", *Journal of Economic Literature*, Vol. 31 No. 3, pp. 1263–1289.

Wireko-Gyebi, S., Adu-Frimpong, G.K., and Ametepeh, R.S. (2017), "Work-related stress: Coping strategies of frontline hotel employees in Ghana", *Anatolia*, Vol. 28 No. 2, pp. 197–208.

Wirtz, J. and Jerger, C. (2016), "Managing service employees: Literature review, expert opinions, and research directions", *The Service Industries Journal*, Vol. 36 No. 15-16, pp. 757–788.

Wirtz, J. and Lovelock, C.H. (2016), *Services marketing: People, technology, strategy*, Eighth edition, World Scientific Publishing, New Jersey.

Wirtz, J., Patterson, P.G., Kunz, W.H., Gruber, T., Lu, V.N., Paluch, S., and Martins, A. (2018), "Brave new world: Service robots in the frontline", *Journal of Service Management*, Vol. 29 No. 5, pp. 907–931.

Witell, L., Snyder, H., Gustafsson, A., Fombelle, P., and Kristensson, P. (2016), "Defining service innovation: A review and synthesis", *Journal of Business Research*, Vol. 69 No. 8, pp. 2863–2872.

World Trade Organization (2019), "World trade statistical review", available at: https://www.wto.org/english/res_e/statis_e/wts2019_e/wts19_toc_e.htm (accessed 4 June 2020).

Wu, L.-Y., Chen, K.-Y., Chen, P.-Y., and Cheng, S.-L. (2014), "Perceived value, transaction cost, and repurchase-intention in online shopping: A relational exchange perspective", *Journal of Business Research*, Vol. 67 No. 1, pp. 2768–2776.

Xanthopoulou, D., Bakker, A.B., Demerouti, E., and Schaufeli, W.B. (2007), "The role of personal resources in the job demands-resources model", *International Journal of Stress Management*, Vol. 14 No. 2, pp. 121–141.

Xanthopoulou, D., Bakker, A.B., Demerouti, E., and Schaufeli, W.B. (2009a), "Reciprocal relationships between job resources, personal resources, and work engagement", *Journal of Vocational Behavior*, Vol. 74 No. 3, pp. 235–244.

Xanthopoulou, D., Bakker, A.B., Demerouti, E., and Schaufeli, W.B. (2009b), "Work engagement and financial returns: A diary study on the role of job and personal resources", *Journal of Occupational and Organizational Psychology*, Vol. 82 No. 1, pp. 183–200.

Xia, L., Monroe, K.B., and Cox, J.L. (2004), "The price is unfair! A conceptual framework of price fairness perceptions", *Journal of Marketing*, Vol. 68 No. 4, pp. 1–15.

Yang, J. and Diefendorff, J.M. (2009), "The relations of daily counterproductive workplace behavior with emotions, situational antecedents, and personality moderators: A diary study in Hong Kong", *Personnel Psychology*, Vol. 62 No. 2, pp. 259–295.

Yang, R.-J., Yang, J.-Y., Yuan, H.-R., and Li, J.-T. (2017), "Techno-stress of teachers: An empirical investigation from China", *DEStech Transactions on Social Science, Education and Human Science*, pp. 603–608.

Yates, D., Jodlowski, S., and Court, Y. (2017), *The global food & beverage market: What's on the menu?*, London, UK, available at: http://www.cushmanwakefield.de/en-gb/research-and-insight/2017/report-global-food-and-beverage-market-2017 (accessed 2 July 2019).

Yeo, A., Legard, R., Keegan, J., Ward, K., McNaughton Nicholls, C., and Lewis, J. (2013), "In-depth interviews", in Ritchie, J., Lewis, J., Nicholls, C.M. and Ormston, R. (Eds.), *Qualitative research practice: A guide for social science students and researchers*, SAGE Publications, pp. 177–210.

Yoo, J. and Arnold, T.J. (2016), "Frontline employee customer-oriented attitude in the presence of job demands and resources", *Journal of Service Research*, Vol. 19 No. 1, pp. 102–117.

Yoon, H.M., Seo, H.J., and Yoon, S.T. (2004), "Effects of contact employee supports on critical employee responses and customer service evaluation", *Journal of Services Marketing*, Vol. 18 No. 5, pp. 395–412.

Yu, T., Patterson, P.G., and de Ruyter, K. (2013), "Achieving service-sales ambidexterity", *Journal of Service Research*, Vol. 16 No. 1, pp. 52–66.

Zablah, A.R., Franke, G.R., Brown, T.J., and Bartholomew, D.E. (2012), "How and when does customer orientation influence frontline employee job outcomes? A meta-analytic evaluation", *Journal of Marketing*, Vol. 76 No. 3, pp. 21–40.

Zaichkowsky, J.L. (1985), "Measuring the involvement construct", *Journal of Consumer Research*, Vol. 12 No. 3, p. 341.

Zeithaml, V.A., Berry, L.L., and Parasuraman, A. (1993), "The nature and determinants of customer expectations of service", *Journal of the Academy of Marketing Science*, Vol. 21 No. 1, pp. 1–12.

Zeithaml, V.A., Bitner, M.J., and Gremler, D.D. (2017), *Services marketing: Integrating customer focus across the firm,* Seventh edition, McGraw-Hill Education, New York, NY.

Zeithaml, V.A., Parasuraman, A., and Berry, L.L. (1985), "Problems and strategies in services marketing", *Journal of Marketing*, Vol. 49 No. 2, pp. 33–46.

Zeithaml, V.A., Parasuraman, A., and Malhotra, A. (2002), "Service quality delivery through web sites: A critical review of extant knowledge", *Journal of the Academy of Marketing Science*, Vol. 30 No. 4, pp. 362–375.

Zeng, Z., Chen, P.-J., and Lew, A.A. (2020), "From high-touch to high-tech: COVID-19 drives robotics adoption", *Tourism Geographies*, Vol. 22 No. 3, pp. 1–11.

Zhang, J., Farris, P. W., Irvin, J. W., Kushwaha, T., Steenburgh, T. J., and Weitz, B. A. (2010), "Crafting integrated multichannel retailing strategies", *Journal of Interactive Marketing*, Vol. 24 No. 2, pp. 168–180.

Zhang, L., Gao, Y., and Zheng, X. (2020), "Let's talk about this in public: Consumer expectations for online review response", *Cornell Hospitality Quarterly*, Vol. 61 No. 1, pp. 68–83.

Zhang, R.Y., Liu, X.M., Wang, H.Z., and Shen, L. (2011), "Service climate and employee service performance: Exploring the moderating role of job stress and organizational identification", *The Service Industries Journal*, Vol. 31 No. 14, pp. 2355–2372.

Zhang, T., Omran, B.A., and Cobanoglu, C. (2017), "Generation Y's positive and negative eWOM: Use of social media and mobile technology", *International Journal of Contemporary Hospitality Management*, Vol. 29 No. 2, pp. 732–761.

Zhang, Z., Ye, Q., Law, R., and Li, Y. (2010), "The impact of e-word-of-mouth on the online popularity of restaurants: A comparison of consumer reviews and editor reviews", *International Journal of Contemporary Hospitality Management*, Vol. 29 No. 4, pp. 694–700.

Zhao, X., Lynch, J.G., and Chen, Q. (2010), "Reconsidering Baron and Kenny: Myths and truths about mediation analysis", *Journal of Consumer Research*, Vol. 37 No. 2, pp. 197–206.

Zuur, A.F., Ieno, E.N., and Elphick, C.S. (2010), "A protocol for data exploration to avoid common statistical problems", *Methods in Ecology and Evolution*, Vol. 1 No. 1, pp. 3–14.

Printed in the United States
by Baker & Taylor Publisher Services